HELLENIC STUDIES 19

WEAVING TRUTH
Essays on Language and the Female
in Greek Thought

Other Titles in the Hellenic Studies Series

Plato's Rhapsody and Homer's Music
The Poetics of the Panathenaic Festival in Classical Athens

Labored in Papyrus Leaves
Perspectives on an Epigram Collection Attributed to Posidippus
(P.Mil.Vogl. VIII 309)

Helots and Their Masters in Laconia and Messenia
Histories, Ideologies, Structures

Archilochos Heros
The Cult of Poets in the Greek Polis

Master of the Game
Competition and Performance in Greek Poetry

Greek Ritual Poetics

Black Doves Speak
Herodotus and the Languages of Barbarians

Pointing at the Past
From Formula to Performance in Homeric Poetics

Homeric Conversation

The Life and Miracles of Thekla
Victim of the Muses: Poet as Scapegoat, Warrior and Hero
in Greco-Roman and Indo-European Myth and History

Amphoterōglossia
A Poetics of the Twelfth Century Medieval Greek Novel

Priene (second edition)

Plato's Symposium
Issues in Interpretation and Reception

http://chs.harvard.edu

WEAVING TRUTH
Essays on Language and the Female in Greek Thought

Ann Bergren

Center for Hellenic Studies
Trustees for Harvard University
Washington, D.C.
Distributed by Harvard University Press
Cambridge, Massachusetts, and London, England
2008

Weaving Truth: Essays on Language and the Female in Greek Thought
    by Ann Bergren
Copyright © 2008 Center for Hellenic Studies, Trustees for Harvard University
All Rights Reserved.
Published by Center for Hellenic Studies, Trustees for Harvard University, Washington, D.C.
Distributed by Harvard University Press, Cambridge, Massachusetts and London, England
Production: Kristin Murphy Romano
Printed in Ann Arbor, MI by Edwards Brothers, Inc.

Editorial Team
Senior Advisers: W. Robert Connor, Gloria Ferrari Pinney, Albert Henrichs, James O'Donnell,
    Bernd Seidensticker
Editorial Board: Gregory Nagy (Editor-in-Chief), Christopher Blackwell,
    Casey Dué (Executive Editor), Mary Ebbott (Executive Editor), Olga Levaniouk,
    Anne Mahoney, Leonard Muellner, Ross Scaife
Production Editors: M. Zoie Lafis, Ivy Livingston, Jennifer Reilly
Web Producer: Mark Tomasko

Library of Congress Cataloging-in-Publication Data:
Bergren, Ann.
 Weaving truth : essays on language and the female in Greek thought / by Ann Bergren.
    p. cm. -- (Hellenic studies series ; 19)
 ISBN 978-0-674-02372-7
 1. Homer--Criticism and interpretation. 2. Homer. Iliad. 3. Homer. Odyssey. 4. Femininity
in literature. 5. Femininity (Philosophy) I. Title. II. Series.
 PA4037.B463 2008
 883'.01--dc22

                                                                                2007037289

For
Taylor

ACKNOWLEDGMENTS

THIS BOOK CONTAINS TEN ESSAYS that have been edited and revised – and in the case of the final one, substantially expanded for this collection. The essays have been arranged so as to indicate relations that suggested themselves as I reviewed the group.

The first one, "Language and the Female in Early Greek Thought," sets the stage for those that come after by introducing the basic theme of the book, the nexus of language, the female, weaving, and the construction of truth. In Greek thought, truth in language has a special relation to the female by virtue of her preeminent art form, weaving. The male Homeric bard inherits from Indo-European culture the designation of poetry as a weaving, the female's art. Like her tapestries, his "texts" can suspend, reverse, and re-order time. He can weave the content from one world, whether real or imagined, into the interstices of another. As a virtual "mistress" of invention and of spatio-temporal ordering, the male poet shares the ambiguous power of the female Muses whose speech he channels: "we can," they tell the poet Hesiod, "say false things like to real things, and whenever we wish, we can utter the truth."

After this first essay, the others are arranged in three groups of three each, under rubrics that describe the relations I sense among them. I describe these rubrics by connecting them to aspects of this book's cover image in the Preface. And in the analytical Table of Contents of the book, I try to convey this organization synoptically through titles for the groups and captions for the articles.

This order of the essays is also roughly chronological. As it moves through the various periods and places of my work, this book is increasingly gifted with debts.

Jean-Pierre Vernant, Marcel Detienne, Gregory Nagy, Jacques Derrida – without them, nothing. As this quartet shows, the essays in this book derive from the intellectual and cultural milieu of structuralist/post-structuralist thought.

In 1976, as an Assistant Professor at Princeton, I had the opportunity to organize one of the first conferences that focused upon the relation between Classics and structuralist/post-structuralist thought. Among the participants at that conference were three great exemplars – Pietro Pucci, Charles Segal, and Froma Zeitlin – whose influence has been a constant inspiration and permeates all of my work.

Other pioneers in this period created an atmosphere of amazing creative energy. Nancy Felson, John Peradotto, Carl Rubino – I remember with special thanks how they not only inspired me with their own writing, but also gave me ideas and occasions to present my work in lectures, and edited it for publications. And it is a pleasure to recall with fond gratitude the many projects and the personal impact of Deborah Boedeker, Page duBois, Helene Foley, and Marilyn Arthur Katz.

For us in the USA at this time, much of our inspiration came from Paris. I am grateful to all of those there whose work meant so much to us, and especially to Marcel Detienne and Nicole Loraux for the opportunity to present in their seminars the first version of "*Homeric Hymn to Aphrodite*: Tradition and Rhetoric, Praise and Blame" in this collection. The audience there lavished their learning upon the text with penetrating questions and suggestions. In particular, I thank Françoise Frontisi-Ducroux, François Lissarrague, and Giulia Sissa.

Moving to Los Angeles in 1980 brought me into the orbit of four scholars whose brilliance is matched only by their generosity. I thank Bernard Frischer for his boundless intellectual *philoxenia* and constructive energy. I thank Daniel Selden for the range of his knowledge – with every conversation, I learned something new about Classics or contemporary theory – and for his acute and tirelessly supportive editing of "Architecture Gender Philosophy." The insights of Bruce Rosenstock into the philosophies of Plato and Derrida were a source of abiding pleasure and an essential stepping-stone, in particular, toward "Sacred Apostrophe: Re-Presentation and Imitation in *Homeric Hymn to Apollo* and *Homeric Hymn to Hermes*" in this collection. And for his ever ready willingness to help me, drawing from his command of the Greek language and philosophy, both ancient and modern, I will be ever thankful to David Blank.

In the mid-'80s my work turned toward architecture, when Michael Rotondi, the director of the Southern California Institute of Architecture, invited me to teach theory there. I am grateful to him for opening this door. With the kind permission of my Chair Bernard Frischer and Dean Herbert Morris, I was able to accept this invitation, while continuing my regular teaching at UCLA. This was the time when the philosophy of Derrida was making its impact upon architectural theory and practice. Thanks to the support of SCI-Arc (as the Southern California Institute of Architecture is abbreviated), I was able to attend the conference on architecture and deconstruction that first stimulated "Architecture Gender Philosophy" in this collection. This essay was first presented in 1988 at a conference at the Chicago Institute for Architecture and Urbanism organized by its director, John Whiteman, and Jeffrey Kipnis. I am grateful to the Institute for a fellowship there in 1989–1990, where the essay was completed, to John Whiteman for an enduring example of the sophisticated blend of architectural philosophy and practice, and to Jeffrey Kipnis for the influence of his unique architectural genius.

Two other essays in this collection stem from this period of blending Classics with architectural thought. Each was graced with expert editing by dear friends. Sarah Morris provided "The (Re)Marriage of Penelope and Odysseus" with incisive advice and cross-references. The urban design and theoretical writing of architect Diana Agrest inspired "Female Fetish Urban Form."

In the mid-'90s my pursuit of architecture led to my becoming a student in the Master of Architecture program at the Harvard Graduate School of Design. I owe the opportunity to acquire this degree to a leave from UCLA granted by the Chairs, David Blank, Sarah Morris, and Robert Gurval. Their support of this unorthodox pursuit reflects the appreciation in our department of interdisciplinary study of Classics. I continue to be strengthened by their colleagueship, along with the fund of knowledge and expertise offered by our other Hellenists, Michael Haslam, Katherine King, Steven Lattimore, Kathryn Morgan, John Papadopoulos, Alex Purves, Giulia Sissa, and Brent Vine.

The making of a book is always a challenging enterprise. In the case of this collection, the labor was lightened by the pleasure of collaboration. I am grateful to Suzanne Lye for careful checking of formatting tags and to Katherine Bergren for eagle-eyed correction. Jill Curry Robbins of the Center for Hellenic Studies lavished her expertise as an art historian and graphic designer on the project, discovering the tapestry by Dora Wheeler at the Metropolitan Museum of Art and choosing the font for the cover. Leonard Muellner shepherded the text with ever ready optimism and elegant advice. For his indefatigable implementation of formatting tags, his acute editorial taste, his comprehensive bibliographical knowledge, and his refined intellectual judgment, I thank Lorenzo Garcia. And for help with proofreading, the checking of references, and the creation of the index, I am immensely grateful to Alex Press.

And finally, I extend my deepest gratitude to Diane Davisson, Carolyn Dewald, Natalie Boymel Kampen, and Laura Slatkin – all along, their creativity and compassion have been a lifeline – and to Taylor Bergren-Chrisman, who lights my way.

CONTENTS

WEAVING TRUTH
Essays on Language and the Female in Greek Thought

Weaving *pseudea homoia etumoisin* "false things like to real things"

Weaving in Architecture: The Truth of Building

PREFACE

O N THE COVER OF THIS BOOK is an image of "Penelope Unraveling Her Work at Night," a "needlewoven tapestry" by Dora Wheeler from 1886. The work is a monument to its content. At 45" × 68", it depicts its Penelope at virtually full scale as a woman about 5' tall, depending upon the length of her legs below the end of her dress. In its choice of subject, the tapestry points to the etymology of "text" from Latin *textus* "that which is woven." This tapestry is a text of a text, a graphic translation of that portion of Homer's *Odyssey* in which Penelope unweaves her weaving of Laertes' shroud. We may recall Penelope's "textual" stratagem. Her husband Odysseus is long absent, gone to fight with the Greeks at Troy, and has not returned, even some twenty years later. Her οἶκος "house" is beset by suitors, each pressing her to become his wife. Wait, she tells each man, until I finish weaving a shroud for Odysseus' father, Laertes. When I complete this garment, I will marry one of you. By each day she weaves the shroud, moving with each turn of woof in warp toward the dissolution of Odysseus' household. But by night, she unweaves her day's work, moving backward toward her position as Odysseus' wife. By blending fabric and words to construct one picture of her mind on the outside, while re-constructing another on the inside, Penelope preserves the integrity of her husband's house. In its choice of this episode from the *Odyssey* and in the details of its construction, Dora Wheeler's tapestry provides a graphic introduction to this book – to the introductory essay and to the three topics under which the remaining essays are arranged.

Introduction

By depicting the figure of Penelope – her manipulation of meaning via the medium of a material text and the relation of this mastery to the maintenance of the οἶκος "house" – Dora Wheeler's embroidery evokes the connection in Greek thought between language, the female, weaving, and the construction of truth. The first essay of this collection, "Language and the Female in Early Greek Thought," explores the foundation of this nexus. It introduces key texts and concepts that will recur throughout the book – in particular, the Muses' transcendent knowledge and the ability it gives them to utter *alêtheia* "true things" and *pseudea homoia etumoisin* "false things like to real things," whenever they wish, and the mythology of *mêtis*, the "transformative intelligence" fundamental to every *technê*, embodied in the goddess Metis, who teaches weaving to women as their defining art.

Weaving in Narrative: Textures of Space and Time

By choosing to focus upon the particular moment of "Penelope Unraveling Her Work at Night," Dora Wheeler's embroidery points to the dimension of time in woven space. It recalls the question at the heart of the relation between weaving and truth: why call a narrative a "text"? Why call a medium that aims to represent non-static phenomena, embedded in temporal flow – changes of time or place, motions, actions, speeches and other sounds – why call this medium a static, silent material object? Why call a stream of words a connection of threads? What aspects of the tapestry does a narrative emulate? The three essays in this section of the book explore this question with regard to Homeric epic.

"Helen's Web: Time and Tableau in the *Iliad*" begins with our first sight of Helen in the *Iliad*. She is weaving a microcosm of the poem, a tapestry of the "many contests that the horse-taming Trojans and bronze-armored Achaeans were enduring for her at the hands of Ares." Her tableau contains the action of the epic within the frame of her web, thus suspending it in time. The essay traces how the poem adopts this temporality of the tapestry – the capture of a given interval of time and its extension in space – to convey the truth of war, its tragic transcendence of historical and local limits.

Besides the tapestry as a whole, a finished product, a text can also mirror the process of weaving. Both "Similes and Symbol in *Odyssey* v" and "Odyssean Temporality: Many (Re)Turns" examine the most basic constructive feature common to weaving and narration: spatio-temporal reversal, the alternation of direction in the movement through space and time.

In "Similes and Symbol in *Odyssey* v," the interweaving is spatial – the "here, there, here again" order of the simile – within a single, simultaneous world. In the Homeric simile, the action of the poem is interrupted. The narrative eye and voice switch – via the phrase ὡς "just as" – to describe another action at another place, and then switch back – via the phrase "just so" – to the first place to declare the actions' common features. Here is an example from the battlefield of the *Iliad*:

νιφάδες δ' ὡς πῖπτον ἔραζε,
ἅς τ' ἄνεμος ζαὴς νέφεα σκιόεντα δονήσας
ταρφειὰς κατέχευεν ἐπὶ χθονὶ πουλυβοτείρῃ·
ὣς τῶν ἐκ χειρῶν βέλεα ῥέον ἠμὲν Ἀχαιῶν
ἠδὲ καὶ ἐκ Τρώων.

Just as snowflakes keep falling to the ground
which the strong-blowing wind, having shaken the shadowy
        clouds,
ever pours thick and fast upon the all-nourishing earth,
just so from the hands of these were the weapons flowing,
        both Achaeans
and Trojans alike.

Iliad XII 156–160

Thus linked by the line of their shared attributes, the different locations and the different actions lose their apparent discontinuity. Revealing them now as sectors of a single spatial fabric, the simile can function as a symbolic commentary upon the action. The montage in Sergei Eisenstein's film *Strike* offers a modern analogue, as the gunning down of striking workers is intercut with knife blows to the neck of an ox being slaughtered in an abattoir.[1] Typically in Homer, the similes in a given book of the epic are independent of one another. But in *Odyssey* v the similes work together to convey the interior, psychological significance of Odysseus' journey – from his departure from Calypso's island, through storms at sea, to arrival at the island of the Phaeacians – to cast this physical passage as a self-generated rebirth of the ψυχή "life-breath, soul."

In "Odyssean Temporality: Many (Re)Turns," a study of *Odyssey* 9-12, the interweaving is temporal. In these books, at the banquet in his honor at Phaeacia, Odysseus takes over the role of "poet" of the *Odyssey*, giving his guests what they ask in return for their hospitality, his identity. His tale displays two chronological circumstructures: both the "present, past, present" order of the *husteron-proteron* "later thing" before "earlier thing" up to the "later thing" again, and the "present, future, present" order of prophetic prolepsis. In its overall structure, Odysseus' "poem" is a *husteron-proteron* "later thing" before "earlier thing," beginning in the present and then recounting the past from the time he left Troy until he reaches the present again. This *husteron-proteron* sequence stages the movement of remembering, the returning of the past to make the present self. At the center of this recollection, Odysseus recounts his descent into Hades where the "present, future, present" sequence of the prophecy by the blind seer Teiresias foretells how he will achieve his goal of νόστος "return" home to Ithaca and later, how he will ultimately die, thus returning again to the realm of the dead, where the two of them stand right now. These temporal circles figure the two dimensions of Odysseus' heroism, his many returns of body and mind.

Weaving *pseudea homoia etumoisin* "false things like to real things"

Unlike depictions of women weaving in ancient Greek art, Dora Wheeler's tapestry focuses not upon the creation, but the "unraveling" of the web.[2] We see Penelope by night, undoing the work of the day. Her eyes gaze at her hand, tracking the grasp of her fingers disconnecting the threads. This act of unweaving belies Penelope's daytime claim to the suitors that she is weaving Laertes' shroud. It makes her words to them an instance of the Muses' capacity to utter *pseudea homoia etumoisin* "false things like to real things," whenever they wish. Penelope's "unraveling" thus alludes to the consummate command ascribed to women by Greek tradition over truth and its perfect imitation. And it recalls the dilemma of the suitors – or any man – confronted with the female's mimesis: how to distinguish the female's true speech from its likeness. Moreover, the scene reminds us that for a human woman, her mastery over mimesis is no certain self-defense. Penelope is not, herself, a Muse.

The essays in this section of the book probe the ambiguous dynamics of *alêtheia* "true things" and *pseudea homoia etumoisin* "false things like to real things" and the variety of efforts by both speaker and interpreter alike to control them. In "Helen's 'Good Drug'," the female's speech is presented as a *pharmakon* "cure, poison" that can tell painful truth without causing pain. At a banquet in Sparta with her husband Menelaus and Odysseus' son Telemachus, their guest, Helen adds to the wine a *pharmakon* that makes even the death of your parents, your brother, or your son a pain-free sight. Under the influence of this "good drug," Helen recounts a tale that enhances her glory in the eyes of her husband and guest, how back at Troy she remained loyal to the Greeks and aided Odysseus when he entered the city as a spy. But the ambivalence of the *pharmakon* turns against its practitioner, when it moves Menelaus to mention what pain might have kept beyond recall, Helen's second Trojan husband, Deiphobus, the man she married after Paris' death, thus belying her claim to pro-Greek allegiance. It is ἄλγιον "all the more painful," says Telemachus, thus registering the re-doubling of his suffering.

In "Sacred Apostrophe: Re-Presentation and Imitation in *Homeric Hymn to Apollo* and *Homeric Hymn to Hermes*," the brotherhood of the two gods, Apollo and Hermes, figures the relation between unerring truth and its imitation – a supplementarity in which each acts as both rival and addition to the other. In the *Hymn to Apollo*, Apollo's first act following his birth is to claim, "May the dear lyre and the curved bow be mine, and I shall unerringly repeat to humankind the unerring plan of Zeus." Apollo's possession of the lyre is thus the prerequisite of his oracular accuracy. Yet in the *Hymn to Hermes*, the first act of Hermes, Apollo's younger brother, after his birth is to invent the lyre himself. Hermes then steals Apollo's cattle by driving them backwards, thus making their hoofs imitate movement in the opposite direction. Upon discovering the ruse, Apollo exchanges the cattle for the lyre, so that now the property of each is his brother's original possession. Following this transaction, Apollo gives Hermes what he had sworn to keep as his own, *manteia* "oracular speech." Now both brothers have oracles, but their truth-telling roles are switched. For the responses of Hermes' *manteia* are said to be discernibly true or false. But to the hapless human who asks more than the god wants him to know, Apollo's oracle will give a vain response, while still accepting his gifts. Now which brother is the unerring prophet and which one the thief?

In "*Homeric Hymn to Aphrodite*: Tradition and Rhetoric, Praise and Blame," the problem of telling *alêtheia* "true things" from *pseudea homoia etumoisin* "false things like to real things" is compounded by the clouds of *eros*. Confronted by the goddess Aphrodite, disguised as an "un-tamed virgin" destined to be his wife, the mortal man Anchises is blinded by erotic desire. In an effort to determine her identity, he tests for two possibilities, that she is a goddess or that she is the mortal woman she pretends to be. He neglects the possibility of duplicitous ambiguity. For were he to "see through" her disguise, he could not consummate his passion. Motivated as he is by *eros*, his quest for truth is pseudo-sincere. Rather than finding *alêtheia*, his desire is that this instance of *pseudea*, this imitation of the truth, should be truthful. Thus beguiled, he yields to the goddess's masquerade. But in her mimetic conquest, the goddess, too, suffers defeat. For her seduction of Anchises results from Zeus' playing "Aphrodite" against the goddess herself. To prevent her from remaining forever exempt from the divine-human unions she causes among the other gods, Zeus instills within her the degrading desire to sleep with a mortal man. Thus does the goddess's hymn frame her mimetic mastery with erotic subordination.

Weaving in Architecture: The Truth of Building

And finally, there is the impact of Dora Wheeler's placement of Penelope in relation to her web. Again Wheeler's design differs from the typical composition in Classical art. Rather than being shown from the back or in profile, as she might walk along from one end of the weft to the other, with the tapestry alone facing us, Penelope, too, is turned forward. She stands upright like the threads of the warp. Her arms are stretched out from her shoulders, in line with the weft threads she pulls away from the web. In this posture, the body of Penelope parallels her weaving. By turning her back upon it, she becomes her web's duplicate. Woman is her weaving.

Wheeler's identification of Penelope with her tapestry recalls Freud's account of the origin of this art.[3] Weaving, he says, is woman's invention. The model and material is her pubic hair, as it lies matted and sticking to her skin. While providing the model, Nature is not herself the artist here. For it is the woman herself who devises the way to transform her natural condition into an artificial copy, a mimesis that transcends its paradigm. For it is the woman who, in an exemplary instance of *mêtis* "transformative intelligence," invents "the step that remained to be taken . . . making the threads adhere to one another." In her weaving, the female makes an artifact – an artifactual instance – of herself.

By virtue of this relation with her weaving, the female becomes the archetype of an architect. For in many cultures, as studied by the 19th century architectural historian Gottfried Semper, the origin of architecture is weaving.[4] The wall is woven – whether of wickerwork, planks of wood, or interlocking courses of masonry. In her weaving, the woman makes the architecture – the vertical space enclosures – of the body and of the house. [Figure 1. Photographer Francesca Woodman assimilates her body to the woven wall.] Here, then, arises a basic question: who designs what the woman weaves? Is it the woman herself? Who, then, designs her? What forms the female's "transformative intelligence"? To the edification of what structures of power, what constructions of identity, what conditions of inside and outside does the female devote her architectural prowess?

The essays in this section of the book investigate this connection between architecture and the female. In "The (Re)Marriage of Penelope and Odysseus," we find the founding exemplars in early Greek thought of the two primary processes of architectural construction, the woven wall, in Penelope's web, and the column, in the living tree that forms the post of Odysseus' marriage bed. In the *Odyssey* these two architectural elements cooperate to construct an ideal of gender relations in which the ambiguity of female mobility – she must be movable in order to be exchanged in marriage, but then she is supposed to stay put – is arrested in the institution of "immovable (re)marriage." The stability of this institution rests upon the philosophical ideal of truth as unique selfsameness. Accordingly, in their culminating act of architectural partnership, Penelope and Odysseus design tests to prove Odysseus' unique identity, a proof only possibly compromised by the maid Actoris, who could have divulged the secret sign of the marriage bed.

In "Architecture Gender Philosophy," I bring the nexus of the female, weaving, and architecture under the rubric of *mêtis* to bear upon the contemporary architectural collaboration between philosopher Jacques Derrida and

Figure 1. Photograph by Francesca Woodman (1958-1981), *Untitled,* New York, 1979. Courtesy of George and Betty Woodman.

Peter Eisenman. For the program of their project, the pair used an essay by Derrida upon the *khôra* "space, place" in Plato's *Timaeus*. Plato's text describes *khôra* "space, place" as a nurse, mother, and receptacle, an absolutely passive medium in which material entities are "built" as perfect copies of their Forms as models. Plato's creator god is the *Demiourgos*, a cosmic architect. In his analysis Derrida concentrates upon *khôra* as that which receives all things, but – so as to produce perfect copies of the Formal models – remains a perpetual *tabula rasa*, never taking on any characteristic herself. He resolutely abjures the "anthropomorphism" of *khôra*'s female gender as mother and nurse. It is this wholly passified, gender-free *khôra* that Derrida and Eisenman use in their effort to create a design that will "dislocate" the foundational tenets of Classical architecture. But in their exclusion of the gender of *khôra* from their model, the collaborators miss the pre-Platonic tradition of the female's *mêtis* and her ambiguous mobility and neglect the aspect of the Platonic *khôra* that might have programmed architectural dislocation – the continual dynamic movement of *khôra* before the institution of cosmic architecture.

What architecture will "dislocate" architectural Classicism? The question arises again in "Female Fetish Urban Form." This essay focuses upon a Greek comedy by Aristophanes, the *Ecclesiazusae*, in which a group of Athenian women, under the leadership of their "general" Praxagora, disguise themselves as men in order to infiltrate the male-only legislative assembly, the *ekklêsia*, there to vote in a new political regime, a communistic gynocracy, thus abolishing the social, political, and economic power structures of father-rule. In Praxagora's new order, the play addresses the question of what women will build if allowed to form the city. The play's answer is unexpectedly ironic – she will build exactly as we have taught her in the "architecture school" of the Classical οἶκος "house." The action of the play recalls other Greek texts, in particular Xenophon's *Oeconomicus*, that describe how the young wife is educated by her husband to mold her household and herself in accordance with male design: she is to emulate the male role of a "general" and to make within the walls of the οἶκος "house" a microcosm of the πόλις "city." In this formation of the female as an imitation-male, the Classical οἶκος "house" parallels the construction of the fetish in Freudian thought, a *Penisersatz* "substitute penis" that the male subconsciously appends to the female genital so as to deny and affirm simultaneously that genital's phallic lack. It is this training as a "para-male" and the indecidable ambiguity of the fetish that constitute Praxagora's urban plan. She extends the borders of her household to coincide with the borders of the city, making the πόλις "city" one large, single οἶκος "house" with herself as general. In this reduction of the formation of the female to female urban form, Praxagora – like the fetish – simultaneously fulfills and abolishes the Classical architecture of father-rule.

Notes

1. On the parallels between Eisenstein's montage and the Homeric narrative, see Garcia 2007.

2. For depictions of women weaving in ancient Greek art, see Barber 1994. For a video demonstration of ancient weaving practices, see Edmonds, Jones, and Nagy 2004.

3. See Freud 1933 [1932]: 132.

4. See Semper 1989:102–103, 254–255 and Herrmann 1984:205.

INTRODUCTION

1

LANGUAGE AND THE FEMALE
IN EARLY GREEK THOUGHT

I. The Speech of the Muses

AT THE START OF THE *THEOGONY,* Hesiod describes his poetic initiation. As he was tending his lambs under Mt. Helicon, the Muses "taught him beautiful singing" (καλὴν ἐδίδαξαν ἀοιδήν, *Theogony* 22), when to him for the first time they made this pronouncement:

> ποιμένες ἄγραυλοι, κάκ' ἐλέγχεα, γαστέρες οἶον,
> ἴδμεν ψεύδεα πολλὰ λέγειν ἐτύμοισιν ὁμοῖα,
> ἴδμεν δ' εὖτ' ἐθέλωμεν ἀληθέα γηρύσασθαι.

> Shepherds of the wild, base reproaches, bellies only,
> we know how to say many false things like to real things,
> and we know, whenever we want, how to utter true things.

> *Theogony* 26–28

The poet then continues:

> So they spoke, these daughters of great Zeus, joiners of words,
> and they gave me a scepter, having plucked a branch of teeming
>   laurel,
> wondrous to see. And they breathed into me divine voice
>   (αὐδὴν θέσπιν)
> so that I might celebrate the things that were and will be.

> *Theogony* 29–32

This text introduces the relation between language and the female in early Greek thought: a male author ascribes a kind of speech to a female and then makes it his own. Let us look more closely.

13

First, what is the nature of the Muses' speech?[1] They claim to know two modes, both "false things like to reality" and "true things," and to be able to switch from one to the other at will. What is their purpose in making this claim? Evidently, it is to declare the extent of their knowledge – note the repetition of ἴδμεν "we know" – to declare the unqualified knowledge and power of speech they must possess, if they are to inspire the "divine voice" of the "things that were and will be."[2] Accordingly, they claim control of both truth and falsehood, since, as Odysseus proves when he tells ψεύδεα ὁμοῖα ἐτύμοισιν "false things like to real things" about himself (*Odyssey* xix 203) (the only other attested instance of this phrase), the ability to utter falsehood implies and requires knowledge of the truth.[3] The Muses can speak both the truth and fictions that imitate fact, with no constraint.[4] No knowledge or power of utterance could be more complete.

These two modes of the Muses' discourse parallel the two kinds of speech attributed to women throughout Greek tradition. Women are both prophets and teachers, voices of truth. Think of the Moirae (Fates) who spin out the future,[5] the Sirens who "know all that comes into being upon the much-nourishing earth" (*Odyssey* xii 191),[6] Nereus' daughters, Nemertes "Unerring" (*Iliad* XVIII 46, *Theogony* 262) and Apseudes "Without-Falsehood" (*Iliad* XVIII 46), the Pythia at Delphi, Teiresias' daughter Manto, Cassandra,[7] Aspasia, teacher of rhetoric to Pericles and Socrates,[8] and Diotima, Socrates' teacher of love.[9] Women are also tricky, alluring imitators in words.[10] Recall the speech in which Aphrodite imitates a "virgin" in order to seduce Anchises (*Homeric Hymn to Aphrodite* 108–142, νύμφαι and παρθένοι, 119)[11] and Hera's similar deception (ἀπάτη) of Zeus.[12] But most females are, like the Muses, capable of both modes – indeed, as we have observed, the ability to falsify implies command of the truth. Remember Calypso and Circe in the *Odyssey*, each a "dread goddess endowed with speech" (δεινὴ θεὸς αὐδήεσσα) who weaves, sings, seduces and prophesies;[13] the Bee Maidens in the *Homeric Hymn to Hermes* whose oracular response is true when they are fed honey and false when they are deprived (*Homeric Hymn to Hermes* 552–563); the Delian Maidens in the *Homeric Hymn to Apollo*, the θεράπναι "ritual substitutes" of Apollo who can imitate voices so well that "every man would say that he himself was speaking" (*Homeric Hymn to Apollo* 157–164);[14] Gaia (Earth) in the *Theogony* who both prophesies (*Theogony* 463, 475, 891–893) and devises plots (μῆτιν, 471) and tricks (Γαίης ἐννεσίῃσι πολυφραδέεσσι δολωθείς, 494) on the basis of her prophetic knowledge (*Theogony* 626–628);[15] and, of course, the Sphinx, whose song of man's essential nature comes in the form of a riddle that "chokes" both the man who cannot and the man who can solve it.[16] In these figures we see a degree of knowledge attributed to the female that results in a capacity for double speech, for both truth and the imitation of truth, a paradoxical speech hopelessly ambiguous to anyone whose knowledge is less than the speaker's. For if the Muses speak truly when they say that they can at will speak either truth or falsehood that is the perfect likeness of truth, who except the Muses themselves can tell whether this very declaration is an instance of the first or the second category, an instance of their true or their apparently true speech?[17]

What, then, do men do when they confront this double nature of female discourse? Again, the Hesiodic text provides the model. Thanks to the Muses' inspiration, the poet acquires their capacity for knowledge and speech. Such appropriation by the male of what he attributes to the female persists throughout Greek literature. What varies, as we shall see, is the degree to which he attempts to demote, divide, or expel the "female" at the same time as he takes on her powers, and then to proceed as if they had always been his own.[18]

But why should this be so? Why should a certain power of language be thought of in terms of gender at all? To pursue this question, I will compare this "female" language with the sign-making activity of women *par excellence* in Greek, namely, weaving. This comparison will reveal that the tricky ambivalence ascribed to the speech of women is consonant with the semiotic character of weaving and of graphic art in general, and that it finds its intellectual counterpart in the Greek concept of *mêtis* or "transformative intelligence," itself portrayed as the goddess, Metis. An instance of this *mêtis*, one that concerns both the production of signs and sexual reproduction, will suggest another comparison, this time between woman's language and her role in marriage exchange, a relation I will explore in the opening chapters of Herodotus' *Histories*. To conclude, I will illustrate the thesis that results from these investigations through the signal example of Helen.

II. The Signs of the Female: Weaving

A significant connection between women and language in Greek thought might seem *prima facie* unlikely, since the semiotic activity peculiar to women throughout Greek tradition is not linguistic. Greek women do not speak, they weave.[19] Semiotic woman is a weaver. Penelope is, of course, the paradigm.[20] When we examine this activity in its cultural context, however, the phenomenon that emerges is not simple. We see first the simple fact: women weave. Why? The Greeks record the fact without analysis. For an aetiology we have to look to Freud whose account is interestingly consonant with but finally inadequate to the ancient evidence. To illustrate the connection between penis-envy and the development of a sense of shame, Freud declares:

> It seems that women have made few contributions to the discoveries and inventions in the history of civilization; there is, however, one technique which they may have invented – that of plaiting and weaving. If that is so, we should be tempted to guess the unconscious motive for the achievement. Nature herself would seem to have given the model which this achievement imitates by causing the growth at maturity of the pubic hair that conceals the genitals. The step that remained to be taken lay in making the threads adhere to one another, while on the body they stick into the skin and are only matted together. If you reject this idea as fantastic and regard my belief in the influence of lack of a penis on the configuration of femininity as an *idée fixe*, I am of course defenseless.[21]

A woman weaves, in Freud's view, in order to hide and compensate for her lack of all that the phallus represents, the capacity to engender life and in patrilinear society to give that life a legitimate name. And indeed, in Greek culture, where women lack citizenship, where men play all the parts in drama, and from which no poetry by women remains except for the lyrics of Sappho and fragments of a few others, the woman's web would seem to be a "metaphorical speech," a silent substitute for (her lack of) verbal art. But this is not a complete picture, for in Greek the utterance of poetry or prophecy is described as "weaving."

Greek culture inherits from Indo-European a metaphor by which poets and prophets define themselves as "weaving" or "sewing" words.[22] That is, they describe their activity in terms of what is originally and literally woman's work *par excellence*. They call their product, in effect, a "metaphorical web." But which, then, is the original and which the metaphorical process? Is weaving a figurative speech or is poetry a figurative web? The question cannot be decided. Weaving as the sign-making activity of women is both literal and metaphorical, both original and derived. It is, like the Muses' speech, ambiguously true speech and an imitation of true speech.

The myth of Tereus, Procne, and Philomela provides a good example. It testifies to the regular limitation of women to tacit weaving, while exposing the magical power of a silent web to speak. When Tereus, the husband of Procne, rapes her sister Philomela, he cuts out the woman's tongue to keep her silent, but Philomela, according to Apollodorus (3.194.5), ὑφήνασα ἐν πέπλῳ γράμματα "wove pictures/writing (γράμματα can mean either) in a robe" which she sent to her sister. Philomela's trick reflects the "trickiness" of weaving, its uncanny ability to make meaning out of inarticulate matter, to make silent material speak. In this way, women's weaving is, as γράμματα implies, a "writing" or graphic art, a silent, material representation of audible, immaterial speech.

This paradoxical capacity of weaving has an intellectual counterpart in Greek. It is the skill known as *mêtis*. As Detienne and Vernant have shown, *mêtis* denotes throughout Greek thought the power of transformation, the power to change shape continuously or to imitate the shape of your enemy and defeat him at his own game.[23] It is both a strategy of deception, the plot itself, and the mental ability to devise one. The connection between the woman, weaving, and *mêtis* is explicit in two divine figures, the goddess Metis and her daughter Athena, goddess of weaving and as she herself says, "famous among all the gods for *mêtis*" (*Odyssey* xiii 299).[24] In the *Odyssey* Athena "weaves a *mêtis*" (μῆτιν ὑφαίνειν, *Odyssey* xiii 303, 386) for Odysseus through which he can take revenge upon the suitors (who themselves "weave a *mêtis*" to kill Telemachus, *Odyssey* iv 678). She changes Odysseus' appearance to that of a beggar (*Odyssey* xiii 397–403), someone with the status his enemies actually occupy, when they are in his home. But this recipient of Athena's *mêtis* had himself already "woven a *mêtis*" when he devised escape from Polyphemus by clutching the belly of the ram (*Odyssey* ix 422).[25] Indeed, through the epithet πολύμητις "he of much *mêtis*," used only of Odysseus from the start of the epic, the text testifies to the hero's prior possession of this quality, and Athena herself admits that she aids Odysseus because of his constant cleverness (*Odyssey* xiii 330–332).

To recapitulate: early Greek thought draws an analogy between woven fabric, poetry, and *mêtis* by making each the object of a verb "to sew" or "to weave," the object, that is, of the woman's sign-making art. If we keep this analogy in mind, the myth of the marriage of the goddess Metis and Zeus becomes an αἴτιον "aetiological myth" of the semiotic power assigned to the female and its (re-)appropriation by the male. According to the Hesiodic account (*Theogony* 886–900), Zeus' first action after securing his kingship was to make Metis his wife, she "whose knowledge was greatest of gods and mortal men" (πλεῖστα θεῶν εἰδυῖαν ἰδὲ θνητῶν ἀνθρώπων, *Theogony* 887). But when she was to give birth, he "deceived her mind with a trick through wily words (δόλῳ φρένας ἐξαπατήσας αἱμυλίοισι λόγοισιν) and put her into his own belly" (*Theogony* 889–890), "so that the goddess might devise on his behalf both good and evil" (ἀγαθόν τε κακόν τε, *Theogony* 900; compare above note 5). Later, he himself gave birth from his head to Metis' daughter Athena (*Theogony*

924). The female as weaver of *mêtis* thus (re-)enters the divine cosmos as a perpetually virgin daughter, loyal solely to her father. And Zeus as sovereign male appropriates a quality that the text has attributed to him from the start. For just as Odysseus alone is πολύμητις "he of much *mêtis*" from the start of his epic, so Zeus is μητίετα "endowed with *mêtis*" from the start of the *Theogony* (56), and just as Odysseus wove a *mêtis* for himself before Athena wove one for him, so Zeus outwits the goddess Metis with his own *mêtis* of wily words.[26] Indeed, even before he swallows the goddess. Zeus is the beneficiary of the one instance in the *Theogony* when a female wields this power, that is, when Gaia and Uranus devise a *mêtis* for Rhea to keep Cronus from swallowing Zeus. But it is this very trick by Rhea that best shows how *mêtis* is related to the power of speech ascribed to the female and why the male needs to possess it.

The fundamental struggle of the *Theogony* is over the power of reproduction. In the three generations that culminate in the rule of Zeus, the male moves progressively closer to appropriating the reproductive process.[27] Uranus tries to block the birth of his children by keeping them within the body of Gaia; Cronus moves closer to the female role by swallowing his children so that they are kept within his own body. But even this measure is not wholly successful, since Rhea, when she is about to give birth to Zeus, asks Gaia and Uranus for a *mêtis* by which to elude Cronus (*Theogony* 468–478). The trick they devise is to substitute a stone wrapped in swaddling clothes for the real infant. Here is the primary *mêtis*, the first imitation, one that seems to symbolize a suppositious child. For Cronus is baffled by the disguise, as any man might be, when his wife presents him with what she says is his child, for who except his wife can vouch for his true child, the legitimate heir to his property and his proper name?[28] Only the female has the knowledge necessary to tell the true from the false heir, but it is this very knowledge that also makes her able to substitute for the truth a false thing that resembles it. Her knowledge gives her the power of falsification in the domain of sexual reproduction, just as on the level of language the knowledge of the Muses makes it possible for them to utter either *alêtheia* "true things" or *pseudea homoia etumoisin* "false things like to real things." The (re-)production of social legitimacy and true meaning are in the hands of the female, but so thereby is the power of *mêtis*, the power of substitution and transformation, the power, therefore, of the *tropos* or "turning" that will later become the foundation of rhetoric.[29]

Yet even in this early mythic text, the semiotic implications of Rhea's *mêtis* are not overlooked. Zeus himself makes them clear. Zeus, as we have seen, improves upon Cronus' attempt to control reproduction by swallowing not the children alone, but the mother Metis as well, thus ensuring that he alone will now possess the knowledge and power she represents. In commemoration of this ascendancy through and over *mêtis*, Zeus sets up "at very holy Pythia in the hollows under Parnassus" the very stone Rhea gave to Cronus "to be a sign (σῆμ') hereafter, a wonder (θαῦμα) for mortals" (*Theogony* 500). He sets up the stone to be a sign of his control of signification, to be a sign to all who come to learn the mind of the father through the oracle of his son, that Zeus' regime is built upon the knowledge necessary to disguise, to imitate, to substitute – a knowledge now securely embodied by the father of men and gods.

If, then, on the divine level, the power of language attributed to the female is (re-)appropriated by the male, it remains the case that the human male is, in the perspective of early Greek thought, forever plagued by his vulnerability to the woman as the ambiguous source of truth and falsehood. In the Hesiodic texts the mortal woman is presented as a duplicitous product of Zeus' power to substitute.[30] For Pandora, the origin of the "race of women" (γένος γυναικῶν, *Theogony* 590), comes to men as a "beautiful (καλόν) evil (κακόν) in place of good (ἀντ' ἀγαθοῖο)" and "in place of fire (ἀντὶ πυρός)" (*Theogony* 570, 585, 602; *Works and Days* 57), another θαῦμα "wonder" (*Theogony* 588) like Zeus' stone/σῆμα "sign." This "sculpted female" (πλαστὴν γυναῖκα, *Theogony* 513, σύμπλασσε 571, πλάσσε, *Works and Days* 70) incarnates the problem of imitation, the problem that disguise presents to anyone without the mind of the disguiser. She comes as a κόσμος "order, ornament" (*Theogony* 587, *Works and Days* 76), a cosmetic composite of all the qualities we have seen so far associated with the language of the female. She can speak "false-hoods" (ψεύδεα) and "wily words" (αἱμυλίους λόγους, *Works and Days* 78); she can "weave a web full of artifice" (πολυδαίδαλον ἱστὸν ὑφαίνειν, *Works and Days* 64); like Aphrodite when she seduces Anchises, she is the "likeness of a reverend virgin" (παρθένῳ αἰδοίῃ ἴκελον, *Theogony* 572). But she is also the maternal source of truth, of the reality that is the next generation.[31]

In Pandora as source of both false words and true offspring and in Rhea's *mêtis* stone as both substitute child and sign of true sovereignty over substitution, we have detected an analogy between the reproduction of legitimate or only apparently legitimate children and the utterance of true or only apparently true words, an analogy that suggests that the power of language ascribed to the female may be a reflex of the role she plays in the social process by which her re-productive role is assured, namely, the process of marriage exchange. To explore this possibility, I have looked to the early Greek text that comes closest to an anthropological analysis of this process, the *Histories* of Herodotus.[32]

III. The Female as Sign in Marriage Exchange

Reflecting the perspective of structuralist anthropology, Claude Lévi-Strauss closes his *Elementary Structures of Kinship* with the observation that women are like words, insofar as they are exchanged in marriage by men so that men can communicate. But the female, he adds, is not "just a sign and nothing more," since she is also "a generator of signs."[33] Women are like words, they are "metaphorical words," but they are also original sources of speech, speakers themselves. They are both passive objects and active agents of linguistic exchange, just as their weaving is both a metaphorical compensation for and the original meaning of poetic speech. In this relation to the linguistic and the social system, the woman, like her weaving, is paradoxically both secondary and original, both passive and active, both a silent and a speaking sign.[34]

Greek tradition has a version of this anthropological and linguistic analysis of the signifying function of the female in the social code. It is contained in the opening chapters of Herodotus' *Histories* (1.1–5). Before turning to the events that precipitate the war, Herodotus looks back in time to the origin of the διαφορά, both the "difference" and the "conflict" between barbarian and Greek, an origin to be found in a series of marriage exchanges. But by virtue of its legendary material and time frame, this opening section seems to act as myth as well as history. The series of particular exchanges seem to illustrate how the system always works.[35] Specifically, as we shall see, the exchange of women and other merchandise always turns out to be uneven, and this unevenness results in "conflict" which constitutes the "difference" between the two sides. Marriage exchange thus becomes the ἀρχή "origin" not just of a given war, but also of social communication and differentiation. And further, insofar as kinship and language are, as Lévi-Strauss maintains, structurally homologous systems of meaning-making, this account of the exchange of women will apply *mutatis mutandis* to the exchange of language as well.[36]

Herodotus begins not with the Greek but with the Persian account, thus exposing at once the problem of competing perspectives and various degrees of knowledge about any given phenomenon. According to the Persians, he says, it was the Phoenicians who originated (αἰτίους γενέσθαι) the διαφορά "difference, conflict," when on one of their stops to trade Egyptian or Assyrian goods in Greece, they stole (ἁρπασθῆναι) the king's daughter Io, along with some other women (*Histories* 1.1.1–4). The Phoenicians, those proverbial traders (it is they who introduced the exchange medium of the alphabet into Greece), are in this case not merchants but pirates, taking goods without making payment, practicing ἁρπαγή "rape, theft" rather than γάμος "marriage" and ξενία "exchange." In return for this ἁρπαγή, the Greeks steal (ἁρπάσαι) Europa from Tyre (*Histories* 1.2.1). By this repetition, theft is transformed into a sort of exchange, for it was, says Herodotus, ἴσα πρὸς ἴσα "equal for equal, tit for tat" (*Histories* 1.2.1). The Phoenicians are simply forced by the abduction of Europa to pay a "fair price" for their abduction of Io. In like manner, rape is turned into a marriage, the union by which a foreign female becomes the origin or perpetuation of the race, a function symbolized here by the fact that the name of the stolen woman, Europa, becomes the name of her new land (*Histories* 1.4.4).[37] Ἁρπαγή "rape, theft", when doubled, becomes ξενία "exchange" and γάμος "marriage."

Then the Greeks initiate (αἰτίους γενέσθαι) a "second illegality" (δευτέρης ἀδικίης) (*Histories* 1.2.2). They initiate the process of theft/exchange again by stealing (ἁρπάσαι) Medea from Colchis. Instead of retaliating with a theft, Medea's father asks through a herald for the return of his daughter, but also for something in addition, δίκας τῆς ἁρπαγῆς "appropriate damages for the rape, theft." In effect, this request turns commerce back to something like robbery, for the Greeks will be giving back more than they took, and accordingly, they refuse on the grounds that they got no δίκας τῆς ἁρπαγῆς "appropriate damages for the rape, theft" of Io (*Histories* 1.2.3). The behavior of the Greeks is then copied by Paris who "steals Helen" (ἁρπάσαντος αὐτοῦ Ἑλένην) and refuses both her return and damages, citing the ἁρπαγή "rape, theft" of Medea (*Histories* 1.3.2). And so again, the situation was equal, since, as Herodotus puts it, there had been only thefts/exchanges (ἁρπαγάς) between the two sides (*Histories* 1.4.1).

But when the Greeks do not accept Paris' refusal and instead mount an army to recover Helen, they escalate the conflict – mindlessly, in the judgment of the Persians, who believe it is illegal to steal women, but irrational to be zealous in revenging the theft, since no woman is ravaged against her will (*Histories* 1.4.2). Nevertheless, the Greeks "on account of a Lacedaemonian woman" (Λακεδαιμονίης εἵνεκεν γυναικός, *Histories* 1.4.3) invade Asia and eradicate the dynasty of Priam. This act of aggression is so excessive that it defines a permanent, polemical opposition between barbarian and European/Greek. The attempt not just to match one ἁρπαγή with another or one ἁρπαγή-plus-δίκαι with another, but instead to re-take the woman by force, this attempt is the origin (ἀρχήν) of the enmity (ἔχθρης) through which the terms "Greek" and "barbarian" acquire their enduring meaning.[38] Such is the *logos* of the Persians (*Histories* 1.5.1).

But theirs is not the only account. The Phoenician version disputes the very foundation of the process, for they claim the abduction of Io was no ἁρπαγή "rape, theft" at all. Rather Io had slept with the Phoenician captain, become pregnant, and run away with him to avoid discovery by her parents (*Histories* 1.5.2). Like the Persians (who think that no woman is unwillingly raped), the Phoenicians believe that Io was a willing captive, but to them this means that there was no ἁρπαγή "rape, theft" at all. If in the Persian account, the women are passive objects of theft/exchange and rape/marriage and thus function like silent signs, in the account of the Phoenicians, they are the active agents of the process and act, as it were, like speakers.

This two-sided account of the origin of Greek/barbarian διαφορά "difference, conflict" reveals a series of irresolvable conflicts, ambiguities and tensions intrinsic to the exchange of women, oppositions that parallel the double status we have seen before in the weaving and the discourse of the female. First, who originates and who merely repeats the ἁρπαγή "rape, theft"? The Persians attribute the "beginning" to the Phoenicians (*Histories* 1.1.1–3) and then to the Greeks (*Histories* 1.4.4). Clearly, any starting point in the process is arbitrary. Is ἁρπαγή theft or rape or marriage? When one abduction is followed by another, the result is termed ἴσα πρὸς ἴσα "equal for equal." Is Europa the barbarian's daughter or the mother of the European Greeks? First one, and then, when she is exchanged, the other? So we might conclude. But these exchanges are not final. A woman can always be re-abducted, as was attempted in the case of Medea and achieved in the case of Helen. The even exchange can (re-)turn into excess, if, again as in the case of Helen, not just the woman but damages are (re-)captured. It is, however, only such an (attempted) excess that (re-)establishes the difference that creates meaning between otherwise equal parties. Signification is both an exchange and a theft of the sign. And, finally, it is possible that the man himself may be deprived of both the power to exchange the female and the control of her (re-)productive capacity. For just as a woman is able herself to speak, so Io may have "stolen or exchanged herself," so to speak, by sleeping with the Phoenician captain. And it may be impossible for any interested male, be he Io's father or the Greeks or the Phoenicians or the Persians or, as Herodotus admits at the end of this opening narrative (*Histories* 1.5.3), even the "father of history" himself, to find out for sure. The institution of marriage attempts to regulate the (re-)productive power of the female, but without total success. The woman can stay exchanged or be (re-)abducted, her offspring can be legitimate or illegitimate, and there is no way for any man either to control her completely or even to know for certain the extent of his control. Only the female knows for sure, and she, like the Muses, can either tell the truth or imitate it.

In Herodotus' account we see marriage exchange not as an even reciprocity, but as a system in which an excess is added to an evenness, thus creating διαφορά, conflict as meaningful difference. In such a system, there is no single status of the female, but her meaning varies according to whether she is being viewed as agent or object, whether as someone to take or someone to be (re-)taken. And there is, accordingly, no univocal origin of truth, but competing versions, one from each perspective upon the woman's role. One woman persistently embodies this mobile doubleness of language and the female throughout Greek tradition – that woman is Helen.

IV. Helen as Female/Rhetorical *Logos*

A. *Helen and Homer*

The figure of Helen in Homer takes us back to the beginning, back, that is, to women and weaving.[39] In each epic Helen is both woven and the weaver of speech, both subject of the song and figure within the text for the poet's own activity. When we first see her in the *Iliad*, she is weaving a tapestry of the ἀέθλους "contests" between the Greeks and the Trojans to possess her (*Iliad* III 121–128). As the scholiast on this passage remarks, "the poet has fashioned a worthy archetype of his own poetic art."[40] Both the role and the tapestry of Helen share the contradictory, double status we noted before in weaving. She is both the passive object of the war and the creator of its emblem. And it is the art of the tapestry – whether Helen's literal web or the "woven words" of the *Iliad* itself – both to represent action and to freeze it at a point before its completion. Helen depicts the contending armies, but she captures them, so to speak, at a point before either side has finally captured her. Helen's art thus ever defers the end of the contest, the final capture of herself. The "text" of the *Iliad* mirrors Helen's web by "weaving the war" up to a point where Achilles' death is certain, but not yet accomplished. It thereby achieves the goal of Iliadic tradition, that is, to keep the glorious death of the hero perpetually alive. In the *Iliad*, therefore, tapestry and text are similarly paradoxical.

In the *Odyssey*, too, Helen acts as both subject and the poet's counterpart. We see her in Book iv reunited with Menelaus in Sparta, giving a double wedding feast. She has acquired some marvelous things from Egypt: equipment for weaving and magic drugs. When the recollections among the men – Menelaus and his visitors, Telemachus and Peisistratus – of the losses at Troy provoke lamentation that would spoil the feast, Helen attempts to turn the evening from Iliadic mourning by means of the Egyptian drugs and an

Odyssean tale. She pours into the wine some drugs (φάρμακα) that are "good" rather than "baneful" (ἐσθλά not λυγρά) and are "full of *mêtis*" (μητιόεντα) (*Odyssey* iv 227–228),[41] drugs that can keep a man from weeping even at the sight of his mother or father or brother or son being slaughtered (*Odyssey* iv 224–226). Shared epithets link these drugs with epic diction itself, so that when Helen follows the pouring of the drugged wine with a recollection of her own, we are led to see in her narration another emblem of the poet's own art, especially since Helen's tale, like the *Odyssey* itself, is about Odysseus, how when he entered Troy disguised as a beggar, she secretly aided him out of re-acquired loyalty to the Greeks (*Odyssey* iv 235–264), and since the *Odyssey*, like Helen's tale, attempts to create Odyssean pleasure in place of Iliadic pain.[42]

But Helen's drug/speech has a curious effect upon its audience. It provokes a second recollection of Odysseus' exploits at Troy, this one by Menelaus. His tale is clearly the doublet of his wife's, since they both begin with the same words: "but such a thing as this the strong man did and endured" (*Odyssey* iv 242 = iv 271). But this doublet counteracts the rhetoric of its model. For Menelaus belies Helen's claim of new-found loyalty to the Greeks, when he mentions (apparently *en passant*) her second Trojan husband, the man she married after the death of Paris (*Odyssey* iv 276). Before beginning her tale, Helen had said "Enjoy these speeches (μύθοις). For I will narrate fitting, seemly things (ἐοικότα)" (*Odyssey* iv 239). But after Menelaus' response, Helen's tale becomes retroactively an imitation of what is fitting. Indeed, Menelaus himself testifies to Helen's mastery of the verbal *mimêsis* "imitation" of truth, when he tells how Helen tested the content of the Trojan horse by imitating the voices of all the Greek wives (πάντων ἀργείων φωνὴν ἴσκουσ' ἀλόχοισιν, *Odyssey* iv 279) and only Odysseus was able to restrain himself and the other men from answering her call (*Odyssey* iv 280–288). And when we recall that the opening description of Helen's drug linked it with epic art, we see that in the effect of this narrative diptych upon the speech of his surrogate Helen, the poet exposes a "pharmacology" that can apply to any storytelling: the double capacity both to represent and to imitate truth can recoil upon anyone who tries to control it.

B. Helen and Stesichorus

The texts of Homer not only reveal but do not attempt to regulate the doubleness of Helen – it is no wonder that an ancient biographical tradition made Metis Homer's mother (*Contest* 314). With the poet Stesichorus, however, we encounter an effort that continues into the 5th century BCE to master the ethical and ontological uncertainty inherent in Helen and the *logos*. Although his traditional *floruit* is about a century after the *Iliad* and the *Odyssey* were probably composed, Stesichorus is to be understood in relation to Homeric and Hesiodic poetry.[43] His lyric is metrically and thematically cognate with hexameter epic, and ancient tradition either parallels him with Homer or makes him the son or grandson of Hesiod.[44] His complex relationship with Homer and Hesiod appears, in fact, to have become an actual theme of his poetry, specifically, his poem called *Helen*.

The orator Isocrates in his own *Helen* (Isocrates, *Helen* 64) summarizes the situation: "Helen demonstrated her power also in the case of the poet Stesichorus. For when at the beginning of his ode he uttered some slander (ἐβλασφήμησε) about her, he stood up deprived of his eyes; but when he recognized the cause of his affliction and composed what is called the recantation (παλινῳδίαν), she restored him again to the same condition." Plato in the *Phaedrus* quotes some lines from this "palinode." He introduces them by saying:

> There is an ancient purification for those who err in story-telling (μυθολογίαν) which Homer did not perceive, but Stesichorus did. For having been deprived of his eyes on account of his slander (κακηγορίαν) of Helen, he was not ignorant like Homer, but being a true servant of the Muse (μουσικός), he recognized the cause (αἰτίαν) and composes at once: "This account (οὗτος λόγος) is not true (οὐκ ἔτυμος), you did not embark upon the well-oared ships, you did not come to the citadel of Troy." And once he had composed the whole of what is called the recantation (παλινῳδίαν), at once he recovered his sight.

> *Phaedrus* 243a–b

If the true Helen never went to Troy, for whom did the armies fight? In Book IX of the *Republic* Plato says "phantoms of true pleasure" (εἰδώλοις τῆς ἀληθοῦς ἡδονῆς) cause themselves to be fought over "just as Stesichorus says that the phantom (εἴδωλον) of Helen was fought over by those at Troy in ignorance of the truth (τοῦ ἀληθοῦς)" (*Republic* 586b–c). The true Helen was in Egypt.

Assuming that Plato is quoting the poet's own terminology, it appears that Stesichorus' *Helen* was another "diptych" (as Kannicht 1969:1.40 terms it): first, a κακηγορία "slander" or βλασφημία "damaging speech" in which he repeats the Homeric account of Helen, a repetition that results in his blinding, and second, a παλινῳδία "recantation" in which he calls the earlier *logos* false (οὗτος λόγος οὐκ ἔτυμος "this account is not true") and tells instead the ἔτυμος "true" story in which an εἴδωλον "phantom" of Helen goes to Troy, while the real Helen stays in Egypt, a recantation that restores his sight.[45] Many aspects of this text would reward close study (in particular, the motif of blindness and insight as signs of false blame and true praise),[46] but for our immediate purposes it is most important to observe what is and is not new about Stesichorus' *Helen*. Stesichorus did not invent the doubleness of Helen and her *logos*. For doubleness is the distinguishing mark of her entire tradition – from her two abductions, first by Theseus before her marriage to Menelaus and afterwards by Paris, to her twin brothers, the Dioscuri, whose alternation between death and divinity parallels the εἴδωλον/ἔτυμος pairing, and above all, her dual paternity, Tyndareus and Zeus. Along with these doublets, we should recall the shape-shifting *mêtis* of Nemesis, the mother of Helen in the *Cypria*, who resisted ἁρπαγή "rape, theft" by Zeus by transforming herself into one dread creature after another (*Cypria* 9). Multiformity in the mother is mirrored in the daughter's ability to imitate the voices of the Greek wives. Even Helen's association with Egypt is reflected in the *Odyssey* where her two mediums of transformation, the equipment for weaving and the magic drugs, are said to be gifts of two Egyptian women, Alcandre (*Odyssey* iv 125–132) and Polydamna (*Odyssey* iv 228–232). Like her Iliadic tapestry and her Odyssean *pharmakon*/tale, Helen is forever double. This ambivalence is, in fact, the essence of her tradition. She is the female forever abducted but never finally captured.

It is against this traditional meaning of Helen that we can appreciate the innovation of Stesichorus. He is not the first to make Helen guilty or innocent. We can see such evaluations in the poetry of Sappho and Alcaeus.[47] What is distinctive in Stesichorus seems to be the attempt to divide the sexual and ethical ambivalence of Helen into two figures, assign them two *logoi*, label one true and the other false, and assign the false one to his older poetic rivals, while arrogating the true one to himself. Yet even separating the female/*logos* into true and false and claiming to represent the true may itself be a traditional device by which a male poet tries to master the semiotic power he attributes to the female and thereby to assert himself *vis-à-vis* his male rivals. For it is often observed that in repeating the Muses' description of their twofold speech, Hesiod means to imply not just that the goddesses have power over both modes, but that in contrast to the ψεύδεα ὁμοῖα ἐτύμοισιν "false things like to real things" of epic, his song of the gods' generation is ἀληθέα "true things."[48] The innovation of Stesichorus may be limited to particular terminology such as ἔτυμος "true" and εἴδωλον "phantom." In any case, it is this treatment of Helen as a competition between a true *logos* of praise and a false *logos* of blame that we see again in the first rhetorical version of the subject, Gorgias' *Encomium of Helen*.

C. Helen and Gorgias

In Gorgias' treatment of Helen, we encounter a parallel to the story of Zeus and Metis.[49] Like the poets, the rhetorician needs to possess the power of signification we have seen attributed to the female. But unlike Homer or Hesiod or Stesichorus who signify this need by identifying themselves with the woman, whether as the Muses' speech or the weaving/drug/speech of Helen or as Helen's ἔτυμος "true" story, Gorgias attempts an appropriation of Helen's *logos* no less total than Zeus' swallowing of Metis. In fact, his procedure in the *Encomium of Helen* is the very essence of *mêtis*, that capacity to take on the shape of the enemy, to win by disguise, to create falsehoods that imitate truth. As many commentators on the text observe, Gorgias' apparent "Praise of Helen" is in fact an encomium of *logos* in general and his *logos* in particular.[50] What has not been seen is how Helen – or rather, more precisely, Helen's traditional meaning – is used by Gorgias. Gorgias proves the power of *logos* over Helen. But that is not all. He endows the *logos* that overpowered Helen with just those characteristics traditionally attributed to the *sêmeiôsis* of women and especially to Helen's signs. And even this is not all, for having appropriated the language of Helen, he tries to regulate its fundamental constitution, its unstable, ever (re-)turning doubleness. Dressed in Helen's costume, as it were, Gorgias' *mêtis*-like *logos* tries to divide the traditional *mêtis* of female speech. But, as often happens, when one creature of *mêtis* hunts another, Gorgias' quarry eludes capture by circling round against the hunter and exposing his ruse. Let us track the turns and counter-turns of this rhetoric.

At the start of his speech, Gorgias defines his goal: it is to be the first to replace the tradition of false speech (ψευδομένους) blaming Helen with a true (τἀληθές) speech of praise (Gorgias *Encomium of Helen* [82] B11.2 DK). He argues that the poets who unanimously assert her guilt are wrong, since she was the victim of irresistible forces, either divine or human. In the human category, he lists "abduction by force" (βίαι ἁρπασθεῖσα), "persuasion by speech" (λόγοις πεισθεῖσα), and "capture by love" (ἔρωτι ἁλοῦσα) (*Encomium of Helen* 6). Gorgias passes quickly over ἁρπαγή "rape, theft" as a literal possibility (*Encomium of Helen* 7), but then returns to it as a metaphor for the power of persuasion by speech. For despite the textual corruption, all readings of section 12 agree that the *logos* is said to have compelled Helen not otherwise than if she had been raped.[51]

But Helen is "raped," as it were, by a *logos/phallos* with the character of female language. Here it is *logos* that makes poetry "divinely inspired" (ἔνθεοι, *Encomium of Helen* 10), just as the Muses inspire the song of Homer and Hesiod. In Hesiod a man is "turned away" (παρέτραπε) from painful memories by poetry as a "gift of the goddesses" (δῶρα θεάων), presented by a poet, the θεράπων "servant" of the Muses (*Theogony* 98–103). But here it is through the *logos* alone that poetry brings "pleasure" and banishes "fear" and "pain" (*Encomium of Helen* 8, 10). Rather than Calypso or Circe or the Sirens, it is the poetic word that "enchants" (ἔθελξε) by "wizardry" (γοητείαι), one type of which are "deceptions" (ἀπατήματα), like those practiced by Hera and Aphrodite (*Encomium of Helen* 10). The deceptive wizardry of the word consists in being, like the "woven song," an uncanny synesthesia of plastic and verbal artforms, a "sculpted word" that "persuades" like Pandora, or more precisely, a "sculpted false word" (πείθουσι δὲ ψευδῆ λόγον πλάσαντες, *Encomium of Helen* 11), just as the "woven words" of the Muses can be ψεύδεα ἐτύμοισιν ὁμοῖα "false things like to real things."[52] Indeed, like the γράμματα "pictures, writing" of Philomela's web, the persuasive *logos* is a kind of writing, another visual and verbal medium, for in legal contests the *logos* "persuades" (ἔπεισε) because it is "written with skill, not spoken with truth" (τέχνηι γραφείς οὐκ ἀληθείαι λεχθείς, *Encomium of Helen* 13).[53]

But it is not just these general characteristics of the signs of women that Gorgias' *logos* shares. In assimilating *logos* and φάρμακα "drugs" (*Encomium of Helen* 14), Gorgias links his speech with the drug/speech of Helen herself in the *Odyssey*.[54] Just as the drugs in the *Odyssey* are divided into "good" and "baneful" (*Odyssey* iv 230), so here Gorgias differentiates between those that end disease and those that end life. With her φάρμακα/speech, Helen attempted to control the emotional response of her audience, and here Gorgias claims a particular effect for a given *logos*: pain, delight, fear, courage. But the question in both texts is whether the "pharmacology" of speech can be controlled. We saw before how the double of Helen's drug/speech reacted against its practitioner, when she attempted to divide Odyssean pleasure from Iliadic pain. What is the fate of him who attempts a similar control over *logos* here?

The speech of Gorgias counteracts its own strategy. Even without knowledge of the tradition of Helen, we can detect that Gorgias is "costuming" the *logos* with Helen's own powers and leaving the woman a mere εἴδωλον "phantom" of her former self. The *logos*, he says, produces the "most divine works" (θειότατα ἔργα), although it is "the most small and invisible body" (σμικροτάτῳ σώματι καὶ ἀφανεστάτῳ) (*Encomium of Helen* 8); "one speech" (εἷς λόγος) in a legal contest "delights and persuades a huge crowd" (πολὺν ὄχλον ἔτερψε καὶ ἔπεισε) (*Encomium of Helen* 13). But earlier in the speech, in a brief passage of direct praise, Gorgias attributes to Helen just this quality of controlling "many" while being "one": her "divine beauty" (τὸ ἰσόθεον κάλλος) activated "the greatest number of desires in the greatest number of men" (πλείστας δὲ πλείστοις ἐπιθυμίας); "in one body it brought together many bodies" (ἑνὶ δὲ σώματι πολλὰ σώματα συνήγαγεν ἀνδρῶν), men of every distinction – wealth, lineage, strength, wisdom (*Encomium of Helen* 4). Similarly, Gorgias claims that if it was a god who willed Helen's going to Troy, she, as only a mortal, was powerless to resist (*Encomium of Helen* 6). But this argument ignores the inborn doubleness of Helen, the divine-plus-human nature that derives from the double paternity cited by Gorgias himself, when he praises Helen's lineage (*Encomium of Helen* 3). Not just the tradition but Gorgias himself ascribes to Helen, what he then denies her and ascribes to the *logos* alone.

But it is in his claims for his own speech that Gorgias is most clearly self-confuting. In the opening words of the *Encomium of Helen*, Gorgias asserts that what gives *logos* its κόσμος "order, ornament" is "truth" (ἀλήθεια) and that the opposite, that is, falsehood, is without κόσμος (τὰ δὲ ἐναντία τούτων ἀκοσμία) (*Encomium of Helen* 1). Here κόσμος implies "the attribute necessary for successful operation," as we can tell from the parallel cases Gorgias lists: the κόσμος of the city is "good manhood" (εὐανδρία), of the body, "beauty" (κάλλος), of the soul, "wisdom" (σοφία). If, then, the κόσμος of a *logos* is ἀλήθεια "truth" and falsehood would mean ἀκοσμία, this implies that for Gorgias' speech to succeed, that is, for it to be persuasive in exonerating Helen, it must be true. But later, as we have seen, he claims persuasive force for ψευδής λόγος "false speech" (πείθουσι δὲ ψευδῆ λόγον πλάσαντες, *Encomium of Helen* 11). Now either way he turns, the sophist is trapped by the principle of exclusive opposites that he introduced to control the doubleness of language. Either way his *logos* fails of its stated goal. If a false *logos* is without κόσμος, it cannot be successful, it cannot be irresistibly persuasive: Helen is still guilty. If there is any false *logos* that can be irresistibly persuasive, then the true *logos* of praise cannot defeat the tradition of false blame: Helen is still guilty. Or at least her ethically double nature, like that of her *logos*, continues to elude capture. The κόσμος of Gorgias' speech becomes a "cosmetic" like the κόσμος of Pandora.[55]

Or is Gorgias a greater master of *mêtis* than we realize? Is he in the *Encomium of Helen* imitating Helen's *logos* to the point of allowing his own text, as did Homer, to demonstrate her uncontrollability? In his last words, he says,

"I wanted to write the *logos*, a praise of Helen on the one hand, and on the other, my plaything" (ἐβουλήθην γράψαι τὸν λόγον Ἑλένης μὲν ἐγκώμιον, ἐμὸν δὲ παίγνιον, *Encomium of Helen* 21). Is this an enigma, an αἶνος "testing discourse" to determine whether we realize that only a demonstration of the ungovernable rhetoricity of language can be both Helen's ἐγκώμιον, "praise," and his παίγνιον, "plaything"?[56] Perhaps. What we can say with security is that Gorgias' encomium of Helen cannot be adequately understood apart from the tradition of Helen and her *logos*, a tradition that is part of the larger phenomenon by which a female is endowed with a degree of knowledge, especially sexual knowledge, that gives her a *mêtis*-like power over the utterance of both truth and imitation, a power that every male from Zeus to Gorgias himself must make his own. As for the degree to which Gorgias, like Zeus, succeeds in his attempt to leave the female bereft of this power, we cannot at this point answer fully, but we can speculate at least on this anecdote contained in a brief report by Plutarch on Gorgias' private life: "When Gorgias, the rhetorician, read to the Greeks at Olympia a discourse about harmony, Melanthius said, 'This man is giving us advice about harmony, when in his private life he has not persuaded himself, his wife, and his maidservant, although being only three persons, to live in harmony.' For there was, as it seems, some passion [ἔρως] on the part of Gorgias and some jealousy on the part of his wife toward the little serving girl."[57]

Notes

An earlier version of this essay appeared in *Arethusa* 16 (Semiotics and Classical Studies) 1983:69–95. I am grateful to Margaret Alexiou, David Blank, Nancy Felson, Bruce Rosenstock, and the UCLA Faculty Seminar on Women, Culture, and Theory for critical reading of that text.

1. Of previous work on the Muses' speech, mine is most indebted to Pucci 1977. Like Pucci, I focus upon the rhetorical structure of the lines and how that structure affects what the lines say about truth and falsehood in language. While Pucci does not treat the speech as specifically female in origin, his brilliant analysis of Pandora as an allegory of discourse points the way for my emphasis on the connection between the operation of the speech and the gender of the speaker.

2. Compare the Muses' omniscience as the ultimate source of epic song at *Iliad* II 484–492.

3. Note also the epithets of the goddess Metis, πολύιδριν "with much knowledge" (Hesiod fr. 343.6 MW) and πλεῖστα θεῶν εἰδυῖαν ἰδὲ θνητῶν ἀνθρώπων "with the greatest knowledge of gods and mortals" (*Theogony* 887); and compare Socrates' argument in Plato's *Hippias Minor* (365d–368a) that the best teller of falsehood must have the best knowledge of truth.

Many studies of the Muses' speech assume that its main purpose is to distinguish two classes of poetry, one, ἀληθέα "true things" and the other, ψεύδεα ὁμοῖα ἐτύμοισιν "false things like to real things," and attempt, consequently, to identify the ψεύδεα "false things" either as epic (Neitzel 1980), the *Theogony* itself (Stroh 1976), or epichoric traditions in contrast to their panhellenic synthesis (Nagy 1982). Pucci (1977:36n11), too, takes the ψεύδεα "false things" to refer to Homeric epic, though with important qualifications. While reference to specific poetic creations cannot be ruled out, the logic of the context and the parallel of invoking the Muses' omniscience in *Iliad* II 484–486 suggest that the immediate aim of the Muses' words is to validate their inspiration, that is, to establish their unqualified veridical authority in contrast to that of humans whose status as "bellies"—creatures who need food to live and ultimately will die— compromises their ability to know the truth and to speak it whenever they wish (on the "belly" as sign of the mortal condition, see Arthur 1982 and for its qualification of human truthfulness, see also Svenbro 1976, esp. 57–73). If that is the purpose of the Muses' speech, then the ψεύδεα ὁμοῖα ἐτύμοισιν "false things like to real things" are mentioned not so much as particular compositions, but as a category of utterance that implies and proves a knowledge of truth. This interpretation is supported by another archaic account of poetic initiation that includes the words of the divinity. The Cretan Epimenides, to whom a *"Theogony"* was attributed among other poetic works, was sent out by his father to search for a sheep (Epimenides [3] A1 DK). When he fell asleep in the cave of Dictaean Zeus, the gods spoke to him in a dream, among them Ἀληθεία "Truth" and Δίκη "Justice" (Epimenides [3] B1 DK). Of Epimenides' report of that epiphany, one line remains: Κρῆτες ἀεὶ ψεῦσται, κακὰ θηρία, γαστέρες ἀργαί, "Cretans, always liars, base beasts, idle bellies" (Epimenides [3] B1 DK). The purpose of this address appears to be to contrast the truth that the divinity is about to reveal with the Cretans' usual falsehood. But the proverbial circularity of the "Cretan lie" is, however, embedded in the account, since if this is the voice of Ἀληθεία "Truth" or some other source of truth, and if she says Cretans *always* lie, then Epimenides' own report of the truth that Cretans always lie, can itself be a lie. As we shall see, there is a similar ambiguity in the Muses' assertion to Hesiod of their command of the truth.

4. In his comprehensive study of true and false speech in archaic thought, Detienne (1967) concludes apropos of the "ambiguity of speech" that "to possess the truth is also to be capable of deception" (77) and of the Muses' speech in particular he observes that "ambiguity" is "here the object of a rational analysis that proceeds in terms of imitation, of *mimêsis*" (77). It is such "ambiguity," the simultaneous capacity for truth and the imitation of truth, that characterizes the language attributed to the female.

5. See *Odyssey* vii 197. At *Theogony* 905 they are named: Κλωθώ "spinner," Λάχεσις "apportioner," and Ἄτροπος "she who does not turn," or as is suggested by Thompson (1966:44) with *a*-intensive, "she who cannot be kept from turning," the spindle itself. The two possible meanings of Ἄτροπος capture the doubleness of the language associated with the female. Note also that the Fates parallel the Muses both in the truth and in the ambivalence of their dispensation: the Muse gives to her best loved poet and the Fates give to mortals ἀγαθόν τε κακόν τε "both good and evil" (*Odyssey* viii 63 and *Theogony* 906). For the same phrase with regard to Metis, see the discussion below of the union of Metis and Zeus.

6. On the Sirens, see Pucci 1974 and Kahn 1980; and for their relation with the Muses, formally evident in the double "we know" (ἴδμεν) declaration and in the tradition that makes the Muse Terpsichore their mother (Apollonius of Rhodes *Argonautica* IV 892–896), see Buschor (1944) who identifies the Sirens as a deadly, underworld double of the Olympian daughters of Zeus. The differences between the Sirens and the Muses marshaled by Pollard 1952, especially that Orpheus as the Muses' champion defeats the Sirens, tend to support rather than invalidate the basic correlation of the two groups. In this connection, note the following parallels: (1) the Sirens "charm" (θέλγουσι, *Odyssey* xii 40, 44) with their "shrill song" (λιγυρῇ ἀοιδῇ, *Odyssey* xii 44); Calypso "charms" (θέλγει) Odysseus with "wily words" (αἱμυλίοισι λόγοισι) so that he will forget Ithaca, but he desires death (*Odyssey* i 56–59); (2) the bones of the Sirens' victims "rot" (πυθομένων, *Odyssey* xii 46); Pytho, the victim of the Olympian god of song Apollo, counterpart of the Muses, gets her name from "rotting" under the Sun, a name that becomes the god's epithet "Pythian" (*Homeric Hymn to Apollo* 368–374); (3) the compensating gain and loss from the Muses (song-craft and blindness for Demodocus, *Odyssey* viii 64; song-craft and mutilation for Thamyris, *Iliad* II 594–600), from the Sirens (knowledge and death), and from the Fates (good and bad).

7. See Davreux 1942 who points out the ambivalence in the epic cycle tradition over whether Cassandra was a "seer," whose speech is directly inspired by divinity, or a "reader of auspices," the god's secondary signs (10–11).

8. See Plato *Menexenus* 235e. In this dialogue Socrates repeats a funeral oration he heard from Aspasia who composed it of fragments of the one she had composed for Pericles, together with some additional improvisations (236b).

9. See Plato *Symposium* 201d–212a.

10. On "the categories of Greek thought which associate the feminine with *mimesis*," see Zeitlin 1981. In tracing the background of the connection between women and *mimesis* in Aristophanes' *Thesmophoriazusae*, Zeitlin analyzes Pandora and Helen in Homer, Hesiod, Stesichorus, and Gorgias. Zeitlin sees Helen in Homer as the "weaver" of the *Iliad* and her story-telling in the *Odyssey* as a self-reflexive revelation of the nature of fiction (203–205). Zeitlin's analysis also includes the tale of Proteus in relation to those of Helen and Menelaus and the connection of the whole cluster of these stories to the reunion of Odysseus and Penelope. On Stesichorus, Zeitlin focuses upon the poet's use of Helen, the εἴδωλον "phantom" motif, and the palinode to reflect the working of his art. Zeitlin also emphasizes the role of the erotic ("Stesichorus' story also suggests that *eros* is not divided from poetics," 202) and stresses his "invention" of the εἴδωλον "phantom" motif as applied to Helen and of the palinode form (201–203). With regard to Gorgias' *Encomium of Helen*, Zeitlin shows how λόγος "speech, account," δόξα "opinion," ὄψις "visual appearance," and ἔρος "erotic desire" operate to persuade, seduce, and deceive the ψυχή "soul" (208–211).

11. This speech functions as the verbal counterpart of the visual disguise the goddess assumes at the *Homeric Hymn to Aphrodite* 82. Note her effort to lend credence to her story on the topic of language itself, when at line 114 she explains that her Trojan nurse taught her his "speech" (γλῶσσαν), an effort that for the hymn's audience draws attention to her verbal ἀπάτη "deception." And compare her later description (*Homeric Hymn to Aphrodite* 249) of how she used to make all the gods "mix" in sexual intercourse with mortal women through her "gossips" (ὀάρους) and "wiles" (μήτιας). For the correlation of woman's language and *mêtis*, see below. For more on the complex relation between language and the female in this hymn, see "*Homeric Hymn to Aphrodite*: Tradition and Rhetoric, Praise and Blame" in this collection.

12. See *Iliad* XIV 153–360, especially 301–311 and 330–340, the counterparts of the πάρφασις "speech that turns aside, persuasion, deceit" embroidered on Aphrodite's girdle (214–217). For the detailed correspondences between the Διὸς ἀπάτη "Deception of Zeus" and the *Homeric Hymn to Aphrodite*, see "*Homeric Hymn to Aphrodite*: Tradition and Rhetoric, Praise and Blame" in this collection, and for the relation of Hera's βουλή "plot" in the Διὸς ἀπάτη to that of the *Iliad* as a whole, see "Helen's Web: Time and Tableau in the *Iliad*," in this collection.

13. For the meaning of this epithet and the function of the goddesses, see Nagler 1977. Before sharing with Odysseus her knowledge of navigation (*Odyssey* v 275–277), Calypso had "beguiled" him with "soft and wily words" (*Odyssey* i 55–57). When Hermes arrives to release the hero, he finds Calypso "singing as a bard sings (ἀοιδιάουσ', compare ἀοιδός 'singer, bard') with a beautiful voice, as she walks before the loom, weaving with a golden rod" (*Odyssey* v 61–62). Similarly, when Odysseus' shipmates arrive at Circe's threshold, "they heard Circe within singing as a bard sings (ἀειδούσης) with beautiful voice, as she walked before the great loom" (*Odyssey* x 220–222). Along with Teiresias, Circe provides Odysseus with prophecy, describing her prophetic "signs" as antidote to another's malevolent weaving: "And I shall show the way and signify (σημανέω) each thing, so that you may not through grievous evil-stitching (κακορραφίη, compare ῥάπτω 'stitch, sew') come to grief, suffering pain either on sea or on land" (*Odyssey* xii 25–27).

14. On the role of the Bee Maidens and the Delian Maidens, and on the translation of θεράπναι as "ritual substitutes," see "Sacred Apostrophe: Re-Presentation and Imitation in *Homeric Hymn to Apollo* and *Homeric Hymn to Hermes*" in this collection.

15. On Nemesis, Thetis, and Themis, who also embody both prophecy and *mētis*, see Detienne and Vernant 1978:107.

16. For the "popular etymology" connecting the Sphinx with σφίγγω "bind fast, throttle, choke," see West 1966:256–257 on *Theogony* 326.

17. I owe to John Peradotto the observation of the essential paradox in the Muses' speech: if they speak truly, when they say they can speak truth and the perfect likeness to truth at will, no listener whose knowledge is less than theirs can tell whether in this instance they are speaking truly. The Muses' speech is thus a model instance of the capacity of language for τρόπος "turning" from one modality to another. Here the very utterance that proves the speaker's consummate knowledge of truth puts in question the truthfulness of that utterance. This circular structure of expression, shared by the "Cretan lie" noted above n. 3, is later categorized as a περιτροπή or a statement that "turns around on itself," as in the criticism of Protagoras' man-measure doctrine by Democritus and Plato (Democritus [68] A114 DK = Sextus Empiricus *Against the Mathematicians* 7.389). Sextus Empiricus records a version of the "Cretan lie" as περιτροπή: "And indeed we have shown before that those who say that all things are false refute themselves (περιτρεπομένους); for if all things are false, then also the phrase 'all things are false' will be false" (*Against the Mathematicians* 8.55). On the role of περιτροπή in Greek philosophy, in particular, in the criticism by the Stoics of the Skeptic denial of decidability between competing claims on the basis of reason, see Burnyeat 1976.

18. On this process, compare Arthur 1982 who shows how in the *Theogony* the powers of the female are treated "metonymically," that is, displaced and distributed among other goddesses and gods; see especially 64–65, 71, 72, 76. Arthur 1983 argues that the inspiration of Hesiod is "a highly sublimated form of reproduction . . .

facilitated . . . by the belly/womb/mouth equation which becomes explicit in the succession-myth, and which attracts into the same symbolic field the acts of ingesting, conceiving, and receiving poetic inspiration, and of vomiting, giving birth, and singing or speaking." In addition to this reproductive symbolism—the Muses as "male" inseminators of αὐδή "speech" into the "female" poet—we may note the masculine force of the σκῆπτρον "sceptre" they give him. Nagy (1982:52–53) has shown on the basis of a survey of the archaic usage of the term, that the σκῆπτρον "indicates that the poet will speak with the authority of a king—an authority that emanates from Zeus himself." Combining these two readings, we may conclude that in the *Theogony* the poet is cast simultaneously as "male" in social and juridical authority by the σκῆπτρον and as "female" in terms of reproductive capacity by the Muses' infusion and his subsequent emission of poetic αὐδή. The two dimensions of reproduction and sovereignty come together when Zeus, father and ruler of men and gods, gives birth to Athena, after having swallowed her mother Metis, and *mêtis* is, as we shall see, analogous to poetic song at the level of diction, since both are objects of the verb ὑφαίνειν "to weave."

Outside of the *Theogony*, the texts I study below repeat the pattern of appropriation by the male of "female" language. Once the male takes upon himself the power of prophecy and imitation, it is often presented as something he always had (for example, Zeus, see discussion below) and something he can give to others (for example, Zeus' gift of prophecy to Apollo, Teiresias, etc.). Those gods presented as wholly independent sources of this power—Nereus, Proteus, Hermes, Hephaestus, and Prometheus (but note his occasional reliance upon his mother, Themis)—share an "intermediary" status of being "male" in sex but closer to "female" in function, since they are deprived of the regular male prerogative of sovereignty (they rather lend their skills, as women do, to rulers; see Detienne and Vernant 1978:84–130) and often inhabit the margins of civilization. On the capacity for falsehood inherent in the truthfulness of the sea gods Nereus and Proteus, see Detienne 1967:72–77.

19. On the fact that women rather than men weave as a mark of Greek vs. Egyptian culture, see Herodotus *Histories* 2.35 and *Dissoi Logoi* [90] 2.17 DK.

20. Mactoux 1975 argues against the traditional interpretation of Penelope as the exemplar of unwavering faithfulness by pointing to signs of a fundamental ambiguity in her role and conduct at Ithaca that is resolved only with the close of the epic, an ambiguity symbolized by her weaving and unweaving of Laertes' shroud. On the relation between Penelope's weaving and her position as Odysseus' wife, see "The (Re)Marriage of Penelope and Odysseus" in this collection.

21. Freud 1933 [1932]:132.

22. Durante 1960. See also Schmitt 1967:299–301, Durante 1976:48, 167–179, Snyder 1981, Scheid and Svenbro 1996:esp. 111–130, Nagy 1996a:84–92, Nagy 1996b:63–74, Graziosi 2002:18–40, Nagy 2002:70–98.

23. Detienne and Vernant 1978, esp. 27–53.

24. See Detienne and Vernant 1978:179–183 for the *mêtis* of Athena and 299–300 for weaving as *mêtis*.

25. For the role of Odysseus' *mêtis* in this episode in the achievement of his νόστος "return," see "Odyssean Temporality: Many (Re)Turns" in this collection.

26. Detienne and Vernant (1978:57–130, esp. 67–8, 109) observe that by "marrying, mastering and swallowing Metis," Zeus makes himself μητίετα "endowed with *mêtis*" and becomes "more than simply a monarch: he becomes Sovereignty itself." But, as they also point out, Zeus "attacks Metis with her own weapons," the αἱμύλιοι λόγοι "wily words" (*Theogony* 890), and the text calls him μητίετα even before his defeat of the goddess. Such chronological or causal inconsistency is a typical feature of mythic expression, but here it also contributes to the goal of the text to validate Zeus' rule: Zeus is able to acquire *mêtis* and the sovereignty it brings because he has already always possessed it, and to a greater degree than his rival, Κρόνος ἀγκυλομήτις "Cronus of the crooked-*mêtis*." In fact, the need to appropriate *mêtis* through prior possession of *mêtis* is, as Detienne and Vernant show, characteristic of several myths of conquering heroes (for example, Heracles, Menelaus, Peleus). This "inconsistency" is, therefore, at the heart of the "myth" of valid sovereignty or the "right to rule": the ruler takes what has always been inherently his own.

27. See Arthur 1982. In her detailed demonstration of this process in the *Theogony* Arthur treats the homology between the mastery by the male through craft and his mastery of reproduction, Zeus' swallowing of the goddess Metis, the stone/σῆμα "sign" as a duplicitous gift, and the link between the stone/σῆμα "sign" and Pandora as θαῦμα "wonder" (see especially 72–78). Arthur analyzes the stone/σῆμα "sign" as an advance from vengeance in the pattern of social retaliation: "This more subtle form of retaliation now introduces the notion of justice as symbolic exchange or reciprocity ... The stone which he [Cronus] vomits up and which is taken up and established as a *sêma* by Zeus is like a point, albeit achieved through trickery, in that it stands as a symbol of recompense given ... The characterization of Zeus' rule as the reign of justice, then, has to do with the emergence of symbolic exchange and balanced reciprocity" (73). Arthur finds in the word link between stone/σῆμα "sign" and Pandora the fact that each "is a symbol of the intersection between natural and artificial creation, and between the divine and human realms" (72). Arthur's analysis provides essential support for the point I stress, the analogy between sexual reproduction and verbal production, when she describes Zeus' swallowing of Metis as a "transformation of progeny into pro-phecy," since "Metis remains within Zeus as his prophetic voice" (78).

28. Compare Telemachus' response when asked if he is Odysseus' son: "My mother says that I am his, but I do not know. For no man of himself (αὐτός) ever knows his own father" (*Odyssey* i 215–216).

29. On the *tropos* "turning," see Cicero *Brutus* 17.69: *ornari orationem Graeci putant, si verborum immutationibus utantur, quos appellant tropous,* "the Greeks think that a

speech is ornamented if they use transformations of words which they call *tropoi*," and Quintilian *Institutio Oratoria* 9.1.4: *est igitur tropos sermo a naturali et principali significatione tralatus ad aliam ornandae orationis gratia, vel, ut plerique grammatici finiunt dictio ab eo loco in quo propria est tralata in eum in quo propria non est.* "A *tropos* is therefore terminology that has been transferred from its natural and primary signification to another for the sake of ornamenting the speech, or, as most grammarians define it, a saying that has been transferred from that place in which it properly belongs into that in which it is does not."

30. In my interpretation of Pandora I follow Pucci (1977:82–126) and Loraux (1981:75–117). See also Detienne (1967:66n104 = 1996:178n85) on Pandora as a creation of Zeus' *mêtis* in conception and of the *mêtis* of all the gods in execution: "*Toute la mêtis des dieux contribue à en faire la forme plus achevé de la mêtis.*" "All the *mêtis* of the gods combines to make her the most complete form of *mêtis.*"

31. West 1966:405 on *Theogony* 899, 900 draws a parallel between the "Hope" left in the jar of Pandora and Metis in the belly of Zeus, and notes the ancient notion of the belly of Zeus as a source of prophecy. If the "jar" of Pandora is rightly likened to a "belly," then this compound analogy would imply that the "hope" in the jar is comparable to the new generation and would thus further support the idea that the capacity for reproduction was conceived in archaic thought as analogous to the power over deception (*mêtis*) and truth (prophecy). See also Arthur (1982:74–75) on Pandora as "bringer of fertility and of the principle of reproduction" and the founder of the race of women as "drone-bellies," "the belly that consumes," but "brings forth the child as well."

32. The idea of a parallel between the role of women in marriage exchange and the female as source of poetic speech was first formulated through conversation with John Peradotto. The work of Carolyn Dewald led me to investigate this relation in the *Histories* of Herodotus.

33. Lévi-Strauss 1967:548–570 = 1969:478–497.

34. For more on the relation between the woman's weaving and her role in marriage exchange, see "The (Re)Marriage of Penelope and Odysseus" in this collection.

35. Compare Vernant's observation (1974 [1965] = 2006:28) apropos of Hesiod's myth of the Five Ages: "*Pour la pensée mythique, toute généalogie est en même temps et aussi bien explication d'une structure; et il n'y a pas d'autre façon de rendre raison d'une structure que de la présenter sous la forme d'un récit généalogique.*" "In mythical thought, any genealogy is also the explanation of a structure, and there is no way to account for a structure other than to present it in the form of a genealogical narrative."

36. See also Lévi-Strauss 1967:34–79 = 1969:29–68.

37. In historical Greece, of course, children took their father's not their mother's name, but as Dewald (1981:120n27) points out: "It is through myth, after all, that

cultures define their own past, and each of the myths told at the beginning of the *Histories* involves a foreign woman who is brought in and helps thereafter to identify the culture to which she is brought. Io in Greek myth becomes an Egyptian goddess and mother of a god; Medea names the Medes; Europa has a continent named after her; and, finally, Helen is the mythic cause of the first open military split between East and West. In Herodotus' carefully indirect account, it is the act of exchanging women back and forth that causes East and West to define themselves, and to define their differences with each other. This is, perhaps, the essence of exogamy as the Greek understood it, but practiced on a cultural rather than a narrowly familial scale."

38. Herodotus *Histories* 1.4.4: "From this event they always considered that Greece was their enemy (πολέμιον). For the Persians consider Asia and the barbarian tribes living within to be their own, and they hold Europe and Greece to have been separated from them (κεχωρίσθαι)."

39. For the details of the analysis here, see "Helen's Web: Time and Tableau in the *Iliad*" and "Helen's 'Good Drug'" in this collection.

40. Erbse, ed. 1969 on *Iliad* III 126–127: ἀξιόχρεων ἀρχέτυπον ἀνέπλασεν ὁ ποιητὴς τῆς ἰδίας ποιήσεως "the poet has fashioned a worthy archetype or model of his own poetic art."

41. On the correlation of drugs and *mêtis*, compare Detienne and Vernant 1978:120–126, 128n7: Metis provides Cronus with a *pharmakon* that is supposed to increase his strength, but actually forces him to disgorge his children, and later is tricked by Zeus into turning herself into a drug that he can then swallow.

42. For the specifics of the diction linking drugs with epic, see "Helen's 'Good Drug'" in this collection. On Helen's poetic role, see Clader 1976:33n13 who notes that the phraseology preceding Helen's entrance at *Odyssey* iv 120 usually signals the appearance of a goddess and that Helen's own words at *Odyssey* iv 140, ψεύσομαι ἦ ἔτυμον ἐρέω "shall I speak falsehood or shall I say what is real," parallel the Muses' speech at *Theogony* 27–28. The identification of Helen's tale with her *pharmakon* is also an ancient interpretation found in Plutarch *Quaestiones Convivales* 1.14.614 and Macrobius 7.1.18.

43. According to the *Lexicon* of Suidas, *s.v.* Σαπφώ, the *floruit* of Stesichorus was Olympiad 42 (612–609 BCE) and, *s.v.* Στησίχορος, his birth and death are given as Olympiad 37 (632–629 BCE) and Olympiad 56 (556–553 BCE) respectively.

44. Cicero (*Republic* 2.20) records the tradition that Stesichorus was Hesiod's grandson; Tzetzes in his Prolegomenon to Hesiod's *Works and Days* (Gaisford, ed. *Poetae minori Graeci*, vol. 2, pg. 18, lines 3–9) says that Aristotle (compare Aristotle fr. 565 Rose) made him Hesiod's son, but that "this Stesichorus was a contemporary of Pythagoras and Phalaris of Agrigentum." An epigram in the *Palatine Anthology* (7.75) notes a Pythagorean saying that in Stesichorus the soul of Homer had found its second home [Στασίχορον, ζαπληθὲς ἀμέτρητον στόμα Μούσης, / ἐκτέρισεν Κατάνας αἰθαλόεν

δάπεδον, / οὗ κατὰ Πυθαγόρεω φυσικὰν φάτιν, ἁ πρὶν Ὁμήρου / ψυχὰ ἐνὶ στέρνοις δεύτερον ᾠκίσατο]. On the meter and language of Stesichorus, see Haslam 1978.

45. Kannicht's reconstruction (1969:1.38–41) of the two parts of the *Helen* reveals an even more complex structure of doublets. In the first part, the κακηγορία "slander" or βλασφημία "damaging speech," the οὐκ ἔτυμος λόγος "not true account," Stesichorus first recounted the Hesiodic aetiology of Helen's μαχλοσύνη "sexual excess" (Stesichorus 223 PMG, Hesiod fragment 176 MW) and then the Homeric version of her abduction by Paris as the cause of the Trojan War; in the second part, the παλινῳδία "recantation," the ἔτυμος λόγος "true account," Stesichorus (according to the *Peri Stesichorou* of Chamaeleon: see Stesichorus 16 PMG, P.Oxy. xxix fr. 26 col. i) "blamed" (μέμφεται) both Homer and Hesiod—Homer, when he says that only the εἴδωλον "phantom" of Helen went to Troy and Hesiod, when he says that the true Helen remained in Egypt, thus remaining sexually faithful to her one true husband Menelaus. If this reconstruction is correct, Stesichorus' diptych (first a negative, then a positive version of Helen's sexual loyalty) is the mirror image of the two tales of Helen in the *Odyssey* (first a positive, then a negative version). Such a narrative doublet exemplifies the παλίντονος ἁρμονία "bent-back harmony" that Kannicht observes in Stesichorus' *Helen*. For an account of the operation of the double structure in the Homeric text, see "Helen's 'Good Drug'" in this collection.

46. Note the parallel between the traditional blindness of Homer, Demodocus who receives blindness as well as song-craft from the Muses (*Odyssey* viii 64), and Thamyris who is "maimed" (πηρός, compare πήρωσις "mutilation, blindness," πηρόω "mutilate" and see Chantraine s.v. πηρός) for challenging the Muses (*Iliad* II 594–600). Blindness and mutilation (with the suggestion of castration) as marks of the male poet suggest that his craft is something conceived of as "female" or feminizing. Compare the case of Teiresias who receives prophecy from Zeus, but blindness from Hera because he "saw" and revealed the secret of female sexuality (that it is greater than the male's) and the fear of Anchises, after his intercourse with Aphrodite, that she will leave him ἀμενός "without μένος" (*Homeric Hymn to Aphrodite* 188; for μένος "strength" as connoting both intellectual and sexual vigor, see Nagy 1974:266–269). To know what the female knows, to speak what she can speak is a gain that is also a loss of the full measure of male identity and power, for it violates the boundary between the sexes. To speak of regaining sight, therefore, as a result of uttering a different, true *logos* of the female as innocent and passive is ironically to retract insight in favor of a new "blindness" about the female, while restoring the sexual and verbal power of the male, a condition we shall observe in Gorgias. See the suggestion of Zeitlin (1981:319n19) that Euripides' second version of the *Hippolytus*, in which he presented a virtuous Phaedra, was in effect a secular version of Stesichorus' palinode on Helen. It was this version that won him the prize from his male audience.

47. For Helen as guilty, see Alcaeus 42 and 283 LP and for a neutral if not positive presentation, see Sappho 16 LP.

48. See above note 3.

49. For the text, see *Gorgias* [82] B11 DK.

50. For Gorgias' philosophy of the *logos*, see especially Segal 1962 and for the role of ἀπάτη "deception," Rosenmeyer 1955.

51. See the apparatus *on Gorgias* [82] B11.12 DK.

52. The πείθω "persuasiveness" of the *logos* "moulds" (ἐτυπώσατο) the soul as it wishes (*Encomium of Helen* 13), just as "through spectacle (ὄψεως) the soul is moulded (τυποῦται) even in its turnings (τρόποις)" (*Encomium of Helen* 15).

53. Similarly, "spectacle" (ὄψις) is said to "write" or "paint" (ἐνέγραψεν) upon the mind "likenesses" (εἰκόνας) of the things seen (*Encomium of Helen* 17).

54. In her study of how Gorgias ascribes to *logos* the traditional characteristics of poetry, de Romilly 1973 notes the earlier connection between drugs and verse, but not the connection between drugs and Helen.

55. I owe the linking of this usage of κόσμος with the κόσμος of Pandora to Charles Segal. For another collocation of κόσμος "order, ornament" with language, see Parmenides κόσμον ἐμῶν ἐπέων ἀπατηλόν "deceptive *kosmos* of my words" (Parmenides [28] B8.52 DK).

56. On the αἶνος, see Nagy 1979:234–241.

57. Plutarch "Advice to Bride and Groom" 43, *Moralia* vol. 2, p. 144 B–C = Gorgias [82] B8a DK.

WEAVING IN NARRATIVE
Textures of Space and Time

2

HELEN'S WEB
Time and Tableau in the *Iliad*

THIS PAPER WAS ORIGINALLY PREPARED FOR A PANEL on "Some Contemporary Approaches to the Homeric Poems."[1] It describes a case in which contemporary critical theory, when combined with our knowledge of formulaic style, helps to interpret a problematic convention of the *Iliad*, namely, the suspension of temporal verisimilitude – the "likeness to the truth" of historical time – in otherwise realistic narrative. Approached through structuralist theory, this convention emerges as one means by which the traditional, formulaic art of the *Iliad* achieves both its historical, its ideal, and its poetic status.

This convention is more widespread in the *Iliad* than we might at first suppose. As a clear and famous example to begin with, take the τειχοσκοπία "viewing from the wall" in Book III. Commentators, both ancient and modern, whether they condemn or defend it, nevertheless agree that the action of this scene is – to use the critical term of the 4th century BCE – ἄλογον "contrary to reason" because it runs counter to chronological verisimilitude.[2] For Priam, after nine years of war, would not need to ask Helen to identify the Achaean chiefs. Such a conversation would be historically realistic only in the early days of the war.[3] Similarly unlikely at this point is Helen's ignorance at the close of the dialogue of whether her brothers have yet arrived in Troy (*Iliad* III 236–242). This aspect of the scene was held by Aristotle to be ἀπίθανον, contrary to realistic probability.[4] The τειχοσκοπία "viewing from the wall" thus fails to cohere with the poem's main plot: Achilles' wrath and the plan of Zeus in the tenth year of the Trojan War. The scene is in this way "a-historical" or "counter-historical," and it does not stand alone.

Besides the τειχοσκοπία "viewing from the wall," all the action from the catalogue of ships in Book II, to the "commencement of hostilities" in Book III through the breaking of the oaths in Book IV and its aftermath in Book V, as commentators have pointed out many times, is appropriate to the account not of an end, but of the beginning of a war.[5] Similarly, the number of lines devoted to the *aristeia* of Diomedes, nearly a thousand, has struck readers as more extensive than is necessary to establish the Greek success that will send Hector back to Troy, to say nothing of its distance from what is demanded by the overall plot, the Greek defeat promised to Achilles. Also faulted as chronologically illogical is the so-called "second duel" of Book VII.[6] And with the *Doloneia* of Book X, the text again moves outside of contemporary chronology and does not come back to the course of Achilles' wrath (except for two brief though critical moments) for the next five books. Together these passages make up 6621 lines, about forty-two percent of the poem, in which temporal verisimilitude is either suspended or contradicted, while the narration is in other respects realistic. This is not a minor phenomenon: by its extent alone it qualifies as a convention of the *Iliad*.

Meeting this convention, critics have chosen either to ignore it as insignificant, while emphasizing the positive and unproblematical achievements of the text, to condemn it as contrary to what the other, realistic conventions of the epic lead us to expect, to rationalize it, or to ascribe it to oral composition. The first is the position most frequently taken: the poetic glories of these passages are so great that their temporal details shrink to insignificance and concern with them to nit-picking philistinism.[7] There remain, however, some for whom these chronological facts are undeniable faults and to these, the defenders of the text have responded either by trying – along with the Aristotelian critics of the 4th century BCE – to resolve the inconsistencies rationally or by claiming that for an audience used to oral poetry the inconsistencies would be unnoticed or at least aesthetically irrelevant. None of these positions proves finally satisfactory. No matter how excellent these passages are in other respects, it is an interpretive repression simply to ignore the existence of their temporal features. Exonerating them as marks of oral composition fails to acknowledge our experience of the *Iliad* as a written text rather than as "winged words." And indeed we may question whether listening to a text rather than reading it makes one less sensitive to its chronologies. The rational explanations offered are often ingenious – for example, that the very detail of Priam's asking Helen to name the chiefs actually increases the verisimilitude of the passage, since an aged man would "naturally" have difficulty seeing from a distance and would need help in recognizing them.[8] Such λύσεις "solutions" cannot be disproved, but neither can they be devised for all of the temporal difficulties we confront. We are left with only the equally unwelcome alternatives of either ignoring or condemning this treatment of time.

For a new interpretive approach, one that would reveal the poetic function of this convention, I have looked in two directions: first, to the formulaic method of composition, that is, to what we recognize as particular to the
Homeric poems, and second, to structuralist theory of convention in general
and verisimilitude in particular. Contemporary theory illuminates the partic-
ularities of the ancient genre, while the need to be consistent with ancient
compositional technique prevents anachronistic application of the modern
generalization. In this case, formulaic composition and structuralist theory
converge in a re-interpretation of the suspension of temporal realism as
the technique by which the *Iliad* creates the time of the tapestry, the time of
Helen's web. By transcending the limit of any single historical moment, the
temporality of tapestry measures the dimension of Achilles' κλέος ἄφθιτον
"unperishing epic fame." This understanding of Homeric "meta-temporality"
makes it possible to re-appraise the artistry of the central Battle Books, to
see how they prove both the temporal transcendence and – through the Διὸς
ἀπάτη "deception of Zeus" – the generic vulnerability of the κλέα ἀνδρῶν
"famous deeds of men."

The suspension of temporal verisimilitude in otherwise realistic narrative is not without parallel in the formulaic method of composition. Beginning
with Aristarchus Homeric scholars have observed that some "formulaic" or
traditional epithets (those termed "generic" by Parry) are used even when
they contradict the "historical moment," for example, a "starry sky" in
daytime.[9] These formulas are analogous to such scenes as the τειχοσκοπία
"viewing from the wall," realistic except from the point of view of time.
Indeed, as a typical scene for epics of war against walled cities (one with counterparts in Mycenaean art, Near Eastern narrative, and other Greek myths),
the τειχοσκοπία is analogous to just such a "generic epithet." It is an enduring
attribute of the start of all such wars, used here in the *Iliad*, in contradiction
of time, at the end instead of the beginning.[10] Similarly, the interpretation
of these epithets by Aristarchus may apply to these scenes as well: they are
used, he says, to add κόσμος "ornament" to the text by expressing the φύσις
"nature" of their nouns, as opposed to epithets that mark only the historical
state, the τότε "then." It is at this point that contemporary theory illuminates
formulaic practice.

Structuralist theory of verisimilitude contributes first of all by revealing
the breadth of this critical category. Particularly in the work of Gérard Genette
it becomes clear that to question the verisimilitude of a text is to ask nothing
less than what it means and what we, or any culture of readers, believe a literary
text can or ought to mean.[11] The answer to the question of verisimilitude

comes, according to this view, from the text itself initially, from its several conventions that together make up a literary genre or "truth" or "world" that readers, then, must learn to recognize. Any literary practice becomes legible when we can recognize its verisimilitude, that is, what genre or world or truth it is about. On the basis of this understanding of the term, Genette and others are able to categorize periods and types of literature according to the level or levels of verisimilitude they include and to specify the conventions that create each level. In their determination of these so-called levels, these critics are aided by a fundamental tenet of the structuralist theory of language, namely, that linguistic signs make their meaning not by reference to external things but by their differential relations with other signs. Consciousness of this fact makes structuralists especially sensitive to the ways in which poetic texts "are about," so to speak, their relations with other texts and thereby are also "about" the poetic process itself. As a result, their analyses are able to show how a given text bears a multi-leveled or complex verisimilitude, a manifold world or truth that could include, for example, the combination of qualities that Aristarchus saw in formulaic epithets, both the historical, the universal, and the poetic.

This theory of complex verisimilitude bears directly upon the conventions of the *Iliad*. It directs us not to ignore or condemn a convention that contradicts others, but to determine whether or not the ensemble portrays a recognizable genre or truth. Specifically, we should look for what is signified by the combination of realistic narrative with the suspension of the plot's history.[12] What we find is that this combination of conventions signifies a complex, but still recognizable verisimilitude and in a genre declared by the τειχοσκοπία "viewing from the wall" itself. It is the genre of the tapestry.

The τειχοσκοπία "viewing from the wall" opens with Iris summoning Helen to watch from the wall as Menelaus and Paris contest to possess her. This is the first time that the epic turns to look at the erotic origin and object of the war, and when it does, we see Helen who "was weaving (ὕφαινε, imperfect) a great web, double, purple, and embroidering (ἐνέπασσεν, imperfect of ἐμπάσσω, literally, "sprinkle in") into it many contests of horse-taming Trojans and bronze-armored Achaeans, which they were enduring (ἔπασχον, imperfect) for her at the hands of Ares" (*Iliad* III 125–128). In this activity we see a reflection of the poetic process in the *Iliad*: in the words of the scholiast, "the poet has fashioned a worthy archetype or model of his own poetic art."[13] The art of the *Iliad* is the art of the tableau. The two conventions of realistic narration and temporal suspension produce a verbal version of what we would see in Helen's tapestry, that is, the action of struggle in stasis, both movement in time – indeed imperfected movement – and metatemporal permanence, both at once. These paradoxical poetics are also those of the τειχοσκοπία "viewing from the wall" as a whole. Not in spite of but because it is a stock scene of the epic tradition, used here anachronistically, the τειχοσκοπία "viewing from the wall" becomes part of a design to show beginnings in ends and by that transcendence of linear time, to show simultaneously both something that happened once and what there is in that "something" that ever recurs. By mixing the suspension of historical temporality with otherwise realistic narration, that is, by retaining the marks of its "origin" as a traditional scene for the start of a siege, the encounter of Priam and Helen is portrayed as both a part of the present conflict and – what is also true of it – as a "formulaic" element, a "generic epithet" of all wars against walled cities. Like a tapestry, the τειχοσκοπία "viewing from the wall" is at once historical and universal and what is more, just as we see not only her web, but also Helen weaving it, so, too, the τειχοσκοπία "viewing from the wall" points by being so obviously traditional to the process of its creation, for it is by means of tradition that epic can make the historical universal. It is by traditional repetition of κλέος that epic makes of men's deeds in the Trojan War, the immortal κλέα ἀνδρῶν "famous deeds of men." This is the complex verisimilitude of the τειχοσκοπία "viewing from the wall" and also of those other portions of the *Iliad* in which the historical development of the plot is either suspended or contradicted.

Of those other portions of the *Iliad,* the most outstanding are the central Battle Books. It is a tradition of Homeric scholarship to observe that Books XI–XV depart from the poem's main plot, the μῆνις "wrath" of Achilles and the βουλὴ Διός "plan of Zeus."[14] The warfare in Books XIII, XIV, and half of XV reverses the advances in XI and XII towards the fulfillment of Zeus' plan. Moreover, the action of these five books is not conceivable in the afternoon allotted to them by the explicit time frame of the text. Before we are halfway through them, we have forgotten what time it is: time has stood still. And at the center of this section lies the Διὸς ἀπάτη "deception of Zeus," customarily viewed as comic relief and not integrally related to the epic as a whole.[15] When analyzed as analogous to traditional generic epithets and according to the notion of complex verisimilitude, however, these very deviations from temporal development are seen to weave into the text another tableau, this time of the κλέα ἀνδρῶν "famous deeds of men" as historical, immortal, and fictional.

By their deviation from the plot of Achilles' wrath, by their stretching of a day into timelessness, and by their overall pattern of action, the Battle Books become more than particular events of the Trojan War. They become the mimesis of the κλέα ἀνδρῶν "famous deeds of men," the epic tradition that Achilles sings when he withdraws from active fighting (*Iliad* IX 185–189) and what the epic sings when it withdraws from him. In his book, *The Story of the Iliad*, Owen points out their grand design, a kind of circumstructure, in which Hector advances to the ditch and to the wall, but then is driven back, and must take the ditch and the wall again. This movement reproduces the forth and back and forth of battle in a period of suspended time.[16] By this schematization the Battle Books, while describing the vicissitudes of one day in the war's tenth year, become as well an emblem of the warfare of all ten years and of warfare of any time. In this design, these books weave a "generic epithet" of war, the eternal reciprocity of victory and defeat.[17] Viewed more closely the design remains, but becomes more complicated.

In the course of Books XI and XII, the deviations from historical development serve to show warfare as a product of the plan of Zeus and epic as its immortalizing compensation – specifically, here, the βουλὴ Διός "plan of Zeus" to give Hector a day of glory that will cause his destruction. As an example, I take the opening of Book XII where the text constructs another τειχοσκοπία "viewing from the wall." The Trojans have in Book XI progressed to the ditch and will at the end of XII break through the Greeks' wall as well. At the start of Book XII, however, the poet turns from the action on the field to describe the destruction of that wall at the end of the war by Poseidon, Apollo, and Zeus. This prediction has no direct bearing upon the war itself; victory and defeat are unaffected by it. The result of this gratuitous forecast is only to dissolve the temporal significance of this moment to a point past the horizon even of the *Iliad* itself, to a point of god-like perspective upon the fighting to come. From this perspective, the permanence of the wall and of the warfare around it is reduced to only that which poetry can give. The gods can preserve or break a wall, but epic can, as it does here, repeat the facts past the point of their obliteration; so heroes can die, but their κλέος "fame" can be undying. It is from this metatemporal point of view, this second "viewing from the wall," that we watch as Hector in rejection of Poulydamas' right reading of the divine sign, insists ironically, "Let us put our trust in the plan of great Zeus (Διὸς βουλῇ) . . . one bird is best: to fight in defense of our fatherland" (*Iliad* XII 241, 243), and as Sarpedon claims that being "not without κλέος" in the eyes of his people is both motive and compensation for heroic death (*Iliad* XII 310–328). In the perspective of this second τειχοσκοπία "viewing from the wall," human war is the product of a divine plot, discernible and redeemable only by epic in its power to transcend time.

So far, then, in this vision of the heroic world, the power of poetry is subordinate to the plan of Zeus. Epic, it appears at this point, can reveal and compensate, but it is powerless to change. The βουλὴ Διός "plan of Zeus" remains the final arbiter of verisimilitude at every level of the text. Thus, for all its lack of chronological realism, this depiction of war appears firmly centered in a truthfulness that transcends simple historical factuality, the universal truthfulness of Zeus. What we are expecting, therefore, at the start of Book XIII is the completion of Zeus' plan, the firing of the ships by Hector and the sundown on his day of glory. What we find, however, is something different, and for the fulfillment of Zeus' promise, we would have to turn ahead to Book XV after line 404, when Patroclus resumes his return to Achilles and the Trojans retake the wall. Instead at the start of XIII, the suspension of historical temporality expands to include the suspension of what has until now been the "unmoved mover" of the Iliadic universe, the βουλὴ Διός "plan of Zeus." During Books XIII and XIV, not only human temporality but divine vision and authority, too, will be subjected to poetic desire.

Book XIII opens with the ultimate violation of verisimilitude in the *Iliad*: Zeus averts his eyes. He no longer sees and can no longer control the progress of the text. This narrative move transgresses not only the poem's historical time frame, but also the timeless realism of its supreme deity. In the absence of its author what happens to the plot of the *Iliad* is the incursion of an opposing plot, traditions kept absent by the central presence of Zeus and the exigencies of his plan for Hector's glory.

What enters the text in opposition to the βουλὴ Διός "plan of Zeus" is the "plot of Poseidon." It is made up of traditions for which there is no room in Zeus' current plan, more κλέα "famous deeds" of the Greeks (Idomeneus, Meriones, Antilochus, and Menelaus), where Zeus' will for Hector requires their defeat. Similarly, traditional narrative forms occur here in ways untypical for the *Iliad*. Most egregious is at the end of Book XIII, when, after two short catalogues of the Trojans and the Greeks and the exchange of challenge and insult by Hector and Ajax, this evident overture to a duel is cut short, and the book ends abruptly with five lines of common attack and outcry.[18] Just as the βουλὴ Διός "plan of Zeus" is stopped by the intervention of Poseidon and will not be resumed until Book XV, so this duel between Ajax and Hector is put off until line 402 of Book XIV. This narrative stroke deviates not just from conventional Iliadic practice, but even from the "plot of Poseidon." It turns our attention from the plots of the gods to the "plotting" of the poet, from the text as mimesis of realistic, if unconventional, action to the text as unstable

49

artifice. In Book XIV, this plotting turns to deception, as the βουλὴ Διός "plan of Zeus" becomes the Διὸς ἀπάτη "deception of Zeus."

Superficially, Book XIV is the simple chronological dependent of XIII: the ἰαχή "shout" that ends the one starts the other (*Iliad* XIII 834, XIV 1), and this outcry motivates the assembly by Nestor of the Greek chiefs and their decision to marshal the troops in person. But here the connection between the two books becomes complicated. Once again, as if he had not done so before, Poseidon intervenes to rouse the Greeks now in the guise of an old man. He first predicts to Agamemnon the ultimate retreat of the Trojans, and then, despite his previous efforts to avoid Zeus' attention, he sweeps over the plain shouting the war cry (*Iliad* XIV 147–152). With that, Hera looks down from Olympus, first at Poseidon, then at Zeus, and proceeds to effect the Διὸς ἀπάτη "deception of Zeus." Once Zeus is asleep, Hypnos informs Poseidon, who again rouses the Greeks. The first encounter of the new wave after the Διὸς ἀπάτη "deception of Zeus" is the duel between Ajax and Hector suspended from the end of XIII. This narrative order has provoked such dismay that previous interpretations all attempt some re-ordering of the text, but still fail to make sense of it.[19] When read as such, however, the design is not meaningless.

As far as the progress of "Poseidon's plot" is concerned, the re-entry of the god is wholly gratuitous: the Greek generals have already decided to marshal their troops themselves. Gratuitous, too, therefore, is anything that depends upon Poseidon's re-intervention and what depends upon it narratively is the Διὸς ἀπάτη "deception of Zeus." Indeed, this dependence of the deception upon Poseidon's re-intervention is the only motivation of the god's re-appearance, although it is a motivation *ex post facto*. As commentators point out, it is only Poseidon's unsolicited bellow that makes it necessary for Hera to distract Zeus.[20] The first scene is the cause of the second, but the first itself has no cause except to cause the second. The combined unit is thus a perfect narrative gratuity. The effect is to manipulate the βουλὴ Διός "plan of Zeus" still further, to transform the text not just into a competing plot but into a deceiving one. In this most radical dislocation of temporal order, the entire world of martial realism – indeed, of reality as war – is de-stabilized, for in the gratuitous Διὸς ἀπάτη "deception of Zeus," the teleology of war is deceived by the ritual of sexuality.

At the center of the κλέα ἀνδρῶν "famous deeds of men" is ritual sexuality – the ritual, the holiday, the comedy and the plotting that is sexuality. For the Διὸς ἀπάτη "deception of Zeus" evokes by detailed parallels one of the most common rituals of the Greek states, the ἱερὸς γάμος "sacred marriage" of the sky-god with the goddesses of earth, the union by which Zeus proves himself the "father of men and gods."[21] The fullest ἱερὸς λόγος "sacred story, account" of the ἱερὸς γάμος "sacred marriage" accompanies the Boeotian festival of the Daedala. In this myth we see how the ἱερὸς γάμος "sacred marriage" of Zeus and Hera celebrates fertility and sexuality as a comic plot of jealousy, disguise, deception, recognition, and laughter.

As recorded by Eusebius and Pausanias the story is this.[22] Once Hera was angry with Zeus and refused intercourse. Zeus could not persuade her to relent, and so at his wits' end, he consulted Alalkomenes (or Kithairôn, king of the Plataeans), who advised him that it was necessary to deceive (ἐξαπατητέον) Hera by pretending to marry another woman. So then in secret Zeus cut from the trunk of a tender oak tree a wooden image which he dressed in a bridal veil. He set the image upon a cart drawn by cattle and announced that he was going to marry this Daidalê (or Plataea, the daughter of Asopus). Amid the singing of the marriage song, the preparation of the bath by the nymphs of the river Triton, and the presentation of flutes and bands of revelers by the cities of Boeotia, Hera could resist no longer, but descended from Kithairôn, followed by the women of Plataea. Angry and jealous, she came running up to Zeus, pulled the clothing from the statue, and upon discovering the deception (ἀπάτη) of a wooden image instead of a bride, she was reconciled. With joy and laughter she rode in the procession as the bride herself, paid tribute to the wooden image by instituting a festival called the Daedala, but nevertheless burned the statue that, although inanimate, had aroused her jealousy. On this αἴτιον "aetiological myth" Frontisi-Ducroux comments:[23]

> These narratives which relate the manufacture of a prototype of a statue are thus put under the category of a ruse. It is to deceive Hera – ἐξαπατητέον τὴν Ἥραν – that Zeus, aided by Cithaerôn or Alalcomenes, manufactures an image. There could be no better way of expressing the fact that art finds its origin in deceit . . . And, as is very often the case when it is a matter of *mêtis*, fraud – *apatê* or *plasma* – , far from being denigrated, bears a quite positive value. The anger of Hera ceases abruptly. There is reconciliation in the joy and in the midst of bursts of laughter that the vision of the artifice provokes (*C'est la réconciliation dans la joie, et au milieu des éclats de rire que provoque la vue du simulacre*).

With these qualities this myth is the double of the Διὸς ἀπάτη "deception of Zeus" except that the roles are reversed.

In light of the ἱερὸς λόγος "sacred story, account" of the Daedala and the other celebrations of the union of Zeus and Hera, it is clear that the Διὸς ἀπάτη "deception of Zeus" in the *Iliad* represents the traditions of this ritual, but with a critical twist: in the epic all phases of the action are in the control not of Zeus, but of Hera. The Διὸς ἀπάτη "deception of Zeus" re-enacts, but in an inverted version, the pan-Hellenic cult of Zeus' and Hera's holy union. The text we have here subverts the authority of Zeus and magnifies the glory of Hera. In this way it is parallel to the *Homeric Hymn to Aphrodite*, which inverts the form of a hymn by overtly aiming to praise the deity to whom it is addressed, while proving in fact her humiliating subordination to Zeus, to his power to tame her with her own power of ἵμερος "sexual passion."[24] Similarly, the *Iliad* here recreates the union by which the Indo-European sky-god makes himself the πατὴρ ἀνδρῶν τε θεῶν τε "father of both men and gods," but with Zeus, too, like Aphrodite, tricked by his susceptibility to sex and mortified (without his knowledge) by the very list of conquests that constitutes his supremacy (*Iliad* XIV 313–328). Indeed the poet's term for this version of the ritual is none other than the βουλή "plan" of Hera (*Iliad* XIV 161).

Hera's technique in prosecuting her βουλή "plan" is the same as that by which the text introduces her plot. Again, the poet provides the term: it is χάρις "gratuitous beauty." At the sight of Hera dressed with ambrosia and the artifice of δαίδαλα "variegated figures," the poet exclaims, "abundant was the χάρις that gleamed forth" (*Iliad* XIV 183). And when Hypnos at first refuses to put Zeus to sleep, the inducement he cannot refuse is marriage to the Χάρις or "Grace" named Pasithea (*Iliad* XIV 267–276). In his eager acquiescence, Hypnos anticipates the reaction of Zeus, who will also bow to the force of χάρις "gratuitous beauty" embodied in his wife and her deception. For just as Hypnos hoped all his life for this "Χάρις," so Zeus has never in all his life been so aroused by the sight of Hera (*Iliad* XIV 293–328). The βουλή "plan" of Hera is the Διὸς ἀπάτη "deception of Zeus" activated by χάρις "gratuitous beauty," just as the episode itself is a deception woven into the center of the κλέα ἀνδρῶν "famous deeds of men" by an act of narrative gratuity.

By this central plot, the weaving of the κλέα ἀνδρῶν "famous deeds of men" emerges as a tapestry that is true to the art of Helen. For by this textual deception, Zeus is proved to be a god who can at the core of his epic be turned from plotting martial tragedy for humans to playing the comic victim of divine χάρις. Even Zeus is vulnerable to the fictionalizing of gratuitous beauty. The seriousness, the illusion of stable significance of the Trojan War is by the Διὸς ἀπάτη "deception of Zeus" deprived of support. The human tragedy of the κλέα ἀνδρῶν "famous deeds of men" is bisected only to reveal a center that has no real origin, no motivation in the text, but only the absence of origin or the fictional origin that is the χάρις of Hera. The truth of war, its verisimilitude, includes this susceptibility to the plotting of *eros*, a plot that does not last long, but long enough. Now the βουλὴ Διός "plan of Zeus" must repeat itself and prove again its narrative authority.

In Book XV, Zeus employs the most effective means of establishing narrative and divine verisimilitude. As supreme divine power, he predicts he will do what the text then does. In turning to this strategy, Zeus wastes no time with motivation of the prophecy itself. Like the preview of the destruction of the wall, Zeus' prediction of the future comes without evident cause, as he is directing Hera to send Apollo to rouse Hector:

> Let him [Hector] stir up strengthless
> panic in the Achaeans and turn them back once more,
> and let them flee and fall into the many-benched ships
> of Achilles, Peleus' son. And he will rouse up Patroclus,
> his companion. And glorious Hector will cut down Patroclus
> with the spear before Ilion, after he has killed many other
> vigorous men, and among them my own son, shining Sarpedon.
> In anger for Patroclus shining Achilles will cut down Hector.
> And from then on I would cause a counter-attack from the ships,
> constant and continuous, until the Achaeans
> capture lofty Ilion through the plans of Athena.
> Before this neither do I cease my anger nor will I let
> any other of the immortals defend the Danaans here
> until the wish of the son of Peleus has been fulfilled,
> just as I first promised and bowed my head to it
> on that day when the goddess Thetis clasped my knees,
> beseeching me to honor Achilles, sacker of cities.
>
> *Iliad* XV 61–77

Although its motivation is hazy, the results of this prophecy are not. First, by recalling the events of Book I and their sequels, it re-collects all the strands of the βουλὴ Διός "plan of Zeus" left hanging, while the κλέα ἀνδρῶν "famous deeds of men" were woven in. Secondly, it summarizes the rest of the βουλὴ Διός, the plot that will take over now and develop relentlessly until the end of the poem. But this prefiguration does not end with the epic, however. Like the prediction about the wall, the end of Zeus' promise is never fulfilled in the *Iliad* itself. What he promises in effect is a sequel to this poem, another story from the epic tradition in which the Greeks take Troy "through the designs of Athena" and the goals of the plots of both Poseidon and Hera will be met. As he solves the problem of opposition in the *Theogony* by incorporating his adversaries in a hierarchy over which he holds sway, so here Zeus checks advances against the βουλὴ Διός by expanding it beyond the confines of the *Iliad* to include all the plots of the Trojan War. Zeus' traditional strategy is to appropriate tradition. At once it begins to take effect, as Hera delivers her messages, Iris restrains Poseidon, Apollo revives Hector, and together the two, like Poseidon and the Greeks before, lead the resurgence that captures again first the ditch and then the wall (*Iliad* XV 78–389). At this point, the weaving of the κλέα ἀνδρῶν "famous deeds of men" is completed and the scene shifts back to Patroclus whose poetic and healing service to the wounded Eurypylus frames and glosses the Battle Books.

For while the poet has been singing the κλέα ἀνδρῶν "famous deeds of men," Patroclus has been sitting and delighting (ἔτερπε) Eurypylus with stories (λόγοι) and sprinkling (ἔπασσε, the same verb as was used to describe Helen's weaving of the contests) healing drugs upon his sore wound (*Iliad* XV 393–394). What are these stories that parallel drugs in healing a wounded warrior? In the proem to the *Theogony*, we are told that κλέα "famous deeds" assuage even the heart whose grief is fresh (*Theogony* 98–103). The stories that would heal Eurypylus are κλέα like those we have just heard in which the Greeks triumphed over the Trojans against the plan of Zeus. Yet to apply this version of the κλέα ἀνδρῶν "famous deeds of men" to the wounds of a Greek would also invoke its "a-centric" center, the Διὸς ἀπάτη "deception of Zeus," the song that is subversive of all glory based in war, death, historical time and tragedy. The "temporal verisimilitude" of the world in which victory and defeat are meaningful is "violated" by sexuality, immortality, ritual repetition, and comedy. Even Zeus, that essence of linear time, is vulnerable to distraction by his own sexual urge. The pretense of the plot of Zeus to supreme narrative authority is vulnerable to disillusionment. Even the κλέα ἀνδρῶν "famous deeds of men," even the κλέος "fame" in epic of Achilles, is a song, the plot finally not of Zeus or Poseidon or Hera, but of bards. Its factuality, its transcendent meaning is the work of bardic will. This is the "complex verisimilitude" of the *Iliad* at its core.

In the *Iliad*, then, deviations from the historical development of the plot are widespread and they range in form from an entire section like the central Battle Books, to a traditional scene like the τειχοσκοπία "viewing from the wall," to extra-narrative predictions, to the indefinite suspension of a plot or an action such as the duel, and even to the gratuitous insertion with no narrative motivation of an actually subversive counter-plot. By bringing the timeless into otherwise realistic narration, this convention permits the text to portray not only the historical, but also the enduring nature of its subject.

By being realistic or historical in every dimension but that of time, the text makes of the Trojan War a classic, if by that we mean the real unbounded by time. This convention is, therefore, not a narrative mistake, as the analytical critics, who detect it best, believe; but it is, as they also claim, a mark of the traditional method and matter of Homeric verse. A scene like the τειχοσκοπία "viewing from the wall" points to the formulaic method of composition precisely because its anachronisms – those anachronisms that mark it as a sort of formula or "generic epithet" – have not been disguised. For it is precisely by anachrony, the contradiction of historical temporality through endless repetition, that epic becomes the immortalizing medium of κλέος ἄφθιτον "unperishing fame." Thus, a third level, that of the poetic process itself, is added by this convention to the historical and the universal meaning of the text. What results is a threefold or complex verisimilitude, one which mirrors in its depiction of time, timelessness, and artifice, the image offered by the text itself of Iliadic art, namely, Helen's web. By these various violations of historical time the epic is given the properties of a woven tapestry – a string of words about heroism is woven into a tableau of permanent, if only poetic significance.

Notes

An earlier version of this essay appeared in *Helios* n.s. 7 (1980) 19–34.

1. APA Panel, "Some Contemporary Approaches to the Homeric Poems," organized by Carl A. Rubino, 28 December 1978, Vancouver, British Columbia. I am grateful to the discussant for the panel, Wallace McLeod, for helpful criticisms and to David Blank, Deborah Boedeker, and Froma Zeitlin for valuable information and suggestions.

2. Aristotle "*Aporhêmata Homêrika*," fragment 147 Rose.

3. See, for example, Faesi 1888 on *Iliad* III 122–244 and Reckford 1964:9–10.

4. Heraklides Ponticus "*Luseôn Homêrikôn*," fragment 172 Wehrli.

5. See, for example, Ameis and Hentze 1877:163–170, Kakridis 1971:32 with bibliography, and Vivante 1970:147–148.

6. Kirk 1978:18–40.

7. See, for example, the defenses of Naegelsbach 1864:391, 396; Leaf 1892 on *Iliad* III 161; Bowra 1930:112–113; Owen 1966 [1946]:34–36. Owen's claim that the scene serves to introduce the major Greek chiefs is countered by the fact that the two most emphasized in the *Teichoscopia*, Agamemnon and Odysseus, are already familiar from Iliad I and II.

8. For another example of this sort of explanation, termed by Aristotle a λύσις "solution" (*Poetics* 1460b6), see Heyne 1834 on *Iliad* III 166: "*Nondum ante hunc diem tam prope ad urbem accessisse Achivos necesse est, et prospectum esse debuisse e muro liberum, ut Priamus singulorum ora discerneret.*"

9. For a summary of the evidence for Aristarchus' analysis of such epithets, see Parry 1971:120–123.

10. For the parallels to the τειχοσκοπία "viewing from the wall," see Kakridis 1971:33–37, and on the traditional character of the scene, Bowra 1930:113: "It was his [the poet's] business to produce the familiar traits as well as his new inventions, and at times he could only do so at some cost to his general design. In themselves the scenes have great beauty and sometimes they are relevant in their immediate context. Perhaps Homer did not mind this." While agreeing with Bowra's observation of the facts, I will try to counter his interpretation by demonstrating a "general design" that is not vitiated by violations of historical chronology within traditional material. By this demonstration, I mean also to suggest that the violations themselves are part of the epic tradition.

11. For the details of what I summarize here, see Genette, "*Vraisemblance et motivation*" (1969:71–99) and Culler, "Convention and Naturalization" (1975:131–160). Among Homeric scholars it is John Peradotto who has realized the importance of this issue and pursued it most profoundly in Peradotto 1974:803–832.

12. On the way in which the elaborate descriptions of objects and places, so characteristic of Homeric style, result in a realistic, "historical" narrative, that is, in the illusion of tangible surfaces in an actual time and place, see, for example, Auerbach 1973 [1953]:3, 6–7, 11, 14, and Barthes 1968:84–89.

13. Erbse, ed. 1969 on *Iliad* III 126–127: ἀξιόχρεων ἀρχέτυπον ἀνέπλασεν ὁ ποιητὴς τῆς ἰδίας ποιήσεως. On Helen's role as poet in the τειχοσκοπία "viewing from the wall" and on weaving as a traditional symbol of poetic composition, see Clader 1976:6–11.

14. This view pervades 19th century English and German commentaries; for contemporary French and English versions see Mazon 1948:183–201; Bowra 1930:4; Owen 1966 [1946]:110–145.

15. See, for example, Owen 1966 [1946]:137–138 and Whitman 1958:283.

16. Owen 1966 [1946]:126–130.

17. This attribute of war is expressed at the level of diction by the line-final noun-epithet formula, ὁμοιίου πολέμοιο "of equal war." Because it is reciprocal, war is equalizing.

18. See Fenik 1968:152–158.

19. See, for example, Leaf 1892:242–244 and Fenik 1968:157.

20. See, for example, Leaf 1892:246 and Mazon 1948:197.

21. See Klinz 1933 and Frontisi-Ducroux 1975:193–216.

22. Eusebius *Praeparatio evangelica* 3.1.3 and 6; Pausanias 9.2.7–3.8.

23. Frontisi-Ducroux 1975:213.

24. See "*Homeric Hymn to Aphrodite*: Tradition and Rhetoric, Praise and Blame" in this collection.

3

SIMILES AND SYMBOL
IN *ODYSSEY* V

SINCE ANTIQUITY, THE *ODYSSEY* HAS INVITED SYMBOLIC INTERPRETATION. When Eustathius pronounces the poem an ethical allegory, and in that, more indicative than the *Iliad* of "Homeric power," he echoes a tradition extending back through early Christian writers to the *Allegoriae (Quaestiones Homericae)* of Heraclitus.[1] Among modern critics, Charles Segal has shown how Books v–xii – the hero's return to Ithaca from the island of Calypso, with his narration to the Phaeacians of his earlier adventures – are symbolic of psychological development.[2] Within this portion of the poem, however, with the exception of a 1966 article by Erling Holtsmark, no developed symbolism has been seen in the action of *Odyssey* v – Odysseus' departure from Calypso, the storm at sea, and his landing upon Phaeacia.[3] The figure of Calypso, "she who covers," has been regularly interpreted as the power of the female – sexual, maternal, and deadly, and her cave as chthonic womb or underworld.[4] In antiquity, she was sometimes read allegorically.[5] And in Segal's elegant and suggestive words, she is "a point of suspension" in whom "are reflected the crossing and binding together of the cosmic substances, earth, sky and sea."[6] But no elaboration of her symbolic meaning has been observed in the action of the book as a whole. She has been taken, to employ Quintilian's distinction, as a single-word trope rather than an extended figure, in an otherwise literal narrative of leaving her.[7] The action by which Odysseus enters his epic is not felt to be figurative in the way, for example, that of its successor, Canto I of the *Inferno*, is held to be.[8] Dante's entry into the *Divina Commedia* displays the extended, systematic symbolization of action designated as allegory, specifically, an allegory of spiritual awakening, while the meaning of *Odyssey* v seems limited to the physical ordeal of escaping Calypso's attractive force. The Homeric narration is full of concrete details with no evident reference outside themselves. The characterization is individual rather than emblematic; the subtle conversations first, between Hermes and Calypso and then, between

Calypso and Odysseus, the building of the raft, and the stages of the storm all tend toward the realism typical of post-allegorical fiction and typically appreciated in Homeric style.[9]

Yet the art of *Odyssey* v both includes and exceeds post-allegorical realism. While Homeric epic is not allegorical in the manner of a medieval text, in *Odyssey* v the genre achieves a similarly extended and systematic symbolization. The critical mechanism is the similes. In Book v the similes function together like those external texts, principally from the Bible, upon which the *allegoria* of *Inferno* I depends. Or, more precisely, the similes are like those Biblical texts when they are compiled in a great commentary such as Singleton's which also specifies the inter-textual connections, a shared code of words and themes, by which Dante allegorizes his narrative.[10] By their lines of contact with the action – the common code of words and themes which they themselves declare through the formal ὡς "as" . . . ὣς "so" – the similes act like a commentary to disclose a ὑπόνοια "undermeaning" in *Odyssey* v similar to that of *Inferno* I, namely, the interior, spiritual or psychological experience "under" or "within" the exterior action of the hero.[11] Both the annotated commentary and the commentating similes participate in a process of symbolization that exemplifies the ancient notion of the *sumbolon*.

Evidently first a means for identifying guest-friends, allies, or depositors of goods, the term *sumbolon* designates an incomplete object, such as a half of a knucklebone or a tablet, which must be brought together (συμβάλλειν) with its counterpart in order to signify the relationship between the bearers.[12] The meaning of the *sumbolon* is an identity constituted by a relationship. The connection between the *sumbolon* and the person who bears it may be arbitrary (in semiotic terms, conventional or unmotivated) – as in the case of a private code or of words as conventional *sumbola* of mental experiences in Aristotle's definition,[13] or it may be natural (motivated) – as in the case of the baby clothes, weaving, necklace, and olive wreath that identify Creusa and Ion as mother and son.[14] In either case, the process of interpreting the *sumbolon* is the same, but the authority of the interpretation may vary. To interpret *sumbolon*-a, one must first establish that *sumbolon*-b is its complement and then determine the relationship between the possessors to which the *sumbola* testify: the symbolic meaning of *sumbolon*-a is the identity of its possessor in that relationship. An instance in Herodotus of conventional *sumbola* illustrates their potential weakness as signs: a creditor "interprets" the *sumbolon* of his debtor by providing its counterpart, but the debtor simply denies that these objects betoken any prior relationship of obligation.[15] Motivated *sumbola* like the contents of Ion's cradle permit a more authoritative reading. This example also illustrates the derived, somewhat metaphorical usage of the term, *sumbolon*, to designate not a half but a whole object. Even in this case, however, the *sumbolon* operates according to the original model and the interpretive process is the same. When Creusa is able to describe, before seeing them, the contents of Ion's cradle, she establishes a "natural" bond of identification between herself and these objects (a sort of *sumbolon*-b) that complements the equally "natural" bond between the objects and Ion (a sort of *sumbolon*-a). Her knowledge of these objects makes them, so to speak, "half-hers," that is, "the other half of the knucklebone."[16] And, because the bond between the objects and their possessors is "natural," that is, true and necessary, Ion can offer no further resistance when Creusa describes the relationship they betoken. He must accept her interpretation of their symbolic meaning, his identity as her son. The relationship signified by "natural" *sumbola* is taken as equally "natural," while the relationship marked by conventional *sumbola* is liable to be denied.

This operation of the *sumbolon* applies to literary symbolism as it occurs in *Inferno* I and *Odyssey* v. As with the concrete *sumbolon*, the meaning of the symbolic text is also constituted by a relationship, in this case, with a complementary "counter-text." The difference between concrete and literary symbolism lies in the fact that when the *sumbolon* is a text, the symbol and its bearer coincide: the meaning of the *sumbolon*, the identity it proves, does not belong to a separate person who possesses it, but to the text itself. The coincidence of *sumbolon* and text results in a simplification of the interpretive process. Since the *sumbolon* is no longer separate from its bearer, what was before a two-step procedure of establishing first the complementarity of the concrete *sumbola* and then the relationship of their owners, is now collapsed into the single need to demonstrate the intertextual relationship through which the symbol acquires its "other meaning." In addition, because the *sumbolon* and its bearer are identical, the authority of an interpretation no longer depends upon whether the symbol is viewed as conventional or natural, but only upon the existence of the intertextual links, the author and "authority" of the symbolism. In the case of an allegory like *Inferno* I, for example, the commentary of Singleton interprets each element in Dante's awakening and movement through the forest (*sumbolon*-a), by repeating the Biblical "counter-texts" (*sumbolon*-b) to which it corresponds through a network of common words or themes. By the internal consistency of the correspondences, he shows how each element in *Inferno* I acts as *res et signum*, both the thing itself and a symbol of its role in Christian experience.[17] More specifically, these textual counterparts together reveal a shared cosmos of analogical oppositions through which spiritual value may be coded in physical terms.[18] Assuming that knowledge of these Christian texts was assured, Dante wrote for those who, like Singleton, could recognize the textual connections that "authorize" the allegory. In *Odyssey* v the process of symbolization is analogous. The epic "annotates" itself by its own intertextual reservoir. It weaves into the action a sequence of similes which, like the Singleton commentary, "allegorize" the narrative. The similes turn the action of *Odyssey* v into a *sumbolon* of self-generated, psychological rebirth.

In *Odyssey* v the similes are not independent of one another. Rather they form a progression comparable to Quintilian's notion of allegory as an extended metaphor. This progression of the similes is interwoven with that of the action through a set of shared oppositions that parallel physical experience with psychological process. This thematic fabric commences, when Hermes begins his mission, having been dispatched by Zeus to break up the union between Odysseus and Calypso:

> αὐτίκ᾽ ἔπειθ᾽ ὑπὸ ποσσὶν ἐδήσατο καλὰ πέδιλα,
> ἀμβρόσια χρύσεια, τά μιν φέρον ἠμὲν ἐφ᾽ ὑγρὴν
> ἠδ᾽ ἐπ᾽ ἀπείρονα γαῖαν ἅμα πνοιῇς ἀνέμοιο.
> εἵλετο δὲ ῥάβδον, τῇ τ᾽ ἀνδρῶν ὄμματα θέλγει,
> ὧν ἐθέλει, τοὺς δ᾽ αὖτε καὶ ὑπνώοντας ἐγείρει.
> τὴν μετὰ χερσὶν ἔχων πέτετο κρατὺς ἀργεϊφόντης.

> Then at once he bound under his feet the beautiful sandals,
> undying, golden, that always carried him over both the water
>   of the sea
> and the limitless earth together with the blasts of the wind.
> And he took the wand by which he forever enchants the eyes
>   of men,
> of whomever he wishes, while others he rouses even as they
>   sleep.
> Having this in his hands he flew, the strong slayer-of-Argos.

Odyssey v 44–49

Hermes' undying sandals, winging their way with the breaths of the wind over land and sea, link "immortality," "wings," and "wind" as intermediaries between the "dry" and the "wet." The ῥάβδος "wand" by which the god enchants men to sleep and awakens them is a parallel agent of change, this time between states of consciousness. Here is the composite:

	MEDIATOR	
sea	immortality	land
	wings	
wet	wind	dry
sleep		wakefulness
	ῥάβδος "wand"	
enchantment		awareness

The basic states of nature, the solid of dry land over against the liquid of the sea, emerge as elemental analogues to human conditions of mind.

Once introduced, this network of terms immediately connects a simile with the action, as the winged god is likened to a bird, one that joins air, land, and water:

> Πιερίην δ' ἐπιβὰς ἐξ αἰθέρος ἔμπεσε πόντῳ:
> σεύατ' ἔπειτ' ἐπὶ κῦμα λάρῳ ὄρνιθι ἐοικώς,
> ὅς τε κατὰ δεινοὺς κόλπους ἁλὸς ἀτρυγέτοιο
> ἰχθῦς ἀγρώσσων πυκινὰ πτερὰ δεύεται ἅλμῃ:
> τῷ ἴκελος πολέεσσιν ὀχήσατο κύμασιν Ἑρμῆς.

> On to Pieria he stepped from the upper air and swooped down
>   upon the sea:
> then rushed over the waves like to a bird, a seagull,
> who along the dread hollows (literally, "bosoms") of the
>   unresting sea,
> hunting for fish, wets his thick wings in the salt water.
> Like to this bird Hermes made his way over the multitude of
>   waves.

Odyssey v 50–54

The comparison achieves its full meaning later, when Odysseus assumes the place and power of Hermes, when the sea is revealed to combine both the nourishing capacity of Calypso (κόλπος) and the dire hostility of Poseidon (δεινός), and when Odysseus himself is compared with an octopus, a creature of the sea. For now, it serves to figure the sea as feminine, nourishing, and dreadful.

Within this figural aura, the god alights upon the island of Calypso. As if following the path of Hermes' eyes, the text describes the two elements regularly taken as symbolic, the goddess and her home. This *ekphrasis* casts Calypso as both sexual and maternal, at the heart of a place of transcendent fertility and sensory satisfaction. Hermes finds a νύμφη "marriageable maiden" inside a μέγα σπέος "great cave," a womb-like pleasure dome (*Odyssey* v 57).[19] For mingled within are offerings to every sense, both from nature and from art: light and heat from the great fire on the hearth, fragrance of burning cedar and lemon wood so intense that it permeates the island, the sound of singing by a "beautiful voice," and the sight of tapestry woven with a golden shuttle (*Odyssey* v 59–62).[20] Outside the cave, the island burgeons with varieties of trees and birds, meadows of soft violet and parsley, and heavy vines. Four springs of "white" water, each flowing in a different direction, capture in one supernatural image the source and totality of all fluids. "At this sight, even an immortal, who happened by, would gaze and delight in his heart." And indeed Hermes, divine mediator that he is, with reason "stood and gazed" (*Odyssey* v 73–75). For here all these qualities blend – earth and water, mother and lover, art and nature, sight, sound, touch, smell – into one all-gratifying, but all-embracing Eden.[21] Calypso – the great "Coveress" – provides all, but encloses all in the ὀμφαλός "navel" of the sea (*Odyssey* i 50), the place that connects life with pre-birth.

Having satisfied his heart with gazing, Hermes enters the cave. Here his encounter with the goddess triggers the transformation of her name and home from *tropos* to *figura*. Calypso asks the purpose of his visit, and after a dinner of nectar and ambrosia, he delivers Zeus' command that she send Odysseus away at once, "for he is not fated to perish here far from his loved ones, but it is still his lot to see his loved ones and arrive at his high-roofed home and fatherland" (*Odyssey* v 75–115). Outraged, Calypso charges, "Cruel you are, gods, and jealous beyond all others, you who always begrudge goddesses that they should sleep beside men openly, if any makes a mortal her beloved bedfellow (φίλον ἀκοίτην)," and cites two such cases, first, the goddess Eos and the human hunter Orion, killed by the arrows of Olympian Artemis, and then, the goddess Demeter and the man Iasion, blasted by Zeus' thunderbolt (*Odyssey* v 118–128). Her examples are ironically revealing. For unlike Orion or Iasion, Odysseus is not to die as a result of Olympian intervention. Hermes is, to be sure, the conductor of ψυχαί "souls" between life and death.[22] But here he has come not to take Odysseus to Hades, but to ensure his return home. Where, then, is Odysseus now? What is the nature of this goddess-man bond? Odysseus is not simply dead. Indeed, it was death at sea from which Calypso saved him "riding on the keel and all alone," after Zeus' thunderbolt shattered his ship. And theirs is more than a simply sexual bond. As she says, "I both loved him as one of my own and nourished him (φίλεόν τε καὶ ἔτρεφον) and I declared I would make him immortal and ageless all his days" (*Odyssey* v 129–136). Emancipation from human death along with everlasting nurture, this is what Calypso gives. Where can a man enjoy such gifts? Only in the maternal cave, the place before mortality. Separation from Calypso by the agency of Hermes would thus be a second birth, not of the body but of that which Hermes conducts, the ψυχή "life-breath, soul" – a psychological rebirth from undying union with the source of life, a birth in which the hero, as consort of the symbolic mother, would be also the figural father, generating his own new self.[23]

Indeed, for Odysseus undying union with Calypso has lost its allure. When Hermes first enters the cave, Odysseus is not himself within. He has gone instead away from the goddess, away from the cave, as far as he can, to the edge of the island, where he can see only water. Matching its "unresting" flow, he "wept sitting upon the shore (καθήμενος ἐπ᾽ ἀκτῆς), there as before, rending his spirit with tears and groans and pains (δάκρυσι καὶ στοναχῇσι καὶ ἄλγεσι θυμὸν ἐρέχθων), and he would look out upon the unresting sea, shedding tears (πόντον ἐπ᾽ ἀτρύγετον δερκέσκετο δάκρυα λείβων)" (*Odyssey* v 81–84). The same terms recur, when Calypso comes to deliver Hermes' message, underscoring the constancy of the hero's grief.

> τὸν δ᾽ ἄρ᾽ ἐπ᾽ ἀκτῆς εὗρε καθήμενον: οὐδέ ποτ᾽ ὄσσε
> δακρυόφιν τέρσοντο, κατείβετο δὲ γλυκὺς αἰὼν
> νόστον ὀδυρομένῳ, ἐπεὶ οὐκέτι ἥνδανε νύμφη.
> ἀλλ᾽ ἦ τοι νύκτας μὲν ἰαύεσκεν καὶ ἀνάγκη
> ἐν σπέσσι γλαφυροῖσι παρ᾽ οὐκ ἐθέλων ἐθελούσῃ:
> ἤματα δ᾽ ἂμ πέτρῃσι καὶ ἠιόνεσσι καθίζων
> δάκρυσι καὶ στοναχῇσι καὶ ἄλγεσι θυμὸν ἐρέχθων
> πόντον ἐπ᾽ ἀτρύγετον δερκέσκετο δάκρυα λείβων.

> She found him sitting upon the shore. Nor were his eyes ever
> dry of tears, but his sweet life was dripping away,
> as he grieved for return, since the nymph was no longer pleasing.
> Indeed by night he would sleep, compelled by force,
> in the hollow cave, unwilling beside her who was willing,
> but by day he would sit upon the rocks and sands,
> rending his spirit with tears and groans and pains,
> and he would look out upon the unresting sea, shedding tears.

> *Odyssey* v 151–158

The hero's "life" has become a liquid, a "sweet" one like honey, that is "dripping away," while his eyes weep "tears," salty like the sea. By these repetitions of δάκρυα "tears" and κατείβω/λείβω "drip away, shed," [24] the life of Odysseus bound to Calypso is allied with the earlier terms, "sea," "wet," "sleep," and "enchantment." Upon receiving the news of Hermes' mediation, however, Odysseus begins his passage to the opposite pole of "land," "dry," "wakefulness," and "awareness."

Following the period of preparation for his departure, Odysseus' passage to Phaeacia includes two major movements, first, the storm at sea sent by Poseidon and then, the final emergence from "wet" to "dry" under the aegis of Athena. At each phase of the hero's progress, the space of the narrative is widened to include a simile that discloses the action's symbolic meaning. Working together, one after another, the similes confirm the earlier implications of Odysseus' separation from Calypso. They cast the vicissitudes of his entry into the epic as stages in a self-generated psychological rebirth. The first one focuses upon Odysseus building the means of his departure:

> ὅσσον τίς τ' ἔδαφος νηὸς τορνώσεται ἀνὴρ
> φορτίδος εὐρείης, ἐὺ εἰδὼς τεκτοσυνάων,
> τόσσον ἔπ' εὐρεῖαν σχεδίην ποιήσατ' Ὀδυσσεύς.

> As large as a man marks off with a compass the bottom
> of a wide cargo-ship, a man who knows well the skills
>   of carpentry,
> so large did Odysseus make the wide raft.

> *Odyssey* v 249–251

In constructing his raft, Odysseus is like the builder of a wide cargo-ship, the tool of commerce, the vehicle by which men step beyond the "ends of the earth" to travel over the ever-threatening sea and to trade for profit in the sphere of human culture dependent upon and reflective of Hermes' power of transportation. [25] As an essential medium of economic exchange, the cargo-ship parallels the earlier agents of Hermes' mediation, "divinity," "wings," "wind," and the ῥάβδος "wand." Likening the raft to the cargo-ship thus makes of Odysseus, Hermes' human counterpart. In building this raft through his τεκτοσύναι "skills of carpentry" – in thereby transforming the dry material of Calypso's island into the means of travel through the sea – a man, Odysseus, plays the role of cultural mediator, but in the human position, midway between the winged god and the winged animal of the first simile.[26] In the raft, Odysseus makes his wings.[27] Yet for all his skill in building, Odysseus is still dependent upon Calypso for clothes, provisions, navigational instructions, and even the propelling winds (*Odyssey* v 263–277). Figuratively, as the next simile reveals, Odysseus is still enclosed by Calypso's protection.

After casting off from Calypso's island, Odysseus is totally surrounded by the "wet." At sea, the elements of wind and water turn hostile to the hero, as Poseidon plays a "maleficent Calypso," stirring up hurricanes and "covering" (κάλυψε) all land and sea with clouds (*Odyssey* v 292–294). By this storm Odysseus is brought to the verge of death, a λευγαλέος θάνατος "wretched death" without the κλέος "fame" of those who died at Troy (*Odyssey* v 295–312). At this prospect, he yearns to have perished in his moment of greatest martial glory, when he rescued the corpse of Achilles. Rather than saving the hero of the *Odyssey*, he longs to have already died, saving the dead hero of the *Iliad*. Rather than the throes of a new birth, he wishes for death (*Odyssey* v 306–312). As he utters this wish, as if in response to it, a wave twists away his raft, leaving him weighted down by the clothes from Calypso and almost engulfed (*Odyssey* v 313–323). Nevertheless, he manages to regain the raft, but now since the mast has been broken, he must ride wherever the winds direct:

> τὴν δ' ἐφόρει μέγα κῦμα κατὰ ῥόον ἔνθα καὶ ἔνθα.
> ὡς δ' ὅτ' ὀπωρινὸς Βορέης φορέῃσιν ἀκάνθας
> ἂμ πεδίον, πυκιναὶ δὲ πρὸς ἀλλήλῃσιν ἔχονται,
> ὡς τὴν ἂμ πέλαγος ἄνεμοι φέρον ἔνθα καὶ ἔνθα.

> Then the great wave was carrying the raft along the current
>   now here, now there.
> And as when the North Wind in autumn carries thistles
> over the plain, and close they stick to one another,
> so the winds were carrying the raft over the deep, now here,
>   now there.

Odyssey v 327–330

Here again, as in the simile of the cargo-ship, the opening set of elemental contrasts is invoked. Over against the "wet" sea and the hurricane, the simile sets the "dry" plain and the wind of autumn, the season of harvest. In the role of the raft that carries Odysseus we find the ἀκάνθας "thistles," protective "coverings" and carriers of seeds, dispersed as the wind scatters the thistledown. Propelled in such a vehicle, the life of Odysseus is no longer tears or honey, but a seed. Although all alone in the liquid sea, his effort to save himself has turned him into a potential source of life on dry land. Borne by "thistles," however, this "seed" is still enclosed by a protective shell, one he will have to discard in order to germinate. For now, the raft is caught in a state of suspended animation, blown first north, then south, then east, then west:

> ἄλλοτε μέν τε Νότος Βορέῃ προβάλεσκε φέρεσθαι,
> ἄλλοτε δ' αὖτ' Εὖρος Ζεφύρῳ εἴξασκε διώκειν.

> At one time the South Wind would cast it to the North Wind to
>   be carried,
> and at another time again the East Wind would yield it to the
>   West Wind to pursue.

> *Odyssey* v 331–332

The syntax is iconic of Odysseus' alternating, non-progressive movement: ἄλλοτε μέν τε "at one time" matched by ἄλλοτε δὲ αὖτ' "at another time again," Νότος Βορέῃ "the South Wind to the North Wind" by Εὖρος Ζεφύρῳ "the East Wind to the West Wind," and προβάλεσκε φέρεσθαι "would cast it to be carried" by εἴξασκε διώκειν "would yield it to pursue." Each movement is reversed, resulting in no forward motion.

Almost at once, Odysseus is moved off this dead center by the intervention of Ino. In the symbolism of rebirth, her role is that of a midwife, facilitating his separation from those elements, previously protective, that now inhibit his emergence from the sea. She urges him to take off the garments from Calypso that have "covered" him like a placenta, but now hold him back, and to abandon his raft, likened before to a thistle's sheltering case (*Odyssey* v 342–345).[28] As an alternative lifeline, a figural umbilical cord, she offers an ἄμβροτον κρήδεμνον "immortal veil" to fasten below his chest and then to cast off, once he reaches dry land. After this offering, Ino dives back into the sea (*Odyssey* v 346–352). Immediately, the sea again covers (κάλυψεν) Odysseus with a dark wave (*Odyssey* v 353). While he debates whether or not to obey Ino, Poseidon breaks the wave upon him (*Odyssey* v 356–367) and by this convulsion the raft is shattered:

> ὡς δ' ἄνεμος ζαὴς ἠΐων θημῶνα τινάξῃ
> καρφαλέων· τὰ μὲν ἄρ τε διεσκέδασ' ἄλλυδις ἄλλῃ·
> ὡς τῆς δούρατα μακρὰ διεσκέδασ'. αὐτὰρ Ὀδυσσεὺς
> ἀμφ' ἑνὶ δούρατι βαῖνε, κέληθ' ὡς ἵππον ἐλαύνων,
> εἵματα δ' ἐξαπέδυνε, τά οἱ πόρε δῖα Καλυψώ.
> αὐτίκα δὲ κρήδεμνον ὑπὸ στέρνοιο τάνυσσεν,
> αὐτὸς δὲ πρηνὴς ἁλὶ κάππεσε, χεῖρε πετάσσας,
> νηχέμεναι μεμαώς.

67

> And as when the strong-blowing wind shakes a heap of dry
> chaff and scatters it now in this direction, now in that,
> so the wave scattered the raft's long planks, but now Odysseus
> sat astride one plank, like a man riding on horseback,
> and stripped off the clothing that the divine Calypso had
> provided him.
> And at once he stretched the veil of Ino under his chest and
> dove down himself head first in the sea with his arms spread out,
> passionately eager to swim.

Odyssey v 368–375

Like its earlier counterpart, this simile pits the "dry" – before, the thistle and here, the chaff – against the "wet" of the sea, with the wind as the mediating agent in both realms.[29] But now the raft is no longer a protective vehicle, encasing a potential life. Now shattered, the raft leaves Odysseus, separated like a seed from the chaff, able to germinate. Now able to act independently, Odysseus turns a fragment of the broken raft into a temporary carrier. In this transformation of wreckage into mobility, Odysseus is likened no longer to any phase of the life of a seed, but to a man, one who augments the speed of his movement by engaging the energy of a horse. Likened to a horse, the wood of the plank becomes animated. And likened to a rider, Odysseus becomes similarly active – he jettisons the "coverings" from the "Cover-ess" that now weigh him down, puts on a final fabric of female protection, and projects himself, now an unsupported missile, into the sea to swim alone. At once, the second movement of *Odyssey* v ends, with Poseidon departing as he initially intruded, after a short prediction of Odysseus' future trials (*Odyssey* v 377–379; compare 286–290). The third portion of Book v, the ultimate passage from "wet" to "dry," is governed by Athena.

Odysseus has now crossed the πεῖραρ ὀιζύος "boundary of misery" (*Odyssey* v 289), the frontier between the two worlds of the *Odyssey*, the raw, elemental nature of Poseidon and the civilization of Athena.[30] Now Athena directs the winds and the waves to conduct Odysseus to the land of the Phaeacians (*Odyssey* v 382–387). The psychological significance of this land for Odysseus is conveyed in a simile that inverts the conventional associations of its terms:

> ὡς δ' ὅτ' ἂν ἀσπάσιος βίοτος παίδεσσι φανήῃ
> πατρός, ὃς ἐν νούσῳ κεῖται κρατέρ' ἄλγεα πάσχων,
> δηρὸν τηκόμενος, στυγερὸς δέ οἱ ἔχραε δαίμων,
> ἀσπάσιον δ' ἄρα τόν γε θεοὶ κακότητος ἔλυσαν,

ὣς Ὀδυσῆ᾽ ἀσπαστὸν ἐείσατο γαῖα καὶ ὕλη,
νῆχε δ᾽ ἐπειγόμενος ποσὶν ἠπείρου ἐπιβῆναι.

As when gladly welcomed life appears to the children,

the life of the father, who lies in sickness suffering strong pains,
for a long time wasting away, and the hated death spirit
    attacked him,
but then gladly welcomed the gods released him from misery,
so gladly welcomed appeared the earth and woods to Odysseus,
and he swam, pressing himself, so as to set foot on the mainland.

Odyssey v 394–399

Instead of its usual identification with motherhood, the earth here is likened to a father. Failure to reach this land would mean the loss of what only the father confers in father-ruled society, home and legitimate adult identity. Despite its distance from Ithaca, Phaeacia is now psychologically the "father-land" of Odysseus. To set foot on this island is to achieve separation from the mother and identification with the father, to emerge, that is, as a male child.[31] Accordingly, it is to children that Odysseus is compared, children nearly orphaned, too young to assume their patrimony.

Once having seen this "father-land," the "child" Odysseus confronts the remaining onslaughts of the sea with increasing independence and intellectual control, a growth reflected in the progressive decrease of direct intervention by Athena. In the first upheaval after sighting land, Athena gives him the idea of clinging to a rock (*Odyssey* v 424–429). Then when the undertow of the same wave sucks him out to sea again, it is through foresight supplied by Athena that he swims out of the reach of the surf (*Odyssey* v 435–440). But when he comes to the mouth of the river, it is Odysseus alone who begs the current to receive him, and when he steps at last upon the land, Odysseus alone plans how to preserve himself against the elements. The last two similes of *Odyssey* v interpret this action as a development within the ψυχή "life-breath, soul" of the hero.

When Odysseus is again thrown out to sea by the backwash of the wave he had just escaped, his separation from the rock is described by a subtly meaningful simile:

ὡς δ᾽ ὅτε πουλύποδος θαλάμης ἐξελκομένοιο
πρὸς κοτυληδονόφιν πυκιναὶ λάιγγες ἔχονται,
ὣς τοῦ πρὸς πέτρῃσι θρασειάων ἀπὸ χειρῶν
ῥινοὶ ἀπέδρυφθεν· τὸν δὲ μέγα κῦμα κάλυψεν.

And as when an octopus is dragged away from its hole,
dense-packed pebbles are held by the cups of its tentacles,
so by the rocks the skin from his bold hands
was torn off. And a great wave covered him.

Odyssey v 432–435

The image is initially elusive. At the start, the counterpart of Odysseus seems to be the octopus: each is forced away from an object in the sea, Odysseus from a rock, the octopus from his hole (θαλάμης).[32] And as the πουλύποδος "octopus" is literally "he of the many feet," so Odysseus is at the start of the epic πολύτροπος "he of the many turns" (*Odyssey* i 1) and elsewhere, πολύμητις "he of much *mêtis*."[33] Accordingly, when we hear how the octopus holds the pebbles in its tentacles, we expect that Odysseus holds something, too. But what happens is just the opposite: the skin of Odysseus "is being held" by the rock. Now, not Odysseus, but the rock becomes the octopus' parallel. The skin he leaves behind and the wave that then "covered" (κάλυψεν) him mark his remaining physical dependency: he is still within the sea and Athena is still stimulating his mind and his action. But his emergence within the simile from an apparent sea creature to a man suggests an internal, psychological development into adulthood, at the same time as it prefigures the external, physical emergence from the sea that this inner development will make possible. This movement of Odysseus within the simile from an apparent animal to a man recalls the earlier simile when Hermes was likened to the seagull who dives into the deep for its food. Just as Odysseus subsequently sat in the chair Hermes had occupied (*Odyssey* v 195–196), so now it is the hero who is compared, at least initially, to a creature of the sea. But no sooner is he likened to a sea creature than he moves on in the simile to a role with no divine precedent, a role solely his own. Odysseus has become his own "Hermes," first by paralleling the god who came to separate him and then by separating himself.

This figuration of Odysseus as his own "Hermes" is explicit in the final act and simile of *Odyssey* v. Here, indeed, he appropriates the roles of both Athena and Calypso as well. Once he has emerged from the ocean, Odysseus acts alone to insure his passage from "sleep" to "wakefulness," safe from that form of the "wet" one can suffer upon the land, the "evil frost and the feminine dew" (*Odyssey* v 467). He assumes this function of Hermes ψυχοπομπός "conductor of the soul" by transforming the "dry" material of the land – leaves from the olive trees of Athena – into a self-made "Calypso." In the simile that interprets this action, Odysseus' "crafting" of a bed and a "cover" of olive leaves is turned into a *sumbolon* of completed rebirth of the ψυχή "life-breath, soul":

τὴν μὲν ἰδὼν γήθησε πολύτλας δῖος Ὀδυσσεύς,
ἐν δ' ἄρα μέσσῃ λέκτο, χύσιν δ' ἐπεχεύατο φύλλων.
ὡς δ' ὅτε τις δαλὸν σποδιῇ ἐνέκρυψε μελαίνῃ
ἀγροῦ ἐπ' ἐσχατιῆς, ᾧ μὴ πάρα γείτονες ἄλλοι,
σπέρμα πυρὸς σώζων, ἵνα μή ποθεν ἄλλοθεν αὕοι,
ὣς Ὀδυσεὺς φύλλοισι καλύψατο.

Seeing this bed, much-enduring, shining Odysseus was happy,
and so he lay down in the middle of it and poured the profusion
   of leaves over him.
As when a man hides a burning log in a dark heap of ashes
in the remotest part of a field, a man for whom there are no
   others as neighbors nearby,
thus saving the seed of fire, so as not to have to kindle it from
   some other source,
so Odysseus covered himself with the leaves.

Odyssey v 486–491

Through the δαλὸν "burning log" and the σπέρμα πυρὸς "seed of fire," the simile connects itself with all the earlier symbolism of rebirth and with the elemental environment of the action as a whole. Odysseus is again a seed, but now a seed of fire, wholly "dry."[34] Before "covered" by Calypso and then by Poseidon's sea, Odysseus has now completed the "self-generation" implicit in being both consort and child of the goddess and can now "cover" himself. What he thus preserves is the spark of the intelligence of Athena. Such is the implication of the fact that the "seed of fire" is hidden in ashes, the product of fire. For the "fire" common to both the "seed of fire" as Odysseus and the "ashes" as counterpart to the olive leaves is Athena. Odysseus has covered "Athena," now fully revived within him. The two are in concert, as the goddess now proves, when in the last words of the book instead of initiating, she echoes the hero's action by "covering his eyes" (βλέφαρ' ἀμφικαλύψας, *Odyssey* v 493) for sleep.[35]

By its interwoven commentary of similes, the action of *Odyssey* v is made symbolic of self-generated psychological rebirth. Once he departs from Calypso's island, Odysseus progresses in the similes from being a seed enclosed in a thistle, to a seed separated from the chaff, to an independent human rider, to a child whose father near death is restored, to a man who preserves his source of fire. Connected to Odysseus' progress by a common code of opposing elements and states of consciousness, this sequence of similes traces the ὑπόνοια "undermeaning" of the action, the internal development of the hero's ψυχή "life-breath, soul." In an assimilation that anticipates Heraclitus, the ψυχή of the hero grows into a spark of intelligence that saves the fire of life.[36] An external text of natural and human growth serves by its systematic links with the narrative *sumbolon* to reveal the sort of figural significance that the commentary of Singleton reveals in *Inferno* I. Without these external texts, whether supplied by author or reader or annotator, the spiritual or psychological experience symbolized by these narratives remains undetected. Apart from the interpreting (re)statement of its connections with its counter-parts, the textual *sumbolon* is a mute sign.

Notes

An earlier version of this essay appeared in *Classical World* 74 (Symbolism in Greek Poetry) (1980) 109–123. I am grateful to Thomas Habinek, Katherine King, David Quint, Froma Zeitlin, and the referee for *Classical World* for help with that text, and to Nancy Felson for her dedication in fostering the special issue of the journal.

1. Eustathius *Commentarii ad Homeri Iliadem* vol. 1, page 7 in his "Critical Remarks on Homer's *Iliad*" observes: ὅτι ἀνδρώδης μὲν ἡ Ἰλιὰς καὶ σεμνοτέρα καὶ ὕψος ἔχουσα, ἐπεὶ καὶ ἡρωϊκωτέρα· ἠθικὴ δὲ ἡ Ὀδύσσεια, ὡς ἐκεῖ σαφέστερον γέγραπται· καὶ ὅτι τὴν Ὁμηρικὴν ἰσχὺν οὐ τοσοῦτον ἐν τῇ Ἰλιάδι ἔστι καταμαθεῖν, ὅσον ἐν τῇ Ὀδυσσείᾳ, "that the *Iliad* on the one hand is manly and more serious and possesses sublimity, since it is also more heroic, and on the other hand, the *Odyssey* is ethical, as has been written more clearly there [where the point was set out earlier]; and that it is not possible to perceive Homer's power so much in the *Iliad* as in the *Odyssey*." See also *Commentarii ad Homeri Odysseam* vol. 1, pages 1–2 on the Proem: Ἠθικωτέρα δὲ τῆς Ἰλιάδος κατὰ τὴν παλαιὰν ἀλήθειαν ἐστὶν ἡ Ὀδύσσεια ὅ ἐστιν, γλυκυτέρα τὲ καὶ ἀφελεστέρα. ἤδη δὲ καὶ ὀξυτέρα διὰ τὰ ἐν φαντασίᾳ ἐπιπολαίου ἀφελείας βάθη τῶν νοημάτων, ὡς οἱ τεχνικοὶ λέγουσι, "According to the ancient truth [that is, a truth uttered long ago], the *Odyssey* is more ethical than the *Iliad*, that is, it is both sweeter and of greater simplicity. And at the same time it is also more acute on account of the depths of its thoughts in an appearance of superficial simplicity, as the grammarians say." On these passages, see Segal 1962b:17 and Allen 1970:90–93. For the allegorical interpretation of Homeric epic, see also Buffière 1956 and Pépin 1958.

2. See Segal 1962b and 1967. In 1962b:18 Segal explains: "The symbolism of the Return – the possibility for certain images, characters, places, episodes in it to carry a deeper meaning than their literal, surface denotation – is latent in the concern of the *Odyssey*, as perhaps of all epic, with the basic mysteries and conditions of human life, ever changing between an unknown beginning and an unknown end. In the *Odyssey* these possibilities are especially rich, for the poem deals recurrently and under many different forms with death and rebirth, with change of state and the loss and resumption of identity."

3. Holtsmark 1966, a study which points the way for the present essay and to which I am greatly indebted.

4. From antiquity through the Renaissance, the most frequent interpretation of Calypso is as the entrapping sexuality of the beautiful female: for example, Antisthenes, the Cynic, who takes Odysseus' rejection of Calypso's offer of immortality in favor of the "wise" but less beautiful Penelope as proof of the wise man's knowledge that lovers promise the impossible and of his preference for wisdom (see Buffière 1956:371–372 and Pépin 1958:107–108), Plotinus, who in his treatise *On the Beautiful* cites Calypso as an example of sensual beauty (see Pépin 1958:199), and Ludovico

Dolce, who in his *L'Ulisse* of 1573 casts Calypso as libidinous femininity (see Allen 1970:94). Contemporary readings stress what is implicit in Calypso as material body, namely, that she is the source of love and death; for example, Güntert 1919, followed by Anderson 1958 and Holtsmark 1966, who also elaborates her maternal role.

5. Eustathius records a neo-Platonic allegory of Calypso as the shell-like body that imprisons the pearl of the soul and of her sea-dashed, wooded island at the navel of the sea as the watery, material body, exposed to all passions; and of Odysseus' escape from her to Penelope by the aid of Hermes as *logos*, as the passage from corporeal to philosophic existence (Eustathius *Commentarii ad Homeri Odysseam* vol. 1, page 17 on *Odyssey* i 51; see Buffière 1956:461–463). In another allegory transmitted by Eustathius Calypso is interpreted macrocosmically as the heavenly vault "covering" the earth and as the science of astronomy, since she is the daughter or *telos* of Atlas, the axis whose regular rotations constitute the laws of the sky; in this conception, the goddess represents the philosophy of the material world as opposed to the true wisdom of internal contemplation represented by Penelope (Eustathius *Commentarii ad Homeri Odysseam* vol. 1, page 17 on *Odyssey* i 52; see Buffière 1956:388–391).

6. Segal 1962b:20.

7. On *tropos* vs. *figura*, see Quintilian 9.1.1–9 and 9.2.46, where Quintilian shows how irony can occur as a *tropos*, that is, by means of one or two words, and as a *figura*, extended over a whole passage or even over a whole life, as in the case of Socrates. He concludes with the analogy: *quemadmodum ἀλληγορίαν facit continua metaphora, sic hoc schema faciat tropos ille contextus* "just as a continued metaphor creates allegory, so that *tropos* which has been connected creates this *figura*." An allegory is a continued metaphor, and figure, a "contextualized" trope. In these terms, Calypso is, as we shall see, "figural" and the action of *Odyssey* v "allegorical."

8. While Vergil is Dante's stated "master and author," the *Odyssey*, as the first epic of "comic" structure in the Western tradition, is the ultimate antecedent of the *Divina Commedia*. The entrances of the two heroes, Odysseus and Dante, into the poems share several features. Common to both is the initial position of the man, his movement from that position, and, as we shall see, the symbolization of that movement through a code of opposite categories as spiritual experience. Just as Odysseus is at mid-point in his return home, so Dante is *nel mezzo del cammin* "midway in the journey." Each struggles to leave this place, a *selva oscura* "dark wood" for Dante and for Odysseus, too, a thick forest. Exemplary of both the kinship and the disparities between *Inferno* I and *Odyssey* v is the simile of Canto I 22–27, in which the mind (*mio animo*) of Dante looks back on the wood (*selva*) as a man looks back upon the sea he has just escaped, an escape parallel to that of Odysseus in *Odyssey* v. Emergence from the forest and the sea is the common motif of the two works, but the greater interiority of *Inferno* I is shown in the fact that the tenor of the simile is not a person, but the personified "mind." In addition, the specific religious meaning of this spiritual experience is not revealed by the simile alone, but only insofar as it alludes to the crossing of the Red Sea in *Exodus*.

On this allusion, see Singleton 1970:2.8. In *Odyssey* v, on the other hand, the overall pattern of action is parallel to that of *Inferno* I, but the function of the similes is, as we shall see, like that of the episode in *Exodus*.

9. On the effect of realism resulting from the description of *Realien*, see Barthes 1968:84–89. For the way such description contributes to the impression in Homeric epic of tangible surfaces in present time and space, see Auerbach 1973 [1953]:3–14.

10. See Singleton 1970:1.2–11 with 2.3–21.

11. On ὑπόνοια as the word in Plato and Xenophon for what was later termed *allegoria*, see Buffière 1956:45–48, Pépin 1958:85–87, and Allen 1970:viii.

12. See Gauthier 1972:65–71. Implicit in this definition is the fact that only halves of the same object will be able to coincide. This implication may seem to re-emerge in the Romantic assertion of a consubstantiality between symbol and idea that is absent in allegory. For the "material substantiality" and the *"participation mystique"* in the conception of the symbol of Goethe and Coleridge, see de Man 1969:174–177 and Fletcher 1964:17–19. The ancient notion of *sumbolon* does not, however, imply the unbroken unity of figure and concept in the Romantic theory, for it is only by reference to a part from which it is irreparably broken that a *sumbolon* can betoken a relationship between two equally separate parties. What the *sumbolon* symbolizes is a liaison between two parts, a "wholeness" or "identity" constituted by the "fault" of difference, like James' "golden bowl." In this way the operation of the Greek *sumbolon* is closer to allegory as described by de Man, in which the allegorical sign must repeat a previous sign with which it can never coincide (de Man 1969:190).

13. Aristotle *On Interpretation* 16a, 4–8, 20–29, in particular: Ἔστι μὲν οὖν τὰ ἐν τῇ φωνῇ τῶν ἐν τῇ ψυχῇ παθημάτων σύμβολα, καὶ τὰ γραφόμενα τῶν ἐν τῇ φωνῇ, "Spoken words are the *sumbola* of experiences in the soul, and written words are *sumbola* of spoken words" (3–4) and Ὄνομα μὲν οὖν ἐστὶ φωνὴ σημαντικὴ κατὰ συνθήκην ἄνευ χρόνου . . . τὸ δὲ κατὰ συνθήκην, ὅτι φύσει τῶν ὀνομάτων οὐδέν ἐστιν, ἀλλ' ὅταν γένηται σύμβολον, "A noun is a sound significant by convention without reference to time . . . by convention, because nothing is by nature a noun, but only whenever it becomes a *sumbolon*" (19–20, 26–28). On motivated vs. unmotivated signs, see Todorov 1977, esp. 28, 32–33. In an unconventional, motivated sign, the signifier bears some natural relation to the signified, such as similarity or difference (metaphorical relations) or contiguity, causality, or consubstantiality (metonymic relations).

14. Euripides *Ion* 1386–1442. Gauthier 1972 observes: "the memories of Creusa that prove her capable of describing the design of the weaving and the shape of the jewels constitute in effect the counter-part, the equivalent of what was before the other half of the broken knucklebone." The μητρὸς σύμβολα "symbols of the mother" here are "natural" or "motivated" not only because they include Ion's actual clothes, but also because of the Gorgon, fringed with snakes in the manner of the aegis, that Creusa

wove into the "middle warp threads of her robe" (*Ion* 1386, 1418, 1421, 1425). This aegis is the emblem of Athena, patroness of Athens, whose autochthonous king, Erechtheus, is Creusa's father. Similarly "symbolic" of the mother's identity are the golden snake necklace worn at Athena's command in memory of Erechthonius and the wreath from the ἀκήρατος "undefiled" olive tree of Athena on the Acropolis (*Ion* 1427–1429, 1436). The references to virginity point to Ion's conception in the "defiling" of Creusa, while the Gorgon herself, the dreaded female head with the power to petrify, betokens the woman's power of life and death displayed by Creusa alternatively in bearing and in trying to kill her son. These *sumbola* Ion terms θέσφατα "things spoken by god" (*Ion* 1424). This usage illustrates the claim of oracles to being "motivated speech," that is, signifiers with a metaphorical or metonymic relation to the signified.

15. Herodotus *Histories* 6.86.28–35. See Gauthier 1972:67–68.

16. Gauthier 1972:72.

17. For *res et signum*, see Singleton 1970:2.7 on line 17.

18. Principally, in general order of occurrence, these oppositions are: dark/light, crooked/straight, fear/hope, bitter/sweet, death/life, evil/good, sleep/wakefulness, true/false, forest or valley/mountain, low/high, beast/divinity, night/morning, she/he, trembling/peace, woe/happiness.

19. See Holtsmark 1966:206n2.

20. The presence of weaving in Calypso's cave complicates the view of Vidal-Naquet (1970:1278–1279) that in the *Odyssey* the adventures take place in the realm of nature and the return in that of culture, with Phaeacia as a place of transition. In the case of Calypso's island and the home of Circe, as well, where we also find weaving and cooking, there is a more complex admixture of the two realms, suggesting that these two female artifices cannot be comprehended by the nature/culture dichotomy.

21. On Calypso's island as a "paradise," see Anderson 1958:6–7.

22. See, for example, Hermes' conducting of the souls of the suitors to Hades, *Odyssey* xxiv 1–4:

Ἑρμῆς δὲ ψυχὰς Κυλλήνιος ἐξεκαλεῖτο
ἀνδρῶν μνηστήρων: ἔχε δὲ ῥάβδον μετὰ χερσὶν
καλὴν χρυσείην, τῇ τ᾽ ἀνδρῶν ὄμματα θέλγει
ὧν ἐθέλει, τοὺς δ᾽ αὖτε καὶ ὑπνώοντας ἐγείρει.

Hermes of Cyllene called out the souls
of the suitors: and in his hands he was carrying the wand,
beautiful, golden, by which he forever enchants the eyes of the men,
of whomever he wishes, while others he rouses even as they sleep.

23. Segal 1962b:23 points the way toward this interpretation when he calls Odysseus' arrival, sleep, and awakening on Phaeacia "a rebirth after the quasi-death on Ogygia."

24. On λείβω and εἴβω as doublets, see Haslam 1976.

25. For instructions on how to maximize profit in ναυτιλία δυσπεμφέλος "rough and stormy sailing," see Hesiod *Works and Days* 618–694. On Hermes as the mediator of commerce, see Watkins 1971:346–350.

26. For the ancient definition of humans by their medial status between divinities and beasts, see Aristotle *Politics* 1253a25-29, Detienne 1972b, and Segal 1974a.

27. For Odysseus' building of the raft as a "symbolical reengagement of his rational faculties," see Segal 1962b:22.

28. Holtsmark 1966:209 interprets only the raft with its source of food as the placenta, but the initially protective covering of the clothes given by the "mother" Calypso would seem to share this function.

29. See Moulton 1977:125 on the common features of the two similes (*Odyssey* v 328–330 and 368–370).

30. Bergren 1975:57–59.

31. For the Athenian male's movement from childhood to manhood as his physical separation from strictly enclosed female quarters and assumption of relationships with men, see Slater 1971:55–63.

32. Although Odysseus only appears initially to be compared to the octopus, it is still instructive to recall that in Greek culture the octopus was a model in the animal world for *mêtis*, due to its exceptional polymorphy (it takes the shape of the bodies to which it clings) and to its inky cloud, a means of both escape and capture. See Detienne and Vernant 1978:34–43. Odysseus' apparent likeness to an octopus is thus proleptically appropriate for the hero who will be covered in a cloud by Metis' daughter, Athena (*Odyssey* vii 15, 140; compare *Odyssey* xiii 189, 299, 313 and 352, where the goddess temporarily disguises Ithaca, too, in a cloud) and will carry out the *mêtis* "woven" by the goddess and himself (*Odyssey* xiii 303, 386) by taking on the shape of a beggar (*Odyssey* xiii 429–438) and later defeating the real beggar, Iros (*Odyssey* xviii 1–107).

33. In the *Odyssey* the adjective πολύμητις is used only of Odysseus and all but two of its 68 occurrences are in the line-final πολύμητις Ὀδυσσεύς.

34. In addition to his efforts to insure his own sleep and safe awakening, this likening of Odysseus to a burning log with its seed of fire points to his assumption of the powers of Hermes. For Hermes as the inventor of fire and fire-sticks, see *Homeric Hymn to Hermes* 111, and for his identity with the Vedic fire god, Agni, see Hocart 1970 [1963]:17–20 and Watkins 1971:354n41.

35. See Holtsmark 1966:210 for the usage of καλύπτω here and elsewhere in *Odyssey* v. On these last occurrences of the verb he comments: "After he has thus covered himself (καλύψατο, 491) with leaves, Athena finally covers up (ἀμφικαλύψας, 493) his weary eyelids in sleep that he may rest from his toil and gather strength.

The meaning of the name of Calypso, the coverer who is Death, is at the beginning of the book the negation of real life, becomes in the book's central portion a strong intimation of the ambivalently exercised struggle between the claims of life and death (353, 372, 435), and suggests at the end the restorative process by means of which the precariously kindled flame will blaze in full affirmation of life."

36. On the relation between the similes of Homer and pre-Socratic philosophy, see Riezler 1936:253–271; note also Riezler's notion of a "metaphorical" interaction between simile and narrative whereby each transfers its characteristics to the other.

4

ODYSSEAN TEMPORALITY
Many (Re)Turns

The wisdom of the text is self-destructive (art is true but truth kills itself),
but this self-destruction is infinitely displaced in a series of successive
rhetorical reversals which, by the endless repetition of the same figure,
keep it suspended between truth and the death of truth.[1]

Paul de Man

I. Odysseus' Poem and Narratology

I T WOULD BE HARD TO FIND A RECENT STUDY OF THE *ODYSSEY* that fails to
observe its concentration upon poetic craft: in the characters of Demodocus
and Phemius, in its markedly artificial narrative exposition, and, above all,
in the casting of its hero as the poet of the four central books.[2] But for all our
attention to what one critic has called the "aedo-centrism" of the epic, we
have not fully appreciated Odysseus' poetic craft.[3] It is common to point to the
two similes that liken Odysseus to a bard (Alcinous' comparison in the middle
of Book xi and its echo as Odysseus strings his bow)[4] and to observe how this
hero-as-poet serves to accord a kind of heroism to the bard. Making him tell
his own story seems to be mainly a kind of simile to aid exposition, another
"trope" for the polytropic hero.[5] And, of course, it is a simile, but one that is
extended: to adopt Quintilian's terminology, this *tropos* becomes a *figura*.[6]

A more complete appreciation of Odysseus' poetic role in Books ix–xii
emerges from attention to the temporality of his tale. The analytical categories of narratology as defined by Gérard Genette make this temporal structure
clear. In his book, *Narrative Discourse: An Essay in Method*, Genette distinguishes
three levels of narrative:[7]

histoire = story: the events narrated, for example, the adventures of Odysseus from the fall of Troy to his arrival at Calypso's island

récit = narrative: the oral or written text in which the story is narrated, for example, the text of the *Odyssey*

narration = narration: the instance or event of telling the story, for example, Odysseus' narrating of his adventures for the Phaeacians or a poet's narrating of the *Odyssey*

The ultimate goal of Genette's project is to elucidate the variety of relations among these three levels. He categorizes these relations in terms borrowed from the grammar of verbs, supporting his choice with the fact that any narrative is essentially an elaboration of a verbal form, an expansion of a verb:[8] tense, for the temporal relations between narrative and story; mood, for the forms and degrees of "dramatization" or μίμησις "imitation" of something vs. the διήγησις "telling" of it ;[9] and voice, for the ways that the narrating event is implied in the narrative. It is the first of these categories, that of "tense," that directly concerns the temporal patterns of a text. In his analysis of "tense," Genette compares the order of events in the narrative with the order of the same events in the story, in order to determine their differences or what he terms their "anachronies."[10] He finds variations on two basic patterns: retrospection or "analepsis," a present enunciation in the narrative of what is past in the story and then a return to the narrative present; and anticipation or "prolepsis," a present forecast in the narrative of what is future in the story and then a return to the narrative present.

These two patterns, analeptic recollections and proleptic prophecies, comprise the anachronies of the *Odyssey*. In each of them, the text "cuts away" to weave another space and another time, whether earlier or later, into the present narrative flow. This spatio-temporal interweaving creates the textual form of return – from present to past to present again or from present to future to present again – a chronological instance of the common Homeric narrative structure of "ring composition." In the case of present-past-present recollections, we have the chronological order recognized in ancient Homeric criticism as ὕστερον–πρότερον Ὁμηρικῶς "the latter thing before the earlier thing as Homer does it."[11] For when the units of the ὕστερον–πρότερον are those of time, there is no difference between A-B-A "ring-composition" and this chronological inversion, since the text always returns to its original position: the ὕστερον "later" before the πρότερον "earlier" up to the ὕστερον "later," that is, present–past–present again. Like its hero, then, the temporality of the epic is polytropic, made up of many τρόποι "turns" or νόστοι "returns" of time: "many (re)turns" from the past and the future to the present. Just as in the story Odysseus leaves Ithaca, fights at Troy, and returns home, with many landings, departures, and new landings on the way, so the narrative repeatedly departs from the present time to the past or the future in the story and returns to the narrative present again. Both the action and the temporal form of the poem share the structure of (re)turn.

When we turn from the *Odyssey* as a whole to its hero's poetry, we find the same temporality and a similarly analogical relation between content and form. Odysseus' tale is made up of temporal patterns and actions which dramatize (re)turn. In its overall structure, Odysseus' tale is a formal νόστος, a present–past–present "return." Its poetic art is stressed by a simile, coined by his host Alcinous, likening Odysseus to an expert bard and praising both the external form and the internal intelligence of the tale. This narrative νόστος "return" acts as an item of fair exchange in the relation of ξενία "guest-friend exchange" with the Phaeacians. With its poetry – its "making" of the hero – Odysseus' self-identification both repays the hospitality already lavished upon the heretofore anonymous guest and earns for him the νόστος of a passage home. This function of the tale as a whole is mirrored in individual episodes, where we find Odysseus as narrator exploiting temporal τρόπος "turning" to dramatize his πολυτροπία "turning many ways" – the tropic character of his challengers and his corresponding capacity to turn, return, change, and exchange. First, with Polyphemus, the trope takes the form of a λόγος "speech" (re)turned into a δόλος "trap" by means of a punning μῆτις "trick of transformative intelligence" that manipulates the conventions of the ξενία "guest-friend exchange" of ὀνόματα "names." Then with Teiresias, νόστος "return" is revealed by the prophetic νόος "intelligence" to depend upon restraint of θυμός "passion, spirit, appetite." With the blind seer's prediction of Odysseus' homecoming and death, the narrative trajectory reaches to the end of the epic and circles back to return to its origin in Hades. And finally, with the Cattle of the Sun, Odysseus proves his capacity to remember Teiresias' dictates and to restrain his appetite in the ξενία "guest-friend exchange" of food. Both on the large scale and in its smaller parts, Odysseus' tale embodies the form and the action of (re)turn. Thus composed, the account is not a rhetorically neutral reminiscence. This poem of νόστος "return" aims to define and to win νόστος, no matter what the risk. And, in the end, the hero's poem will win νόστος, but at the risk of revealing too well the nature of (re)turn.

II. Odysseus' πολυτροπία "turning in many directions"

Alcinous' Simile: The Form and the Content of νόστος "return"

The temporality of Odysseus' narrative is founded upon the chronological structure of the *Odyssey* as a whole, the structure that itself is built upon asking the hero's name. At the end of Book viii, when Alcinous asks Odysseus to identify himself, his request sets up a long recollection that transforms the entire epic into a large-scale analepsis, a ὕστερον–πρότερον "the latter thing before the earlier thing" in which the present situation in Ithaca, Ogygia, and Phaeacia comes before the past. This διήγησις "narration" is also a μίμησις "imitation" of the self-identification required of the guest in this instance of ξενία "guest-friend exchange." In exchange for the hospitality they have already lavished upon him and for their conveying him home, Odysseus must give the Phaeacians his name and then, like a poet, recall the events that "make" the name. In return for his return to Ithaca, he must give his return from Troy to Phaeacia: a νόστος for a νόστος.

Accordingly, Odysseus shapes his narrative in the manner of its frame, in the form, that is, of temporal return. He starts in the present by stating his name in full:

> "νῦν δ' ὄνομα πρῶτον μυθήσομαι, ὄφρα καὶ ὑμεῖς
> εἴδετ', ἐγὼ δ' ἂν ἔπειτα φυγὼν ὕπο νηλεὲς ἦμαρ
> ὑμῖν ξεῖνος ἔω καὶ ἀπόπροθι δώματα ναίων.
> εἴμ' Ὀδυσεὺς Λαερτιάδης, ὃς πᾶσι δόλοισιν
> ἀνθρώποισι μέλω, καί μευ κλέος οὐρανὸν ἵκει."

> "Now first I will declare my name, so that you too
> may know, and that I hereafter, escaping the day without pity,
> may be your guest-friend, although dwelling in halls far away.
> I am Odysseus son of Laertes, known to all men
> for my traps and my fame goes up to the heavens."[12]

Odyssey ix 16–20

After completing his name with a description of his homeland – the place so dear that neither Calypso nor Circe could keep him away from it – he moves from the present to the past (*Odyssey* ix 21–36). [13] To substantiate his claim to a κλέος that reaches heaven, he will, he says, narrate νόστον ἐμὸν πολυκηδέα "my woeful return" (*Odyssey* ix 37–38). He begins with its earliest point, the departure from Troy, and proceeds from there – over the next three books – all the way back to the present again at Phaeacia (*Odyssey* ix 39–xii 453).[14] Formally, therefore, his narrative is a present–past–present circumstructure. The content of Odysseus's κλέος is connected with the form of his νόστος by Alcinous himself.

To keep the audience from forgetting that Odysseus is the poet of Books ix–xii, the poet of the *Odyssey* weaves into Odysseus' tale another chronological ring from past to present to past and, in the space thus formed, presents a scene of commentary upon the hero's tale. In the middle of Odysseus' journey to Hades described in Book xi, the text returns from the narration of the past to the hero's narrating in the present: "'But I could not tell or name all the women I saw who were the wives and daughters of heroes, for before that the undying night would perish'" (*Odyssey* xi 328–330).[15] Rather than ending a tale, such magnifications of the subject, coupled with a personal disclaimer, elsewhere fan the audience's interest and good will.[16] That is the effect here, too, for the Phaeacians are enchanted. Echoing the return of Odysseus' narrating, the poet, too, declares: "So he spoke, and all of them were hushed in silence and held by enchantment (κηληθμῷ) through the shadowy halls" (*Odyssey* xi 333–334).[17] The silence is broken, when the queen Arete exclaims: "'Phaeacians, how does this man appear to you with respect to both visible form (εἶδος) and size (μέγεθος) and balanced wits within (φρένας ἔνδον ἐΐσας)?'" (*Odyssey* xi 336–337). The queen's pairing of Odysseus' external, visible, physical form with his interior, mental prowess reappears as the king Alcinous describes the hero's tale:

> "ὦ 'Οδυσεῦ, τὸ μὲν οὔ τί σ' ἐΐσκομεν εἰσορόωντες,
> ἠπεροπῆά τ' ἔμεν καὶ ἐπίκλοπον, οἷά τε πολλοὺς
> βόσκει γαῖα μέλαινα πολυσπερέας ἀνθρώπους,
> ψεύδεά τ' ἀρτύνοντας ὅθεν κέ τις οὐδὲ ἴδοιτο·
> σοὶ δ' ἔπι μὲν μορφὴ ἐπέων, ἔνι δὲ φρένες ἐσθλαί.
> μῦθον δ' ὡς ὅτ' ἀοιδὸς ἐπισταμένως κατέλεξας,
> πάντων τ' Ἀργείων σέο τ' αὐτοῦ κήδεα λυγρά."

> "Odysseus, we as we look upon you do not imagine
> that you are a deceiver and a thief, of the sort that in great
>   numbers
> the dark earth breeds, men spread far and wide,
> who fashion false things, stemming from whatever no one
>   can see.
> Upon you there is a beautiful form of words and in you are
>   good wits

and the story, as does a poet, with knowledge you have narrated
   in full,
the baneful sorrows of all the Greeks and of you yourself."

Odyssey xi 363–369

Odysseus' narration of his νόστος "return" is like a skillful poet's in its internal intelligence (ἔνι δὲ φρένες ἐσθλαί) and in the external "shape" or "form" (ἔπι μὲν μορφὴ ἐπέων).[18] By their relative abstractness, many translations of μορφή here – such as "grace" (Lattimore), "shapeliness" (Stanford), "charm" (Heubeck), or *Anmut* (Ameis-Hentze) – tend to obscure the mystery of this phrase μορφὴ ἐπέων. In Greek after Homer μορφή consistently denotes a shape or form, external, visible, material – especially that of the human body and those other entities that can undergo transformation.[19] When that μορφή is beautiful, the word can bear the force of this attribute and mean, in effect, "beauty" – not beauty as an abstraction, but rather as a quality or condition of something that can have a contour, that is, a material entity.[20] To use the word μορφή "shape, form" of ἐπέων "words, epic verse" implies a conception of epic narration as such a material entity, one whose form or shape can be discerned.[21] Such a conception coheres with the model inherited by Greek from Indo-European culture of poetry as a "woven text"[22] and indeed with the very notion of ποίησις "poetry" as "fabrication" – a "making" – and of the καλὴ ἀοιδή "beautiful poem" as a virtually architectural construction like that of the Delian Maidens in the *Homeric Hymn to Apollo* 164: οὕτω σφιν καλὴ συνάρηρεν ἀοιδή "thus was their beautiful song fitted together."[23]

   What, then, might be the particular μορφή, the beautiful "shape" or "form" that Alcinous discerns in Odysseus' tale? The question cannot be answered definitively. For the usage of μορφή here is one of just two in all of hexameter diction, and the other repeats the question, insofar as it, too, attributes μορφή to words. In its verb, however, this second usage is sugges-tive. In Book viii, Odysseus counters the claim that he does not "look the part" of an athlete with a generalization about the relation between exterior appear-ance and interior quality:

> "οὕτως οὐ πάντεσσι θεοὶ χαρίεντα διδοῦσιν
> ἀνδράσιν, οὔτε φυὴν οὔτ' ἄρ φρένας οὔτ' ἀγορητύν.
> ἄλλος μὲν γάρ τ' εἶδος ἀκιδνότερος πέλει ἀνήρ,
> ἀλλὰ θεὸς μορφὴν ἔπεσι στέφει."

> "Thus the gods do not give graces to all
> men, not in stature nor in wits nor in ability to speak.

For one man is more weak in respect to visible appearance
but the god puts beautiful form as a crown around his words."

Odyssey viii 167–170

The god crowns (στέφει, compare στέφος "crown, garland, wreath") the
"words" with a μορφή "beautiful form" as a στέφος "crown, garland, wreath"
crowns a head or the bowl at a symposium. The other usage of στέφει in
hexameter clarifies the metaphor here. In the *Iliad*, Athena prepares Achilles
to show himself in order to strike fear into the Trojans:

> ἀμφὶ δ' Ἀθήνη
> ὤμοις ἰφθίμοισι βάλ' αἰγίδα θυσσανόεσσαν,
> ἀμφὶ δέ οἱ κεφαλῇ νέφος ἔστεφε δῖα θεάων
> χρύσεον, ἐκ δ' αὐτοῦ δαῖε φλόγα παμφανόωσαν.

> Athena
> cast her tasseled aegis around his mighty shoulders
> and around his head she put as a crown a cloud
> golden, and from the man himself she kindled an all-gleaming
> blaze.

Iliad XVIII 203–206

As the goddess Athena "crowns" Achilles with a νέφος "cloud," so the god, in
Odysseus' claim, "crowns" the "words" with a μορφή: as objects of στέφω both
the νέφος "cloud" and the μορφή "beautiful form" share the shape of a στέφος
"crown."[24] The "words" are thus made metaphorically into something – a head
or a bowl at a symposium – that can "wear" the "beautiful form" of a wreath.

What is this narrative μορφή? What form of epic narrative might be
thought to share the coronal's circular shape? The most common formal
feature of Homeric style is, indeed, circular: A–B–A "ring-compositions"
like that of the chronological ὕστερον–πρότερον "the latter thing before the
earlier thing" form taken by Odysseus' tale. By lauding the "beautiful form of
words (μορφὴ ἐπέων)" in Odysseus' narration, does Alcinous (and thereby, the
poet) allude to its overall circumstructural "form," its analeptic arrangement?
Perhaps not – perhaps such an allusion would require a degree of abstraction foreign to characters in epic. The phrase remains mysterious. What we
do know is, on one hand, that the temporal form of Odysseus' tale is that of
analepsis, and on the other, that the tale is likened to that of an expert poet by
virtue of its exterior μορφὴ ἐπέων "beautiful form of words" and its internal
φρένες ἐσθλαί "good wits." Putting those two facts together, we are directed
to ask why an expert poet would use the form we find in Odysseus' narrative,

the ὕστερον–πρότερον "the latter thing before the earlier thing" order, for a νόστος "return" that displays intelligence.

By this point in its development, Odysseus' tale has shown why first-person analepsis with the prolepses it permits is the right form for imitating and narrating the intelligence behind his many returns. As μίμησις "imitation," Odysseus' recollection, because it returns from present to past to present, is a dramatization – a putting into the form of a δρᾶμα "doing" – of the action of memory, a virtual νόστος "return" of the mind, while as διήγησις "narration," it traces the same pattern of νόστος in its cycles of departure and return, death and rebirth.[25] Just as the hero returns from the dead in Hades, so the narrator's memory resurrects the past from the realm of the forgotten.[26] But by this point in Odysseus' narrative, it is also clear that mental and physical return are not just formally parallel but are causally connected. In the Polyphemus and Teiresias episodes, Odysseus as narrator uses anachrony to show Odysseus as a hero learning what νόστος "return" requires: crafty ξενία "guest-friend exchange," especially the exchange of names and food, "crafted" through remembering the dictates of the prophetic νόος "mind, intelligence."[27] And later, in the encounter with the Cattle of the Sun, he will direct the same temporality toward proving that he has met these conditions of νόστος and that the gods thus will his return.

Polyphemus: λόγος "speech" (Re)Turned into δόλος "trap"

Because it is the longest episode that centers upon the hero's action, the Polyphemus story offers the widest scope for the anachronies of first-person recollection, for the interplay between Odysseus as narrator and Odysseus as hero, between what he saw or foresaw then and what he sees now. As poet, Odysseus exploits this potential, but by neglecting the factor of analepsis with its double point of view critics have sometimes simplified or mistaken his complex meaning. Over the central issue of Odysseus' giving his name, they have split into two camps: those who approve the withholding but not the giving of the proper name, and those who criticize the Οὖτις "Nobody"-trick but defend the later revelation.[28] The positions are not wholly exclusive, however. From the narratological perspective, the defense vs. the criticism of revealing the name corresponds, as we shall see, to the hero's vs. the narrator's point of view and thus reflects the anachronic structure of the text. As for the Οὖτις "Nobody"-trick, in this episode both hero and narrator are unequivocally delighted with this λόγος "speech"/δόλος "trap."[29] Indeed, as narrator Odysseus uses anachrony to show what happens when such crafty manipulation of name-exchange is relaxed: the trick returns as and turns into the trickster.

From the start of the episode Odysseus as narrator employs prolepsis within the over-all analepsis to evaluate his actions as hero. After directing the rest of his comrades to remain behind while he goes with his crew to test the inhabitants of the island (*Odyssey* ix 172–176), he recounts sailing close enough to the shore to see a great cave and then gives the following description of its inhabitant:

"ἔνθα δὲ πολλὰ
μῆλ', ὄιές τε καὶ αἶγες, ἰαύεσκον: περὶ δ' αὐλὴ
ὑψηλὴ δέδμητο κατωρυχέεσσι λίθοισι
μακρῇσίν τε πίτυσσιν ἰδὲ δρυσὶν ὑψικόμοισιν.
ἔνθα δ' ἀνὴρ ἐνίαυε πελώριος, ὅς ῥα τὰ μῆλα
οἶος ποιμαίνεσκεν ἀπόπροθεν: οὐδὲ μετ' ἄλλους
πωλεῖτ', ἀλλ' ἀπάνευθεν ἐὼν ἀθεμίστια ᾔδη.
καὶ γὰρ θαῦμ' ἐτέτυκτο πελώριον, οὐδὲ ἐῴκει
ἀνδρί γε σιτοφάγῳ, ἀλλὰ ῥίῳ ὑλήεντι
ὑψηλῶν ὀρέων, ὅ τε φαίνεται οἶον ἀπ' ἄλλων."

"There many
flocks, both sheep and goats, used often to sleep. And a lofty
courtyard had been built around with deep-dug stones
and tall pines and oaks with lofty foliage.
There a monstrous man used to spend his nights, who
used often to shepherd his flocks alone and afar: nor did he
used to mingle with others, but being apart from them he knew
  no civilized customs.
For he was created as a monstrous marvel, and was not like
a man who eats bread, but like the wooded peak
of lofty mountains, which appears alone, away from the others."

Odyssey ix 183–192

This proleptic description has been interpreted as an attempt to "mislead" the audience by implying that Odysseus the hero "already knows" the Cyclops' character so that his taking of the Ismarian wine will not seem unmotivated.[30] But the tenses of the verbs – the imperfects, ἐνίαυε "used to spend his nights," πωλεῖτ' "used to mingle" and the frequentatives, ἰαύεσκον "used often to sleep," and ποιμαίνεσκεν "used often to shepherd" – imply that this prolepsis expresses the perspective not of Odysseus the hero, not what he can see and thus "already knows" at that moment of sailing by the cave, but rather the perspective of Odysseus the narrator, who now knows what Polyphemus used frequently to do. The purpose of the narrator's foreshadowing does not seem to be to mislead, but rather to enable the audience to anticipate what is coming and to applaud what Odysseus does next, that is, to foresee as hero what as narrator he has just established as fact. For it is now that Odysseus describes the fabulous wine (*Odyssey* ix 196–213) and explains why he took it along:

> "αὐτίκα γάρ μοι ὀίσατο <u>θυμὸς</u> ἀγήνωρ
> ἄνδρ' ἐπελεύσεσθαι μεγάλην ἐπιειμένον ἀλκήν,
> ἄγριον, οὔτε δίκας ἐὺ εἰδότα οὔτε θέμιστας."

> "For my manly <u>spirit</u> had suspected that
> very soon a man would come upon us clothed in great strength,
> savage, who knew well neither rights nor civilized customs."

Odyssey ix 213–215

The focus on the θυμός "spirit, passion" here initiates a careful and critical usage of the term in the Polyphemus and Teiresias episodes by which, as we shall see, Odysseus both displays and evaluates the two sides of his character: the defensive, preservative ingenuity we see now and the aggressive, excessive appetite which will nearly destroy him later and which Teiresias will declare he must curb in order to reach home. At this point, the foresight provided by the θυμός is complimentary to the hero, but it also sharpens the critical edge of the narrator's next prolepsis. For after relating how his companions begged him just to take some food and escape, Odysseus adds: "'but I did not obey – and indeed it would have been much more profitable – in order that I could both see the creature himself and whether he would give me guest-presents (ξείνια)'" (*Odyssey* ix 228–229). If he can anticipate the Cyclops' character, he should be all the more able to heed his companions' warning. Now, as narrator, he says that it would have been more advantageous to do so, but then, as hero, he was determined to pit the skills of culture against nature's rude force, to extract the recognition of ξενία "guest-friend exchange" even from a monster.

Odysseus as narrator still sees the contest in these terms. His use of two narrative devices, the simile and the pun, stamp his former weapons as cultural products. He likens his olive beam to tools of civilized crafts, one of which, shipbuilding, the Cyclopes specifically lack: he and his men twist the beam as others drill a ship plank with a brace-and-bit, and its point sizzles in the Cyclops' eye like a hot axe or plane in tempering water (*Odyssey* ix 125–130,

383–388, 391–394). This olive beam blinds Polyphemus, but escape from the beast – whose name means "he of the many speeches" – ultimately depends upon manipulation of λόγος "speech," the cultural tool *par excellence*.

Odysseus wins the contest of speech-as-weapon because he can turn λόγος "speech" into δόλος "trap" – or so the narrator implies by glossing the Οὖτις "Nobody"/οὔ τις "not anybody" trick with a pun on μῆτις "trick of transformative intelligence" and μή τις "not anybody."[31] After recalling the other Cyclopes' answer to Polyphemus' call for help:

> "'εἰ μὲν δὴ μή τίς σε βιάζεται οἶον ἐόντα,
> νοῦσον γ' οὔ πως ἔστι Διὸς μεγάλου ἀλέασθαι,
> ἀλλὰ σύ γ' εὔχεο πατρὶ Ποσειδάωνι ἄνακτι.'"

> "'If then indeed <u>not anybody</u> does violence to you, alone
>   as you are,
> by no means is it possible to avoid a sickness from great Zeus.
> But do you rather pray to your father, the lord Poseidon.'"

> *Odyssey* ix 410–412

Odysseus adds his own reaction:

> "ὣς ἄρ' ἔφαν ἀπιόντες, ἐμὸν δ' ἐγέλασσε φίλον κῆρ,
> ὡς ὄνομ' ἐξαπάτησεν ἐμὸν καὶ <u>μῆτις ἀμύμων</u>."

> "So then they spoke as they went away, and my heart within me
>   laughed at how
> my name and my <u>flawless trick of transformative intelligence</u>
>   utterly deceived him."

> *Odyssey* ix 413–414

After creating this pun, Odysseus as narrator reinforces it, repeating the word μῆτις in the same metrical position and assimilating the word-play to a δόλος "trap":

> "πάντας δὲ <u>δόλους</u> καὶ <u>μῆτιν</u> ὕφαινον
> ὥς τε περὶ ψυχῆς· μέγα γὰρ κακὸν ἐγγύθεν ἦεν."

> "I was weaving all kinds of <u>traps</u> and a <u>trick of transformative
>   intelligence</u>
> as one always does when life is at stake. For great was the evil
>   close upon us."

> *Odyssey* ix 422–423

By this reinforcement of his "flawless" pun, Odysseus as narrator registers his continued pride in what the pun implies: Odysseus is the "master-troper," for he can turn a thing into the same–but–different thing.[32] Odysseus can assimilate μῆτις and μή τις, just as his μῆτις "trick of transformative intelligence" made the Cyclopes say μή τις "not anybody," and just as his Οὖτις "Nobody"/ δόλος "trap" made Polyphemus say in his call for help:

"'ὦ φίλοι, Οὖτίς με κτείνει δόλῳ οὐδὲ βίηφιν .'"

"'O loved ones, Nobody is killing me by means of a trap
 or by violence.'"

Odyssey ix 408

By thus repeating Odysseus' Οὖτις "Nobody" even as he calls it a δόλος "trap," Polyphemus turns speech against himself. The speech/trap of Odysseus as the "master-(re)turner" is that Polyphemus must (re)turn his speech into and as a trick. Whose speech? Not "Nobody's." For it is the speech of Polyphemus himself that turns against Polyphemus, as long as his is the only "proper" name available to the contesting parties. With another proper name to say, however, the direction of Polyphemus' speech will be turned.

In the second round of name-exchange, the narrator's view diverges again from the hero's. With emphasis on the θυμός "spirit, passion" that over-ruled his comrades' arguments, Odysseus recalls his boast to the giant:

"ὣς φάσαν, ἀλλ' οὐ πεῖθον ἐμὸν μεγαλήτορα θυμόν,
ἀλλά μιν ἄψορρον προσέφην κεκοτηότι θυμῷ:
'Κύκλωψ, αἴ κέν τίς σε καταθνητῶν ἀνθρώπων
ὀφθαλμοῦ εἴρηται ἀεικελίην ἀλαωτύν,
φάσθαι Ὀδυσσῆα πτολιπόρθιον ἐξαλαῶσαι,
υἱὸν Λαέρτεω, Ἰθάκῃ ἔνι οἰκί' ἔχοντα.'"

"So they spoke, but did not persuade my great-hearted spirit
 but once again I spoke to him in the anger of my spirit:
 'Cyclops, if ever anyone of mortal men
 asks about the shameful blinding of your eye,
 say that Odysseus, sacker of cities, blinded you,
 the son of Laertes, who has his home in Ithaca.'"

Odyssey ix 500–505

By giving the true, powerful version of his name, Odysseus activates the powerful version of his adversary's name. In the name "Polyphemus"

(Πολύφημος) – "he of the many speeches (φῆμαι)" – the "speeches" may be subjective or objective, "he who speaks" or "he who is spoken of" and the sense of φήμη, either an unmarked "report" or a marked "prayer or curse."[33] Context alone regulates the polysemy, and in this context "Polyphemus" is now subjective and marked, "he who utters many curses." For Odysseus has (re)turned to him and against himself the power of speech, the "divine" power – expressed by the optative mood used in prayers – to cause what it says. Now Polyphemus can with two such optatives – ὀψὲ κακῶς ἔλθοι "'may he come home late and badly'" and εὕροι δ᾽ ἐν πήματα οἴκῳ "'and may he find miseries in his home'" – curse a known, namable man, "Odysseus, sacker of cities" (*Odyssey* ix 530–535). The validity of the curse is confirmed by Odysseus as narrator, when, after describing his sacrifice to Zeus of the ram he rode to safety, he adds the prolepsis:

> "ὁ δ᾽ οὐκ ἐμπάζετο ἱρῶν,
> ἀλλ᾽ ὅ γε μερμήριξεν ὅπως ἀπολοίατο πᾶσαι
> νῆες ἐύσσελμοι καὶ ἐμοὶ ἐρίηρες ἑταῖροι."

> "But he [Zeus] took no heed of my offerings,
> but indeed was pondering how all my well-benched
> ships might perish and all my trusty companions."

> *Odyssey* ix 553–555

By exploiting the double focus of first-person recollection through prolepsis, simile, and pun, the poet Odysseus shows what he now knows about the exchange of names. If your host proves to be as uncivilized as you expected by inverting the code of ξενία "guest-friend exchange" – asking your identity before feeding you, making a meal of instead of for his guests, escape lies in complementary inversions of the conventions – giving wine to your host, who drinks it alone, and giving "Nobody" as your name.[34] If your host is huge but brainless, you may blind him with the tricks of intellect and the tools of culture. But, if your host is savage, you must restrain all desire to gain more from him than escape. To extort personal credit for victory requires giving your name, thereby restoring the creature's sight and canceling the intellectual advantage you won with your λόγος "speech"/δόλος "trap." Only culture can accord κλέος "fame." When ξενία is inverted, νόστος "return home" requires πολυτροπία, the continual, controlled (re)turning of λόγος into δόλος, despite the claims of θυμός.[35] What made this (re)vision of the encounter clear to Odysseus was the prophecy of Teiresias.

Teiresias: The Full Circle of Prolepsis

At the end of Book x, Circe tells Odysseus what he must do to return home:

"'διογενὲς Λαερτιάδη, πολυμήχαν' Ὀδυσσεῦ,
μηκέτι νῦν ἀέκοντες ἐμῷ ἐνὶ μίμνετε οἴκῳ.
ἀλλ' ἄλλην χρὴ πρῶτον ὁδὸν τελέσαι καὶ ἱκέσθαι
εἰς Ἀίδαο δόμους καὶ ἐπαινῆς Περσεφονείης,
ψυχῇ χρησομένους Θηβαίου Τειρεσίαο,
μάντηος ἀλαοῦ, τοῦ τε φρένες ἔμπεδοί εἰσι:
τῷ καὶ τεθνηῶτι νόον πόρε Περσεφόνεια,
οἴῳ πεπνῦσθαι, τοὶ δὲ σκιαὶ ἀίσσουσιν.'"

"'Son of Laertes and seed of Zeus, resourceful Odysseus,
no longer remain in my house against your will.
But first you must accomplish another journey and arrive
at the halls of Hades and dread Persephone,
there to consult as oracle the soul of Teiresias the Theban,
the blind prophet, whose wits are always firm-set.
To this one, even though he has died, Persephone granted
    intelligence,
to him alone to be wise, while the others are flittering
    shadows.'"

Odyssey x 488–495

Here we meet two paradoxes, each with the same bearing on νόστος "return" and νόος "intelligence." To return to life Odysseus must suffer a death. The way home from Hades can be learned only from one who can see while blind, whose soul alone among the shades possesses oracular intelligence. In its formal and thematic relation to the rest of Odysseus' poem, Teiresias' prophecy displays this "homecoming" power.

At the heart of Odysseus' recollection lies the prophecy of Teiresias. The two narrations are complementary in their anachronic structures. Odysseus' tale is analeptic, tracing an arc from present to past to present, while Teiresias' vision stretches from present to future to present. In the order of the text the hero's account frames the prophet's. Here is the composite:

HERO: Present to Past [PROPHET: Present to Future to Present] Past to Present

In this double anachronic μορφή, a circle toward the future interrupts, opposes, and complements a circle toward the past. When the content, too, is considered, the construction emerges in its reach and extent as an emblem of the hero's many (re)turns.

Odysseus' recollection puts in the center of the *Odyssey* all of his νόστος "return" that precedes the epic. His analepsis reaches back to his first stop after leaving Troy, extends through nine more cycles of coming and going, and ends where the poem begins, with the hero enthralled by Calypso.[36] Teiresias' prophecy bisects this recollection of the past with a vision of Odysseus' future νόστοι "returns." Through these anachronies the "line" that is the text imitates the circles of departure and return that make up heroic experience. For the two parts of Teiresias' prophecy sweep forward, the first reaching to the end of the epic and the second beyond the end, round again and back to the center of the poem in Hades.

Teiresias first explains what νόστος "return" in the second half of the *Odyssey* will require.

> "'<u>νόστον</u> δίζηαι μελιηδέα, φαίδιμ' Ὀδυσσεῦ:
> τὸν δέ τοι ἀργαλέον θήσει θεός: οὐ γὰρ ὀίω
> λήσειν ἐννοσίγαιον, ὅ τοι κότον ἔνθετο θυμῷ
> χωόμενος ὅτι οἱ υἱὸν φίλον ἐξαλάωσας.
> ἀλλ' ἔτι μέν κε καὶ ὣς κακά περ πάσχοντες ἵκοισθε,
> αἴ κ' ἐθέλῃς σὸν <u>θυμὸν</u> ἐρυκακέειν καὶ ἑταίρων,
> ὁππότε κε πρῶτον πελάσῃς ἐυεργέα νῆα
> Θρινακίῃ νήσῳ, προφυγὼν ἰοειδέα πόντον,
> βοσκομένας δ' εὕρητε βόας καὶ ἴφια μῆλα
> Ἠελίου, ὃς πάντ' ἐφορᾷ καὶ πάντ' ἐπακούει.'"

> "'Glorious Odysseus, you are seeking honey-sweet <u>homecoming</u>,
> but the god will make this grievous for you. For I think you
>   will not
> escape the Shaker of the Earth, who has stored up wrath in
>   his spirit,
> being angry because you blinded his dear son.
> But even so and still you might come back, after much suffering,
> if you are willing to restrain your own <u>spirit</u> and your companions',
> at that time when you first bring your well-made vessel near
> to the island Thrinakia, escaping the violet-colored deep,
> and there find the pasturing cattle and fat sheep
> of Helios, who sees all things, and listens to all things.'"

Odyssey xi 100–109

The hero's νόστος "return" demands restraint of θυμός "spirit, passion" in accord with what the prophetic νόος "intelligence" can see will determine his goal. Teiresias sees that Odysseus must restrain his hunger to eat the Cattle of the Sun. If he wants a day of homecoming, he must observe correct ξενία "guest-friend exchange" with the bringer of all days. If he wants to expel the Suitors, guests who eat their host's food by force, he must leave the herds of this host unscathed. With the ability to make the body serve the devisings of the mind, one man can defeat many.

Teiresias' prophecy does not stop, however, where the poem ends, with the defeat of the Suitors. The reach and extent of his prophecy include the future beyond the border of the epic, just as Odysseus' tale embraces the past before its start. After killing his rivals, Odysseus must take up an oar and travel until he reaches men who have never seen the sea or tasted salt (*Odyssey* xi 119–125). This will be his final cycle of departure and return:

> "'σῆμα δέ τοι ἐρέω μάλ' ἀριφραδές, οὐδέ σε λήσει:
> ὁππότε κεν δή τοι συμβλήμενος ἄλλος ὁδίτης
> φήῃ ἀθηρηλοιγὸν ἔχειν ἀνὰ φαιδίμῳ ὤμῳ,
> καὶ τότε δὴ γαίῃ πήξας ἐυῆρες ἐρετμόν,
> ῥέξας ἱερὰ καλὰ Ποσειδάωνι ἄνακτι,
> ἀρνειὸν ταῦρόν τε συῶν τ' ἐπιβήτορα κάπρον,
> οἴκαδ' ἀποστείχειν ἔρδειν θ' ἱερὰς ἑκατόμβας
> ἀθανάτοισι θεοῖσι, τοὶ οὐρανὸν εὐρὺν ἔχουσι,
> πᾶσι μάλ' ἑξείης. θάνατος δέ τοι ἐξ ἁλὸς αὐτῷ
> ἀβληχρὸς μάλα τοῖος ἐλεύσεται, ὅς κέ σε πέφνῃ
> γήραι ὕπο λιπαρῷ ἀρημένον: ἀμφὶ δὲ λαοὶ
> ὄλβιοι ἔσσονται. τὰ δέ τοι νημερτέα εἴρω.'"

> "'And I will tell you a very clear sign and it will not escape
> your notice.
> Whenever indeed, another wayfarer meets with you
> and says that you have a winnowing-fan on your bright shoulder,
> then indeed you must fix your well-fitted oar in the earth
> and make beautiful sacrifices to the lord Poseidon,
> a ram and a bull and wild boar, mounter of sows,
> and then go away back home again and render holy hecatombs
> to the immortal gods who hold the wide heaven,
> all of them in order. And for you yourself a very gentle
> death away
> from the sea will come which will slay you

overcome by shining old age. Your people about you
will be blessed. These things I say to you are unerring.'"

Odyssey xi 126–137

In this final return of the hero, the *Odyssey* itself circles around to reconnect
with itself. After leaving home, sailing again, and reaching so far inland that
men interpret the oar as a winnowing-fan, Odysseus will plant this instrument
in which commerce at sea and cultivation of the land now coincide. Coming
back to Ithaca from this farthest, most foreign land, will be Odysseus' last
homecoming, but not his last νόστος. For from this ultimate reunion with
his own people, a "very gentle death" will return Odysseus to the place
where he and the poem stand now.[37] In Teiresias' proleptic perspective these
oppositions – commerce and agriculture, sea and land, foreign peoples and
family at home, death and life – dissolve in a "still point" at the turning of the
epic in Hades.

The Cattle of the Sun: ὕστερον-πρότερον of Memory

Odysseus does not end his tale without attempting to validate Teiresias' grand
prophecy. Here there is none of the uncertainty that closes the *katabasis* of
the *Aeneid*, no shade from the ivory gate (Vergil *Aeneid* VI 893–898). Odysseus
is unambivalent in his desire for conveyance by his hosts, and his elaborate
precautions and strenuous efforts since arriving at Phaeacia imply that their
response cannot be taken for granted. But just as another tale by Odysseus
will wangle a mantle from Eumaeus and another by Penelope will elicit gifts
from the Suitors (*Odyssey* xiv 459–517, xviii 250–283), so this story may win
passage from the Phaeacians if it persuades them of two things, that Teiresias'
prophecy is true and that Odysseus can meet its demands. To prove himself
and corroborate Teiresias, Odysseus again applies the rhetorical force of
prolepsis.

In Book xii Odysseus as narrator risks the tedium of repetition in order
to establish a pattern of proleptic admonition and subsequent response. After
rehearsing in full Circe's forecast of his coming trials (*Odyssey* xii 37–141), he
then describes how he survived them all by remembering her instructions and
acting upon them.[38] By this sequence he demonstrates the "death" of the man
who indulged his θυμός "spirit, passion" in his encounter with Polyphemus
and his "rebirth" as one who can fulfill Teiresias' conditions for homecoming:
to remember a prophecy and to restrain his θυμός accordingly. Conversely, the
hero's success in the trials ratifies the prophet's conditions.

Besides Odysseus' own behavior, the fate of his crew confirms the truth of Teiresias' predictions. At every point, Odysseus repeats Circe's directions to his comrades. Encountering the Sirens, all remember and obey, and no one is lost. Next, preparing for Scylla and Charybdis, Odysseus tries to encourage his men by reminding them of their escape from the Cyclops' cave.

> "'ἀλλὰ καὶ ἔνθεν ἐμῇ ἀρετῇ, βουλῇ τε νόῳ τε,
> ἐκφύγομεν, καί που τῶνδε μνήσεσθαι ὀίω.
> νῦν δ' ἄγεθ', ὡς ἂν ἐγὼ εἴπω, πειθώμεθα πάντες.'"

> "'But even from there, by my excellence, both my counsel and
>   my intelligence,
> we escaped. I think that somehow all these things, too, will be
>   remembered.
> But now, come! As I said, let us all be persuaded.'"

Odyssey xii 211–213

Besides remembering past success, the men are to look into the future to the point where present peril becomes remembered escape. They should project upon the future their recollection of the past. Again they comply, and the losses are kept to the predicted minimum (*Odyssey* xii 108–110, 222–250).

On Helios' island, however, the outcome is different. At the outset Odysseus recalls the warnings of Teiresias and Circe and conveys them to the crew, but this time to no avail.[39] They steal the god's cattle and a shipwreck results. Through prolepsis, Odysseus makes this calamity the rhetorical climax of his tale. He repeats the premonition of disaster he had as soon as the crew rejected his plea:

> "καὶ τότε δὴ γίγνωσκον ὃ δὴ κακὰ μήδετο δαίμων."

> "And then indeed I was recognizing that the god was indeed
>   devising evils."

Odyssey xii 295

This anticipation of divine vengeance soon blossoms into the words of the gods themselves. Praying to Zeus, Helios threatens, in effect, to eliminate all days:

> "'εἰ δέ μοι οὐ τίσουσι βοῶν ἐπιεικέ' ἀμοιβήν,
> δύσομαι εἰς Ἀίδαο καὶ ἐν νεκύεσσι φαείνω.'"

> "'If these will not pay me fitting recompense for my cattle,

> I will go down into the house of Hades and shine my light
> among the dead.'"

Odyssey xii 382–383

In ignoring Teiresias' prophecy, the shipmates have committed a crime tantamount to turning the cosmos inside out, to putting the source of life in the place of death.[40] Zeus promises to restore the natural order:

> "'Ἥέλι', ἦ τοι μὲν σὺ μετ' ἀθανάτοισι φάεινε
> καὶ θνητοῖσι βροτοῖσιν ἐπὶ ζείδωρον ἄρουραν:
> τῶν δέ κ' ἐγὼ τάχα νῆα θοὴν ἀργῆτι κεραυνῷ
> τυτθὰ βαλὼν κεάσαιμι μέσῳ ἐνὶ οἴνοπι πόντῳ.'"

> "'Helios, indeed for your part do not fail to shine among the
> immortals
> and mortal men upon the grain-giving earth.
> And I myself quickly with my shining thunderbolt will strike
> their swift ship
> and split it into small pieces in the middle of the wine-dark
> deep.'"

Odyssey xii 385–388

This prediction defines the shipwreck, before Odysseus recounts it, as confirmation by the world's undying realities of Teiresias' ontology of νόστος "return." The shipwreck derives Teiresias' prophecy and Odysseus' homecoming from the righteousness of Zeus. Who now could doubt the truth of the prophecy or Odysseus' right to fulfill it? Who would refuse the hero's return?

III. The Economy of νόστος "return"

In the world of the *Odyssey* poetry is exchanged. Sometimes, as between Odysseus and the Phaeacians, the process is part of ξενία, an exchange between "guest-friends." And sometimes it is more "economic" with the parties clearly identified as producer and consumer and the recompense set beforehand.[41] A θέσπις ἀοιδός "divine singer" is one of the δημιοεργοί "those who do the people's work" (*Odyssey* xvii 382–385), a professional who makes his living by trading his stories for shelter, clothes, food, or conveyance. In either case, the exchange proves that poetry has "economic value." A tale is rewarded, if it tells the truth or what the listeners want the truth to be.[42]

Conversely, a poem's worth in the eyes of the listeners is measured by what it elicits, what it "makes." In these terms, the response to Odysseus' tale makes it a masterwork.

Like a good audience, the Phaeacians in Book viii indicate beforehand what they want to hear. Although they have already offered gifts and expressed their willingness to escort Odysseus home, their πομπή "conveyance" still requires his self-identifying tale. Alcinous asks his name and country so that the Phaeacians' self-piloting ships may know where to take him (*Odyssey* viii 550–563) and even specifies the guiding theme for his story, the observance or violation of ξενία "guest-friend exchange," the Phaeacians' pre-eminent virtue:

> "ἀλλ' ἄγε μοι τόδε εἰπὲ καὶ ἀτρεκέως κατάλεξον,
> ὅππη ἀπεπλάγχθης τε καὶ ἅς τινας ἵκεο χώρας
> ἀνθρώπων, αὐτούς τε πόλιάς τ' ἐὺ ναιετοώσας,
> ἠμὲν ὅσοι χαλεποί τε καὶ ἄγριοι οὐδὲ δίκαιοι,
> οἵ τε φιλόξεινοι, καί σφιν νόος ἐστὶ θεουδής."

> "But come now, tell me this and narrate exactly
> both where you have wandered and what lands of men
> you have reached, both the people and their populous cities,
> both as many as are cruel and savage and not just,
> and those who are kind to guests and have a god-fearing mind."

> *Odyssey* viii 572–576

But between his promise of conveyance and his request for Odysseus' tale, Alcinous recalls his father's gloomy prophecy:

> "ἀλλὰ τόδ' ὥς ποτε πατρὸς ἐγὼν εἰπόντος ἄκουσα
> Ναυσιθόου, ὃς ἔφασκε Ποσειδάων' ἀγάσασθαι
> ἡμῖν, οὕνεκα πομποὶ ἀπήμονές εἰμεν ἁπάντων.
> φῆ ποτὲ Φαιήκων ἀνδρῶν ἐυεργέα νῆα
> ἐκ πομπῆς ἀνιοῦσαν ἐν ἠεροειδέι πόντῳ
> ῥαισέμεναι, μέγα δ' ἧμιν ὄρος πόλει ἀμφικαλύψειν.
> ὣς ἀγόρευ' ὁ γέρων: τὰ δέ κεν θεὸς ἢ τελέσειεν
> ἤ κ' ἀτέλεστ' εἴη, ὥς οἱ φίλον ἔπλετο θυμῷ."

> "But this story I once heard from my father,
> Nausithoos, who used to say that Poseidon begrudged
> us, because we are safe conductors of all men.
> He said that some day a well-made ship of the Phaeacians

returning from conveyance in the misty deep
Poseidon would shatter and cover our city with a great
    mountain.
So that old man used to speak, and these things the god
    might fulfill
or they may be unfulfilled, as is pleasing to his spirit."

Odyssey viii 564–571

Along with his request for a poem in return for Odysseus' νόστος "return" goes the king's awareness of what this νόστος may cost. The "economic" challenge here for Odysseus is clear: his tale must persuade his audience to give him a homecoming at a mortal risk. The impact of the prophecy Odysseus will narrate must counteract the prophecy that Alcinous remembers now. And, at the end of Odysseus' story, the truth of Teiresias seems unassailable. The Phaeacians act at once to take their guest home.

And the final cost in this exchange of νόστος for νόστος, the poem for the deed? Now we find something like the poignancy and ambiguity that end *Aeneid* VI. For in Book xiii, immediately after the Phaeacians leave Odysseus on Ithaca, the text confirms that his was indeed the conveyance predicted by Nausithoos. Like Zeus and Helios before the shipwreck, Zeus and Poseidon debate the Phaeacians' fate. Poseidon declares his intention to turn their ship to stone and to bury their city beneath a mountain (*Odyssey* xiii 146–152). Zeus replies:

> "ὦ πέπον, ὡς μὲν ἐμῷ θυμῷ δοκεῖ εἶναι ἄριστα,
> ὁππότε κεν δὴ πάντες ἐλαυνομένην προΐδωνται
> λαοὶ ἀπὸ πτόλιος, θεῖναι λίθον ἐγγύθι γαίης
> νηΐ θοῇ ἴκελον, ἵνα θαυμάζωσιν ἅπαντες
> ἄνθρωποι, μέγα δέ σφιν ὄρος πόλει ἀμφικαλύψαι."

> "Dear brother, here is how it seems to be best to my spirit:
> whenever all the people are watching her from the city
> as she is drawn in, then turn her into a stone that looks like
> a fast ship, close off shore, so that all men may wonder,
> and veil around their city with a great mountain."[43]

Odyssey xiii 154–158

And what does Poseidon do? We never learn. In what John Peradotto calls a "prophecy degree zero," the outcome here is left uncertain, as indeterminable within the text as Teiresias' prophecy of Odysseus' death.[44] This uncertainty raises questions that challenge the ontology upon which the truthfulness of Odysseus' tale is based. Can a divinely ordained homecoming necessitate the divinely ordained destruction of those that accomplish it? If the two prophecies seem to conflict, was one of them a fiction? Neither is confirmed in the text. Can any prophecy or recollection be trusted as true? What is true, in any case, is that the prophecy of Teiresias is coupled with another that opens the question of prophetic truth, just as Odysseus' recollection in Books ix–xii is matched in the course of xiii–xxiv by his explicitly false "memories" of Crete, two apparent instances of ἀληθέα "true things" followed by ψεύδεα ὁμοῖα ἐτύμοισιν "false things like to real things."[45]

In admitting these questioning counterparts, the text makes its final disclosure on the nature of νόστος. It acknowledges the inherent instability of (re)turn. It implies that if Odysseus can turn from controlled λόγος "speech"/ δόλος "trap" to indulgence of θυμός "spirit, passion" and back to controlled θυμός, he can turn back again.[46] There can be no final return of time, for the truth of the past or future always eludes its only verification, occurrence in a present that never returns. The truth of memory or prophecy can be only a verisimilitude, achieved by the similarity between temporal and causal relations.[47] In admitting the radical uncertainty of anachrony, Odyssean temporality takes its own risk in the economy of νόστος "return." In order to disclose the nature of the poetic "trope," it risks (re)turning as an Οὖτις "Nobody" trick against the rhetorical mastery of its hero and poet.

Notes

An earlier version of this essay appeared in *Approaches to Homer*, edited by C. Rubino and C. Shelmerdine, Austin, 1983:38–71.

1. de Man 1979:115.

2. See, for example, Stewart 1976:146–195.

3. The term belongs to Frontisi-Ducroux 1976:538–548, a review of Genette, "Discours du récit," in *Figures III* (Genette 1972:67–282). In this book, Genette (1980:25–29) describes the three narratological levels of a text as outlined below. Frontisi-Ducroux's review points the way for my essay by illustrating these three levels with the case of Odysseus as bard.

4. The similes are at *Odyssey* xi 366–369 and xxi 406–409.

5. Pucci (1982) describes the implications of Odysseus' epithet πολύτροπος "of many turns" used in *Odyssey* i 1 in place of his proper name: (1) its attribution to the hero of "manyness" – the repetition of the same or the similar, that is, the "disguised" same; the constant economic accumulation and loss; and perpetual arriving and leaving – and the efforts of the text to direct this "manyness" toward a fulfillment in conclusive victory; (2) its possible reference to the text itself as tropological or rhetorical; and (3) its illustration of the excessive or supplementary property of language to "trope on" or multiply its literal meaning, and how such πολυτροπία "turning many ways" precludes a single, "proper" name with its attendant κλέος "fame in epic poetry." While different in range, methodology, and emphasis, Pucci's essay inspires my analysis of the "tropic" structure of (re)turn in the temporal form and the critical action of the poem.

6. On the one- or two-word *tropos* vs. the extended *figura*, see Quintilian 9.1.1–9 and 9.2.46 and note 7 of "Similes and Symbol in *Odyssey* v" in this collection.

7. Genette 1980:25–29.

8. Genette 1980:30–32.

9. This distinction comes from *Republic* 392c–395, where Plato condemns narration through deceptive μίμησις "imitation" in which the poet speaks as someone else, in favor of ἁπλῆ διήγησις, narration pure and simple in which the poet always speaks in his own voice. These two narrative forms correspond to "mood" defined by Genette 1980:161 as the "name given to the different forms of the verb that are used to affirm more or less the thing in question, and to express . . . the different points of view from which the life or the action is looked at."

10. Genette 1980:35–48. While the "story" is logically prior to the "narrative" by providing the chronological order that the narrative can either follow or change, it can be the case, when other sources are lacking, that the narrative is our only source of the events of the story. The two narrative levels are nonetheless clearly distinct, when the

narrative makes it clear – as in the case of the *Odyssey* – that it is presenting events out of their chronological order.

11. See Bassett 1920:39. In this article Bassett argues that ὕστερον-πρότερον "the latter thing before the earlier thing" originally meant not just a simple inversion of natural order (for example, *Odyssey* iv 208: γαμέοντί τε γεινομένῳ τε "both marrying and coming into being"), but complete A–B–A or A–B–B–A sequences.

12. Odysseus' claim of κλέος "fame" here on the basis of δόλοι "traps" reflects a development from his identification with his previous martial glory in the episode with Polyphemus. See below, note 35.

13. At the level of the story, these brief mentions of Calypso and Circe are analeptic, recollections of what is past. At the level of the narration, that of Calypso remains analeptic, recalling the action of Book v, while that of Circe is proleptic, looking forward to Odysseus' account in Book x of his encounter with the goddess.

14. Last of all Odysseus mentions his sojourn with Calypso, but he does not elaborate: "why should I tell you these things? For just yesterday I told it to you and your wife in your home" (*Odyssey* xii 450–453). Note the narrative effect of making Odysseus recount his departure from Calypso separately (*Odyssey* vii 240–297), before his grand narration of the νόστος "return" that ends with that separation: the end of Odysseus' tale recalls both his earlier account in *Odyssey* vii to Arete and the poet's account of the same action in Book v and at the start of the epic in Book i. The end of Odysseus' story thereby curves back to the three "same but different" points at which the *Odyssey* as the narration of Odysseus' νόστος begins. Compare Genette 1980:45–46 on how the repeated analepses at the start of Proust's *À la recherche du temps perdu* attempt by "propitiatory mimesis" to "exorcize" the difficulty of any beginning. As the "repeated starts" of *Odyssey* v and xiii testify, this effort to control the difficulty of beginning by imitating it belongs to the earliest stage of Western narrative.

15. Frontisi-Ducroux 1976:541–542 observes how this return to Odysseus' narrating and the comments of Arete and Alcinous stress the double role of Odysseus as hero and bard.

16. Compare the disclaimers of Nestor (*Odyssey* iii 113–117), Helen (*Odyssey* iv 240–241), and Odysseus (*Odyssey* xiv 193–198, compare *Odyssey* xiv 463–467) and the similar gesture in the *Iliad* at the start of the Catalogue of Ships (*Iliad* II 488–492).

17. The use here of the term κηληθμός "magic charm of song" marks Odysseus as poet. See Stanford 1961:1.394 on *Odyssey* xi 334.

18. See Stanford 1961:1.395 on *Odyssey* xi 367: "Note the antithesis between the outward form (ἔπι = ἔπεστι) and inner meaning (ἔνι = ἔνεισι)." Note, too, that if Koller 1972:16–24 is correct in claiming that in epic diction ἔπος designates a hexameter verse, then the plural, ἔπεα, would denote an aggregate of such verses, that is, an epic narrative, and μορφὴ ἐπέων here should be translated as "the form of an epic narration."

19. See Sandoz 1971:55–67.

20. In Homeric poetry, "beauty" – as indicated by usages of the adjective καλός "beautiful" and the noun κάλλος "beauty" – is preeminently an attribute of works of art and craft: 60% in the *Iliad* and 48.25% in the *Odyssey*.

21. See Sandoz 1971:56: "In the *Iliad* and the *Odyssey*, in fact, the author lends to ἔπεα ["words"] a material existence." For the conception of ἔπεα "words" as constituting material objects that occupy tangible space, see also *Iliad* XX 246–249:

> ἔστι γὰρ ἀμφοτέροισιν ὀνείδεα μυθήσασθαι
> πολλὰ μάλ', οὐδ' ἂν νηῦς ἑκατόζυγος ἄχθος ἄροιτο.
> στρεπτὴ δὲ γλῶσσ' ἐστὶ βροτῶν, πολέες δ' ἔνι μῦθοι
> παντοῖοι, ἐπέων δὲ πολὺς νομὸς ἔνθα καὶ ἔνθα.

> For there are for both of us blame-speeches to tell,
> very many, nor would a ship of a hundred benches bear the load.
> Ever-turning is the tongue of mortals, and in it are many stories
> of all kinds, and the field of words is wide on this side and that.

For the image of a νομός "place of pasturage, field, range" of ἐπέων "words," see also Hesiod, *Works and Days* 403: ἀχρεῖος δ' ἔσται ἐπέων νομός "the field of your words will be useless."

22. Durante 1960. See also Schmidt 1967:299-301, Durante 1976:48, 167-179, Snyder 1981, Scheid and Svenbro 1996:esp.111-130, Nagy 1996a:84-92, Nagy 1996b:63-74, Graziosi 2002:18-40, Nagy 2002:70-98.

23. For the Delian Maidens' song, see "Sacred Apostrophe: Re-Presentation and Imitation in *Homeric Hymn to Apollo* and *Homeric Hymn to Hermes*" in this collection.

24. Sandoz (1971:56–57) attempts to derive the meaning of μορφή in hexameter diction by means of the verb, στέφω. He cites *Iliad* XVIII 203–206 where the object of the verb is νέφος "cloud" and *Odyssey* v 303–304 where the compound of the verb, περιστέφω, is used in relation to clouds: οἵοισιν νεφέεσσι περιστέφει οὐρανὸν εὐρὺν Ζεύς, which he translates as "*de quelles nuées Zeus couvre l'immensité du ciel*." From these usages, together with that of ἐπιστέφανω at *Odyssey* i 148 = iii 339 = xxi 271, he concludes that "men of the heroic period conceived μορφή as a kind of rain or vapor of beautification." This interpretation emphasizes and assimilates the two objects of the verb: μορφή shares the characteristics of νέφος "cloud," whereas I emphasize the form inherent in the verb: when an object of στέφω both μορφή and νέφος share the form of the στέφος "crown, garland, wreath." In the post-Homeric usages of μορφή studied by Sandoz, the word is shown to denote physical, visible, changeable form: the beautiful figure of the human body, in particular, the external form as opposed to the inner ψυχή "soul," when μορφή "designates the body in its tangible reality" whether beautiful or ugly; the conformation of an organism in medical texts; the visible form of a corpse or the changing shapes of the moon or a metamorphosing god; the profile of a sphere in materialist philosophy; a "form" that undergoes "transformation" as the

103

object of the nouns μετάστασις "change" or τρόπος "turning," like a degree of color or the profiles of flames; the curvilinear contour of a circle (as opposed to a rectilinear σχῆμα "configuration") or an animal; the outline of a σχῆμα in the more general sense of a "figure" or an imprint; the form emanating from an object and imprinting its surroundings in the materialist theory of vision; and the metaphorical sense of a phase in an evolving situation. Sandoz concludes that μορφή "is essentially the form of entities in a situation of transformation, then, in the language of geometry, the form of inflected lines, the contour" (67).

25. The formal and thematic relation between return and intelligence in the *Odyssey* coheres with the etymology of νόος "mind, intelligence" offered by Frame 1978. On the basis of evidence in the Homeric epics and the *Rig-Veda*, and from parallels in other Indo-European languages, Frame argues that both νόστος "return" and νόος "mind, intelligence" are deverbative substantives of the same root, **nes*. According to his derivation, νόστος and νόος make up an unmarked/marked pair of nouns: νόστος, the more general term, means a return from darkness, death, forgetfulness, or sleep to light, life, consciousness, and home, while νόος, restricted to mental activity, denotes what may be termed a νόστος or "return" of the mind. Throughout his book, Frame notes with regret that only vestiges of the proposed connection between νόος and νόστος are found in the language of the Nekyia. Homeric diction regularly indicates awareness of etymological connection by the so-called *figura etymologica*, and it is true that in Odysseus' "poem" there is no such figure at the level of diction for νόος and νόστος. The thematic connection between νόος and νόστος in Odysseus' tale may, however, be so deeply embedded in the tradition that his narration is by itself such an etymological figure.

26. As Plato will later maintain that μάθησις "knowledge" is ἀνάμνησις "recollection" in the present of what was learned in the past (see, for example, Plato *Phaedo* 72e), so the return of the past to the present in the *Odyssey* is the homecoming of the mind. It is self-constituting, "self-poetic."

27. Note the parallel inversions in the Polyphemus and Cattle of the Sun episodes of the motifs of eating and speech: in the first, the issue for Odysseus and his crew is what to say, while for Polyphemus it is what to eat; in the second, the crew's improper eating is signified by the equally improper φωνή "sound" of the pieces of meat which bellow like cattle (*Odyssey* xii 396).

28. Most representative of those who defend revealing the name is Dimock 1956. Dimock's reading is informed by the tenets of ego-psychology and its foundation in Existentialist philosophy. For Odysseus, to enter Polyphemus' cave and there to name himself "Nobody" is to return to the womb and pre-birth anonymity. Both the blinding of the giant and the subsequent exclamation of his name are necessary for rebirth: "This cry of defiance is thought to be foolish of the wily Odysseus, no less by his crew than by the critics, but it is in reality, like the boar hunt, a case of deliberate self-exposure for the purpose of being somebody rather than nobody . . . To pass from the

darkness of the cave into the light, to pass from being 'nobody' to having a name, is to be born. But to be born is to cast one's name in the teeth of a hostile universe" (55–56). For Dimock the blinding and the true naming are not separable: both are necessary, if Odysseus is not to remain a "nobody" in the womb.

In direct opposition to this reading is the ethnographic approach of Brown 1966. Invoking the 1857 *Die Sage von Polyphem* of Wilhelm Grimm and citing the studies of Hackman, Radermacher, Frazer, Carpenter, and Page, Brown attempts to demonstrate that the Polyphemus episode exemplifies a folktale common in Europe and Asia, and that the concealment and revelation of the name, along with Polyphemus' curse, must be understood as an instance of "name taboo" or belief in "the power of the name" common in ancient societies. Brown documents "the belief that the personal name is a vital part of the self, that it is dangerous for anyone to know it and to reveal it puts one in the power of the other," in order to show how by giving his name Odysseus "makes it possible for Polyphemus to lay a curse upon him" (196). From this comparative, ethnographic perspective, the concealment of the name is not a psychological regression, but a mature, self-preserving restraint, while its revelation is the opposite, just as "Nobody" is the opposite of the proper name (rather than the alternate, but not incorrect, answer, "Myself," which appears in all the versions of the folktale except the Homeric). The risk to Odysseus' selfhood thus lies in his improper naming, rather than in his proper non-name.

29. With regard to assessing the Οὖτις "Nobody"–trick, Austin 1972 accepts Brown's demonstration of the power of the name, but shares the values of Dimock. Austin shows how this false naming or non-naming is one in a series of strategic concealments of real identity either through language or physical disguise (at Troy as beggar and inside the Trojan horse, at the Phaeacians' island, Scheria, and at Ithaca). These concealments amount, in his view, to self-negations that "undercut" the identity and achievements of the "superhero" (15–16). In a pun on Odysseus' pun that is worthy of the hero himself, Austin writes, "Odysseus *polymêtis*, when he is exercising his *Mêtis*, then is he invariably *Outis*. His mask is his *Mêtis*; the face it displays to the world is *Outis*" (16). From my perspective, however, with its roots in structuralist anthropology, narratology, and theory of meaning by analogous oppositions, it remains a question whether in the ideology of the *Odyssey* itself these manipulations of the *nom propre* undermine the hero or whether, on the contrary, they precisely define the polytropic heroism of the master of δόλος "trap," the lure of false appearance (see the usages of δόλος at *Odyssey* viii 276 of Hephaestus' net, *Odyssey* viii 494 of the Trojan horse, *Odyssey* xii 252 of bait, *Odyssey* xix 137 of Penelope's weaving, Hesiod *Theogony* 589 and *Works and Days* 83 of Pandora, and *Odyssey* ix 19–20, where Odysseus attributes to all his δόλοι "traps" the κλέος "fame" he is about to recount). It is at least true that within the text Odysseus never suffers from or fails to achieve victory from "impersonating" Οὖτις "Nobody" except in the episode with Polyphemus, when he gives up control of the role and the rate of recognition. Indeed, the successful "structure of revelation" constructed by Odysseus at Scheria and Ithaca (Austin 1972:17), his successful working

of the magic, trickster-like power of visibility and invisibility, identity and disguise, is discernible by its contrast with the earlier failure.

30. Page 1955:19n14.

31. This pun has often been noticed: for example, Eustathius *Commentarii ad Homeri Odysseam* vol. 1, p. 353 on *Odyssey* ix 413: δόξοι δ' ἂν τὸ, "ἐμὸν δ' ἐγέλασε φίλον κῆρ" καὶ ἑξῆς, καὶ Ὁμηρικῶς [reading Ὁμηρικῶς, as in the phrase ὕστερον–πρότερον Ὁμηρικῶς, for the apparent misprint, Ὁμηρικὸς] ἐμφαίνειν χαρὰν ἐπὶ τῇ δεξίᾳ πλάσει τοῦ τοιούτου σοφίσματος "And this would seem – the 'and my dear heart laughed' and following – also in the Homeric manner to display delight in the clever invention of such an ingenious device"; Stanford 1961:1.361 (commentary at *Odyssey* ix 408); Podlecki 1961:130n11; Frame 1978:71; Austin 1972. Stanford (1972:105) notes: "This is the only place in Homer where ambiguity and paronomasia motivate a whole episode. Technically, it is possibly the cleverest use in all Greek. The symmetry of Οὖτις – οὔ τις – μή τις – μῆτις and the echo in οὐτιδανός anticipate the most ingenious constructions of the sophists."

32. See Austin 1972:13: "Odysseus derives almost excessive pleasure from outwitting Polyphemus with his punning pseudonym *Outis*, No-Man. It is a good pun because a double pun in Greek. Polyphemus, when blinded, wails that Οὖτις is killing him and his neighbors reply with the alternative negative μή τις, thus unwittingly punning on μῆτις, intelligence, the suffix of Odysseus' destructive epithet *polymêtis*. Odysseus, hearing their exchange on *Outis* and *Mêtis* as the cause of Polyphemus' pain, laughs that his name and his wit (*onoma* and *mêtis*) have deceived them." We should note, however, that it is Odysseus as narrator, and not the neighboring Cyclopes, who is ultimately responsible for the pun: both hero and poet are laughing.

33. In hexameter diction φήμη with its alternate form, φῆμις, means either unmarked "speech," whether report or rumor (*Iliad* X 207) or marked "speech with the force of action, often about the future," whether omen, prayer, or blame (*Odyssey* ii 35, vi 273, xiv 239, xvi 75, xix 527, xx 100, 105, xxiv 201, Hesiod *Works and Days* 760–764, fr. 176.2 MW, and note also, *Odyssey* xv 468, where φῆμις is local, the "place of the speech of the people" and the name of the poet Phemius, *Odyssey* i 337, xvii 263, xxii 331). The two usages in epic of the adjective πολύφημος reflect the diathetic ambiguity of the compound: the ἀγορὴν πολύφημον of *Odyssey* ii 150 and the πολύφημος ἀοιδός of *Odyssey* xxii 376 can be either "much speaking" or "much spoken of."

34. Compare the earlier instances of ξενία "guest-friend exchange" in the *Odyssey* in which the guest is asked for his name only after and in return for what he has received: *Odyssey* i 119–176, *Odyssey* iii 22–71, *Odyssey* iv 37–64, and *Odyssey* vii 133–239. Note also Odysseus' account of his stay at Aeolus' island, where hospitality is followed by questioning and story-telling: *Odyssey* x 14–16. From Aeolus as from the Phaeacians, Odysseus receives the ὁδός "road" and the πομπή "conveyance" he requests in return for his recitation: *Odyssey* x 17–18.

35. In the naming of himself at the start of his "poem," Odysseus registers the recognition, following the encounter with Polyphemus, of δόλοι "traps" as essential to his κλέος "fame" (*Odyssey* ix 19–20). We can see now how this naming marks a progression from the identification with his earlier martial glory displayed in his exchanges with Polyphemus, when he calls his men "the troops of Agamemnon" whose κλέος "fame" for sacking Troy is "now the greatest under heaven" (*Odyssey* ix 263–266) and names himself πτολιπόρθιος "sacker of cities," the epithet the Cyclops repeats in his curse (*Odyssey* ix 504, 530).

36. The ten arrivals are: the Cicones, the Lotus Eaters, the Cyclopes, Aeolus (twice), the Laestrygonians, Circe (twice), Hades, and the island of the Sun.

37. It is no wonder that generations of readers have found the end of the *Odyssey* to be somehow not an "ending," for Odysseus' νόστος "return" ends only here, in the center of the poem, in the place where the epic's essential oppositions are finally resolved. On the tradition of dispute about the end of the *Odyssey*, see Wender 1978 and Finley 1978, Appendices I and II.

38. In preparing to encounter Scylla (*Odyssey* xii 226–231) Odysseus seems to have deviated from perfect adherence to Circe's instructions. When the goddess directs him to lose six men to Scylla rather than confront Charybdis, Odysseus asks if he cannot somehow fight off Scylla to save the six men (*Odyssey* xii 112–114). Circe answers:

> There is not any defense. It is best to run away from her.
> For if you delay by arming yourself beside her rock,
> I fear she will spring forward and catch you
> with the same number of heads and snatch away as many men as before.
> Rather drive on with all vigor and call upon Krataiïs.
> She is the mother of Scylla, who bore her as a misery for mortals,
> and she then will make her cease from springing forth again.
>
> *Odyssey* xii 120–126

Upon approaching Scylla, however, Odysseus "forgets" this advice, arms himself, and stands at the prow, looking intently for the monster's attack (*Odyssey* xii 226–231). The sight of Charybdis then diverts his attention, while Scylla takes the six men from behind his back (*Odyssey* xii 244–250). Contrary to what Circe "feared," Odysseus does not suffer any further losses (perhaps because he only arms himself and does not "delay" further by stopping to fight). Whether or not he forestalls a second attack by invoking Scylla's mother is not clear, for Odysseus ends his narration of the episode with the sight of the six being captured, the "most pitiful scene" of all his sufferings, and turns at once to the landing at Thrinakia (*Odyssey* xii 258–262). That Circe herself, in telling him to invoke Krataiïs, gave him a "weapon" by which to escape the consequences of arming himself does suggest, however, that this limited retention of martial spirit does not contradict divine injunction.

39. Note that Odysseus' periphrasis at *Odyssey* xii 266–268 makes his θυμός "spirit, passion" the seat of his remembering: "'καί μοι ἔπος ἔμπεσε θυμῷ μαντῆος ἀλαοῦ Θηβαίου Τειρεσίαο Κίρκης τ' Αἰαίης'" "'and upon my spirit fell the word of the blind prophet Teiresias of Thebes, and of Aeaean Circe.'"

40. On the eating of the Sun's cattle as a violation of religious, social and alimentary codes, see Vernant 1972:xiv–xvii: through their confusion of hunting and sacrifice, domestic and wild animals, and their use of leaves instead of grain and water instead of wine, the crew perform a perverted sacrifice, as the crawling skins and the bellowing meat, both raw and cooked, attest.

41. As recompense for the κλέος "fame" he sings, the professional poet receives material sustenance and a good κλέος for himself that will increase the "market value" of his songs. Phemius is paid with shelter and food, but is forced to accept the transaction (*Odyssey* i 154). Demodocus receives similar support, along with a choice cut of meat from Odysseus and a promise to spread his fame in return for singing the "Wooden Horse" (*Odyssey* viii 477–498). Disguised as a wandering beggar, Odysseus tries to ply the same trade without the advantage of a permanent position, when he offers his stories in return for clothing from Eumaeus (*Odyssey* xiv 459–517) and Penelope (*Odyssey* xvii 549–550) and promises to spread Alcinoos' κλέος in return for food (*Odyssey* xvii 418).

42. See Svenbro 1976:11–45.

43. Reading, with the manuscripts, μέγα rather than the Alexandrian μή.

44. Peradotto 1985:429–455. This study provides a comprehensive morphology of prophecy in the *Odyssey*.

45. Odysseus' "Cretan lie" is termed ψεύδεα ὁμοῖα ἐτύμοισιν "false things like to real things" at *Odyssey* xix 203. On the two categories of the Muses' speech in Hesiod *Theogony* 27–28, see "Language and the Female in Early Greek Thought" in this collection.

46. Readers of Paul de Man's analysis of Nietzsche's rhetoric of tropes (de Man 1979:103–118) will recognize in this theme of the *Odyssey* an allegory of the philosopher's view of figures. As de Man puts it, "All rhetorical structures, whether we call them metaphor, metonymy, chiasmus, metalepsis, hypallagus, or whatever, are based on substitutive reversals, and it seems unlikely that one more such reversal over and above the ones that have already taken place would suffice to restore things to their proper order. One more 'turn' or trope added to a series of earlier reversals will not stop the turn towards error" (113).

47. Compare de Man 1979:108, paraphrasing Nietzsche: "Logical priority is uncritically deduced from a contingent temporality."

WEAVING *PSEUDEA HOMOIA ETUMOISIN* "FALSE THINGS LIKE TO REAL THINGS"

5

HELEN'S "GOOD DRUG"

I.

δύο τὰ πολλὰ τῶν ἀνθρωπίνων.[1]

Alcmaeon

WERE SOMEONE TO FORMULATE a Foucaultian *epistêmê* for archaic Greek thought, it might be some version of "polarity."[2] To begin to study Greek is to learn of its pervasive antitheses, built around the particles, μέν, "on the one hand," and δέ, "on the other hand." Supported by such syntax are the dualities of myth, philosophy, and social organization, pairs so various, subtle, and interconnected by opposition and analogy that the principle of analogous bi-polar oppositions would seem to be the mental paradigm of the age. From the magisterial study of G. E. R. Lloyd, *Polarity and Analogy: Two Types of Argumentation in Early Greek Thought*, come vivid examples: the Pythagorean "Table of Opposites" listing ten pairs of opposite principles – limited and unlimited, odd and even, one and plurality, right and left, male and female, at rest and moving, straight and curved, light and darkness, good and evil, square and oblong; the various pre-Socratic theories of what determines the sex of the child – for Parmenides, the position in the womb (right for males, left for females), for Empedocles, the temperature of the womb at conception (hotter for men, colder for women), and for Anaximander, the side from which the father's seed came (right for males, left for females); and the repeated claim in the Hippocratic corpus that disease is caused by an imbalance in a pair of opposites and that, as a result, counterbalancing opposites effect cures: τὰ ἐναντία τῶν ἐναντίων ἰήματα "opposites are cures for opposites."[3] To Lloyd's data from philosophy and science, we may add the evidence of Homeric epic.

Structuralist analysis shows how the Homeric world is based upon systems of analogical oppositions.[4] In his study of Odyssean poetics Norman Austin concludes that "whatever the original impulse, it is clear that Homeric man sees the world through the structure of polarity" and that "analogical thought is fundamental to Homer; it is through analogy that the various phenomena and experiences are attributed to one or the other of the polar oppositions."[5] This declaration is borne out by technical studies of the Homeric *Kunstsprache*, the artificial and traditional diction of which the epics are composed. Here formulations of structuralist linguistics, such as marked vs. unmarked pairs and the fundamental tenet that the meaning of a word resides in its differential relations with other words, intersect with such insights of Milman Parry as the economy of formulas (the tendency to use only one form to fill a given metrical and semantic function) and the generation of formulas by analogy. To cite one elegant instance, Leonard Muellner demonstrates in the economy of their formulaic usage a marked vs. unmarked pair of the verbs, φημί "to say," vs. εὔχομαι "to say with sacral, legal, or heroic force."[6] At all levels, from diction to theme, Homeric epic reveals fundamental analogous polarities and nowhere more so than in the opening of *Odyssey* iv.

II.

> I'm a man of medicine, not a medicine man.
>
> *The Wizard of Oz*

When with Telemachus at the start of Book iv, we come to the palace of Menelaus and Helen, we enter a world of dualities. The first evening there is divided into two movements: the one, extending from the start of the banquet up to Menelaus' attempt to put an end to the after-dinner speeches, and the other, from Helen's re-introduction of speeches up to the retirement of everyone for the night (*Odyssey* iv 1–218, 219–305). Each of these movements is itself divided into two. The first, presided over by Menelaus, begins as a wedding feast for his children and ends as a funeral with eulogies and lamentation for the Greek losses, chiefly the absent Odysseus. In the second, governed by Helen, her story about Odysseus is matched by another by Menelaus. And within these units, the polarities proliferate.

The wedding celebration keynotes this evening in Sparta. With it we encounter the original locus of the Trojan War, the marriage of Menelaus and

Helen, as it is now recreated and about, it would seem, to reduplicate itself in the marriages of its children. For this is a double wedding. Not only are there two weddings, that of Hermione, the daughter of Helen and Menelaus, to Achilles' son, Neoptolemus, and that of Megapenthes, the son of Menelaus and a slave woman, to the daughter of Alector, but one is present, taking place in Sparta, and one is absent, taking place at Achilles' home (*Odyssey* iv 3–14). The existence of war is acknowledged – it was at Troy that Menelaus promised Hermione to the son of "man-breaker" Achilles – but it is kept absent, in the past. Now Neoptolemus has returned home from Troy and is joined not in battle but in marriage to the lovely (ἐρατεινή) Hermione, the incarnation of golden Aphrodite (*Odyssey* iv 8–9, 13–14). The erotic reigns, and amid the banqueting neighbors and the dancer-acrobats, the poet stations another poet singing what must be epithalamia (*Odyssey* iv 15–19). But then, following a declaration of the function of ξενία "guest-friend exchange," this marriage song changes into a funeral dirge.

In the midst of the wedding feast arrive Telemachus and Peisistratus, two who are ξεῖνοι, that is, "guests" or "others" than those who belong at Sparta. This fundamental opposition of "friend, own" vs. "guest, other" (φίλος vs. ξεῖνος) is mediated by the principle and practice of ξενία "guest-friendship." Menelaus' reply, when asked if the two strangers should be received, encapsulates the norm:

> "οὐ μὲν νήπιος ἦσθα, Βοηθοΐδη Ἐτεωνεῦ,
> τὸ πρίν· ἀτὰρ μὲν νῦν γε πάϊς ὣς νήπια βάζεις.
> ἦ μὲν δὴ νῶϊ ξεινήϊα πολλὰ φαγόντε
> ἄλλων ἀνθρώπων δεῦρ' ἱκόμεθ', αἴ κέ ποθι Ζεὺς
> ἐξοπίσω περ παύσῃ ὀϊζύος."

> "You were never a fool, Eteoneus, son of Boethous,
> before, but now indeed you babble foolishness, like a child.
> Surely it was by having eaten many gifts of guest-friendship
> from other men that we two came back here. May Zeus
> only make an end of misery hereafter."

> *Odyssey* iv 31–35

Because Menelaus received hospitality when he was a wanderer, he, too, should give it, now that he is home. His suffering may recommence at any time, whenever Zeus so moves. Life oscillates between suffering and safety, and to counterbalance the system for all, those in times of good fortune must aid those who are not by treating them as "own" (φιλεῖν "to treat the ξεῖνος as a φίλος").[7] Such aid consists, as we notice, of a bath by servant women and a generous share of the feast (*Odyssey* iv 48–67).

By mediating the social opposition between ξεῖνος and φίλος, Menelaus' act of ξενία "guest-friendship" moves his portion of the evening from one ritual with its particular kind of song to its antipode. For it is the welcomed ξεῖνος "guest," Telemachus, who initiates the modulation from marriage song to funeral dirge, when he compares the glittering wealth he sees all around him – the gleam of bronze, gold, electrum, silver, and ivory – to the palace of Zeus on Olympus (*Odyssey* iv 71–75). Menelaus replies with the first of two speeches (another doublet) that end by arousing lamentation. He acknowledges his riches, but then exposes the economy by which they were bought with irremediable loss: his brother Agamemnon murdered while he was away wandering and collecting the wealth, and before that, the deaths of the Greeks who fought at Troy (*Odyssey* iv 80–99). Thus he has no joy in his wealth, but only the delight of lamentation that alternates with its opposite, the surfeit of lamentation.

> "ἀλλ' ἔμπης πάντας μὲν ὀδυρόμενος καὶ ἀχεύων
> πολλάκις ἐν μεγάροισι καθήμενος ἡμετέροισιν
> ἄλλοτε μέν τε γόῳ φρένα τέρπομαι, ἄλλοτε δ' αὖτε
> παύομαι· αἰψηρὸς δὲ κόρος κρυεροῖο γόοιο."

> "But nevertheless mourning all these men and sorrowing
> over and over as I sit in our halls
> at one time I delight in my heart in lamentation, and at another
> time again
> I stop. For surfeit of gloomy lamentation is quick."

> *Odyssey* iv 100–103

In particular he laments for Odysseus, who, when remembered, divides Menelaus' life into food and sleep, on the one hand, and mournful recollection on the other:

> "τῶν πάντων οὐ τόσσον ὀδύρομαι, ἀχνύμενός περ,
> ὡς ἑνός, ὅς τέ μοι ὕπνον ἀπεχθαίρει καὶ ἐδωδὴν
> μνωομένῳ, ἐπεὶ οὔ τις Ἀχαιῶν τόσσ' ἐμόγησεν,
> ὅσσ' Ὀδυσεὺς ἐμόγησε καὶ ἤρατο."

> "For all of these I do not mourn so much, despite my sorrow,
> as for one, who makes sleep and food hateful to me

when I remember him, since no one of the Achaeans toiled
    so much
as Odysseus toiled and endured."

Odyssey iv 104-107

In like manner, as if mourning is contagious, by recollecting these sorrows of the past, Menelaus arouses in the son of Odysseus ἵμερος γόοιο "desire for lamentation" (*Odyssey* iv 113). A few minutes later Menelaus answers his first eulogy with another memory of the war gone by – how he wanted to settle Odysseus upon their return in one of his client cities, where "we would mingle together (ἐμισγόμεθ'), and nothing would separate us, loving and delighting ourselves two together (note the duals: φιλέοντέ τε τερπομένω τε), until the blood-dark cloud of death covered us over" (*Odyssey* iv 178–180). Again his recollection excites ἵμερος γόοιο, and all weep, even Peisistratus who remembers his brother killed at Troy (*Odyssey* iv 183–188).

It is now Peisistratus, however, who moves to close the occasion, to switch it back from funeral to feast.

"οὐ γὰρ ἐγώ γε
τέρπομ' ὀδυρόμενος μεταδόρπιος, ἀλλὰ καὶ ἠὼς
ἔσσεται ἠριγένεια."

"For I myself
take no delight in dinner mixed with tears, but indeed dawn
will be early-born."

Odyssey iv 193–195

The alternation of night and day forbids suspending animation in prolonged mourning. Menelaus readily accedes: he and Telemachus can exchange more stories in the morning (*Odyssey* iv 212–215). Upon his direction, water is poured and all the men, their hands now washed of these Iliadic recollections of war, turn back to the feast (*Odyssey* iv 216–218).

In its two-part structure, in its contrary rituals and in its detailed dualities, this first portion of the evening at Sparta enacts, it would seem, the working of the world and of language as mediation or exchange or alternation of opposites. Two rituals, wedding/funeral; two poetic genres, epithalamium/ dirge; two sexes, male/female; two times, past/present; two places, present/ absent; two categories of person, own/other; of economy, gain/loss; of activity, remember and weep/sleep and eat. Between the members of each pair there exists a relation variously named in this portion of the text as marriage (γάμος), exchange (ξενία) and alternation (ἄλλοτε . . . ἄλλοτε). Such is the constitution here of both κόσμος "order" and λόγος "speech." And when Helen intervenes, inaugurating the second half of the evening and delaying the closure upon speeches, this character of the Homeric λόγος is initially confirmed.

III.

And if, in the two texts we are now going to look at together, the formal structure of the argument is indeed the same; if in both cases what is supposed to produce the positive and eliminate the negative does nothing but displace and at the same time multiply the effects of the negative, leading the lack that was its cause to proliferate, the necessity for this is inscribed in the sign *pharmakon*.[8]

Jacques Derrida

In opposition to her husband's attempt to regulate the production of speeches, Helen ἄλλ᾽ ἐνόησε "thought otherwise" (*Odyssey* iv 219). Her counter-action divides this evening into two parts, but parts that match, insofar as each is made up of speeches and actions that exemplify a world of polarities. It is to continue the exchange of μῦθοι "stories" that Helen intervenes, to imitate, thereby, her husband's portion of the evening. Her action differs from that of her husband by being described in terms that cast the wife as a poet, one who works, like the poet of the *Odyssey*, within a poetics of analogous polarities. For tracing the terms of her action reveals another double opposition: two contrary poetic genres parallel to two contrary kinds of drugs.

Here is the description of Helen's intervention:

αὐτίκ᾽ ἄρ᾽ εἰς οἶνον βάλε <u>φάρμακον</u>, ἔνθεν ἔπινον,
<u>νηπενθές</u> τ᾽ <u>ἄχολόν</u> τε, <u>κακῶν</u> <u>ἐπίληθον</u> <u>ἁπάντων</u>.
ὃς τὸ καταβρόξειεν, ἐπὴν κρητῆρι μιγείη,
οὔ κεν ἐφημέριός γε βάλοι κατὰ δάκρυ παρειῶν,
οὐδ᾽ εἴ οἱ κατατεθναίη μήτηρ τε πατήρ τε,
οὐδ᾽ εἴ οἱ προπάροιθεν ἀδελφεὸν ἢ φίλον υἱὸν
χαλκῷ δηιόῳεν, ὁ δ᾽ ὀφθαλμοῖσιν ὁρῷτο.
τοῖα Διὸς θυγάτηρ ἔχε <u>φάρμακα</u> <u>μητιόεντα</u>,
ἐσθλά, τά οἱ Πολύδαμνα πόρεν, Θῶνος παράκοιτις
Αἰγυπτίη, τῇ πλεῖστα φέρει ζείδωρος ἄρουρα
<u>φάρμακα</u>, πολλὰ μὲν <u>ἐσθλὰ</u> <u>μεμιγμένα</u> πολλὰ δὲ <u>λυγρά</u>·
ἰητρὸς δὲ ἕκαστος ἐπιστάμενος περὶ πάντων

ἀνθρώπων: ἦ γὰρ Παιήονός εἰσι γενέθλης.
αὐτὰρ ἐπεί ῥ᾽ ἐνέηκε κέλευσέ τε οἰνοχοῆσαι,
ἐξαῦτις <u>μύθοισιν</u> ἀμειβομένη προσέειπεν.

At once into the wine they were drinking she cast a <u>drug</u>,
both <u>grief-less</u> and <u>anger-less</u>, a <u>forgetfulness</u> of <u>all</u> <u>evils</u>.
Whoever should drink it down, once it was mixed in the bowl,
for that day indeed would not let a tear fall down his cheeks,
not if both his mother and father should die,
not if right before him men should slay with the bronze
his brother or his own son, and with his eyes he should see it.
Such were the <u>crafty</u> <u>drugs</u> the daughter of Zeus possessed,
good ones, given to her by the wife of Thon, Polydamna,
of Egypt, where the fertile earth bears the most
<u>drugs</u>, many <u>good</u> when <u>mixed</u> and many <u>baneful</u>,
and every man there is a doctor, with knowledge beyond all
humankind. For indeed they are of the race of Paeëon.
Now when she had cast in the drug and ordered the wine
　　to be poured,
beginning again the <u>stories</u> she spoke.

Odyssey iv 220–234

The contexts of the word φάρμακον "drug" in hexameter diction depict drugs
in their capacity to cure or to destroy as analogous to two faces of poetry.
Parallel terminology displays the following corresponding doublets:

two genres of φάρμακον "drug"

Helen's φάρμακον "drug"	Circe's φάρμακα "drugs"[9]
νη–πενθές "grief-less"	
ἐσθλά "good" (vs. λυγρά "baneful")[10]	λυγρά "baneful" (vs. ἐσθλόν "good")[11]
produces	makes one
"forgetfulness (ἐπίληθον) of all evils"	"forget (λαθοίατο) the fatherland"[12]

two genres of poetry

κλέος "fame"[13]	λυγρός "baneful"[14]
about κλέα "famous deeds"[15]	about λυγρά ("baneful deeds")
makes one	produces
ἐπιλήθεται κηδέων "forget cares"	πένθος ἄλαστον "unforgettable grief"
(vs. πένθος "grief" in a νεοκηδέι θυμῷ "spirit with fresh care")	

117

Mediator between drugs and poetry is Paeëon, both a god and an epithet of Apollo, in his role as dispenser of healing and song.[16] As divine doctor, Paeëon heals Hades and Ares by sprinkling ὀδυνήφατα φάρμακα "pain-slaying drugs" upon their wounds (*Iliad* V 401, 900).[17] And as the καλὸς παιήων "beautiful *paeëon*," Paeëon is himself a type of poetry, the one sung by the Achaean youths to appease Apollo upon his lifting of the plague. Upon hearing his *paeëon*, Apollo τέρπετ' "was delighted" (*Iliad* I 472–474). Such delightful speech parallels healing drugs and counters the "baneful," when Patroclus treats Eurypylus, whom he "was delighting with words" (ἔτερπε λόγοις) as he "was sprinkling drugs as cures" (φάρμακ' ἀκέσματ' ἔπασσε) upon his "baneful wound" (ἕλκεϊ λυγρῷ).[18] By locating her φάρμακον within this network of terms – by invoking Paeëon as its ultimate source, by calling it νη-πενθές "grief-less," a "forgetfulness (ἐπίληθον) of all evils," and one of those that are ἐσθλά "good" as opposed to λυγρά "baneful" – the poet's description implies that Helen's "good drug" is analogous to the poetry of κλέος "fame," the antidote of πένθος "grief" and an oblivion of κηδέων "cares."

Helen's φάρμακον "drug" is, then, like the poetry of κλέος "fame." It is so effective an antidote to grief that at the tragedy of your family, you would sense only glory and would not weep. With this drug Helen can now supply what the banquet has lacked heretofore, remembrance of the past without pain. For indeed, just as she adds a φάρμακον "drug" with the power of poetic κλέος, so she will now supply a μῦθος "story" with the properties of her "good drug."[19] Unlike Menelaus' earlier recollections, Helen's μῦθος will be a painless painful memory. By this drug-like narrative supplement, events naturally tragic for some of the audience will be detoxified. A song of the λυγρός "baneful" genre for some will sound like κλέος and will be heard by all without loss or suffering. By thus describing her drug and its verbal counterpart, the poet casts Helen in the role played by himself and by the Odyssean tradition he repeats – the role of making past deeds present with κλέος for the actors and τέρψις "delight" for the audience. Helen's φάρμακον "drug"/μῦθος "story" will be, therefore, the opposite of Menelaus' part of the evening – just as female is the opposite of male, wife of husband, and *Odyssey* of *Iliad* – but it will be the equal of its mate in constitution. For both are based upon the assumption of analogous polarities, controllable and mutually exclusive, to which poetry and drugs offer no exception.

At least initially, the content of Helen's drug-story maintains this identity. After naming her audience, she abruptly invokes the alternation of opposites at the heart of the universe:

"Ἀτρεΐδη Μενέλαε διοτρεφὲς ἠδὲ καὶ οἵδε
ἀνδρῶν ἐσθλῶν παῖδες: ἀτὰρ θεὸς <u>ἄλλοτε ἄλλῳ</u>
Ζεὺς ἀγαθόν τε κακόν τε διδοῖ: δύναται γὰρ ἅπαντα."

"Son of Atreus, god-nourished Menelaus, you and these
children of good men: however, the god <u>at one time to one and
at another to another,</u>
Zeus, gives both good and evil. For he has all power."

Odyssey iv 235–237

And after this invocation, she declares herself a bard:

"ἦ τοι νῦν δαίνυσθε καθήμενοι ἐν μεγάροισι
καὶ <u>μύθοις τέρπεσθε</u>: <u>ἐοικότα</u> γὰρ καταλέξω."

"Now indeed feast yourselves, seated in the hall,
and <u>delight yourselves</u> with <u>stories</u>. For I will narrate the <u>likely</u>."

Odyssey iv 238–239

Her tale will consist of ἐοικότα: things like to the truth, fitting for the occasion,
and not hard to believe. [20] From this sphere of the persuasive comes the μῦθος
"story" of Odysseus that Helen now tells:

"I could not tell you all the number nor could I name
how many are the struggles of enduring-hearted Odysseus,
but such a thing as this the strong man endured and
accomplished
in the Trojans' country, where you Achaeans suffered woes.
He beat himself with unseemly blows,
then threw a cheap sheet around his shoulders, and in the
likeness of a servant,
he crept into the wide-wayed city of the enemy men.
By hiding himself he looked like another man,
a beggar. Never was there such a man beside the ships of
the Achaeans.
Like to this one he crept into the Trojans' city, and they
were taken in –
all of them. I alone recognized him even so disguised,
and I questioned him. But he by his craftiness eluded me.
But when indeed I was bathing him and anointing him with
olive oil

119

and I put clothing upon him and swore a great oath
not to reveal to the Trojans that this was Odysseus
until he reached the swift ships and the shelters,
then at last he told me the whole plan of the Achaeans.
Then after killing many Trojans with the thin-edged bronze,
he returned to the Argives and brought back much intelligence.
At that the other Trojan women were crying out shrill,
    but my heart
was happy, since already my heart had turned to going
back home again, and I was mourning over the delusion that
    Aphrodite
gave, when she led me there from my own fatherland,
forsaking my child and my bedroom and my husband,
a man who lacks nothing either in sense or in appearance."

Odyssey iv 240–264

With this account of his exploit in Troy, Helen becomes a poet of Odysseus' κλέος "fame." And indeed, as is often noted, her tale, while concerned with the Trojan War, forecasts as well the "fame" Odysseus attains in the *Odyssey* itself, when he again enters a city covertly and kills those he succeeds in tricking with his disguise as a beggar.[21]

Besides praising Odysseus, Helen's story is perfectly concocted to present an image of herself that will impress and delight her audience of Greek partisans. As the only one to have recognized Odysseus, she shows herself even more than he, a master of disguise. The revelation of her heart's own reaction to the murder of the Trojans sets her apart as a true ally of the Greeks, only an apparent collaborator with their enemy. How appealing for Menelaus, Telemachus, and Peisistratus to be able to see Helen, the object of all the sacrifices they were just lamenting, as a victim of Aphrodite's machinations. How flattering to her husband to conclude with these compliments. Her aim, it appears, is not only the κλέος of Odysseus, but also her own "fame" among the assembled men.

Yet Helen's recollection is oddly elliptical and when questioned, its foundations slip.[22] How did this mendicant Odysseus come to be received in the royal house and bathed by none other than Helen herself? Earlier it was servant women who bathed Telemachus and Peisistratus. What was Helen doing bathing a naked beggar? Why did Odysseus permit himself to be bathed, anointed, and clothed by a woman whose earlier recognition and questioning he had to elude? Why is it necessary to omit the answers to these questions, if Helen's "good drug" can cure any negative side-effects of the story? And, indeed, what in Helen's story would be λυγρός "baneful" without the "good drug" and for whom? Would Odysseus' victory by violation of ξενία "guest-friendship" be shameful to Telemachus? Would Helen's intimacy with Odysseus be painful to Menelaus? And if so, why does she include it? Is she trying not only to enhance her glory and to flatter her husband, but to seduce her young guest with glimpses of a sexual scene with his father? Recollections in the *Odyssey* are modes of characterization. Is the poet here showing how Helen does it, how she once seduced Paris, another young guest, and can ever re-seduce her husband by representing reality as these men want to hear it? This would be a magnificent κλέος "fame" for Helen, comparable to Odysseus' victories through deceit.

If such a κλέος "fame" is the aim of Helen and of the poet, too, it does not last for long. It is as brief as Menelaus' previous attempt to end the recollections of the past. For to the supplement of Helen's φάρμακον "drug"/μύθος "story" comes the supplement of Menelaus' antiphonal reply. The "good drug" of Helen's representation of the past engenders a doublet that is also a rival. Menelaus' μύθος "story" is a product of the same φάρμακον "drug," the same power to recall the past without pain. But now by its very working, this drug loses its positive valence and poisons the κλέος "fame" of Helen that it has just produced.[23]

Menelaus' tale is clearly marked as the doublet of Helen's. He opens by repeating her line, "but such a thing as this the strong man endured and accomplished" (*Odyssey* iv 271 = iv 242). His tale, too, is a glorification of Odysseus, another victory through disguise:

> "Inside the wooden horse we who were greatest of the Argives
> were all sitting
> and bringing death and destruction to the Trojans.
> Then you came there; you will have been ordered
> by some divine spirit, who wished to extend glory to the Trojans.
> And godlike Deiphobus followed beside you as you came.
> Three times you circled the hollow ambush, feeling it all
> around,
> and you called out to the best of the Danaans by name,
> likening your voice to the voices of the wives of all the Argives.
> Now I myself and the son of Tydeus and shining Odysseus
> were sitting in the middle of them and heard you as you
> cried out.

121

Diomedes and I started up, both determined
to go outside or to answer at once from inside,
but Odysseus pulled us down and held us, for all our desire.
Then all the other sons of the Achaeans were silent,
but Anticlus alone wanted to answer you with words;
but Odysseus pressed his mouth
mercilessly with his strong hands and saved all the Achaeans,
and he held him thus, until Pallas Athena led you back away."

Odyssey iv 272–289

In this addition to the addition, however, the element of disguise has reduplicated, for now Helen, too, is an imitator and Odysseus, the one who sees through the ruse. Here the bi-polar opposition collapses, as both Odysseus and Helen fill the same category of "disguiser" – he by means of the horse and she by the voices – while Odysseus simultaneously occupies the contrary category of "discerner."

Similarly, the sign, "recollection without pain," slips from the status of a "good" producer of κλέος "fame" to that of a κλέος-deconstructor, for it permits Menelaus to recall the one fact that belies Helen's previous self-portrait and retroactively renders her μύθος "story" yet another fictitious imitation of the voice of a Greek wife. As if he caught it from the end of her tale, Menelaus opens his own with the same explanation for Helen's anti-Greek activity, the interference of a god. But inserted between this defense and his full account of her trick, as if recollected by accident along the chain of associations, is the crucial detail: "and godlike Deiphobus followed beside you as you came" (*Odyssey* iv 276). This Deiphobus is Helen's second Trojan husband, the man she married after the death of Paris, a figure who belies her claim that even back when Odysseus infiltrated the city, her allegiance was already with the Greeks.[24] Helen's φάρμακον "drug" has recoiled upon its practitioner. By permitting Menelaus to recall without pain what pain might have kept beyond recall, Helen's "good drug" and her "good tale" have reminded Menelaus of another, similar feat of Odysseus, one that violates her claim to κλέος and to narrating ἐοικότα "things like to the truth."

Yet by counteracting the effect of Helen's μύθος "story," Menelaus also de-activates his own, for they share the same pharmacology. Both result from the same attempt to recall the past without pain, to divide drugs and poetry into governable opposites. But the opposite of Helen's φάρμακον-μύθος "drug-story" is a double with a difference, both drug and antidote (just as inside Menelaus' tale, Helen is disguiser and Odysseus both disguiser and discerner).

Once invoked, in a manner that forecasts the patterns of tragedy, the power of drugs and poetry defeats all attempts to divide and control it: in both speeches, by its successful operation the "good drug" fails. Here the recollection of Iliadic traditions about Odysseus in order to produce Odyssean pleasure imperfectly represses Iliadic pain. Such is the testimony of our counterpart, Telemachus. In response to both tales he says, "It is all the more painful (ἄλγιον), for even these exploits did not guard my father from baneful (λυγρόν) destruction" (*Odyssey* iv 292). Come, he says, let us turn to sleep. And with that, the couples return to the earlier polarities and sleep apart, the men outside, and the man and woman inside, beside one another (*Odyssey* iv 294–305).

IV.

Who knows if to live is to be dead, and to be dead, to live?[25]

Euripides

Is such a return to the earlier model of meaning by polarity open to the audience? We have seen Helen attempt to apply to painful recollection a remedy defined, according to an ontology of governable opposites, as "good" (vs. "baneful") and watched the drug (re)assert its ambivalence against this attempt at logical domination. We have seen Homeric language change from a structure of analogical opposites into differing doublets, whose difference is not stable. The "good drug" of Helen's story becomes the "good-baneful drug" of its non-identical twin: in repeating itself it reverses itself, leaving each tale an indistinct "gain-loss." With such a constitution, Helen's half of the evening no longer appears to be the equal opposite of her husband's. Rather, like Menelaus' complement to Helen's story, Helen's half of the evening comes as a double with something different, something in excess. It now appears that the text has changed from working according to structuralist semiotics to enacting the operation of the sign as described by Derrida.[26] Yet, this appearance is deceiving. No such change could occur, or at least not in these terms. If it ever worked by pure oppositions, no text can be an allegory of the Derridean analysis of language. If the polarities of Menelaus' part of the evening are mutually exclusive, all we may see, after Helen adds her "good drug" to the wine, is a temporarily inebriated text. For the text to exemplify the Derridean analysis of language, any return to the earlier polarities must reveal them to have been "always already" imperfect.

After observing the effects of Helen's "good drug," we may notice its traces in the first part of the evening. None of the earlier terms now gives the impression of unalloyed identity. First, marriage. In the names of the couples, this union is occupied by adversaries. War is not successfully kept in the past, for even as a groom, "Neo-ptolemus" (Νεο-πτόλεμος) is the one to whom not a wedding, but "war (πτόλεμος) is new (νέος)." To his marriage "Mega-penthes" (Μεγα-πένθης) contributes "great grief," that πένθος "grief" supposedly absent from Helen's drug (νη–πενθές "grief-less," *Odyssey* iv 221) and forgotten upon hearing a song of κλέος "fame." This double wedding does and does not reproduce the marriage of Menelaus and Helen, for this "Great-Grief" is the child of Menelaus and a slave woman, a union within and without the legitimate family. While uniting opposite sexes for legitimate procreation, marriage here imperfectly excludes war, grief, and illegitimate intercourse with an extra female. Within the epithalamium sound the notes of a dirge.[27]

The funeral-like recollections by Menelaus that follow the announcement of this double marriage are similarly impure. Here terms belonging to the discourse of sexuality and the κλέος "fame" genre of poetry are coupled with the language of lamentation. By using the verb τέρπομαι "I delight" with γόῳ "in lamentation" (*Odyssey* iv 102), Menelaus says, in effect, that he gains from mourning the pleasure produced by poetry or by "golden Aphrodite." [28] In his second recollection Menelaus applies the diction of sexual intercourse to the relationship he longed for with Odysseus, limiting its span to their lifetimes: "and going there we would mingle together (ἐμισγόμεθ'), and nothing would separate us, loving and delighting ourselves two together (duals: φιλέοντέ τε τερπομένω τε), until the blood-dark cloud of death covered us over" (*Odyssey* iv 178–80).[29] Yet by the litany that follows each of Menelaus' speeches, "and he aroused the desire for lamentation (ἵμερος γόοιο)" (*Odyssey* iv 113, 183), this separation between sex and death is bridged. For in addition to its unmarked sense of "desire," ἵμερος bears in hexameter diction the marked meaning of "sexual urge," a meaning brought to mind now by the earlier focus on marriage, by Menelaus' own use of erotic terminology, and, in retrospect, by the sexual relations described in the speeches of Helen and Menelaus.[30] In this context, the phrase ἵμερος γόοιο becomes, like γόῳ τέρπομαι, an oxymoron. Just as Helen's imitation of the voices of the Greek wives aroused in the Greeks the sexual urge to break open the horse and meet certain death, so Menelaus' recollections arouse a "lust for lamentation." As a ritual to separate opposite states of being, this funeral imperfectly represses the erotic bond between the living and the dead. Within this dirge are heard the strains of delight.

Within the first half of the banquet, therefore, and particularly within these two funereal recollections by Menelaus, we now see that the oppositions are as unstable as they are within the second half. We see that the terms there – life and death, lust and lamentation, sexual and poetic delight over against mourning, the ritual of marriage with its music over against a funeral with its song – are in motion, with one inhabiting, however temporarily, the territory of the other. This first movement of the banquet is, indeed, structured upon analogous polarities – in detecting them we are not deceived. But the opposites are not fixed forever, their exclusion of one another is not total or permanent, and we are moved to notice their movement and admixture – to supplement our first reading with its insufficiently close attention to the potential for the dynamic – through the working of Helen's "good drug." We are similarly not mistaken to analyze Homeric language and thought in structuralist terms. The "post-structuralist" theory of language supplements, rather than cancels, Saussure. The structures of polar and analogous oppositions should be discovered, along with their movements as well. As structuralist methodology elucidates the one, so the Derridean critique uncovers the other.

V.

Some of the Homeridae also recount that Helen appeared to Homer by night and ordered him to compose an epic on those who fought at Troy, because she wished to render their death an object of greater envy than the life of others, and they say that while it is partly through the craft of Homer, it is chiefly through her this poem has become so charming (ἐπαφρόδιτον) and named by all.[31]

Isocrates

Through the action of Helen's "good drug," this banquet in Sparta becomes an allegory of the movement of opposing terms within two opposing forms of relationship, "marriage" and "funeral." By neither of these relations, either marriage that joins or death that separates, are countervalent forces excluded. Neither unification nor division is final. Marriage and the marriage song include πόλεμος "war" – in the form of "Neo-ptolemus" (Νεο-πτόλεμος), the one to whom "war (πτόλεμος) is new (νέος)" and πένθος "grief" – in the form of "Mega-penthes" (Μεγα-πένθης), the one who contributes "great (μέγας)

125

grief (πένθος)." And in funeral and dirge there is ἵμερος "sexual desire" and τέρψις "erotic and poetic delight." The lamentation and its poetic counterpart, Menelaus' painful, Iliadic recollections, do not expel their lustful impulses and satisfactions. And when Helen attempts to separate recollection from pain by the dividing of drugs and of poetry, her "good" drug–story moves against her, (re)forming itself as "good-baneful." Her impulse toward creating a pure κλέος "fame" from the Iliadic past results in comic, Odyssean tales that do not exclude pain.

When it (re)turns upon Helen, the text turns upon itself, for the division of drugs and of poetry belongs, as we have seen, to Homeric diction as a whole. Indeed, the words that attempt to separate drugs belong not to a character in the epic, but to the poet alone, and, like Helen's μῦθος "story," they contain their own contradiction:

φάρμακα, πολλὰ μὲν ἐσθλὰ μεμιγμένα πολλὰ δὲ λυγρά.

drugs, many on the one hand good mixed, many on the other baneful.

Despite the construction with μέν "on the one hand" . . . δέ "on the other," the order of the words here imitates what the operation of Helen's drug–story proves: between the two kinds of φάρμακα "drugs," there is not exclusive division, but "mixture" (μεμιγμένα "mixed") that moves with its semantic force in either direction, both toward the ἐσθλά "good" before and the λυγρά "baneful" thereafter. The two categories are opposites – indeed, exclusive – but the relationship between them is one of potential movement and ambivalent combination.

Notes

An earlier version of this essay appeared in *Contemporary Literary Hermeneutics and the Interpretation of Classical Texts*, edited by S. Kresic, Ottawa, 1981:200–214.

1. Alcmaeon [24] A1 and A3 DK.

2. For Foucault's use of *epistêmê* to designate the mental paradigm of a period, see Foucault 1971b.

3. Lloyd 1971:16, 17, with bibliography, 20–23.

4. See, for example, the studies of myth and ritual by Vernant and Detienne (Vernant 1965, Detienne 1967 [= 1996], 1972a [= 1977b], 1972b [= 1981], 1977a, Detienne and Vernant 1974 [= 1978]) and the anthropologically informed analyses by Vidal-Naquet 1970, Redfield 1975, and Foley 1978.

5. Austin 1975:90, 105.

6. Muellner 1976. For other studies that combine the methodology of comparative structural linguistics with the formulaic analysis pioneered by Parry, see Boedeker 1974, Nagler 1974, Nagy 1974, 1979, Shannon 1975, Clader 1976, and Frame 1978. For the distinction, "marked vs. unmarked," see Trubetzkoy 1969 and for its status as a "language universal" that applies to phonology, grammar, semantics, and kinship terminology, see Greenberg 1966.

7. For the opposition between φίλος and ξεῖνος and the meaning of the verb φιλεῖν, see Benveniste 1969: I.341–342.

8. Derrida 1972a:113=1981:100.

9. For Circe's drugs, see κακὰ φάρμακ᾿ "evil drugs" (*Odyssey* x 213), φάρμακα "drugs" (x 290), φάρμακον "drug" (x 317), φάρμακ᾿ "drugs" (x 326–327), φάρμακον "drug" (x 392), φάρμακον οὐλόμενον "accursed drug" (x 394).

10. For φάρμακα ἐσθλά "good drugs," see *Iliad* XI 830–831 where Eurypylus begs Patroclus to heal his wound with "gentle drugs, the good ones they say you have been taught by Achilles."

11. For Circe's drugs as λυγρά "baneful," see *Odyssey* x 235–236. To counteract the force of Circe's drugs, Hermes gives Odysseus a φάρμακον "drug" that is ἐσθλόν "good" (*Odyssey* x 287, 292).

12. *Odyssey* x 235–236: "In their food she [Circe] mixed baneful drugs (φάρμακα λύγρ᾿), in order that they might forget their fatherland (λαθοίατο πατρίδος αἴης)."

13. For κλέος "fame" as what the bard relates, having heard it from the Muses, see *Iliad* II 484–487:

ἔσπετε νῦν μοι Μοῦσαι Ὀλύμπια δώματ᾿ ἔχουσαι·
ὑμεῖς γὰρ θεαί ἐστε πάρεστέ τε ἴστέ τε πάντα,
ἡμεῖς δὲ κλέος οἶον ἀκούομεν οὐδέ τι ἴδμεν·

οἵ τινες ἡγεμόνες Δαναῶν καὶ κοίρανοι ἦσαν.

Tell me now, Muses, having homes on Olympus,
for you are goddesses and are present beside and know all things,
but we hear only the fame and know nothing:
who were the leaders and the lords of the Danaans.

Compare Nagy 1974:244–261.

14. The adjective λυγρός "baneful" designates a song by modifying either the ἀοιδή "song" or the subject of the song that produces πένθος "grief," as in the case of the ἀοιδή "song" of the περικλυτὸς ἀοιδὸς "famous singer," Phemius, who "sang the baneful homecoming (νόστον ἄειδε λυγρόν) of the Achaeans." Upon hearing this song, Penelope pleads: "Cease from this baneful song (ἀοιδῆς λυγρῆς) which ever wears away the heart in my breast, since upon me most of all has come unforgettable grief (πένθος ἄλαστον)" (Odyssey i 325–327, 340–342). For the νόστος λυγρός "baneful homecoming" of the Achaeans, see also Odyssey iii 132. Compare the ἄτη λυγρή "baneful folly" of Helen in sleeping with Paris that brought πένθος "grief" to the Achaeans (Odyssey xxiii 223–224). Note also the λυγρὸς ὄλεθρος "baneful destruction" of the Greeks, heard of by Telemachus (Odyssey iii 87), that of Odysseus which he asks first Nestor and then Menelaus to "narrate" (Odyssey iii 92–93, iv 323), and that of Agamemnon at the hands of Aegisthus and Clytemnestra (Odyssey iii 194–198, xxiv 96). Compare the death of Agamemnon as λυγρά plotted by Aegisthus (Odyssey iii 303) and Clytemnestra (Odyssey xi 432), and the revenge of Orestes, the κλέος "fame" of which the Greeks will spread "widely even for men of the future to learn" (Odyssey iii 203–204), and the κήδεα λυγρά "baneful sorrows" of the Greeks narrated by Odysseus ὡς ὅτ' ἀοιδὸς ἐπισταμένως "as does a singer, with knowledge" (Odyssey xi 368–369).

15. See Hesiod Theogony 98–103:

εἰ γάρ τις καὶ πένθος ἔχων νεοκηδέι θυμῷ
ἄζηται κραδίην ἀκαχήμενος, αὐτὰρ ἀοιδὸς
Μουσάων θεράπων κλέεα προτέρων ἀνθρώπων
ὑμνήσῃ μάκαράς τε θεούς, οἳ Ὄλυμπον ἔχουσιν,
αἶψ' ὅ γε δυσφροσυνέων ἐπιλήθεται οὐδέ τι κηδέων
μέμνηται· ταχέως δὲ παρέτραπε δῶρα θεάων.

For if someone who has even grief in his spirit afflicted with fresh care
is parched with sorrowing in his heart, yet a bard,
the servant of the Muses, hymns the famous deeds of men gone by
and the blessed gods, who hold Olympus,
at once this man indeed forgets his anxieties and none of his cares
does he remember: and swiftly the gifts of the goddesses turn them aside.

16. Nagy 1979:136–137, 231.

17. For additional instances of the healing of wounds with φάρμακα "drugs," see Iliad IV 218, XI 515.

18. *Iliad* XV 392–394.

19. The identification of Helen's μῦθος "story" with her φάρμακον "drug" is an ancient interpretation found in Plutarch *Quaestiones Conviviales* 1.1.4, 614c and Macrobius *Saturnalia* 7.1.18; see Dupont-Roc and Le Boulluec 1976:35.

20. For these meanings of ἐοικότα see Dupont-Roc and Le Boulluec 1976:37n13.

21. See Andersen 1977:5–18, with bibliography.

22. Dupont-Roc and Le Boulluec 1976:31, 37n11, correlate this speech with the rhetorical figure of "*enigma*": specifically, with the kinds of *enigma* listed in the ancient treatise of Trypho, "*la seconde, kat' enantion, pourrait s'appliquer à Hélène, amie des Achéens tout en étant leur ennemie*," "the second, the one 'in accordance with the opposite,' could be applied to Helen, friend of the Achaeans, all the while being their enemy."

23. Dupont-Roc and Le Boulluec 1976:37n13, claim that the force of Helen's drug applies only to her tale and not to that of Menelaus, but do not explain why. The two speeches are marked as doublets by the same opening line (iv 242 = iv 271) and by their similar themes of role-playing, unmasking, and divine manipulation of Helen. There is no reason to think that Menelaus did not drink the wine that Helen mixed and that his speech is not thereby covered under its analgesic powers. What is true is that the drug does not work as advertised in the case of Menelaus' speech and that this dysfunction then claims Helen's speech as well.

24. See Andersen 1977:10–12; Dupont-Roc and Le Boulluec 1976:30–31, and Kakridis 1971:45.

25. Plato *Gorgias* 492e7–493a1.

26. For the critique by Derrida of Saussure's structuralist linguistics, see Derrida 1967:46–64. The version of Derrida's own views most relevant to this Homeric text is "La pharmacie de Platon" [= Derrida 1972a:71–197].

27. Other archaic Greek wedding songs also fail to suppress the war and death that counteract marriage. Sappho 44 LP, the wedding of Hector and Andromache, ends with indirect allusions to the death of Hector in the *Iliad* through the agency of Apollo and Achilles; see Nagy 1974:135–139. Similarly, in Alcaeus' hymn to Helen and Thetis, 42 LP, the wedding of Peleus and Thetis is framed by descriptions of the deaths in the war at Troy over Helen, the losses that result from and include the child of that marriage, Achilles.

28. For τέρπειν "to delight" and τέρψις "delight" as produced by poetry, see *Odyssey* i 346–347, 421–422, viii 45, 91, 367–368, 429, xii 52, xvii 385, xxii 330; *Iliad* IX 186–189, XVIII 603–604; Hesiod *Theogony* 36–37, fr. 274 MW; and by sex, see Mimnermus, 1.1 West: τίς δὲ βίος, τί δὲ τερπνὸν ἄτερ χρυσῆς Ἀφροδίτης "What is life, what is delight without golden Aphrodite?" For the opposition between τέρπειν and mourning, see *Odyssey* xix 513.

29. In addition to being the regular term for sexual intercourse, the verb μείγνυμι "to mix" is also used of "mixture" in hand-to-hand combat (*Iliad* XV 510) or in ξενία "guest-friendship" (*Odyssey* xxiv 314). In context with the dual forms, φιλέοντέ τε τερπομένω τε, and the collocations, γόῳ τέρπομαι "I take poetic and sexual delight in mourning" and ἵμερος γόοιο "sexual urge for lamentation," however, the erotic connotation of the verb is paramount. With regard to the relationship between Menelaus and Odysseus, note also the subtle distinction between how Menelaus and Helen regard the Trojan war: for him it was the Greeks fighting for him, a case of "men and a man," while for Helen it was a case of "men and a woman," the Greeks fighting for her (*Odyssey* iv 145–146, 170). Love among men who fight together is not un-Homeric: Achilles and Patroclus are the paradigm, as Plato recalls in the *Symposium* 179e–180b.

30. When Hera begs from Aphrodite the girdle with which she can seduce Zeus, she says, δὸς νῦν μοι φιλότητα καὶ ἵμερον "now give me love and sexual desire," and the same terms are used by the poet to describe what the love charm contains (*Iliad* XIV 198, 216). Compare also *Homeric Hymn to Aphrodite* 2, 45, 53, 57, 73, where the essential nature of the goddess is the power to arouse ἵμερος, a power that threatens Zeus and that he must reappropriate. The adjective, ἱμερόεις modifies χορός "dancing place," when it is the scene of sexual arousal or rape: Boedeker 1974: 46–48, 50–51. For the collocation of ἵμερος and death, compare Sappho 95 LP, evidently concerning the beloved Γογγυλα (4), in which the speaker says, κατθάνην δ᾿ ἵμερός τις [ἔχει με] "a kind of erotic urge to die possesses me" (11). Note also the adjective modifying the face of a groom suffused with *eros* (ἔρος δ᾿ ἐπ᾿ ἱμέρτῳ κέχυται προσώπῳ) in the epithalamium (Sappho 112.4 LP).

31. Isocrates *Helen* 65.

6

SACRED APOSTROPHE
Re-Presentation and Imitation in *Homeric Hymn to Apollo* and *Homeric Hymn to Hermes*

I. Genre and History

FROM THE BEGINNING, the Homeric hymns mark both beginning and end. They come before the recitation of epic, but after Homeric epic has reached its peak. The evidence is scanty, but so far as we can tell, the works in this somewhat paradoxical category of "Homeric hymn" represent an elaboration by the rhapsodes of the invocation that had traditionally begun an epic song. Demodocus, at the start of his third song at Phaeacia, is said to "begin from the god" or "goddess" (*Odyssey* viii 499).[1] Similarly, the Homeridae, according to Pindar *Nemean* 2.1–3, "generally begin their woven epics with a *prooimion* to Zeus," the same term "*prooimion*" with which Thucydides (3.104) in our earliest explicit reference to the hymns designates the *Homeric Hymn to Apollo*.[2] According to the scholiast on *Nemean* 2.1 (3.28.16–3.29.18 Drachmann), the Homeridae were "originally sons of Homer who sang by right of succession" and later rhapsodes who performed Homeric epic without claiming direct descent.[3] The Homeridae performed at such contests as those described in the *Contest Between Homer and Hesiod*, local gatherings like the funeral at Chalcis where Hesiod triumphed (see also *Works and Days* 654–659) and larger festivals like the *panêguris* at Delos (see also Hesiod fr. 357 MW). While questionable as biography, the *Contest* does seem to preserve a plausible picture of the process by which the works of the poets canonized as "Homer" and "Hesiod" were gradually disseminated and finally fixed in their Panhellenic form.[4] So we have this chain of evidence: Demodocus begins his song with an invocation of the deity; the "sons of Homer" who recite epic at contests during the period of its progressive fixation begin with a *prooimion* to Zeus; and our earliest reference to a Homeric hymn is as a *prooimion*.

This evidence, to quote the commentary of Allen, Halliday, and Sykes (1936:lxxxviii–lxxxix) seems "to show the 'Homeric hymn' in the light of a πάρεργον of the professional bard or rhapsode, as delivered at an ἀγών, whether at a god's festival or in honor of a prince." The Homeric hymn is a πάρεργον "subordinate or secondary business" of the "sons of Homer" in relation to their primary job of repeating the father's words. A πάρεργον, yes, but not merely so, for as the major hymns of the corpus testify, this "preface" develops into a genre in its own right, and it does so as the paternal genre declines. The period and the process of the dispersal, fixation, and Panhellenization of Homeric epic is also the period and process of epic's decline. During that period, the agents of the process, the "sons of Homer," develop the old preface into a genre of their own. The old beginning of Homeric epic begins as a vital genre when Homeric epic ends.[5]

Why did the Homeridae choose to elaborate the *prooimion*? What was it about the hymn form that appealed to them? With such scarcity of data, any reconstruction can, of course, be only speculative, but within that limitation, can we make any correlation between the nature of the hymnic genre and such evidence as we have of its historical function? The rhetorical figure at the heart of the genre seems to point the way. That figure is apostrophe or the direct address by the poetic voice, as when, for example, the hymnist addresses the god. Tracking the operation of apostrophe in the Homeric hymns leads to an analysis of the hymn in which it is most prominent, the *Homeric Hymn to Apollo*. This is also the hymn in which the poetics of the genre – for example, the context of performance, the relation between the hymnist and his subject, his audience, and his "father" Homer – are an overt theme. The *Homeric Hymn to Apollo* presents a vision of poetic and prophetic practice that assimilates the hymnist's achievement to the power claimed in the hymn by Apollo himself. This text would seem to offer a complete picture of what the Homeridae were attempting to accomplish with the elaborated *prooimion*, except that its version of Apollo is both expanded and qualified by the other major hymn that concerns poetry and prophecy, the *Homeric Hymn to Hermes*. The complementary and contradictory relation between these two hymns sheds light upon the genre and its history.

II. Sacred Apostrophe and Sacred Presence

The formal feature that distinguishes the Homeric hymn from Homeric epic is not the narrative core of the poems, for hexameter narration is what the hymns share with epic, what makes them formally "Homeric." What makes the Homeric hymn a "hymn" is its particular use of the most poetically marked, but also the most rare and restricted convention of epic, namely, apostrophe.[6] The difference between apostrophe in epic and in a hymn is not solely one of quantity. To be sure, the figure is more frequent in the hymns, closing thirty-two of the thirty-four poems (the other two lack closings), opening five, and occurring sporadically (or in the case of the *Homeric Hymn to Apollo*, profusely) in the body. But this quantitative difference is significant only as a reflection of the more fundamental difference of function. The epic is cast by its opening invocation as the voice of the Muse – "Sing, Goddess, the wrath" and "Sing, Muse, the man" – but the closing apostrophe makes the hymn the poet's own speech.

In its complete form, the final apostrophe casts the hymn as the inverse of epic, not a goddess's words, but the poet's product, one he will try to exchange with a god. The obligatory χαῖρε "farewell" is followed by imperatives that ask the god to grant victory or some other blessing in return for the hymn. (It is the judges of the contest, of course, who will "act for the god" in awarding the prize.)[7] Then, after leaving unstated but implied the necessary connective – "If you accept this offer," – the poet concludes with the promise to initiate another exchange, "I will remember you and another song." This ending that promises another beginning is, in fact, the opening of most of the hymns. About a third of the hymns imitate epic by calling upon the Muse to "sing the god," but the rest start either with an apostrophe of the god or with the words, "I will remember . . ." or "I begin to sing . . ." or "I will sing . . . ." The conventional hymnic beginning (apostrophe or "I will remember . . .") matches the hymnic close (apostrophe and "I will remember . . ."), a close that promises another beginning.[8] This frame casts the hymn as a single direct address of the god, one grand "sacred apostrophe." Why is a such a product worth the response of the god/audience? What does "sacred apostrophe" aim to effect? Culler's analysis (1977) of the secular function of the figure points to the answer.

Starting from Quintilian's definition of apostrophe as a "turning away from" the judge, Culler bases his analysis upon the communicative context of the trope. This context includes three parties: the speaker, the addressee, and the judge – a triangle parallel to the rhapsode, the god, and the judges of the contest. Culler shows how the function of apostrophe in this situation is twofold. The poet apostrophizes not simply to elicit the response of the addressee, but also to prove to his "judging" audience the poetic power of his speech. By invoking Nature, the Romantic poet implies that Nature itself responds to his call. Invocation tends to animate even lifeless objects: when called upon, who knows if they may not answer? Apostrophe of non-existent objects demonstrates the most basic capacity of the voice, to "re-present," to "make present" something by the sheer act of uttering it. The claim of the apostrophizing voice is that of a "motivated signifier," namely, to indicate the signified not by an arbitrary connection, but by a natural semiotic constitution.[9] The effect of "sacred apostrophe" would therefore be the re-presentation of the "transcendental signified," divinity itself. In exchange for the prize, the hymnist offers nothing less than an epiphany of the god.

If sacred apostrophe establishes the poetic voice in the eyes of the judges as able to re-present divinity, consider how well it would seem to serve the Homeridae in their complex relation to Homeric epic. When epic was "winged words," individual bards could win praise and prizes, while avoiding self-reference in their songs. Many may have even called themselves by the same name, if "Homer" denoted the bardic function rather than a single poet.[10] In order to concentrate on the κλέα ἀνδρῶν "famous deeds of men," the conventions of epic minimize the presence of the singer – the poetically marked apostrophe is correspondingly rare – but foster the display of individual skill in the composition of the narrative. Since each prize-winning composition was a unique performance, bards could share the prestige of "Homer," but no "Homer" could repeat another's song and thus steal his prize. With the advent of writing, however, a fundamental change in the means of poetic (re-)production in Greece takes place.

With writing comes the possibility of preserving and canonizing a monumental Homeric composition, but the process involves both gain and loss for the Homeridae. As Homeric epic becomes a fixed text, the chance for innovation or variation in the genre diminishes, along with proper attribution and compensation of the product. In elevating Homeric epic to Panhellenic preeminence, the Homeridae give up the chance to develop the form in their own right. The more they increase their patrimony, so to speak, the less they can spend it themselves. Now defunct through the prestige of fixation, the epic genre is no longer a living tradition, but a virtuoso repetition.[11] As far as the "son of Homer" is concerned, such a "repeatable" legacy is not even his own. The text of "Homer" may be the ultimate epic, but because it is fixed in writing, it is no longer the possession of a proper Homeric line, handed down only to legitimate heirs. It is rather the common property of any "son" who can (re-)write a copy for himself. What can a "son of Homer" do to avoid this unprofitable trade-off? How can he continue to profit from the prestige of Panhellenization, without the loss of his identity as a Homeric poet? How can he, like the oral bard, win the prize for his own Homeric composition?

What can the "son of Homer" do, after the fixation of Homeric epic? He can develop a new Homeric genre, a new and more self-referential Homeric speech, out of the single convention of epic that points to the poet's voice. The opening apostrophe of epic can be expanded, via a relative clause, into a narrative of the god's traditional ἔργα "works," where the Homeridae can emulate (or parody) epic art. And when apostrophe is not just expanded but also exploited, the hymn can be more than an emulation of epic. While shorter and introductory, this πάρεργον "subordinate or secondary business" can exceed the primary genre in its glorification of the poetic voice. For when its close matches its opening, the hymn becomes one grand invocation, one grand display of the power not just to describe, but to epiphanize a god through speech.

This function of the apostrophe is most clear in the hymn where the figure is most prominent, the hymn to the gods' own hymnist, Apollo. In the *Homeric Hymn to Apollo* we find a profusion of apostrophe and doubling (even the "number" of the text, whether it is singular or a plural, is in question), a profusion sometimes faulted as proof of careless or multiple authorship. These formal features demonstrate the re-presentational capacity of the hymnic voice: apostrophe makes present again its addressee, while doubling re-presents particular diction or themes. This doubling becomes the form and apostrophe the figure for the power attributed in the content of the hymn to its three poetic/prophetic speakers – Apollo, the Delian Maidens, and the hymnist himself – the power of unerring re-presentation. Apollo's oracle re-presents the will of Zeus; the chorus of Delian Maidens, θεράπναι "attendants" of Apollo, re-present the voices of those attending the festival at Delos and sing a hymn to Leto, Apollo, and Artemis; the hymnist re-presents himself singing at the Delian festival this very *Homeric Hymn to Apollo*. For in the midst of describing the scene at the festival, the hymnist apostrophizes the Delian Maidens: O Maidens, he says, remember me and whenever you are asked to name the pre-eminent poet, answer "the blind man from Chios," that is, "Homer" (166–172). Through this extended apostrophe, the hymnist turns narration into a demonstration of his own voice re-presenting the voice of the pre-eminent poet, the father "Homer." This, it would seem, is what the hymnic apostrophe offered the "son of Homer," a mode by which to re-present the voice of the father, the voice of poetic supremacy, a re-presentation that emulated Apollo's own poetic and prophetic role.

But the *Homeric Hymn to Apollo* does not tell the whole story of that god's relation to poetry and prophecy. The rest of the tradition comes in the *Homeric*

Hymn to Hermes, the "sequel" to the *Homeric Hymn to Apollo* both in content and in the order of our corpus. The *Homeric Hymn to Hermes* revises and adds to the earlier account. Here the first act of Hermes after his birth is to invent the lyre, while in the earlier hymn the first act of Apollo after his birth is to claim possession of the lyre as the precondition of his oracular accuracy. Hermes then tries to steal Apollo's cattle by the trick of driving the herds backwards so that their hoofs point in the opposite direction from their actual movement. When the ruse is discovered, he exchanges the lyre for the stolen cattle. Now the defining "property" of each god is an original possession of the other. No sooner is this trade completed than Apollo gives Hermes what he had sworn to retain as his exclusive possession, μαντεία "oracular speech." He describes the responses of Hermes' new μαντεία as discernibly true and false, while revealing the similarly double but indistinguishable voices of his own oracle. Now who is the unerring prophet and who the thief? Each god seems to imitate the other.

Taken together, therefore, the hymns to Apollo and Hermes reveal a competition between the two gods over the issues of ownership, accuracy, temporal primacy, and origin. This competition centers around the problem of repetition. The hymns present divergent forms of repetition, two modes of doubling: the "re-presentation" of the *Homeric Hymn to Apollo* and the "imitation" of the *Homeric Hymn to Hermes*. In re-presentation, something is repeated or presented again but at a different time or place – for example, when the hymnist apostrophizes Apollo at one time and the same Apollo later, or when he begins and ends a hymn with the same words. In re-presentation, there is no effort to disguise the difference between the first and the second instances and no effort by the second instance to take the place of the first. In imitation, on the other hand, something is repeated but without distinct, stable difference between an "original" and a "copy" – for example, when Hermes (re-)invents the lyre.[12] What are we to make of this divergence between the two hymns?

Before we can pursue this question, we must answer a more basic one. By what justification do we treat these two texts together, if like the other Homeric hymns they were originally composed separately of traditional material, performed orally, and juxtaposed in our written corpus only centuries later?[13] The interpretive position of ancient listeners and modern readers is not the same, but there is a bridge: because the hymns are traditional poetry, thematic interdependence in our texts reflects thematic interdependence in the tradition. The relationship between the *Iliad* and the *Odyssey* provides a parallel. Because we have the written texts, we can read the *Odyssey* in terms of the *Iliad* or even ignore chronology and read the *Iliad* in light of its sequel. But the same sort of interpretation, even the anachronic, could be made before the fixation of the texts, since the audiences knew the traditions from which epic was composed. Because their thematic interconnection is traditional, there was never a time when the "*Iliad*" and the "*Odyssey*" as traditions did not imply one another, when any version of either one was meaningful except in relation to its complement. The intertextuality of our *Iliad* and *Odyssey* mirrors this "inter-traditionality." In the same way, the thematic integrity and formal placement of the hymns to Apollo and Hermes represent the traditional brotherhood and rivalry of the two gods. (Indeed, pairing hymns to Apollo and Hermes may itself be a traditional mechanism for expressing the traditional relationship of the two gods.)[14] Any correlations or inconsistencies we observe by comparing the hymns with each other, early listeners could also observe by comparing either hymn with this tradition. It is the traditional character of the affinity and competition of Apollo and Hermes that entitles us to treat the hymns to these gods as cognate and competing accounts of poetic, prophetic, and economic supremacy.

If, then, it is not anachronistic to read these two hymns together, how are we to interpret their contradictions? We could simply take them as marks of mythic subject matter. Two versions of the same myth are often inconsistent, and mythic temporality often ignores historical sequence. But a parallel pairing of two gods recorded in Plato's *Phaedrus* suggests that the inconsistencies and temporal anomalies between these two hymns are themselves germane to the meaning of the tradition of Apollo and Hermes. For the relation between Apollo and Hermes and between the two modes of repetition exemplified in their hymns corresponds to the relation between the Egyptian deities Ammon and Theuth as described by Socrates in the *Phaedrus*, when he is trying to illustrate the superiority of "living speech" over "dead writing" (274c–277a). In his analysis of the *Phaedrus* Jacques Derrida points out the shared characteristics of Theuth and Hermes and describes for speech and writing the sort of complex kinship and competition that we have seen between Apollo and Hermes.[15] We may have in the relation between Apollo's re-presentation and Hermes' imitation a pre-conceptual version of the relation between speech and writing in the *Phaedrus*. In view of the role of speech and writing in the historical situation of the Homeridae, it is not implausible that the two "hymns about Homeric hymning" may be concerned with these two modes of poetic (re-)production.

III. *Homeric Hymn to Apollo*: The Invocation of Presence

Formal doubling and its thematic counterpart commence with the first words of the hymn, μνήσομαι οὐδὲ λάθωμαι Ἀπόλλωνος ἑκάτοιο "I shall remember and I shall not forget Apollo who works from afar" (1). There is a place or category of being remembered and another of being forgotten. The hymnic voice claims to control the difference between the two and to put Apollo in the place of the wholly remembered, the fully present. This mastery over μνήμη "memory" and λήθη "forgetfulness," this ability to re-member, re-peat, and re-present the absent past, is expressed in the form of the repetition we find here – first, the μνήσομαι "I will remember" and then, the litotes of "remembering," that is, οὐδὲ λάθωμαι "I will not forget." In this doubling there occurs a return of the same – that is, the "remembering" – but at a later time and place in the sequence of the narrative. As in Platonic ἀνάμνησις "recollection," there is an assertion of – a striving and a desire for – full re-presentation now in the present of what was fully present in the past.

In the next example, the repetition of verbal doublets marks the first apostrophe of the poem. Leto "rejoices" (χαίρει) because she "gave birth" (ἔτικτεν) (12–13). The poet then repeats, "rejoice (χαῖρε), O blessed Leto, because you gave birth (τέκες)" (14). By commanding in the first person what it has just narrated in the third person as a fact, the poetic voice displays its power both to present and to re-present, both to present a fact and to bring about its accurate re-presentation by the sheer act of invocation. Indeed, this control over presence and absence is demonstrated in the apostrophe alone, since χαῖρε signals the conventional hymnal close, the separation from the god. As a result, there is a nuance here of closure upon a mini-hymn to Leto, but a closure that will also re-open the hymn to her son.[16] For it is this same topic, how Leto gave birth to Apollo, that the poet now brings forth, via the priamel of lines 19–27, as the subject of the hymn. This priamel is also the place where apostrophe and doubling next coincide and where these opening motions toward hymnic practice become an explicit theme.

In the first of two invocations in this priamel, Apollo is characterized by two parallel totalizations:

πῶς τ' ἄρ ς' ὑμνήσω πάντως εὔυμνον ἐόντα;
πάντη γάρ τοι, Φοῖβε, νομοὶ[17] βεβλήατ' ἀοιδῆς,
ἠμὲν ἀν' ἤπειρον πορτιτρόφον ἠδ' ἀνὰ νήσους.

How then shall I hymn you, when you are in every way
    well-hymned?

For everywhere upon you, Phoebus, the whole range of song
has been cast,
both upon the cattle-nourishing continent and upon the
islands.

Homeric Hymn to Apollo 19–21

Apollo is always present "everywhere" and always well re-presented in song. The implication of this parallelism and of the possible pun in νομοί is that the hymning of Apollo must represent the reality of the god: as he covers all geographical νομοί (νομός "place of pasturage, field, range"), so too his hymn must contain all the νόμοι (νόμος "melody, type of song") or the entire "range" of its possibilities, a total re-presentation that would transcend the limits of time and space. And indeed, the whole of the *Homeric Hymn to Apollo* is an attempt to realize that goal.

The next phase of the effort is the second apostrophe of the priamel:

ἦ ὥς σε πρῶτον Λητὼ τέκε, χάρμα βροτοῖσι,
κλινθεῖσα πρὸς Κύνθου ὄρος κραναῇ ἐνὶ νήσῳ,
Δήλῳ ἐν ἀμφιρύτῃ;

Shall I sing how at first Leto gave birth to you, a joy to mortals,
having leaned against Mt. Cynthus in the rocky island,
in sea-surrounded Delos?

Homeric Hymn to Apollo 25–27

This question answers the question of line 19, "How then shall I hymn you?" This subject may not encompass the whole range of possibilities, but it is the subject that the hymn has just presented and moved to re-present through apostrophe in the ending-like opening, χαῖρε, in line 14: "rejoice (χαῖρε), O blessed Leto, because you gave birth (τέκες)." If Apollo is present everywhere – as is asserted by the πάντῃ "everywhere" of line 20, the hymn can re-present him everywhere, as it once again displays, when it addresses Apollo directly in line 120: ἔνθα σέ, ἤιε Φοῖβε, θεαὶ λόον ὕδατι καλῷ "there, great Apollo, the goddesses washed you with beautiful water" and repeats the lines with which this subject was begun:

χαῖρε δὲ Λητώ,
οὕνεκα τοξοφόρον καὶ καρτερὸν υἱὸν ἔτικτεν.

Leto rejoiced
because she gave birth to a bow-bearing and mighty son.

Homeric Hymn to Apollo 125–126

> χαίρει δέ τε πότνια Λητώ,
> οὕνεκα τοξοφόρον καὶ καρτερὸν υἱὸν ἔτικτε.
>
> Revered Leto rejoices
> because she gave birth to a bow-bearing and mighty son.
>
> *Homeric Hymn to Apollo* 12–13

Such "ring-composition" is, of course, a conventional feature of hexameter poetry, but it is used here so reflexively that the form tends to become a theme.[18]

Why a hymn to Apollo must so insist on its power of re-presentation becomes clear when Apollo himself emerges as a speaking presence in the text. Upon bursting his swaddling bands, Apollo's first act is a "speech act." It is introduced formally by an apostrophe that answers the one that earlier at line 120 marked his birth:

> αὐτὰρ ἐπεὶ δή, Φοῖβε, κατέβρως ἄμβροτον εἶδαρ,
> οὔ σέ γ' ἔπειτ' ἴσχον χρύσεοι στρόφοι ἀσπαίροντα,
> οὐδ' ἔτι δέσματ' ἔρυκε, λύοντο δὲ πείρατα πάντα.
>
> But when indeed, Phoebus, having tasted immortal food,
> then you, to be sure, golden bands did not hold, as you
>   struggled,
> nor did the fetters still restrain, but all the bonds were released.
>
> *Homeric Hymn to Apollo* 127–129

Thus unbound, the god avers:

> εἴη μοι κίθαρίς τε φίλη καὶ καμπύλα τόξα,
> χρήσω δ' ἀνθρώποισι Διὸς νημερτέα βουλήν.
>
> May the dear lyre and the curved bow be mine,
> and I shall unerringly repeat to humankind the unerring plan
>   of Zeus
>
> *Homeric Hymn to Apollo* 131–132

Apollo's words identify him as the divine counter-part of the power displayed by the hymnic voice. If he may possess the lyre and the bow, Apollo will re-present to humankind the oracles of Zeus. The basis of this reciprocity is evident in the structure common to the lyre, the bow, and the oracle. As we see in the simile in the *Odyssey* by which Odysseus' testing of the bow is likened to the test of a lyre (xxi 404–410), and as may be implied in Heraclitus' perception of the "palintropic harmony" of the two instruments (Heraclitus

[22] B51 DK), archaic Greek thought perceives in the bow and the lyre the capacity of attaining an exact mark of sound or space, if the string is plucked properly. That such attainment is also the property of the βουλὴ Διός "plan of Zeus" is implied by the metaphor in νημερτέα "unerring," an alpha-privative compound of νη– "not" + the root of ἁμαρτάνω "miss the mark." The "plan of Zeus" is an arrow that never misses its mark, is never sharp or flat. And so, moreover, is the re-presentation of it by Apollo, for the verb χρήσω "I shall unerringly repeat" – a cognate of χρή "it must be" and χρεών "that which must be" – implies the accuracy of cosmic necessity. Zeus is the primary archer of the mind, and Apollo, by virtue of his skill with lyre and bow, is his unerring *porte-parole*. To hymn Apollo, therefore, the hymnic voice must re-present the god's straight arrow, his ideal re-presentation of Zeus' similarly unerring will. Like Apollo, the hymnist must be ἕκατος "he who works from afar" or more precisely, ἑκατηβόλος "he who can cast from afar" the straight shaft of speech that hits the present mark.

Accordingly, the hymn responds to Apollo's voice with a sequence in which apostrophe, doubling, and the thematization of poetic re–presentation are no longer intermittent but in fact take over the text. The poet's first "cast" is the next apostrophe, the five-word, line-filling invocation of Apollo:

αὐτὸς δ', ἀργυρότοξε, ἄναξ ἑκατηβόλ' Ἄπολλον.

And you yourself, of the silver bow, lord Apollo who can cast
from afar.

Homeric Hymn to Apollo 140

A five-word, line-long apostrophe occurs earlier as well, when the island of Delos addresses Leto: Λητοῖ, κυδίστη θύγατερ μεγάλου Κοίοιο "Leto, most glorious daughter of great Koios" (62). But here the device calls attention to itself by the four word-initial alphas (αὐτὸς, ἀργυρότοξε, ἄναξ, Ἄπολλον) and by its placement of the two parallel epithets, ἀργυρότοξε "of the silver bow" and ἑκατηβόλ' "he who can cast from afar" on either side of ἄναξ "lord" and surrounding them, the two defining terms, the pronoun αὐτός "you yourself" and the proper noun Ἄπολλον. Then, as in the opening priamel, the invocation of presence is answered by a description of geographic omni-presence (141–145 ~ 21–24), a doubling marked by the repetition in lines 144–145 of lines 22–23. Such rings conventionally signal closure, but here, in a repetition of the opening manipulation of invocation and dismissal, the closed subject is at once re-opened with a second apostrophe and the selection once again of Delos out of the god's spatial range:

ἀλλὰ σὺ Δήλῳ, Φοῖβε, μάλιστ' ἐπιτέρπεαι ἦτορ.

But you, Phoebus, in Delos especially delight your heart.

Homeric Hymn to Apollo 146

In this new end/beginning, however, the hymn becomes completely self-referential, as the subject of this hymn to Apollo now becomes its very performance at the Delian *panêguris* by the hymnist who identifies himself as "Homer."

At this Delian festival, all parties reflect one another. Like the voice of the hymn in its first line, the Ionians remember Apollo with the contests in which he delights:

οἱ δέ σε πυγμαχίῃ τε καὶ ὀρχηθμῷ καὶ ἀοιδῇ
μνησάμενοι τέρπουσιν, ὅτ' ἂν στήσωνται ἀγῶνα.

By remembering you with boxing and dancing and
    epic song
they delight you, whenever they mount their contest.

Homeric Hymn to Apollo 149–150

In the eyes of one beholding them, the Ionian celebrants assume the god's attributes, ἀθανάτους "immortal" and ἀγήρως "ageless," such is their χάριν "grace" (151–153). Their gathering includes a great θαῦμα "wonder," endlessly re-presented through a κλέος "fame" that never dies, that of the Delian Maidens:

πρὸς δὲ τόδε μέγα θαῦμα, ὅου κλέος οὔποτ' ὀλεῖται,
κοῦραι Δηλιάδες, ἑκατηβελέταο θεράπναι·[19]
αἵ τ' ἐπεὶ ἄρ πρῶτον μὲν Ἀπόλλων' ὑμνήσωσιν,
αὖτις δ' αὖ Λητώ τε καὶ Ἄρτεμιν ἰοχέαιραν,
μνησάμεναι ἀνδρῶν τε παλαιῶν ἠδὲ γυναικῶν
ὕμνον ἀείδουσιν, θέλγουσι δὲ φῦλ' ἀνθρώπων.

In addition there is a great wonder, whose fame will never
    perish,
the Delian Maidens, attendants of the one who can cast from afar:
when these have hymned Apollo first
and then both Leto and Artemis who delights in arrows,
remembering the men and women of old
they sing a hymn and enchant the races of men.

Homeric Hymn to Apollo 156–161

The Delian Maidens resemble Apollo: their name and title fills an entire line, as did the god's (140, 157) and they are called his θεράπναι "attendants." They also echo the hymnist, for after celebrating Apollo, Leto, and Artemis, they too turn to the subject of Homeric epic, the men and women of the past. The Maidens "enchant" their audience, and of what does their enchantment consist? The Delian Maidens enchant their audience through mimesis of the voice: πάντων δ' ἀνθρώπων φωνὰς καὶ κρεμβαλιαστὺν μιμεῖσθ' ἴσασιν "They know how to imitate the voices and melodic contour of all men" (162–163). Theirs is an ideal verisimilitude – φαίη δέ κεν αὐτὸς ἕκαστος φθέγγεσθ' "for each man would say that he himself was speaking" – resulting from ideal harmony – οὕτω σφιν καλὴ συνάρηρεν ἀοιδή "thus was their beautiful song fitted together" (163–164). It is in this way, perhaps, that the Maidens are the θεράπναι "attendants" of Apollo: their song shares the quality he claimed for his repetition of the βουλή "plan" of Zeus, perfect accuracy. Accordingly, the hymnist couples a prayer to Apollo and Artemis with an invocation of the Maidens as well: χαίρετε δ' ὑμεῖς πᾶσαι "farewell, all you Maidens" (165–166).

Like the earlier instances of the verb, this apostrophic χαίρετε "farewell" signals an ending, and this time the closure seems confirmed, since the vocative is followed by the imperatives of exchange between divinity and poet with which the hymns regularly conclude. Indeed, this exchange seems to complete the movement of the hymn toward self-reference through the harmony of its poetic and prophetic speakers:

> χαίρετε δ' ὑμεῖς πᾶσαι: ἐμεῖο δὲ καὶ μετόπισθεν
> μνήσασθ', ὁππότε κέν τις ἐπιχθονίων ἀνθρώπων
> ἐνθάδ' ἀνείρηται ξεῖνος ταλαπείριος ἐλθών·
> ὦ κοῦραι, τίς δ' ὕμμιν ἀνὴρ ἥδιστος ἀοιδῶν
> ἐνθάδε πωλεῖται, καὶ τέῳ τέρπεσθε μάλιστα;
> ὑμεῖς δ' εὖ μάλα πᾶσαι ὑποκρίνασθαι ἀφήμως·
> τυφλὸς ἀνήρ, οἰκεῖ δὲ Χίῳ ἔνι παιπαλοέσσῃ
> τοῦ πᾶσαι μετόπισθεν ἀριστεύουσιν ἀοιδαί.
> ἡμεῖς δ' ὑμέτερον κλέος οἴσομεν, ὅσσον ἐπ' αἶαν
> ἀνθρώπων στρεφόμεσθα πόλεις εὖ ναιεταώσας·
> οἳ δ' ἐπὶ δὴ πείσονται, ἐπεὶ καὶ ἐτήτυμόν ἐστιν.

> Farewell, all you Maidens, and also hereafter
> remember me, whenever someone of the men upon the earth,
> a stranger with many trials behind him, comes here and asks,
> "O Maidens, who do you believe is the sweetest man of the
>   singers

that come here, in whom do you most delight?"
Then answer, one and all of you, with a single voice,
"The blind man. He lives in rugged Chios.
All of his songs will be supreme hereafter."
And in return I will carry the fame of you over the entire
distance
I cover in my circuit of the well-placed cities of men.
And you may be sure they will believe me, since it is indeed
accurate.

Homeric Hymn to Apollo 166–176

The content of the *Hymn* has become its performance. More precisely, the narration has become the appeal for the prize of poetic preeminence. As narration has become narrating, so the hymnist seeks perpetual victory in and through a display of the poetic and prophetic capacity he shares with Apollo and the Delian Maidens. As with Apollo and Zeus, this "son" describes his unique function as a re-presentation of the "father" – the "blind man from Chios," "Homer" himself. Like Apollo's oracle, the κλέος "fame" that he offers the Delian Maidens is ἐτήτυμόν "accurate." His speech also resembles that of Apollo's θεράπναι "attendants" and would be a fair recompense, therefore, for their words of praise. For he re-presents the speech of a man who comes to Delos, just as they re-present the voice of "each man" there, and he even re-presents the speech of the Delian Maidens themselves, the very words for which he asks. In this virtuoso performance, prize-winning re-presentation re-presents the prize-winning it seeks. After such a sign of completion, we expect an end to the hymn.

But no, the ending we expect after this elaborate, apparent ending is immediately revoked:

αὐτὰρ ἐγὼν οὐ λήξω ἑκηβόλον Ἀπόλλωνα
ὑμνέων ἀργυρότοξον, ὃν ἠύκομος τέκε Λητώ.

But I myself shall not cease hymning far-casting Apollo
of the silver bow whom beautiful-haired Leto bore.

Homeric Hymn to Apollo 177–178

At once the hymnist makes good this hyperbole of a song without end by more apostrophe and doubling: first, by another apostrophe, ὦ ἄνα "O lord," another expression of Apollo's omni-presence, "you hold both Lycia and Maeonia and Miletus, lovely city by the sea," another singling out of Delos "but you yourself rule in power over wave-girt Delos" (179–181), and then by the transformation

144

of the apparently completed Delian hymn into only the first half of a double hymn, "the all-glorious son of Leto, goes to rocky Pytho, playing upon his hollow lyre, clad in ambrosial, perfumed garments" (182–183).[20] For it is, of course, in its overall "Delian-plus-Pythian" structure that the text most overtly manifests its duple form. To the omni-presence of Apollo corresponds this formal attempt at limitless re-presentation.

The Pythian hymn carries out this double framework both in its apostrophe, in its confirmation of Apollo's original claim to the lyre, the bow, and the oracle, and in the resulting augmentation of the god's proper name. The invocation at the start of the Delian hymn – "How then shall I hymn you, when you are in every way well-hymned?" – opens the Pythian as well (207 = 19). Here, the figure achieves an almost egregious prominence, as this opening apostrophe is extended over the next seventy-three lines through twenty second-person singular verbs. The narrative, too, reflects its Delian half by recounting how Apollo realized his first words: "May the dear lyre and curved bow be mine and I shall unerringly repeat to humankind the unerring plan of Zeus" (131–132). At the start of the Pythian hymn, the lyre indeed belongs to Apollo, as he plays for the Muses on Olympus. Then, after the opening apostrophe, the hymn selects as its subject, via another priamel, none other than the founding of Apollo's oracle, a founding that depends, as in the god's original utterance, upon his possession of the bow and the lyre. For he slays the dragoness with his κρατεροῖο βιοῖο "mighty bow" (301), kindles the fire in his ἄδυτον "sanctuary" by showing forth the gleam of his arrows (443–445), plays the lyre to lead his paean-singing priests to the temple (514–519), and characterizes his oracular speech as ἐμὴν ἰθύν "my straight direction" (539).

In this conquest that proves his claim to the bow, the god adds through his power of speech two epithets to his proper name. As the dragoness breathes her last, Apollo exults, "Now rot (πύθευ) there on the man-nourishing earth" (363). As if in sympathetic harmony, "the holy strength of Helios made her rot (κατέπυσ᾽) there. As a result now the place is called Pytho, and they call the lord 'Pythian' as an epithet, because there on that spot the strength of piercing Helios made the monster rot (πῦσε)" (371–374). The god commands a natural transformation, nature obeys, and at once the transformation becomes the name of the place and of the god. The property of the place is now the property of Apollo. In the same way, Apollo acquires the name of the spring Telphousa, who had tried to restrict the "name" of her property to her own proper name. She at first persuaded Apollo to build his temple elsewhere, "so that the fame (κλέος) upon the land might belong to Telphousa herself and not to him who works from afar" (275–276). Once Apollo sees through her ruse, however, he charges, "Telphousa, so you were not destined to possess this lovely place by tricking my mind and to pour down beautifully-flowing water. Here indeed there will be my fame (κλέος) as well and not yours only" (379–381). With that, he buries her streams under a crag and builds an altar nearby, where "all pray to the lord with the epithet 'Telphusian,' because he shamed (ἤσχυνε) the streams of holy Telphousa" (382–387). Apollo's oracular "straight direction" thus proves itself preeminently in the case of Apollo himself: his words to Pytho and Telphousa are an efficacious prophecy of his property and proper names.

In the *Homeric Hymn to Apollo*, therefore, the harmonious lyre, the straight arrow, accurate speech, and proper naming all embody the power of unerring re-presentation. This mode is claimed for the voice of the god, for the voice of his surrogates, the Delian Maidens, and for the voice of the hymnist who re-presents the voice of the "blind man from Chios." But in the *Homeric Hymn to Hermes*, this "straight arrow" of ideal invocation is deflected by the competing and completing mode of imitation, the mode, that is, of writing.

IV. *Homeric Hymn to Hermes*: The Deflection of Writing

In our collection, the *Homeric Hymn to Apollo* is followed by the *Homeric Hymn to Hermes*, a text that rivals and adds to its mate.[21] There, the younger, belated god (re-)invents what "always already" existed as the property of another, in particular, the lyre, the possession of which Apollo claimed in the earlier *Hymn* as a condition of his oracular accuracy. In this (re-)invention of the lyre – with its repercussions in the theft of Apollo's cattle, the exchange of the lyre for the cattle, and the subsequent character of Apollo's oracular speech – the relation between Hermes and Apollo shows the effect of imitation through writing upon re-presentation through speech. This effect may be traced by looking at the three mediums of exchange in the hymn – the lyre, the cattle, and oracular speech – somewhat outside of chronological order: first, at the lyre, from its (re-)invention up to the point when Hermes is about to exchange it for the stolen cattle; second, at the theft for which the lyre is supposed to pay; and then, again, at the exchange of the lyre for the cattle and how that exchange affects the status of oracular speech.[22]

Lyre

Right after his birth, at the point when Apollo spoke and said that his oracular power depended upon his ownership of the lyre and the bow, Hermes invents the lyre his older brother has already appropriated. He encounters it upon his threshold in the form of a living tortoise. He then apostrophizes it with the hymnal χαῖρε "hail" as χοροιτύπε "struck for the dance" and as one who "would sing very beautifully," when dead (31, 37–38). The hymnist then calls the lyre an ἄθυρμα "plaything" (40). These terms parallel attributes of writing as analyzed by Derrida: a τύπος "struck mark," a dead shell of the sound it reflects, living speech (λόγος ζῶν καὶ ἔμψυχος "speech living and breathing," Plato *Phaedrus* 276a8),[23] a frivolous substitute, like the gardens of Adonis, for serious dialectic and the agriculture of Demeter.[24] But the analogy goes much further.

In the invention and subsequent exchange of the lyre, Hermes and Apollo themselves enact the relation between writing and speech. Hermes gives to Apollo that which Apollo originally had, that of which he is the origin, his "original" meaning, but in so doing, Hermes belies any stable, originary attribution. Here in the *Homeric Hymn to Hermes*, this double origin of the lyre is not like the controlled pairings of the *Homeric Hymn to Apollo*, where presence and absence, memory and oblivion, Delian and Pythian are clearly defined. It is the mobile doubling of inebriation, the doubling of deceptive imitation, in which the mind's eye cannot logically separate the two origins, or at least not without calling one false and the other true. That sort of control by true/false opposition is, in fact, attempted in the *Homeric Hymn to Hermes*, but without total success.

When Apollo first hears the sound of the lyre, his reaction is to insist on the absolute worth and originality of the instrument. After Hermes sings him a "Theogony" of the "deathless gods and the dark earth, how they first came into being and how each one received a portion" (427–428), Apollo declares the lyre worth fifty cattle (437) and asks about its source by posing two alternatives: was it yours "from birth" (ἐκ γενετῆς) or was it a gift from a god or a mortal? (440–442). "For," he adds, "I hear this marvelous new-spoken voice (νεήφατον ὄσσαν), which I declare that no one ever yet has learned (δαήμεναι), neither of men nor of the immortals with homes on Olympus, except you, you thief, son of Zeus and Maia. What is this technique (τέχνη), what is this music (μοῦσα) of irremediable cares, what is this worn path (τρίβος)?" (443–448). "For although I am an attendant of the Olympian Muses," he adds, "never have I cared for any of the clever accomplishments (ἐνδέξια ἔργα) at young men's feasts as I care in my heart for this" (450, 453–454). So, to elicit the lyre for himself, he swears:

> ἷζε, πέπον, καὶ <u>μῦθον</u> ἐπαίνει πρεσβυτέροισι:
> νῦν γάρ τοι <u>κλέος</u> ἔσται ἐν ἀθανάτοισι θεοῖσι

147

σοί τ' αὐτῷ καὶ μητρί· τὸ δ' <u>ἀτρεκέως</u> ἀγορεύσω·
<u>ναὶ μὰ τόδε κρανέινον ἀκόντιον</u>, ἦ μὲν ἐγώ σε
κυδρὸν ἐν ἀθανάτοισι καὶ ὄλβιον ἡγεμόν' ἔσσω[25]
δώσω τ' ἀγλαὰ δῶρα καὶ ἐς τέλος οὐκ ἀπατήσω.

Sit down, dear brother, and agree to this <u>speech</u> of your elders,
for there will be <u>fame</u> for you among the immortal gods,
for you and your mother. This I will declare <u>accurately</u>.
I <u>swear</u> <u>by</u> <u>this</u> <u>shaft</u> <u>of</u> <u>cornel</u> <u>wood</u>, truly I myself shall seat you as
a leader renowned and blessed among the immortals
and I will give you shining gifts and to the end I will not
    deceive you.

Homeric Hymn to Hermes 457–462

By this solemn oath, he guarantees his "speech."

Hermes responds to this μῦθος of the elder with a κερδαλέος μῦθος "gainful speech" (463) in which he describes Apollo and the lyre in a way that would seem appropriate to the god. Just as Apollo had insisted on the originality of the lyre, so Hermes first insists on Apollo's complete "knowledge" of divine utterance:

καὶ τιμάς σέ γέ φασι <u>δαήμεναι</u> ἐκ <u>Διὸς ὀμφῆς</u>
<u>μαντείας</u> θ' Ἑκάεργε, Διὸς παρά, <u>θέσφατα</u> πάντα.

And they say that from the <u>voice of Zeus</u> you indeed have
    <u>learned</u> the gods' honors
and the <u>oracles</u>, O Far-Worker, from Zeus, all the <u>divine decrees</u>.

Homeric Hymn to Hermes 471–472

Then, as Apollo had called it a νεήφατος ὄσσα "new-spoken voice," so Hermes casts the lyre as a sort of oracular voice, an instrument that accurately reflects the presence or absence of "knowledge" in its player:

ὅς τις ἂν αὐτὴν
τέχνῃ καὶ σοφίῃ <u>δεδαημένος</u> ἐξερεείνῃ,
φθεγγομένη παντοῖα νόῳ χαρίεντα διδάσκει
ῥεῖα συνηθείῃσιν ἀθυρομένη μαλακῇσιν,
ἐργασίην φεύγουσα δυήπαθον· ὃς δέ κεν αὐτὴν
<u>νῆις ἐὼν</u> τὸ πρῶτον ἐπιζαφελῶς ἐρείνῃ,
μὰψ αὔτως κεν ἔπειτα μετήορά τε θρυλλίζοι.
σοὶ δ' αὐτάγρετόν ἐστι <u>δαήμεναι</u>, ὅττι μενοινᾷς.

Whoever
<u>through</u> <u>knowledge</u> inquires of it with technique and skill,
speaking it teaches all sorts of things pleasing to the mind,
since it is played easily with gentle familiarities,
for it flees miserable labor. Whoever
<u>in</u> <u>ignorance</u> for the first time inquires of it violently,
then just at random and off-pitch it would make a false note.
But you have only to choose to <u>know</u> whatever you have a
    mind to.

Homeric Hymn to Hermes 482–489

Such an oracular instrument would appear an appropriate λιγύφωνος ἑταίρη "clear-voiced companion" (478) for Apollo, a curved shell for the arrow of knowledge and straight speech. The voice of the lyre will accurately repeat the "knowledge" of its questioner, Apollo, just as Apollo's oracular voice will accurately repeat his "knowledge" of the βουλὴ Ζηνός "plan of Zeus" (538), the knowledge that in turn repeats Διὸς ὀμφή "the voice of Zeus" (471). The doubling here seems stable and proper, therefore, to Apollo: the lyre first belonged to Hermes and it now belongs to Apollo; to knowledgeable questioning the lyre responds harmoniously and to ignorant questioning it returns dissonance.

These doublets befit the Apollo of the double hymn. They make the lyre a proper possession for him and thus promise an even exchange for the cattle that were his property. But as soon as the exchange is made, the earlier, ambivalent character of the lyre reasserts itself. A look at the intervening theft of the cattle makes clear why. After retracing the theft for which this lyre is supposed to pay, we see that no exchange of property is even.

Cattle Exchange/Theft

When Hermes first plays the lyre, he "names his own famous-named birth" (54–59): he plays the poet of his own origin, that is, the poet of the *Homeric Hymn to Hermes*. This "auto-tropic" naming is not satisfactory to the polytropic god, however, for it is during this song that Hermes conceives the desire for meat (κρειῶν ἐρατίζων "having *eros* for meat," 64). To satisfy this craving, he initiates the exchange that is also a theft of the cattle of the gods, through the technique that is also the trick of writing. He makes the cattle walk backward and disguises his own tracks by attaching branches to his feet. As a result, the connection here between cattle and signs is more than the homologous exchange of cattle, women, and words noted by Lévi-Strauss and exemplified in the Greek meta-poetic tradition when Archilochus is said to trade his cattle for the Muses' "gift" of poetry.[26] Here, the cattle are literally signs, or rather, it is their imprints or τύποι "struck marks" in the sand that signify. For this trick, the cattle are driven πλανοδίας (75), as the gloss of Hesychius puts it, "askew of the straight path," by reversing the direction of their hoofs, so that these signs, like those of writing, reverse the apparent direction of the exchange and reverse also the apparent difference between owner and thief. When the hoofs are straight, they, like speech, signify their proper owner. But when they are reversed by Hermes, they are like writing, since their tracks seem to lead to Apollo, just as writing seems to signify the signified, but they in fact move away from Apollo toward the home of Hermes. Like the written sign, a secondary sign of a sign, the tracks in fact belong to or signify not the signified, but another signifier, namely, Hermes, the disguised owner, the thief who signifies the absent owner. As such, this writing is another of Hermes' non-original originations, just as Hermes' sacrifice will be a parodic αἴτιον "aetiological myth" of sacrifice.

Hermes' writing is another non-original origin, this time of language, the exchange of words. Before Hermes' theft, all the cattle were the property of the gods. Like *le nom propre*, they signified their "proper," unique owner and thus could not be exchanged. But now by turning their cattle into writing signs, Hermes steals them from their proper owner and puts them into circulation. Now the cattle/signs are the property of a thief, who with his bushy sandals disguises his own footprints as those of an unidentified creature, a creature with no proper name.[27] Now the cattle/signs are like common nouns, the noun "kleenex," for example: they can be the property of any thief, of any referent who happens to possess them.[28]

Thus the threat posed by the writing of Hermes to the speech of Apollo is the loss of original, proper identity. Unlike invocation, which takes the name in order to re-present the god, this writing attempts to appropriate Apollo's property, to create a double with the same property as the signified. Unlike apostrophe, in which doubling is re-presentation in a different place and not an imitation, the appropriation of writing attempts to imitate the original. Hermes makes himself a double with the same property as Apollo. He disguises his own identity and takes on Apollo's "proper name."

Hermes' exchange/theft is not, however, without evidence, for the path of the cattle's tracks can be back-tracked by Apollo. Nor is Hermes' appropriation of the stolen property totally successful, for in the parodic αἴτιον "aetiological myth" of sacrifice, the ritual that defines humans and gods, Hermes plays the role of both the god who eats and the human who craves to do so.[29] Instead of being eaten – a consummation that would separate the new owner of the cattle forever from the gods – the fat and the flesh, the leftovers of the original goods, are put up on a shelf to be the σῆμα νέης φωρῆς "sign of the recent theft" (136). The theft is not without evidence, but Apollo's desire to re-appropriate his property is deflected by an *eros* for the lyre (434), just as *eros* for meat drives Hermes to rustle the cattle. Apollo proposes an exchange of the lyre for his cattle, and indeed, as we have seen, Hermes offers the instrument as one that would in its structure of distinct presence and absence be a suitable substitute for Apollo's property, a gift Apollo could own. But this gift of the lyre, too, turns out to be an imperfect theft, for the lyre is revealed to retain the property of its non-original/original owner.

Oracular Voice

No sooner have Apollo and Hermes concluded the deal than Hermes invents another instrument, the voice (ἐνοπή) of the pipes, which, like "far-working" Apollo, is "heard from afar" (τηλόθ᾽ ἀκουστήν, 512). At once Apollo fears for his property, this time for both the bow and the lyre: "Son of Maia, leader, you of dazzling intelligence, I fear that you will steal from me the lyre and the bow together. For you have as your sphere of honor (τιμὴν) from Zeus to establish works of exchange (ἐπαμοίβια ἔργα θήσειν) among men throughout the fruitful earth" (514–517). In response to this fear, Apollo tries to control the movement of Hermes' ἐπαμοίβια ἔργα, first by exacting from Hermes what he himself gave earlier to seal his word: the "swearing of a great oath" (μέγαν ὅρκον ὀμόσσαι, 518), an utterance that aims, like Apollo's oracle, at the status of necessity, a speech that would regulate the action of writing by re-establishing proper ownership.[30] To Hermes' promise not to steal from his possessions, Apollo promises his friendship (521–526), sealing the bond with the additional pledge to give Hermes an identifying instrument of his own:

> αὐτὰρ ἔπειτα
> ὄλβου καὶ πλούτου δώσω περικαλλέα ῥάβδον,
> χρυσείην, τριπέτηλον, ἀκήριον ἥ σε φυλάξει
> πάντας ἐπικραίνους᾽ θεμοὺς ἐπέων τε καὶ ἔργων
> τῶν ἀγαθῶν, ὅσα φημὶ δαήμεναι ἐκ Διὸς ὀμφῆς.

> Moreover,
> I will give you the exceedingly beautiful wand of wealth and
> riches,

golden, with three branches, which will keep you unharmed,
accomplishing all the laws of both words and deeds that are
good, as many as I declare I have <u>learned</u> from the <u>voice of Zeus</u>.

Homeric Hymn to Hermes 528–532

The exchange would seem even: in return for being allowed to keep his "property," his bow and his lyre, Apollo will give to Hermes the "property" of Hermes, his ῥάβδος "wand." And in relation to oracular authority, Hermes would remain properly distinct from Apollo. The ῥάβδος "wand" may effect what Apollo has "learned," but the μαντεία itself, the "oracular voice" Hermes "mentioned" before (471) – this, Apollo insists, must remain his own. Again he seeks the support of an oath, this time by appealing to the one he once swore to retain exclusive possession of oracular knowledge.

αὐτὰρ ἐγώ γε
πιστωθεὶς κατένευσα καὶ ὤμοσα καρτερὸν ὅρκον,
μή τινα νόσφιν ἐμεῖο θεῶν αἰειγενετάων
ἄλλον γ᾽ εἴσεσθαι <u>Ζηνὸς</u> πυκινόφρονα <u>βουλήν</u>.
καὶ σύ, κασίγνητε χρυσόρραπι, μή με κέλευε
θέσφατα πιφαύσκειν, ὅσα μήδεται εὐρύοπα Ζεύς.

Moreover I myself
gave a pledge and vowed and swore a strong oath,
that no other apart from me of the everlasting gods
would know the wise-witted <u>plan of Zeus</u>.
And so you, my brother of the golden wand, do not bid me
declare those divine decrees, as many as wide-seeing Zeus
intends.

Homeric Hymn to Hermes 535–540

But here the distinction between the two gods breaks down. For the oracular speech that Apollo retains is no longer the unerring re-presentation he appropriated in the *Homeric Hymn to Apollo*.

Apollo is now "peritropaic" himself, "greatly bewildering (περιτροπέων) the tribes of unenviable men" (542). For the mantic god will not simply re-present his knowledge of the "plan of Zeus," but will present to humans two sorts of signs, a double in which the true cannot be distinguished from its imitation:

ὅς τις ἂν ἔλθῃ
φωνῇ καὶ πτερύγεσσι τεληέντων οἰωνῶν·

οὗτος ἐμῆς <u>ὀμφῆς</u> ἀπονήσεται, οὐδ' ἀπατήσω.
ὃς δέ κε μαψιλόγοισι πιθήσας οἰωνοῖσι
<u>μαντείην</u> ἐθέλησι παρὲκ νόον ἐξερεείνειν
ἡμετέρην, νοέειν δὲ θεῶν πλέον αἰὲν ἐόντων,
φήμ', ἀλίην ὁδὸν εἶσιν. <u>ἐγὼ δέ κε δῶρα δεχοίμην</u>.

> Whoever comes
> by the sound and flight of significant birds,
> this man will profit from my <u>voice</u>, nor will I deceive.
> But whoever trusts in empty-speaking birds
> and wishes to question our <u>oracular voice</u> outside our purpose
> and to know more than the immortal gods,
> I declare, he will come on a vain journey. <u>But</u> I <u>would accept
> the gifts</u>.

> *Homeric Hymn to Hermes* 543–549

Apollo's oracular speech is now a double in which one sign, like writing, is the indistinguishable imitation of the other, meaningful sign of speech. It offers two kinds of signs – ones not unlike the two categories of the Muses' speech in Hesiod or the two gates of dreams in the *Odyssey* – one of which is common, meaningless in itself, but indistinguishable by humans from proper, meaningful speech. These signs can be read only by those who know ahead of time whether their desire to know exceeds the divine desire to reveal, that is, whether their desire transgresses the division between divine and human knowledge. But this is an exclusively divine knowledge, as far as humans are concerned. For in yet another exchange/theft, Apollo, now the twin of his younger, mercantile brother, will, as he says, "take the gifts" in any case. Apollo's signs bear no diacritical mark.

The μαντεία "oracular voice" of Apollo is now a deceptive double, an imitation of Hermes' writing. But the proliferation of imitative doubles does not stop here. No sooner does Apollo swear to retain μαντεία as his exclusive property than he accords to Hermes the μαντεία of the Bee Maidens (552–564).[31] He attempts to differentiate their prophecy in time, space, and authority from his current prophetic charge: the Maidens were "teachers apart (ἀπάνευθε) of the μαντεία which I practiced when still a child. But my father paid no attention" (556–557).[32] Why did the father pay no attention? Why does Apollo say so? Why other than to stress that the Maidens do not re-present what Apollo swore that he alone would re-present, namely, the βουλὴ Διός "plan of Zeus" (538)? But Apollo then counteracts this differentiation by attributing to the Maidens' μαντεία the structure and authority of his own oracular voice: when fed honey, the Maidens "are willing to speak truth" (ἐθέλουσιν ἀληθείην ἀγορεύειν), but when deprived, they "speak false things" (ψεύδονται) (560–563).[33] Both Apollo and the Maidens speak both truth and falsehood. The one repeats the βουλὴ Διός, but the others utter ἀλήθεια "truth." Unless the βουλὴ Διός "plan of Zeus" can be distinguished from ἀλήθεια "truth," the two oracles are cognate. The Maidens' μαντεία now belongs to Hermes: "inquire of them accurately," urges Apollo, and "if you should teach a mortal man to do so, often he will hear your own voice (σῆς ὀμφῆς)" (564–566).[34] Thus the "oracular voice" of Hermes is now the deceptive double of the "exclusive" μαντεία of Apollo.

This movement of distinct into indistinct doubles, of origin into shared originality, of proper into common property, of speech into speech with the structure of writing – this movement deflects the "straight arrow" of ideal representation and blurs the target. This is the movement embodied by Hermes, by his theft of Apollo's cattle, by his gift of Apollo's lyre, and, finally, by Apollo too, whose prophetic speech now imitates Hermes' writing. "Polytropic" Hermes has turned the "palintropic" harmony of Apollo's instruments into a movement that literally "turns back" upon the god. What is the extent of this movement? Does it affect only the Apollo of the Homeric Hymn to Hermes or does it include the Apollo of the earlier hymn as well? Does the ideal representation of the Homeric Hymn to Apollo remain intact?

V. The Epiphany of Apollo/Hermes

If we look at the two hymns together, their modes of doubling no longer appear distinct. As the Derridean analysis "deconstructs" the distinction between original, living logos and derivative, dead writing by showing that speech "always already" shared the origin-less structure of writing, so the operation of imitation in the Homeric Hymn to Hermes exposes Apollo's re-presentation as an imitation itself. By depriving Apollo of original possession of the lyre, the Homeric Hymn to Hermes dispossesses the earlier hymn of all that depends upon (that) original possession: the epiphany of Apollo as unique(ness) in name, prior(ness) in time, ubiquitous(ness) in space and accurate(ness) in speech. In light of the Homeric Hymn to Hermes, what Apollo re-presents is not a/the "real thing," but its appearance; not reality, but its compelling illusion. The insistent hymnic apostrophe does not completely re-present the god, but rather attempts to persuade the judging audience that the re-presentation is complete. This effort is unmistakable once the Homeric Hymn to Hermes supplements the story, but even in the Homeric Hymn to Apollo alone, it was "always already" evident. Consider again the three poetic/prophetic speakers.

In establishing the prophetic authority of Apollo, the hymn ignores the contradiction between a unique, original, ubiquitous godhead and the non-original origin of his name and place of prophecy. The territorial epithets "Pythian" and "Telphusian" reflect not "proper" naming, but the taking of another's "proper-ty." Apollo's name/place is stolen property, just as the cattle Hermes stole were Apollo's "proper name." By exposing his "own" as originally "other," Apollo's theft denies any stable, originary opposition between the terms: the opposition is imposed out of a desire for ownership, but all we can "own" is the property of another. The place of Apollo's unique role, the original re-presentation of the father, is the place of his imitative appropriation of the property of the female/earth.

A similar contradiction marks the claim of the hymnic voice to poetic preeminence. The voice of the *Homeric Hymn to Apollo* asks to be awarded the status of "the best," whenever the Delian Maidens are questioned, and to be awarded it by name. Yet the name he gives to the Delian Maidens is not his "own." In its effort to demonstrate ideal re-presentation, the hymnic apostrophe imitates the voice of "Homer." Like generations of bards before him, the "son" tries to win the prize for his own composition by taking the name of the "father." But now such name-taking means more than claiming the composition just performed; it means posing as the author of the fixed epic about to be repeated. Taking the name of Homer means a Hermes-like "theft" of an older poet's "property." This appropriation of a product "made" through writing shares the imitative structure of writing and, ironically, it will also share the ambivalent fate of the fixed epic text. For through the Hermes-like operation of writing, the *Homeric Hymn to Apollo* is itself fixed and "stolen"/Panhellenized by such rhapsodes as Kynaithos of Chios who (we are told in the Pindaric *skholion* on the Homeridae) was said to have "written" the *Homeric Hymn to Apollo* and first performed it in Syracuse.[35]

And what of the Delian Maidens themselves, the θεράπναι "attendants" of Apollo? It is in their song that the indecidability of re-presentation and imitation is most clear. On the one hand, the presence of the original speaker, the "each man," establishes the difference between original and copy. But "each man" is so enchanted by the Maidens' song that he can no longer distinguish between himself and this repetition of himself: "each man would say that he himself was speaking" (163–164). By his own testimony, the subject both asserts and denies his unique, prior status. "Each man" attributes to the Delian Maidens a re-presentation so ideal that it is indistinguishable from imitation. Like the double origin of the lyre, the mode of the Maidens' "enchanting verisimilitude" cannot be decided. They are the θεράπναι of Hermes no less than of Apollo.

But if the imitative structure of re-presentation in the *Homeric Hymn to Apollo* could be detected from the start, why not do so? Why first present the claims of the *Homeric Hymn to Apollo* as if they were successful, and demystify them only later, in light of the *Homeric Hymn to Hermes*? This is the traditional order of the hymns to these two gods, an order that facilitates their epiphany: to "see" Apollo/Hermes, we must experience the theft of what we thought we owned. The rhetoric of re-presentation must be felt in all its detail, insistence, and apparent disingenuity, if we are to realize the intensity of the will behind the rhetoric, the desire of the subject to name (itself) properly.[36] We must recognize this desire in our confident acceptance of the hymn's apparently regulated repetition: ring-composition that seems to divide space and time into distinct presence and absence and thereby to formulate true definition, the return to the origin. We must empathize with the attempt to control difference: in the separation of unerring re-presentation from deceptive imitation in the *Homeric Hymn to Apollo* and in the claim of the Homeridae to a living Homeric speech in the Homeric hymn over against the declining genre of epic.[37] Without partaking in the power of Apollo, we cannot see the god epiphanized in its loss. For the epiphany of Hermes is the theft of the epiphany of Apollo, a theft in exchange for the epiphany of Apollo/Hermes. What the *Homeric Hymn to Hermes* reveals is the indecidability of the two gods: Apollo's desire for unique identity is a desire for what belongs to Hermes, just as Hermes' desire is for what belongs to Apollo. In the traditional conjunction of the hymns, we see the uneasy φιλότης "affection" (*Homeric Hymn to Hermes* 575) of the two brothers, the compelling ἔρως "desire" for original identity, and the deconstruction of originality as the imitative desire for the origin.

Notes

An earlier version of this essay appeared in *Arethusa* 15 (American Classical Studies in Honor of Jean-Pierre Vernant), edited by A. Bergren and F. Zeitlin (1982) 83–108. It is a pleasure to thank David Blank, Rebecca Bushnell, Judith Engle, Bernard Frischer, and Bruce Rosenstock for invaluable assistance with that text.

1. See Stanford 1961:1.344–345 on ix 499 for the difficulties of the construction.

2. For the evidence on the archaic προοίμιον, see Koller 1956.

3. Fehling (1979) argues that the notion of a clan of rhapsodes from Chios named "Homeridae" may be explained as a conflation of two traditions invented independently, (1) of rhapsodes as Homeridae, an invention of Pindar to honor the rhapsodes, and (2) of a γένος in Chios called Homeridae, an invention by the genealogists on the basis of *Homeric Hymn to Apollo* 172, since the sources of (1) do not mention (2) and vice versa. It is the first of the two traditions that is germane to this essay.

4. On this process, see Nagy 1979:5–9. My argument in this essay accords with Nagy's demonstration of the traditional character of archaic Greek poetry. In particular, I accept his theory that the names "Homer" and "Hesiod" originally denoted a traditional bardic function, rather than a single individual. The term "Homeridae" in that case would mean "sons of those poets who compose in the Homeric manner." It is true, however, that if Homer and Hesiod were individual poets, my analysis of the connection between Homeric epic and the Homeric hymn would remain essentially the same. The issues that govern the relation between Homer and the Homeridae do not depend upon whether the "father" was one man or a whole tradition. On the sources of the *Contest Between Homer and Hesiod*, see Richardson 1981.

5. The relation between Homeric epic and the Homeric hymn would thus be a complex version of what Guillen (1971:135–58) calls genre and "counter-genre."

6. For the rarity and function of apostrophe in epic, see Parry 1973.

7. Compare Svenbro (1976:16–34) who analyzes the Muses in epic as the embodiment of the audience's control over the content of the poet's song: in order to receive payment or support for his composition, the poet must express what the audience wants to hear, the local traditions of their heritage, values, and beliefs. In the case of both Homeric genres, it is the audience who would actually supply or determine what the poet attributes to the god invoked.

8. The complex beginning/end status of the Homeric hymn *vis-à-vis* Homeric epic is reflected here in the conventional diction of the genre.

9. On the "motivated" or "natural" signifier, see Todorov 1977:14–33. For an example, see Jakobson 1971 on "Mama" and "Papa" and the analysis of the pa/ma structure by Fineman 1980.

10. See above, n. 4.

11. Compare Svenbro 1976:42–45.

12. The difference between re-presentation and imitation in language is parallel to the distinction drawn by Vernant in the realm of plastic art between "symbol" and "image." See Vernant 1975 and 1975–1976, in particular 1976:23: "The symbol supposes two levels, the natural and the supernatural, levels opposed but between which, by a play of correspondences, communication sometimes is established, the supernatural bursting into nature in order to 'epiphanize' there in the form of those double entities one of whose faces is visible, while the other face remains turned toward the invisible. The image is not of the order of an epiphany; it is a semblance, a simple appearance. Product of an imitation, it has no other reality than a similarity with that which it is not. Its semblance is a false-semblance. Over against the dualities, nature–supernature and visible–invisible, it establishes a new dimension, another domain: the fictive, the illusory, that indeed which defines the nature of *muthos* in the eyes of the Greeks, when they wish to devalue it by opposing it to the true discourse of proofs, to the *logos*: a fiction" (translation mine). Vernant locates the "symbol" in the archaic period and sees the "image" as a product of the post-Parmenidean experience of Attic drama (1977–1978:454). In archaic poetry, however, we find "imitation" when Helen imitates the voices of the Greek wives (*Odyssey* iv 278–279; see "Helen's 'Good Drug'" in this collection) and in the visual sphere when Apollo makes an εἴδωλον "image" of Aeneas around which the Greeks and the Trojans fight (*Iliad* V 449–52).

13. On the dating of the hymns by linguistic criteria, see Janko 1982, and on their arrangement in our corpus, Van der Valk 1976.

14. Page (1955:244) notes: "The first book of Alcaeus in the Alexandrian edition began with two hymns, the first addressed to Apollo, the second to Hermes." Compare the frequent depiction of Apollo and Hermes together in vase painting, in particular the late 6th century BCE skyphos with Apollo playing the lyre on one side and Hermes playing the pipes on the other (Zanker 1965:56–58, 71–76, plates 1 and 2).

15. Derrida 1972a, esp. 95–107.

16. This manipulation of the signals of close and opening depends upon the conventional linkage of these two critical points in a Homeric hymn via the same phraseology: the opening (apostrophe or "I will remember . . .") matching the close (apostrophe and "I will remember . . .").

17. The reading here of νομοὶ follows Cassola 1975. In his Oxford text, Allen reads νομός, adjusting the accent from the manuscript's νόμος. On the question of whether the noun should be singular or plural here and whether νομοί from νομός "place of pasturage, field, range" or νόμοι from νόμος "melody, type of song" should be read, see AHS:204 on 20.

18. On the formal, unifying function of ring-composition in the Delian hymn, see Niles 1979.

19. For the translation of θεράπνη and θεράπων as "ritual substitute" on the basis of cognate usage in Hittite, see Nagy 1979:33 with bibliography.

20. On the basis of close analysis of archaic hymnic conventions, especially the diction of opening, transition, and closing, Miller (1979) argues convincingly for the unity of the Delian and Pythian hymn(s) against the "*Ruhnkenite*" separatists. He shows how "both the epilogic force of 165–76 and the proemial force of 177–78 make perfect sense . . . if the passage as a whole is understood as transitional rather than final, effecting a return to the main subject from a subsidiary topic of merely temporary interest" (181), and attributes the appeal of the separatist view to an "*a priori* skepticism that automatically denies rhetorical sophistication to 'primitive' poets and rejects its imputation by others as rampant subjectivism" (184). My analysis is based upon the assumption of just such "rhetorical sophistication," insofar as I am trying to prove that Miller's "unity of two parts" is both a persistent formal feature and also an overt theme of the text.

21. The entire *Homeric Hymn to Hermes* is studied by Kahn 1978 in an example of the interpretive potential of *lexicologie structurale*. Each critical term, every important theme is analyzed both in the hymn itself and throughout Greek literature according to structuralist principles; the result is a dazzling network of insights.

22. Applying the semiology of Roland Barthes, Klein (1980) establishes a homology between poetry and cattle exchange in the hymn.

23. Compare Derrida 1972a.

24. For the relation between the gardens of Adonis and writing in the *Phaedrus*, see Toubeau 1972, a review of Derrida 1972a and Detienne 1972a.

25. For the reading, see Cassola 1975:538–539 on 461.

26. On the exchange of women and signs, see Lévi-Strauss 1967:548–570 = 1969:478–497. For the "Life of Archilochus" preserved in the Mnesiepes inscription from Paros, see Treu 1959:40–45. Compare Nagy 1979:303.

27. When he sees the tracks, Apollo himself declares he cannot name the maker of the second set: "Oh, oh! Truly a great marvel (θαῦμα) is this I behold with my eyes. These, indeed, are the tracks of straight-horned cattle, but they have been turned back toward the flowery meadow. But these others are not the footprints of either man or woman or grey wolves or bears or lions, nor do I expect that they are those of a shaggy-necked Centaur—whoever makes such monstrous footprints with swift feet" (*Homeric Hymn to Hermes* 219–225).

28. The example of "kleenex," now a common noun meaning "tissue" and before the proper name of "Kleenex tissue," is offered by Bruce Rosenstock.

29. Kahn 1978:43–47. Kahn makes an astute point about the temporal status of Hermes' sacrifice: in the world of the hymn, sacrifice as the mark of human/divine definition already exists before Hermes' slaughter of the cattle, for his conversation with the old vine worker (87–93) proves that the human world of agriculture is already constituted apart from the world of the gods. Hermes' sacrifice is thus not a true "first," but an *aition* of what "always already" existed.

30. Apollo's trust in a μέγαν ὅρκον "great oath" from Hermes here would seem to forget his earlier offer to swear a μέγαν ὅρκον that he had not stolen Apollo's cattle, "whatever cattle may be" (274–277). Perhaps Apollo's confidence stems from the fact that this is to be a "great oath of the gods" sworn either "by nodding with your head or by the mighty water of the river Styx" (518–519). Compare AHS:264 on 518.

31. On the identity and connotations of the Bee Maidens, see Scheinberg 1979.

32. On the possible senses of ἀπάνευθε "apart" here, see Scheinberg 1979:10.

33. These two categories of the Bee Maidens' speech parallel those of the Muses who speak ψεύδεα ἐτύμοισιν ὁμοῖα "false things like to real things" and ἀληθέα "true things" εὖτ᾽ ἐθέλωμεν "whenever they wish" (Hesiod *Theogony* 26–28). Compare Scheinberg 1979:11 and "Language and the Female in Early Greek Thought" in this collection.

34. For the linkage of the oracular power of Apollo to repeat the voice of Zeus with that of the Bee Maidens and Hermes through the use of the noun ὀμφή "voice" and the common property of uttering both truth and falsehood, see Scheinberg 1979:11, 27–28.

35. On Kynaithos, see Wade-Gery 1967.

36. This will to unique identity seems no less inevitable than its deconstruction. Compare de Man (1979:111) apropos of the critique of metaphysics in Nietzsche: "the idea of individuation, of the human subject as a privileged viewpoint, is a mere metaphor by means of which man projects himself from his insignificance by forcing his own interpretation of the world upon the entire universe, substituting a human-centered set of meanings that is reassuring to his vanity for a set of meanings that reduces him to a mere transitory accident in the cosmic order. The metaphorical substitution is aberrant but no human self could come into being without this error. Faced with the truth of its nonexistence, the self would be consumed as an insect is consumed by the flame that attracts it."

37. In its effort to control difference the *Homeric Hymn to Apollo* anticipates the text of Plato, where the problem of repetition is also treated through attempted regulation of its two forms: the two kinds of εἴδωλα, the εἰκών and the φάντασμα (*Sophist* 236a–c, 241e3); the two kinds of memory, μνήμη and ὑπόμνησις (*Phaedrus* 275a); and the two forms of linguistic signification, the living *logos* and the written word (*Phaedrus* 274c–277a).

7

HOMERIC HYMN TO APHRODITE
Tradition and Rhetoric, Praise and Blame

I. Introduction

THE HOMERIC HYMN IS A TRADITIONAL FORM OF PRAISE POETRY. Employing traditional diction, theme, and structure, the hymn presents an epiphany of the god and an aetiology of his or her powers.[1] The traditional rhetoric of the *Homeric Hymn to Aphrodite* is, however, subversive of the genre, producing a complex and ambiguous αἴτιον "cause" that both praises and blames its goddess.[2]

The opening of the *Homeric Hymn to Aphrodite* inaugurates a structural antagonism that marks a sexual antagonism between Aphrodite and Zeus. The hymn resolves this structural and sexual rivalry by narrating how Zeus finally but equivocally imposes sexual domination upon Aphrodite. It reveals how Zeus arouses ἵμερος "sexual passion" in Aphrodite, so that for the first time, she seduces and sleeps with a mortal male – so that the goddess may no longer boast of making gods "mix" with mortals, herself exempt from such mating. In this epiphany of Aphrodite – her successful seduction and intercourse – the hymn discloses its rhetorical and aetiological ambiguity.

In Aphrodite's seduction of Anchises, heteroerotic ἔρως "erotic desire" confronts the human male as an insoluble problem of knowledge: how to discern a sexually available virgin from Aphrodite disguised as a virgin, how to tell the truth from an imitation of the truth, when "either/or" logic is blinded by ἔρως, when the very desire for knowledge is born of a desire not to know (that the imitation is not true and available). As this ἔρως blurs diacritical difference in the eyes of the mortal man, so it blurs the distinction between praise and blame of the goddess as well. For her successful seduction praises her powers of visual and verbal allure, while testifying also to their subordination to the erotic domination of Zeus.

The rhetorical force of Aphrodite's intercourse with Anchises is, according to the goddess herself, even more degrading. She terms their union – and thereby the hymn that reveals it – an ὄνειδος "reproach" (247), a specialized term within the diction of praise poetry denoting blame.[3] The aetiological import of Aphrodite's union with Anchises is less certain. Does Aphrodite's subjection to divine–human intercourse mean an end to such matings, with immortality henceforth available to humans only through progeny? Or will Aphrodite continue to mate gods with mortals, but just cease to boast about it? Will the force of sexual and ontological mixture thereby elude a system of meaningful distinction between men and gods? Here the rhetorical strategy of praise and/in blame, of acknowledgment and/in negation deprives the hymn of an ultimately stable aetiology.

II. Cosmos of Aphrodite vs. Cosmos of Zeus

The antagonistic structure of the hymn is set up in the first fifty-two lines, which divide into two versions of the poem's essential opposition: A (1–6) vs. B (7–33), and A´ (34–44) vs. B´ (45–52).[4] In lines 1–6 the hymn starts off with an invocation to the Muse to narrate the ἔργα "works" of its subject, Aphrodite.[5]

> μοῦσά μοι ἔννεπε ἔργα πολυχρύσου Ἀφροδίτης,
> Κύπριδος, ἥτε θεοῖσιν ἐπὶ γλυκὺν ἵμερον ὦρσε
> καί τ' ἐδαμάσσατο[6] φῦλα καταθνητῶν ἀνθρώπων
> οἰωνούς τε διιπετέας καὶ θηρία πάντα,
> ἠμὲν ὅσ' ἤπειρος πολλὰ τρέφει ἠδ' ὅσα πόντος·
> πᾶσιν δ' ἔργα μέμηλεν ἐυστεφάνου Κυθερείης.

> Muse, narrate for me the <u>works</u> of golden <u>Aphrodite</u>[7]
> the Cyprian, who <u>rouses</u> <u>sweet</u> <u>sexual</u> <u>passion</u> in gods
> and <u>tames</u> the races of mortal men
> and winged birds and all creatures,
> as many as the dry land rears and as many as the sea,
> to <u>all</u> the <u>works</u> of well-crowned Cythereia are a care.

> *Homeric Hymn to Aphrodite 1–6*

The repetition of ἔργα closes off the unit in which these "works" of the goddess are defined in relation to the three categories that in early Greek thought make up the sphere of animate being: gods, humans, and beasts. In the gods she "rouses sweet sexual passion" (γλυκὺν ἵμερον ὦρσε, 2), and she "tames" (τ' ἐδαμάσσατο, 3) the races of mortals and every variety of beast. This opening section of the hymn asserts the ἔργα Ἀφροδίτης as a cosmic power, extending to "all" (πᾶσιν, 6).[8] But in the use of the verb δαμνάω "tame," a traditional term for the workings of the goddess,[9] there is a suggestion that a cosmos ruled by Aphrodite runs counter to the regular order of things.

Structuralist analysis has shown how in early Greek thought the entities of the universe are constituted by virtue of their differential relations.[10] Thus the human condition is defined by its difference from that of divinity, on the one hand, and bestiality, on the other. This differential relation is hierarchical and proportional, with mortals positioned below gods but above beasts: divinities are to humans as humans are to beasts.[11] But it is the function of the ἔργα Ἀφροδίτης "works of Aphrodite" to confuse this meaningful differentiation. The verb δαμνάω denotes the power of men to "tame" wild creatures into civilized form – beasts through domestication, children through education, and virgins through marriage.[12] Thus in her "taming," Aphrodite blurs the distinction between humans and beasts by exercising over them all, the power of men over beasts: Aphrodite is to humans and beasts as humans are to beasts. And while not going so far as to name the gods explicitly as objects of δαμνάω, the use of πᾶσιν "all" in line 6 suggests that this "taming" is synonymous with the "rousing of sweet sexual passion" in them, an implication confirmed at the start of A´ (34–44), where gods and men are paired.[13]

> τῶν δ' ἄλλων οὔ πέρ τι πεφυγμένον ἔστ' Ἀφροδίτην
> οὔτε θεῶν μακάρων οὔτε θνητῶν ἀνθρώπων.
>
> Of all others there is nothing that has escaped Aphrodite,
> neither of the blessed gods nor of mortal men.
>
> *Homeric Hymn to Aphrodite* 34–35

Thus even at this point Aphrodite's sway threatens to reduce divinities, as well as humans and beasts, to a single status parallel to that of beasts: Aphrodite is to divinities and humans and beasts as humans are to beasts. Such a cosmos results in an "illicit mixture" of categories, recalling the fact that sexual intercourse is denoted in Greek by the verb μείγνυμι "to mix." The ἔργα Ἀφροδίτης produce a cosmos of "mixture" that challenges the distinctions that make for cosmic meaning.

But is not this "mixture" essential to the human and the cosmic order?[14] Is it not necessary for the propagation of all living species? Does it not bring joy? Outside of calling ἵμερος "sexual passion" γλυκύς "sweet" and alluding

in the use of δαμνάω "tame" to procreation through marriage, the opening
of the hymn mentions none of the benefits of Aphrodite.[15] We hear nothing
like τίς δὲ βίος, τί δὲ τερπνὸν ἄτερ χρυσῆς Ἀφροδίτης "what is life, what is
delightful without golden Aphrodite?" (Mimnermus 1.1), but only the extent
of Aphrodite's power.[16] And indeed, once articulated, her power is immediately
qualified, as if its working had to be countered at once.

Juxtaposed with the praise in A (1–6) comes the delimitation in B (7–33) of
Aphrodite's dominion. Here we meet three rival "mini-hymns" – each nearly
as long as or longer than Aphrodite's invocation – to the virgin goddesses who
elude her, Athena (8–15 = 8 lines), Artemis (16–20 = 5 lines), and Hestia (21–32
= 12 lines).[17] Over against the ἔργα Ἀφροδίτης "works of Aphrodite" (9) are set
the ἔργα of Athena (15);[18] the occupations of Artemis, whom Aphrodite cannot
"tame" (δάμναται, 17); and the abstinence of Hestia, a καλὸν γέρας ἀντὶ γάμοιο
"fair gift of honor instead of marriage" given by Zeus (29). The section as a
whole is marked by the repetition of its first and last lines:

> τρισσὰς δ' οὐ δύναται <u>πεπιθεῖν</u> φρένας οὐδ' <u>ἀπατῆσαι</u>:

> But there are three whose wits she is not able to <u>persuade</u>
>   or <u>deceive</u>.

> τάων οὐ δύναται <u>πεπιθεῖν</u> φρένας οὐδ' <u>ἀπατῆσαι</u>.

> Of these three she is not able <u>to persuade</u> or <u>deceive</u> the wits.

> *Homeric Hymn to Aphrodite 7, 33*

These terms πεπιθεῖν "persuade" and ἀπατῆσαι "deceive" introduce the verbal
and intellectual dimensions of the ἔργα Ἀφροδίτης "works of Aphrodite," but
only under the cover of their incapacity – a figure of negated acknowledgment
that is repeated in the hymn and ultimately sums up its rhetoric, as we will
see later, for example, in the use of alpha-privatives.[19] For now, this almost
verbatim repetition frames B (7–33) as a unit parallel and opposed to A (1–6)
with its similar repetition of ἔργα "works" in lines 1 and 6. No sooner is it
completed, however, than this opposition between A and B is itself repeated.

In A′ (34–44), the opening lines 34–35 recapitulate the force of A (1–6) by
asserting that apart from these three virgin goddesses, neither god nor mortal
has πεφυγμένον "fled, escaped" Aphrodite.[20] This claim is then proved by the
exemplum of none less than Zeus himself:

> καί τε[21] <u>παρὲκ</u> Ζηνὸς <u>νόον ἤγαγε</u> τερπικεραύνου,
> ὅστε μέγιστός τ' ἐστὶ <u>μεγίστης</u> τ' ἔμμορε <u>τιμῆς</u>.

καί τε τοῦ, εὖτ' ἐθέλοι,²² πυκινὰς φρένας ἐξαπαφοῦσα
ῥηιδίως συνέμιξε καταθνητῆσι γυναιξίν,
Ἥρης ἐκλελαθοῦσα, κασιγνήτης ἀλόχου τε,
ἣ μέγα εἶδος ἀρίστη ἐν ἀθανάτησι θεῆσι.
κυδίστην δ' ἄρα μιν τέκετο Κρόνος ἀγκυλομήτης
μήτηρ τε Ῥείη· Ζεὺς δ' ἄφθιτα μήδεα εἰδὼς
αἰδοίην ἄλοχον ποιήσατο κέδν' εἰδυῖαν.

She even subverted the mind of Zeus who delights in thunder,
he who is ever greatest and has the greatest honor as his share.²³
Even of this one, whenever she wished, she utterly deceived the
    clever wits
and easily made him mix with mortal women,
by making him forget Hera, his sister and wife,
who is best by far in visible form among the immortal
    goddesses.
She is the most glorious of those whom Cronus of the crooked
    counsel bore
and the mother Rhea. Zeus knowing imperishable schemes
made her his revered wife, who knows what is trustworthy.

Homeric Hymn to Aphrodite 36–44

This example makes explicit the threat detected in the earlier rivalry of
cosmic orders. For Aphrodite does not limit herself to the promotion of
mating within the natural kind – divine, human, or beast – or within the
culturally sanctioned bond, but rather has made even Zeus exceed the limits
of legal marriage in liaisons that adulterate the divine/human boundary.²⁴
Easily and at will, Aphrodite makes the greatest of the gods engender children
through a "misce-genation" that blurs the divine difference.²⁵ In the cosmos
of Aphrodite, the hierarchical order dependent upon the preeminence of Zeus
collapses, as he joins the other gods, men, and animals whom the goddess
can interbreed. Aphrodite reigns supreme, exempt from her own workings:
Aphrodite is to divinities (including Zeus) and humans and beasts as humans
are to beasts.

But Zeus does not take this lying down. In Β´ (45–52), the ratio of power is
rewritten, as Zeus usurps the role of Aphrodite – himself now wielding γλυκὺς
ἵμερος "sweet sexual passion"²⁶ with the goddess as the object – and puts her
in his place among divinities subject to sexual desire across the divine/human
line. Aphrodite, too, will assume, for once at least, the passive role to which

she reduces others, lest her speech among the gods survive unsubordinated by the "negative purpose" of Zeus that renders her boast hypothetical:

τῇ δὲ καὶ αὐτῇ Ζεὺς <u>γλυκὺν ἵμερον</u> ἔμβαλε θυμῷ
ἀνδρὶ καταθνητῷ μιχθήμεναι, <u>ὄφρα</u> τάχιστα[27]
<u>μηδ᾽</u> αὐτὴ βροτέης εὐνῆς <u>ἀποεργμένη</u> <u>εἴη</u>,
καί <u>ποτ᾽</u> ἐπευξαμένη <u>εἴπῃ</u> μετὰ πᾶσι θεοῖσιν
ἡδὺ γελοιήσασα, φιλομμειδὴς Ἀφροδίτη,
ὥς ῥα θεοὺς συνέμιξε καταθνητῇσι γυναιξί,
καί τε καταθνητοὺς υἱεῖς τέκον ἀθανάτοισιν,
ὥς τε θεὰς ἀνέμιξε καταθνητοῖς ἀνθρώποις.

And even in the heart of the goddess herself Zeus cast <u>sweet sexual passion</u>
to be mixed with a mortal man, <u>so that</u> as quickly as possible
she herself <u>might not be separated</u> from a mortal bed
and <u>ever say</u> boasting among all the gods,[28]
laughing sweetly, smile-loving Aphrodite,
how she makes gods mix with mortal women
and they bear mortal sons to the immortals,
and she makes goddesses mix with mortal men.

Homeric Hymn to Aphrodite 45–52

As before, when Aphrodite's power of persuasion and deceit was acknowledged only via negative example, here her words are allowed utterance only in the negative purpose clause – "so that she might not ever say" – that unsays them.[29] The narrative voice of the hymn thus acts as a proleptic ἀντιλογία to the λόγος of Aphrodite among the gods. The goddess is not to remain forever on top, separate from the mixture that frustrates separation. Her speech and the cosmos it represents are here subordinated to the hierarchical order of Zeus that the hymn will henceforth represent. For the remainder of the *Homeric Hymn to Aphrodite* – its account of Aphrodite's love for the human Anchises – will demonstrate Zeus' reduction and replacement of the goddess, while at the same time exemplifying her power over mortal men and beasts. Thus the hymn will attempt to resolve the tension between a cosmos controlled by Aphrodite and a cosmos controlled by Zeus into a stable hierarchy in which the immortal male "tames" the principle of sexuality as an immortal female, who herself "tames" the mortal male.

The mode of Zeus' (and the hymn's) subordination of Aphrodite is rhetorical, in the strong sense of a will that manifests itself in the metaphorization –

the forcible transfer – of the power of speech and action. In the case of Aphrodite's voice, the transference is proleptic, as the narrative voice renders her words a bygone potentiality, muted by the "negative purpose" of Zeus. This "purpose" is realized in an action, the arousing in Aphrodite of sexual desire for a human, that reverses the roles of goddess and god, leaving Zeus in the position of a "metaphorical Aphrodite" – Zeus is to divinities (including Aphrodite) and humans and beasts as humans are to beasts.[30] Yet it is the aim of the hymn to show that this metaphorical divinity of sex is, insofar as he "tames" Aphrodite, more truly "Aphrodite" than the goddess of sex herself, more able than she to control the power she embodies.[31] The very distinction, therefore, between figurative and literal, imitation and original, becomes blurred in the hymn and ultimately indecisive.

In the same way, Zeus' exercise of the power of Aphrodite upon Aphrodite will subvert the genre of the hymn itself, leaving the generic aim of praise contradicted by the goddess's own words, and leaving the text itself unique among the Homeric hymns, an ambiguously exalting and degrading document. But before returning to the overarching contest between Aphrodite and her metaphorical/literal supplanter, the hymn recounts the erotic blindness by which Anchises ultimately sees the goddess.

III. Aphrodite's Visual Epiphany

A "Cosmos" of Sight, Smell, and Sound

The locus of Aphrodite's conquest is pastoral, where *epos* "speech in epic"[32] and *eros* "sexual desire" work in analogous ways. The critical senses are sight, smell, and sound. Once Zeus casts γλυκὺν ἵμερον "sweet sexual passion" for Anchises into her heart (53), "then as soon as she saw him, laughter-loving Aphrodite loved him, and passion (ἵμερος) seized her wits utterly" (56–57). At once she retires to her temple at Paphos in Cyprus, where she prepares the "cosmetic" that rules her cosmos, overwhelming fragrance and visual adornment.[33] Her temple and altar are θυώδης "incense-smelling" (58, 59; compare θύω "burn as offering"). The Graces anoint her with "immortal oil such as blooms out upon (ἐπενήνοθεν) the everlasting gods,[34] for her immortal gown, which had been perfumed for her" (ἀμβροσίῳ ἑανῷ, τό ῥά οἱ τεθυωμένον ἦεν, 62–63).[35] Such is her fragrance that all of Cyprus becomes "sweet-smelling" (εὐώδεα, 66). Thus perfumed, Aphrodite incarnates the metonymy of allure, the part that promises a hidden whole.[36] As if to mark the cosmetic nature of fragrance, as well as to foreshadow its transformation into verbal seduction, the text structures this perfuming around the similarly decorative and intense sonic artifice of a triple, successive, line-initial anaphora: (1) ἐς Κύπρον, ἐς Πάφον (58, 59); (2) ἔνθ᾽, ἔνθα (60, 61); and (3) ἀμβρότῳ, ἀμβροσίῳ (62, 63).[37] This appeal to smell and sound is capped by a brief indication of Aphrodite's visual "cosmos" – χρυσῷ κοσμηθεῖσα "ornamented with gold" (65).[38] But the text dramatically postpones our first full sight of the goddess until it can coincide with the gaze of her mortal lover.

The epiphany of Aphrodite is a θαῦμα ἰδέσθαι "wonder to behold" that evokes both *eros* "sexual desire" and *epos* "speech in epic." As she approaches Anchises' pastoral hut, wild animals follow (69–72).[39] Beholding this parade, Aphrodite "was delighted in her heart" (τέρπετο θυμόν, 72)[40] and in turn casts ἵμερον "sexual passion" into the breasts of the beasts, who lie down at once by twos in their shady glens (73–74). Having displayed her power over beasts, Aphrodite turns to her mortal lover, whom she finds all alone, playing the lyre (75–80). Is he, like so many pastoral poets, singing of love?[41] We never learn. But in the epiphany that interrupts his playing, the hymn stages his initiation as a mortal male into the problem of *eros* as a divine female and the *epos* by which he attempts to solve it.

Ambiguous Imitation

From the male perspective of Anchises and of the hymn itself, the appearance of Aphrodite presents a problem of knowledge and interpretation. The epiphany of Aphrodite – the form in and by which Anchises "sees" the goddess – is a "deception that persuades" (compare πεπιθεῖν and ἀπατῆσαι, 7, 33). More precisely, the epiphany of Aphrodite is an imitation:

> στῆ δ᾽ αὐτοῦ προπάροιθε Διὸς θυγάτηρ Ἀφροδίτη
> <u>παρθένῳ ἀδμήτῃ</u> μέγεθος καὶ εἶδος <u>ὁμοίη</u>, [42]
> μή μιν ταρβήσειεν ἐν ὀφθαλμοῖσι <u>νοήσας</u>. [43]

> Aphrodite, daughter of Zeus,[44] stood before him,
> <u>like</u> to an <u>untamed</u> (ἀδμήτῃ: ἀ "not" + δαμνάω "tame") <u>virgin</u> in
>   size and appearance,
> lest he tremble in fear, having <u>recognized</u> her with his eyes.

> *Homeric Hymn to Aphrodite* 81–83

Direct sight, direct knowledge of Aphrodite would cause a man to "tremble in fear" and certainly not feel free to make love to her, for intercourse with goddesses was maiming, if not lethal.[45] So Aphrodite disguises herself as a female without experience of sexuality, an "untamed virgin," like the goddesses posed against Aphrodite in the opening of the hymn (compare δάμναται, 17; παρθένος, 28).

To forestall the realistic reaction of the male, the goddess disguises herself as her opposite. But her opposite is not – as the alpha-privative, ἀ "not" + δμήτη "tamed," and the principled, perpetual virginity of Athena, Artemis, and Hestia might suggest – a true absence of sexuality.[46] The opposite of female sexuality is not "female non-sexuality," for any female old enough to be called παρθένος "virgin" is always "tame-able," always potentially sexual. Even virgin goddesses can be made pregnant. In the logic of heterosexuality, the opposite of female sexuality is only a temporal, temporary precondition. The only real absence marked by the alpha-privative here is that of the phallus, for the virgin has not yet experienced the instrument by which the female is "tamed." No wonder, then, that an "untamed virgin," this absence heretofore of "Aphrodite" as sexual experience, is so attractive to Anchises, for it incites the presence of what is always only temporarily lacking.

An elaborate "costume" – evocative of the first "untamed virgin" – supports the goddess's disguise:

> πέπλον μὲν γὰρ ἔεστο φαεινότερον πυρὸς αὐγῆς,
> εἶχε δ' ἐπιγναμπτὰς ἕλικας κάλυκάς τε φαεινάς,
> ὅρμοι δ' ἀμφ' ἁπαλῇ δειρῇ περικαλλέες ἦσαν
> καλοὶ χρύσειοι παμποίκιλοι· ὡς δὲ σελήνη
> στήθεσιν ἀμφ' ἁπαλοῖσιν ἐλάμπετο,[47] θαῦμα ἰδέσθαι.

> For she was dressed in a gown more shining than the gleam
>   of fire,
> and she wore spiral armlets and shining flower-cup earrings,
> and around her tender neck were exceedingly beautiful
>   necklaces,
> beautiful, golden, all-variegated. And like the moon
> there was a glow around her tender breasts, a wonder
>   to behold.

Homeric Hymn to Aphrodite 86–90

Coupled with her description as "like to an untamed virgin," this account of Aphrodite's appearance evokes the creation of Pandora, the first human female, herself an artificial production παρθένῳ αἰδοίῃ ἴκελον "like to a respected virgin" (*Theogony* 572) and ἀθανάτῃς δὲ θεῇς εἰς ὦπα ἐίσκειν "like to the immortal goddesses in face" (*Works and Days* 62–63).[48] As Aphrodite is "ornamented" (κοσμηθεῖσα, 65) with gold, so Athena "ornamented" (κόσμησε)

169

Pandora (*Theogony* 573 = *Works and Days* 72). Each woman is a θαῦμα ἰδέσθαι "wonder to behold":[49] Aphrodite for the glow of the golden jewelry around her breasts (89–90)[50] and Pandora for her embroidered veil (*Theogony* 574–575) and for the many creatures wrought in her golden crown (*Theogony* 581) – "as many creatures as the land and sea nourish" (*Theogony* 582),[51] the same number as Aphrodite at the start of the hymn is said to "tame" (5). Aphrodite's necklaces are παμποίκιλοι "all-variegated" (89), and both the veil and the crown of Pandora are "intricately wrought" (δαιδαλέην, δαίδαλα, *Theogony* 575, 581). When in the *Theogony* the dressing of Pandora as virgin bride is complete, "wonder (θαῦμα) possessed the immortal gods and mortal men" (588), just as Anchises "wondered" (θαύμαινεν, 84) at the sight of the disguised goddess. And in the *Works and Days*, after describing her dress, the account of Pandora mentions her ψεύδεα "falsehoods," αἱμύλιοι λόγοι "tricky speeches," and ἐπίκλοπον ἦθος "thief's nature" (*Works and Days* 78), just as Aphrodite follows her visual disguise with its verbal counterpart.

The description of Aphrodite's "costume" refers, then, to every aspect of Pandora's appearance, every accoutrement of the virgin bride,[52] except for two essential items, the ζώνη "girdle" and the καλύπτρη or κρήδεμνον "veil."[53] Among the Greek woman's garments, the girdle and the veil are the two most basic symbols of female sexuality as something "inside" to be "uncovered," something, therefore, paradoxically pointed to by its own "covering." And in keeping with this paradoxical phenomenon of revealing by covering, the failure here to refer overtly to the girdle and veil of Aphrodite does not turn out, upon examination, to indicate their absence. Just as the description of Aphrodite's dress is delayed (from the scene of her toilette) until it coincides with Anchises' first sight of it, so reference to the ζώνη is delayed until the moment when Anchises "loosens" it (164), an act that is, like the lifting of the veil, both preliminary to and symbolic of intercourse itself.[54] The narrative does not allow us to "see" the "covering" that marks Aphrodite's sexuality until we are allowed, like voyeurs, to see it uncovered. Similarly, there is no sign of the goddess's veil until – and even then, it would be only indirect and after the fact – Anchises sees her face uncovered and recognizes, at last, divinity in the κάλλος ἄμβροτον "immortal beauty" that ἀπέλαμπεν "was glowing forth" from her now visible cheeks (παρειάων), "the beauty that belongs to well-crowned Aphrodite" (174–175).[55] What "glows" at first (ἐλάμπετο, 90) is the golden jewelry – the necklaces and armbands – around the goddess's breasts. By directing our eyes in this first description to the shining jewelry, the text emphasizes what Anchises saw, the golden aura at the borders of the veil, the sign of all the veil promises.

So Aphrodite would appear here to be imitating Pandora, the prototype of the human virgin bride. But this imitation is far from simple, for what is the human bride except an imitation of Aphrodite?[56] Golden jewelry – both crown and necklaces – are as characteristic of Pandora (see above for her golden crown and *Works and Days* 74 for her ὅρμοι χρύσειοι "golden necklaces") as of Aphrodite "of much gold" (πολυχρύσου 1, 9), "golden" (χρυσέη 93; *Iliad* IX 389; *Odyssey* iv 14; viii 337, 342, xvii 37 = xix 54) and "well-crowned" (ἐϋστεφάνου/-ῳ 6, 175, 287; *Odyssey* viii 267, 288; xviii 193). And in creating Pandora, Hephaestus "likened the beautiful, lovely form of a virgin to the immortal goddesses in face" (*Works and Days* 62–63), just as it is from her face that Aphrodite's "immortal beauty" will shine upon Anchises (174–175). Thus in imitating a human virgin bride, Aphrodite imitates an imitation of herself. In this presentation of herself to Anchises, the "real" Aphrodite comes as an imitation of an imitation of the "real" Aphrodite. Is there any way by which a man could "see through" this imitation, could know that this is "really" Aphrodite in disguise? Some readers have thought the answer is "yes."

According to Podbielski, "despite the fact that she [Aphrodite] plays the quasi-theatrical role of a chaste maiden, she does not lose her divine character at any moment. Her appearance and her dress, by which Anchises is stupefied, are proof of it."[57] Despite the fact that the text says she is ὁμοίη "like, equal to" a virgin in εἶδος "appearance, that which is seen," Aphrodite's appearance, Podbielski argues, remains that of a goddess, since her πέπλος "gown" is termed "more shining than the gleam of fire," a phrase applied elsewhere in hexameter only to the armor of Achilles (*Iliad* XVIII 610); earrings and twisted armbands like hers are attributed elsewhere only to goddesses; and her necklaces are qualified by four epithets, περικαλλέες "exceedingly beautiful," καλοί "beautiful," χρύσειοι "golden," and παμποίκιλοι "all-variegated," and are said to glow like the moon. Aphrodite here may resemble Pandora in kind, as it were, but exceed her in degree. The goddess's necklaces are more beautiful, her gown more resplendent, and her earrings and armbands are extra, something Pandora does not wear at all.[58] To Podbielski, "it is incontestable that this portrait of Aphrodite represents her as the goddess of beauty. The ornaments presented with such precision are connected even aetiologically with her most frequent and most venerable epithet, χρυσέη."[59]

We must conclude, it seems, that Aphrodite's disguise is deliberately ambiguous. She likens her εἶδος "appearance" and μέγεθος "size" to that of a virgin, so that Anchises will not see her for who she is (82–83), and Anchises, when he does see (ὁρόων, 84) this εἶδος and μέγεθος (85, repeated from 82), "wondered" (θαύμαινεν, 84), as do those who view Pandora. But in her

171

"shining apparel" (εἵματα σιγαλόεντα, 85), also the object of Anchises' sight and wonder, Aphrodite permits an excess of golden glow and specific jewels that demarcate her from the model of her imitation (the virgin imitating Aphrodite). She permits one to see signs of her divinity and maybe even of her uniqueness as golden goddess of love. In her attempt to seduce Anchises, Aphrodite does not give up her inimitable singularity. Despite her disguise as human so as not to be "recognized with the eyes," she remains recognizably divine so as not to give up her unique allure.

But can this be right? We have to ask whether Aphrodite could have deliberately included the visual marks that can unmask her disguise, the signs of her real identity, without forfeiting the imitation upon which her goal, as the "real" Aphrodite, depends.[60] Will such an ambiguous imitation – the εἶδος "appearance" of a human virgin, but still visibly divine – not be doomed to the either/or logic of the viewer? Or can Aphrodite have it both ways? Perhaps we are to conclude that the goddess's epiphany is a "wonder to behold" precisely because it presents an ambiguity that confounds or, better, seduces the analytical capacity of the seer/knower – that such is the strange epistemology of the θαῦμα. And perhaps, then, Aphrodite's ambiguous epiphany works such thaumaturgy by virtue of what is left unmentioned, "unseen" or not yet seen in this vision of the goddess – her veil. Is it by covering her face that Aphrodite's unique glamour can work on her victim without giving her away? We must look to the victim's reaction.

IV. Aphrodite's Verbal Epiphany

ἔπος *of the Male Seized by* ἔρος

Anchises' reaction to the θαῦμα of Aphrodite's appearance is described thus:

> Ἀγχίσην δ' ἔρος εἷλεν, ἔπος δέ μιν ἀντίον ηὔδα.
>
> *eros* seized Anchises, and he spoke an *epos* in reply.
>
> *Homeric Hymn to Aphrodite* 91

Only gradually does the full significance of this line emerge. In a poem where the repetitions of structure, theme, word, and sound are, as Pellizer has demonstrated,[61] singularly extensive and meaningful, and the oppositional structures are so overtly thematic, we may notice the alliteration between ἔρος "eros, sexual desire" and ἔπος "epos, speech in epic," two ἐ-initial, dissyllabic, –ος-ending words, framing the ἐ-initial εἷλεν "seized." This specific collocation is unparalleled in extant hexameter, but the use of *eros* as subject elsewhere is so restricted as to suggest a special relationship between the two words here.

In the *Iliad*, *eros* appears in the nominative as subject only in the Διὸς ἀπάτη "deception of Zeus" of Book XIV and in the scene in the bedroom between Paris and Helen in Book III. In the "deception of Zeus," *eros* figures in a pattern of sight and speech parallel to the one we find here in the hymn.[62] Hera suddenly appears before Zeus on Mount Ida, just as Aphrodite has suddenly appeared in the same place to Anchises:

ἴδε δὲ νεφεληγερέτα Ζεύς.
ὡς δ᾽ ἴδεν, ὥς μιν ἔρως πυκινὰς φρένας ἀμφεκάλυψεν[63]
οἷον ὅτε πρῶτόν περ ἐμισγέσθην φιλότητι,
εἰς εὐνὴν φοιτῶντε, φίλους λήθοντε τοκῆας.
στῆ δ᾽ αὐτῆς προπάροιθεν ἔπος τ᾽ ἔφατ᾽ τ᾽ ὀνόμαζεν.

Cloud-gathering Zeus <u>saw</u> her.
And as he <u>saw</u> her, so <u>eros</u> <u>veiled</u> his <u>clever</u> <u>wits</u>,
as when for the very first time they were mixed in love-making,
going together into the bed, having escaped the notice of their
  parents.
And he stood right in front of her, spoke an *epos* and called her
  by name.

Iliad XIV 293–297

In this *epos* Zeus calls Hera by name (for she is not visually disguised) and asks her purpose in coming, but in her reply Hera δολοφρονέουσα "devising a deception (δόλος)" claims to be on her way to reconcile Oceanus and Tethys, long estranged from love-making (*Iliad* XIV 297–298, 300–306). Accepting this verbal disguise, Zeus replies by urging that they turn to love-making:

οὐ γάρ πώ ποτέ μ᾽ ὧδε θεᾶς ἔρος οὐδὲ γυναικὸς
θυμὸν ἐνὶ στήθεσσι περιπροχυθεὶς ἐδάμασσεν . . .
ὡς σέο νῦν ἔραμαι καί με γλυκὺς ἵμερος αἱρεῖ.

for not ever before has <u>eros</u> of goddess or woman so
flooded and <u>tamed</u> the heart in my breast . . .
as now I <u>have</u> <u>eros</u> for you and <u>sweet</u> <u>sexual</u> <u>passion</u> seizes me.

Iliad XIV 315–16, 328

In their bedroom, Paris lures Helen with the same language:

οὐ γάρ πώ ποτέ μ᾽ ὧδε γ᾽ ἔρως φρένας ἀμφεκάλυψεν, . . .

173

ὥς σεο νῦν ἔραμαι καί με γλυκὺς ἵμερος αἱρεῖ.

for not ever before has *eros* so veiled my wits, ...
as now I have *eros* for you and sweet sexual passion seizes me.

Iliad III 442, 446

Both Hera and Helen yield to their husbands' *eros*, a desire stronger than that of their first clandestine intercourse, a desire that "veils the wits."

In the Διὸς ἀπάτη "deception of Zeus," then, we see the relation between *eros* "sexual desire" and *epos* "speech in epic" unfold in the following sequence:

1. The male's *eros* "veils his wits" and provokes an *epos* asking why the female has come.
2. A δόλος "deception" speech by the female disguises the truth.
3. Accepting the female's verbal deceit, the male urges indulgence of *eros*.
4. The *eros* is consummated.

This sequence raises the possibility that a similar proceeding may follow the conjunction of *eros* and *epos* in the hymn. And indeed, without awareness of the Iliadic pattern, one can miss the full significance of Anchises' first *epos*.

Anchises' speech seems to ignore the ambiguity of the goddess's epiphany. As if the θαῦμα "wonder" of Aphrodite were so dazzling that he did not notice her likeness to a παρθένος "virgin," Anchises speaks as if she is unambiguously divine.[64] That is, he responds with a speech that bears, as Podbielski has shown, all the elements of a cult hymn: the hymnic invocation χαῖρε "hail"; a catalogue of alternate names; the promise to build her an altar and make seasonal offerings, in short, to found a cult; and the request for blessings in return, here, a long, wealthy, and prestigious life among the Trojans and a vigorous progeny (92–106). Unlike Odysseus who, when confronted by an unknown female in the countryside, seeks the identity of Nausicaa by posing both alternatives, "if you are a goddess" and "if you are a mortal" (*Odyssey* vi 149–153), Anchises acts as if he has not even considered the possibility that this apparition is not divine. His words would be the expression not of *eros* but of σέβας "reverential awe."[65] And indeed his speech does work as the proper human response to Aphrodite's true identity: his petition does foretell the true outcome of the encounter.

But we deduce such simplicity of motive – that Anchises has no idea that this female is not a goddess – at the cost of the same omission it imputes to the hero: we ignore the text's clear insistence that Aphrodite appears "like an untamed virgin," that is, as a sexually available mortal woman, and that "*eros* seized" Anchises. The evidence of the *Iliad* indicates that the *epos* following *eros* is an attempt to determine the reason why the female has come. And considered in light of the conventions of indirect speech in early Greek, Anchises' words here could be in service of such an effort. Compare the αἶνος "testing discourse" by which the disguised Odysseus tells Eumaeus how the "real" Odysseus gave him a cloak at Troy, so as to test whether the swineherd will be hospitable to his master's guest-friend and give him a cloak as well.[66] On analogy with this αἶνος, Anchises' speech may be an attempt to resolve the ambiguity of this female's appearance, to determine just who she is and to obtain from her satisfaction of his *eros*, should her identity permit. If such is his motive, a "cult hymn" is definitely the right way to begin.

Assuming the exclusivity of the options it presents, ambiguity can be resolved logically by treating one possibility as true and seeing what results. In the case of Aphrodite's ambiguous epiphany, which possibility should be tested first? Surely that the female is a goddess, for if she were divine, any suggestion of mortality – especially an erotic overture – could be a dangerous insult. A fully detailed "cult hymn" is the right first response, whether Anchises believes she is a goddess or is not sure. Anchises' speech can thus conform to the order of *eros* and *epos* in the *Iliad*, and need not imply that Aphrodite's disguise as a mortal virgin has been in vain. What we should rather say is that as yet Anchises' own belief cannot be certainly determined. In motivation his *epos* is as ambiguous as is the epiphany itself. But it is the right speech, whether he already recognizes or is testing her divinity.

Aphrodite's Erotic Fiction

Just as Hera replies to Zeus' *epos* with a δόλος "deception" speech, so Aphrodite now answers Anchises with a deceitful *epos* of her own.[67] The effect of her speech is specified at its conclusion:

> ὣς εἰποῦσα θεὰ <u>γλυκὺν ἵμερον ἔμβαλε</u> θυμῷ
> Ἀγχίσην δ' <u>ἔρος εἷλεν</u>, <u>ἔπος</u> τ' ἔφατ' ἔκ τ' ὀνόμαζεν.

> By speaking thus, the goddess <u>cast</u> <u>sweet</u> <u>sexual</u> <u>passion</u> into his
>   heart.
> <u>eros</u> <u>seized</u> Anchises, and he spoke an <u>epos</u> and called her by
>   name.

> *Homeric Hymn to Aphrodite* 143–144

By recalling line 73, where Aphrodite "casts sexual passion (ἵμερον)" into the breasts of the beasts; lines 45 and 53, where Zeus "casts sweet sexual passion (γλυκὺν ἵμερον)" for Anchises into Aphrodite's own heart; and line 2, where Aphrodite is said to "rouse sweet sexual passion (γλυκὺν ἵμερον)" in the gods, line 143 implies that Aphrodite's "speaking thus" here is an instance of the power of "Aphrodite" in action. And by repeating the *eros/epos* conjunction that followed her earlier, visual epiphany ("*eros* seized Anchises, and he spoke an *epos* in reply," 91), line 144 implies that the speech just concluded is that visual epiphany's analogue, a verbal version of its deceptive ambiguity, a verbal θαῦμα "wonder" to parallel the earlier "cosmos" of sight and smell. By what means does the goddess's speech achieve its erotic ἀπάτη "deception"? How does it succeed in persuading Anchises that she is an "untamed virgin" meant to be his own?

Wielding at will, like the Muses in the *Theogony*, both ἀληθέα "true things" and ψεύδεα ὁμοῖα ἐτύμοισιν "false things like to real things," Aphrodite first denies the truth (her divinity) and then produces an imitation of truth, a convincing verisimilitude.[68] Successful imitation depends, as again the Speech of the Muses confirms, upon knowledge – knowledge in this case of what will "really" seduce a male of the heroic tradition, not only what plot will prove irresistible, but also the rhetorical means by which this tradition creates the "effect of the real."[69] Accordingly, having contradicted Anchises' earlier list of divine names (one of which is her own) with a fictitious human parentage (111–112), Aphrodite covers her fiction with the mechanics of persuasive credibility. Before being asked, she answers the question of how she knows Anchises' language:

> γλῶσσαν δ' ὑμετέρην καὶ ἡμετέρην σάφα οἶδα.
> Τρωὰς γὰρ μεγάρῳ με τροφὸς τρέφεν· ἡ δὲ διαπρὸ
> σμικρὴν παῖδ' ἀτίταλλε, φίλης παρὰ μητρὸς ἑλοῦσα.
> ὣς δή τοι γλῶσσάν γε καὶ ὑμετέρην εὖ οἶδα.

> And I know clearly your language and mine,
> for a Trojan nurse raised me in my home: and right from
> the time
> I was a small child she nursed me, after taking me from my
> dear mother.
> So indeed I know well your language too.

> *Homeric Hymn to Aphrodite* 113–116

Chronological circumstructure (present result – past cause – present result), a figural guarantor of narrative reliability in epic, marks not only this "how I know the Trojan language" story, but also Aphrodite's "how I got here" story:[70]

> νῦν δέ μ' ἀνήρπαξε χρυσόρραπις Ἀργειφόντης
> ἐκ χοροῦ Ἀρτέμιδος χρυσηλακάτου, κελαδεινῆς.
> πολλαὶ δὲ νύμφαι καὶ παρθένοι ἀλφεσίβοιαι
> παίζομεν, ἀμφὶ δ' ὅμιλος ἀπείριτος ἐστεφάνωτο.
> ἔνθεν μ' ἥρπαξε χρυσόρραπις Ἀργειφόντης·
> πολλὰ δ' ἔπ' ἤγαγεν ἔργα καταθνητῶν ἀνθρώπων,
> πολλὴν δ' ἄκληρόν τε καὶ ἄκτιτον, ἣν διὰ θῆρες
> ὠμοφάγοι φοιτῶσι κατὰ σκιόεντας ἐναύλους.

> And now Hermes the Slayer of Argus, he of the golden wand,
>   abducted me
> from the dancing group of Artemis, she of the golden arrows,
>   sounding loudly as she hunts.
> Many of us, maidens and marriageable virgins,
> we were playing, and an immense crowd was circling around.
> From there Hermes the Slayer of Argus, he of the golden wand,
>   abducted me.
> Over many worked fields of mortal men he led me
> and over much earth [sc. γαῖαν], both unapportioned and unset-
>   tled, where wild beasts
> who eat raw flesh roam through shadowy glens.

> *Homeric Hymn to Aphrodite* 117–124

And since the appearance of being a virgin, indeed, a helpless virgin, is the essential element in her disguise, she adds a plaintive intensity to her account of being abducted from the maidens' chorus through insistent line-initial anaphora: πολλαί "many" (νύμφαι "virgins," 119), πολλά "many" (ἔργα "worked fields," 122), πολλήν "much" (sc. γαῖαν, 123), linked through the word-initial π's with the crucial phrase παρθένοι παίζομεν "we virgins were playing" (119–120). These formal structures ornament the most seductive of epic plots: the ἁρπαγή "abduction."

The plot of the ἁρπαγή "abduction" is appealing to men – as the *Iliad* might testify – because it provides the opportunity for both transgression and rectification of society's social order: both the illicit pleasure of taking another man's woman and the glory of (re-)appropriating the woman in legitimate marriage, often through mortal combat.[71] Aphrodite makes her version of this plot especially seductive by maximizing the glory and pleasure of its "hero" Anchises, while minimizing his guilt and risk. Anchises' honor is not only preserved, it is actually increased by having a god abduct the woman he is supposedly to take for his own. The goddess's tale then speaks of both legitimate and illegitimate love-making with the woman – and in that order, thus intimating the possibility (taken up later by Anchises) of the first as a justification for the second. Aphrodite first portrays a legal, fruitful marriage between the two of them as divine dictate (126–127): "And he [Hermes] used to declare that I would be called Anchises' wedded wife beside the bed and would bear you glorious children." She describes her coming as nothing less than κρατερὴ ἀνάγκη "strong necessity" (130).

Having thus established their legitimate marriage as divinely ordained, the goddess then puts into words the unlawful union that is her true desire. Her *modus dicendi* is the alpha-privative:

> ἀλλά σε πρὸς Ζηνὸς γουνάζομαι ἠδὲ τοκήων
> ἐσθλῶν· οὐ μὲν γάρ κε κακοὶ τοιόνδε τέκοιεν·
> <u>ἀδμήτην</u> μ᾽ ἀγαγὼν καὶ <u>ἀπειρήτην</u> φιλότητος
> πατρί τε σῷ δεῖξον καὶ μητέρι κέδν᾽ εἰδυίῃ
> σοῖς τε κασιγνήτοις, οἵ τοι ὁμόθεν γεγάασιν.
> <u>οὔ</u> σφιν <u>ἀεικελίη</u> νυὸς ἔσσομαι, ἀλλ᾽ εἰκυῖα.

> But I beg you by Zeus and your noble
> parents – for no base-born folk could beget such a man as you –
> lead me <u>untamed</u> (ἀ-<u>δμήτην</u>) and <u>inexperienced</u> (ἀ-<u>πειρήτην</u>) in
>   love-making
> and present me to your father and your careful-minded mother
> and your relations descended from the same stock.
> <u>Not</u> an <u>unseemly</u> (ἀ-<u>εικελίη</u>) daughter- and sister-in-law shall
>   I be to them, but seemly.

> *Homeric Hymn to Aphrodite* 131–136

Just as her visual epiphany manifested the goddess of sexuality as her opposite – the un-/not-yet-tamed virgin – so the alpha-privatives here present the "premarital" union of Aphrodite and Anchises in its negated form. The effect is like that of a *praeteritio*: "I shall pass over saying that . . . etc." What is denied and expelled at the level of the narrating is (re–)admitted at the level of the narration. One gets the satisfaction of saying something without the technical responsibility. Similarly, here, by means of the alpha-privatives, Aphrodite can include the pleasure of forbidden sex in her abduction plot. Or we should rather say that she gives a slight peek at such pleasure behind the "veil" of the negated adjectives – untamed (ἀ-δμήτην), inexperienced (ἀ-πειρήτην), οὔ ἀεικελίη (not unseemly), for she no sooner utters these seductive terms than she provides her tale with a "festive conclusion," the marriage, complete with lavish dowry to enrich the groom and the prestigious wedding feast itself (137–142).[72] The "peek" of the alpha-privatives is enough, however. As we saw before in the case of the ἀδμήτη παρθένος "untamed virgin" (82), alpha-privative adjectives, expressing the lack of sexual experience are, when applied to human virgins, not complete negations – not absolutely "no," but only "not yet." They signify only the absence heretofore of the phallus and thus incite its presence. Such is the testimony of Anchises' reaction to this tale.

ἔρος *and Epistemology*

In the pattern of *eros* and *epos* in the *Iliad*, the δόλος-speech of the female is followed by another *epos* by the male in which, without verifying the claims of the female's verbal disguise, he urges consummation of his desire. Here in the hymn the male would seem to be more careful. In the *epos* in which Anchises displays the *eros* aroused by Aphrodite's "epic" imitation of an untamed virgin, the hero makes his call for immediate love-making conditional upon the truth of the female's tale:

> εἰ μὲν θνητή τ' ἐσσι, γυνὴ δέ σε γείνατο μήτηρ,
> Ὀτρεὺς δ' ἐστὶ πατὴρ ὀνομακλυτός, ὡς ἀγορεύεις,
> ἀθανάτου δὲ ἕκητι διακτόρου ἐνθάδ' ἱκάνεις
> Ἑρμέω, ἐμὴ δ' ἄλοχος κεκλήσεαι ἤματα πάντα·
> οὔ τις ἔπειτα θεῶν οὔτε θνητῶν ἀνθρώπων
> ἐνθάδε με σχήσει, πρὶν σῇ φιλότητι μιγῆναι
> αὐτίκα νῦν· οὐδ' εἴ κεν ἑκηβόλος αὐτὸς Ἀπόλλων
> τόξου ἀπ' ἀργυρέου προΐῃ βέλεα στονόεντα.
> βουλοίμην κεν ἔπειτα, <u>γύναι εἰκυῖα θεῇσι</u>,
> σῆς εὐνῆς ἐπιβὰς δῦναι δόμον Ἄιδος εἴσω.

> If on one hand you are mortal, and a woman was the mother
>   who bore you,
>   and famous-named Otreus is your father, as you say,
>   and you come here by the will of the immortal guide

Hermes, and you will be called my wife all our days,
no one then of gods or mortal men
will here restrain me from being mixed with you in love-making
immediately now. Not if far-shooting Apollo himself
should cast forth baneful arrows from his silver bow.
I would wish then, <u>woman like to the goddesses</u>,
if I could mount upon your bed, to go down into the house
of Hades.

Homeric Hymn to Aphrodite 145–154

This speech complements Anchises' first *epos* (92–106) in that it seems carefully constructed to test the second alternative of Aphrodite's ambiguity, the possibility that she is a human virgin. If the first speech, while piously eschewing an overt conditional construction, nevertheless meant in effect, "if you are a goddess, I shall establish your cult here, and do you bless me accordingly," this second speech is openly and profusely conditional. Anchises' determination to make love immediately – even at the cost of death itself – is made dependent, for all its vehemence, on a five-fold protasis, listing the key items of Aphrodite's tale.

By the logic of this grammar, everything depends upon the veracity of Aphrodite's claimed identity. But how can Anchises' conditional construction determine the identity of the female? The implied reasoning seems to be that if she is not a human virgin destined to be his wife, she certainly would not persist in her story and acquiesce to premarital loss of virginity.[73] If she is who she claims to be, she would have no need to resist, especially if her intended flatters her with a hyperbolic expression of desire – and what could be more flattering or hyperbolic than Anchises' final vow? If she does not resist, her claim and Anchises' reaction to it must be correct. The calculation would seem flawless: this female is ambiguously divine and human; to the conventionally correct treatment of a goddess, she has not responded as a goddess; if she is not the virgin she claims to be, she will not maintain the claim at the cost of an unlawful liaison that would jeopardize her subsequent marriageability. She must be, as the text with perfect irony makes Anchises call her, a "woman like to the goddesses" (153).

The only fault in this reasoning is the prior assumption of innocent ambiguity on the part of the veiled stranger. Anchises' αἶνος-like speeches will determine the truth only if Aphrodite responds with truth and not its imitation. For all their accord with traditional protocols and sound logic, Anchises' speeches ignore the possibility of duplicitous ambiguity, ever present in the capacity of language embodied in the Speech of the Muses:

ἴδμεν ψεύδεα πολλὰ λέγειν ἐτύμοισιν ὁμοῖα,
ἴδμεν δ' εὖτ' ἐθέλωμεν ἀληθέα γηρύσασθαι.

we know how to say many false things like to real things,
and we know, whenever we want, how to utter true things.

Theogony 27–28

As Aphrodite has disguised herself as "like to (ὁμοίη) an untamed virgin" (82) so the Muses know how to utter falsehoods "like to (ὁμοῖα)" the truth. Why is this alternative of knowledge-based ambiguity not anticipated by a male so cultivated as is Anchises in epic conventions? The repetition of *eros* as the motive of his *epos* suggests the answer: to discern the "truth" of this situation would be to discover the prohibition of his *eros*. Just as *eros* for Hera "veiled the clever wits" of Zeus, so the *eros* aroused by Aphrodite's imitation "veils" the one logical alternative that Anchises' speeches fail to take into account, that her story is an erotic fiction, one that covers not a "woman like to the goddesses" but a goddess deliberately (dissimulating by) simulating a mortal virgin. Aphrodite's costume with its glow of gold blinds Anchises to this possibility, for were he to "see" it, he would "see through" it, he would "recognize the goddess with his eyes" (83) and could not "lift the veil." Thus, through a sort of sympathetic magic, *eros* provoked by imitation turns the logical process of truth determination into an imitation of a sincere epistemological quest.[74] For when motivated by erotic desire, the goal of the process is not really to find the truth, but to find that the imitation of the true – the sexually available virgin – is truthful.

No man whose ardor is aroused by the "veiled Aphrodite" could discern that she is "really" the goddess of sexuality imitating a virgin and not his destined bride. But it would not make any difference, even if he could. For Pandora, the virgin bride, is herself an imitation of Aphrodite, and thus the "veiled Aphrodite" is the model of how all mortal virgins present themselves to men. The female is an "imitation" either way, and which way the imitation is "really" going can be decided only after the male – like Anchises here or Epimetheus in the Hesiodic texts – lifts the καλύπτρη and loosens the ζώνη, and thereby learns for himself what they conceal. But this knowledge cannot come from sight alone.

181

A Disguised Bridal Scene

Following Anchises' second *epos*, Aphrodite's answer – the reply that would parallel her earlier fiction – comes in the form of ambiguous silence, not denying and so apparently confirming the truth of the conditions he posed. This phase of her verbal disguise works so quickly that without the expectation of the female's δόλος "deception" speech following the male's erotically motivated *epos*, one would almost miss it. For at once the mode of encounter moves for the first time from sight and speech to action – more precisely, to actions suggestive of a marriage ceremony.

In keeping with the ambiguity of Aphrodite here, the ensuing bridal scene is both real and unreal. For the man, it is an actual passage from the "untamed virginity" of adolescence as a hunter to an adulthood productive of children – and to this degree a "real" marriage.[75] And if she were who she seems, it would be a similar sexual initiation for the goddess as well. It is at least her first liaison with a mortal. Accordingly, Anchises "takes her hand" – the initiatory gesture of the wedding ceremony – and she "walks, with her face turned around and her beautiful eyes downcast" with the shyness of a virgin bride (155–156).[76] From their sexual union she will give birth to Anchises' child and become the mother of his race. But this "Pandora" is also a goddess in disguise, about to consummate her seduction of a mortal. And this "wedding" outside the city, apart from the company of the families it would unite, is an untamed imitation of the civilized institution.

Such is the symbolism of the coverings upon their marriage bed:

αὐτὰρ ὕπερθεν
ἄρκτων δέρματ' ἔκειτο βαρυφθόγγων τε λεόντων,
τοὺς αὐτὸς κατέπεφνεν ἐν οὔρεσιν ὑψηλοῖσιν.

And on top
were laid the skins of bears and deep-roaring lions,
that he himself had killed in the high mountains.

Homeric Hymn to Aphrodite 158–160

As Anchises' own trophies, these wild animal skins signal his success as a hunter, the status preliminary to legitimate marriage and the assumption it brings of the adult male's role in the *polis*, where he will be called upon to father future citizens and to devote his hunting skills to defending the city as a warrior. The skins are thus the male counterpart to the accoutrements of the female virgin, marks of being ripe for the union from which new life is born.

Specifying the animals killed by Anchises, the bear and the lion, reinforces this association with fertility by recalling the earlier mention of the beasts, including lions and bears, who respond to the advent of Aphrodite by lying down two by two (69–74). Now the goddess's power embraces Anchises, too, as the killer of beasts will join the beasts in procreative coupling.[77] But this recollection of Aphrodite's sway over beasts also points to the disparity of status between the man and the goddess and to the irregularity of their union.

By themselves the skins testify to Anchises' prowess, his capacity to "break" wild beasts on high mountains.[78] Making love to the goddess upon these furs would seem a similar act of domination, a "breaking" of the παρθένος ἀδμήτη "unbroken virgin." Yet by recalling the goddess's earlier epiphany, these blankets also bespeak the universality of Aphrodite's power – a power of confounding the distinction between real and imitation, and a universality confirmed in this imitation of domination wherein Anchises is actually subjected and, indeed, subjects himself to the goddess's will. In "taking" his bride, every husband yields to Aphrodite, but his bride is not usually that goddess in disguise – or is she? Can he know for sure? This is a marriage outside the city. Can the city by its institution of father-rule securely exclude such a wildly paradoxical union in which the man "puts himself underneath by putting himself on top" – upon fur skins that figure this self-imposed sexual trope?[79]

This intertwining of sexual context and deception culminates in what is stated and unstated, seen and not seen, in the final act of the seduction. There is first a movement toward the ultimate moment in a wedding, the moment, in fact, usually hidden from all outside view, the deflowering of the bride. The hymn provides more than a brief, discreet glimpse. The text stages the progress of erotic arousal, as it describes Anchises detaching the goddess's "cosmos" object by object, garment by garment – in the same words used to describe his first sight of them: the γναμπτάς θ' ἕλικας κάλυκάς τε καὶ ὅρμους "spiral armlets and shining flower-cup earrings" (163 and 87) and the εἵματα σιγαλόεντα "shining apparel" (164 and 85).[80] We are offered the voyeuristic satisfaction of watching him strip off what he gazed at before. But shared terms also link this undressing with Aphrodite's dressing of herself at Paphos: Anchises takes the "ornament from her skin" (κόσμον . . . ἀπὸ χροός, 162) as she was before "ornamented about her skin with gold" (περὶ χροῒ . . . χρυσῷ κοσμηθεῖσα, 64–65). The εἵματα σιγαλόεντα "shining apparel" he now lays upon the "silver-studded seat" (164–165) recall the εἵματα καλά "beautiful apparel" we saw her assume inside her redolent temple (64). As we watch Anchises take off what we saw the goddess put on before, we are forced to see, at the pinnacle of his erotic victory, his epistemological defeat – and to see it in the larger context of divine will.

This ironic vision of mortal deception and divine knowledge is what the hymn ultimately stresses about this mortal-plus-immortal union. After describing his removal of Aphrodite's clothes, the text moves silently past any mention of how the goddess looked to Anchises or of how he felt. As if to save its hero and its audience as well from the penalty for seeing a goddess naked,[81] the hymn moves immediately to pronounce their union a function of human ignorance, with all the hieratic solemnity of a double expression of divine will (166–167):

> ὁ δ' ἔπειτα θεῶν ἰότητι καὶ αἴσῃ
> ἀθανάτῃ παρέλεκτο θεᾷ βροτός, οὐ σάφα εἰδώς.

> Then he by the will of the gods and by fate
> lay beside an immortal goddess, he a mortal, not knowing
>   clearly.[82]

Homeric Hymn to Aphrodite 166–167

Now Anchises has taken off Aphrodite's clothes. Now he could see her without any veil, but whatever else it may have offered, the sight was not enough to solve the ambiguity of her appearance. Here we do not have to wonder about the actual state of Anchises' awareness – whether he is only pretending ignorance and did, as he will claim later to Aphrodite, recognize her from the start. It is not that he saw she was the goddess and just did not care, for we have him οὐ σάφα εἰδώς "not knowing clearly" on the authority of the hymnic voice itself.

In this context, it is significant that what we do not see, the part of the undressing that the text does not explicitly describe, is the actual removal of Aphrodite's veil, the action that would parallel the ἀνακαλυπτήρια "unveiling" in an actual wedding.[83] Unless she is not wearing one – unless her disguise as an "untamed virgin" lacks this essential mark of modesty – Anchises must have lifted her veil, but the text says nothing about him doing so. It says nothing about his seeing the goddess's face, the locus of unique identity, or more specifically, the mouth, the displaced parallel of the private parts below. By this omission, the hymn may reproduce Anchises' own visual and mental experience. By not saying that he removes the veil, the text suggests that Anchises saw but did not really see, and that this would-be bride thus remained unrecognized in the very moment when a groom can view her in her uniqueness most intimately. As before when he questioned her, Anchises' *eros* blinds him to Aphrodite's true identity, even as he sees her. Thus does the goddess remain disguised, even when naked. Even seeing the goddess unveiled and even – as is perhaps silently implied – the knowledge that comes with love-making itself is not enough to give the clear knowledge that resolves ambiguity.

From the perspective of an Anchises – of any man whom Aphrodite and *eros* deceive – the inside of the woman, her truth, remains impenetrable even to intercourse. In its desire to tame, the phallus is blinded. A man can lift the veil of the goddess disguised as a virgin. He can see her body naked. He can "know" it, but such knowledge is not insight. The man can recognize the truth only after his *eros* is spent, when the woman herself "lifts her veil" and shows who and what she is.

V. Aphrodite's Epiphany Unveiled

It is only when Aphrodite herself (αὐτή, 171) puts on her clothes, thus recalling the previous sequence of her dressing and undressing,[84] and stands to her full height that her true face is unveiled. Indeed, we see it before Anchises, upon whom she has "poured sweet, deep sleep" (170–171): the "immortal beauty, such as is characteristic of well-crowned Cythereia"[85] that now "shone (ἀπέλαμπεν) from her cheeks" (174–175), as before it was the glow of her jewelry that "shone around her tender breasts" (ἐλάμπετο, 90).[86] Thus is inaugurated the revelation to the mortal male of the goddess's true identity, an epiphany that reverses their apparent positions in this confrontation, rendering the human male submissive and the goddess openly supreme. Yet this reversal itself reverses, as defeat becomes victory and praise becomes blame.

Aphrodite couples the visual revelation of her true identity with the speech that might have come, instead of silence, after the five-fold protasis of Anchises' erotic *epos* (145–154), in which he called the goddess a "woman like to (εἰκυῖα) the goddesses" (153), ironically recalling the goddess's initial disguise as "like to (ὁμοίη) an untamed virgin" (82) and its goal of clouding his vision, μή μιν ταρβήσειεν ἐν ὀφθαλμοῖσι νοήσας "lest he tremble in fear, having recognized her with his eyes" (83). In terms that recall this earlier disguise as well as its goal, she now addresses her sleeping lover:

> ὄρσεο, Δαρδανίδη: τί νυ νήγρετον[87] ὕπνον ἰαύεις;
> καὶ φράσαι, εἴ τοι ὁμοίη ἐγὼν ἰνδάλλομαι εἶναι,
> οἵην δή με τὸ πρῶτον ἐν ὀφθαλμοῖσι νόησας.

> Rise, son of Dardanus! Why do you sleep the sleep from which there is no waking?

> And consider if I seem to you to be like to such a one
> as I seemed, when you first recognized me with your eyes.

Homeric Hymn to Aphrodite 177–179

Anchises' reaction, upon seeing her neck and the beautiful eyes no longer "cast down," is the trembling (τάρβησεν, 182) her disguise aimed before to forestall, and in a repetition of her previous, bridelike gesture, "he turned his eyes askance in the other direction" (182).

The reversal is figured in privative-form adjectives that now characterize Anchises' condition. Just as Aphrodite had disguised herself as a virgin un-tamed by sex, so now Anchises' sexual initiation leaves him the mirror image – parallel but opposite – of his lover in a sleep termed "un-waking" (νήγρετον, 177), a state in which the phallus cannot rise again to tame. And so he now supplicates his earlier supplicant:[88]

> αὐτίκα ς' ὡς τὰ πρῶτα, θεά, ἴδον ὀφθαλμοῖσιν,
> ἔγνων ὡς θεὸς ἦσθα· σὺ δ' οὐ νημερτὲς ἔειπες.
> ἀλλά σε πρὸς Ζηνὸς γουνάζομαι αἰγιόχοιο,
> μή με ζῶντ' ἀμενηνὸν ἐν ἀνθρώποισιν ἐάσῃς
> ναίειν, ἀλλ' ἐλέαιρ'· ἐπεὶ οὐ βιοθάλμιος ἀνὴρ
> γίγνεται, ὅς τε θεαῖς εὐνάζεται ἀθανάτῃσι.

> Immediately, when I first saw you, goddess, with my eyes
> I recognized that you were divine. But you did not speak
>   unerringly.
> But by Zeus who holds the aegis, I beseech you –
> do not allow me, living but without strength,[89]
> to dwell among men, but have pity. For no man's life blooms
> who sleeps with immortal goddesses.

Homeric Hymn to Aphrodite 185–190

Sympathy with Anchises' dread of impotence might obscure his masterful use of traditional rhetoric to bolster a proposal that is in fact far from timid and that bears something of the same ambiguity with which he first addressed the disguised goddess.

Submissive Anchises: Erotic Hero or God?

Why should a plea to escape the punishment of one who sleeps with a goddess be prefaced by an insistence that he knew she was a goddess from the start? Would not a claim of simple and total ignorance be more logical? Anchises knows better. He knows the traditionally proper response to the epiphany of a previously disguised goddess, just as he knew before the right way to test her ambiguous appearance. This much is clear from comparing his words with those of Odysseus, after Athena dispels her disguise as a "grand, beautiful woman, who knows glorious handiwork" – another case of the goddess imitating a human imitation of herself (*Odyssey* xiii 289).[90] To Athena Odysseus says: "It is difficult, goddess, for a man to recognize you on meeting, even one exceedingly knowledgeable. For you liken yourself to everything" (xiii 312–313).[91] In both cases the hero aggressively defends his powers of perception, so that his defeat both proves and compliments the superiority of the goddess's powers of deception, while making his mistake no more avoidable than his human condition.

If Anchises is more aggressively self-justifying and, by the logic of this approach, thereby more complimentary, it is because, unlike Odysseus, he is asking for something. He is asking for nothing less than the pinnacle of sexual success for a mortal male: to see the naked Aphrodite and get away with it, to sleep with her and not "go down into the house of Hades" (154). In this moment the rightness of his first response to the disguised Aphrodite shows most clearly. For his having hailed her as a goddess is now plausible evidence of having then recognized her as such. And reiterating that recognition now serves to acknowledge her divinity once again. So also, indirectly, does the charge that she spoke οὐ νημερτές "not unerringly" – again a privative form, here testifying to human error (ἁμαρτάνω) whose absence (ν-) is not absolute, but able itself to be negated (οὐ) simply by a goddess's deceptive speech. The human knowledge that cancels error is itself cancelled when it comes up against divine lies.

Anchises' *apologia* thus amounts to a reestablishment of the boundary that divides divine from human, the boundary crossed by his "mixture" with the goddess. In his intercourse with Aphrodite, Anchises has intruded upon divine knowledge. He has seen and thus knows what only a god should see and know, the goddess's naked body. The normal compensation in early Greek thought for such an elevation above the level of the human mind is a corresponding degradation at the level of the body: blindness, maiming, impotence, or death.[92] For sexual access to divinity, a man pays with a loss of his capacity for sexual reproduction. Anchises seems to ask, in effect, that for reassuming the human condition of acknowledged powerlessness over against divine ambiguity, his body may be allowed to retain its human vigor. In epic tradition, this combination of experiencing divine knowledge with unimpaired human life is not without parallel. Odysseus braved Hades to gain wisdom from

Teiresias and returned home successfully thereafter. What Anchises wants from Aphrodite would seem to be an erotic counterpart to Odysseus' heroism, just as he earlier besought the goddess for distinction among the Trojans and a flourishing progeny (103–104).[93]

But Anchises may also be asking for something more, an experience of divine sexuality that ends not in erotic heroism but in immortality itself. It is the claim of van der Ben that we must give full force to ἐν ἀνθρώποισιν ναίειν in 188–189 and realize that Anchises is asking not "to dwell among men" but to dwell among the gods.[94] Taking ζῶντα as conditional, he translates: "But I beseech you, by Zeus who holds the aegis, not to let me, if I shall live [i.e., escape the normal punishment for intercourse with a goddess], dwell strengthless among humankind." This interpretation is required, van der Ben argues, to make sense of Aphrodite's reply that effectively grants Anchises erotic heroism, but refuses immortality by adducing the negative examples of Ganymede and Tithonus. Anchises seeks to resolve their illicit mixture not by returning to mortal status but by himself becoming Aphrodite's undying lover.

To recapitulate the turnings of this scene: At the epiphany of Aphrodite unveiled, Anchises trembles and looks away. For the first time, he does not gaze directly at the goddess. Shielding his eyes is a sign of fearful submission. But it also affords a chance for Anchises to see apart from Aphrodite's blinding beauty. From that point of view he can voice a prayer that perfectly reflects the double meaning of this gesture: he fearfully acknowledges violating the division between divine and human, in the same words that seek, instead of punishment, either heroism or divinity in the erotic sphere. The ambiguity seems as intentional here as in his first words to the veiled goddess. As Aphrodite's reply to his plea will indicate, Anchises has suggested immortality for himself. But his prayer also leaves open the possibility of a vigorous life, if he cannot be divine. As he aimed before to determine from Aphrodite's answer whether she was divine or human, so he now presents two options that ask the same question of her with regard to himself.

So important is this question that the rest of the hymn is devoted to Aphrodite's response. Her answer – that he is to be mortal, not her divine lover, but sexually prolific, not impotent – focuses the hymn upon what most scholars take to be its key theme and αἴτιον, the boundary between immortality and mortality, mediated no longer by intercourse between divinities and humans but henceforth by mortal procreation alone.[95] It is thus Aphrodite's own prophecy that voices Zeus' success in staging this erotic encounter, the end of her cosmos of divine/human mixture and the stability of his own order.

VI. Aphrodite's Prophecy

The rest of the hymn except for its last three lines is made up of the prophecy of Aphrodite, some ninety-nine lines (192–290). No other Homeric hymn has such a long stretch of narration by its divinity, and, indeed, Aphrodite speaks *in toto* far more lines in proportion to her whole hymn than does any other god.[96] More than of any other deity, the ἔργα "works" of Aphrodite are presented as speech. Yet the hymn never permits the goddess wholly direct discourse, never an expression unmediated by the ruling desire of Zeus. Her potential boast among the gods of mixing gods with women and goddesses with men is uttered only as indirect statement, subordinated to Zeus' "negative purpose." Her formally direct speech so far in the hymn serves a ἵμερος "sexual passion" that is at once both her own and originated by Zeus precisely to preclude this potential boast. In her prophecy to Anchises, Aphrodite's words continue to bear this double origin. They are hers – they express her desire and her knowledge. But even though her passion is now fully spent, the expenditure leaves the goddess's speech still subject ultimately to Zeus' presiding will.

It is in light of this complex authorship – Aphrodite as herself authored by the hymnic voice that represents and implements the plan of Zeus – that the conflicting forces and apparently illogical turns of this long prophecy can be understood. Like the hymn itself, the prophecy is structured as an antagonism between Aphrodite's cosmos of mixtures and the hierarchical order of Zeus. In this conflict, the effort to subordinate the goddess will serve finally by its success, however, to make her subordination uncertain.

The Structure of the Prophecy

Aphrodite's long prophecy is structured in a ring-composition of three main movements:[97]

    i. Aeneas: Anchises' κῦδος "victory" vs. Aphrodite's ἄχος "grief"
       A   About Anchises: 192–195
              κῦδος "victory " for Anchises
       B   About Aeneas and Aphrodite: 196–99
              ἄχος "grief" for Aphrodite
    ii. Ganymede and Tithonus
       C   About Anchises' race: 200–201
              Examples of Ganymede and Tithonus: 202–238
      About Anchises and Aphrodite: 239–255
            θάνατος "death" for Anchises: 239–246

Within this circular structure is an opposition, recalling the opening antagonism between Aphrodite and Zeus, between praise of Anchises and blame of Aphrodite because of their son, Aeneas. The prophecy thus mirrors in reverse the submissive grandiosity of Anchises' plea. With all the power of the unveiled goddess to foretell the future, Aphrodite predicts a grief and shame for herself that are given voice even as she orders their silencing.

i. Aeneas: Anchises' κῦδος "victory" vs. Aphrodite's ἄχος "grief"

Aphrodite begins by responding both to the fear and to the implied question in Anchises' appeal. She hails him with an epithet that reveals he is, indeed, to be mortal, not her divine lover, but far from impotent: κύδιστε καταθνητῶν ἀνθρώπων "most gifted with κῦδος of mortal men" (192) – the epithet bearing here the primary sense of κῦδος "magic talisman of victory given by a god."[98] Anchises is to be granted a transcendent victory over the loss of procreative μένος "strength" (188) that normally follows intercourse with a goddess, and even over the mortality to which he remains consigned. Thus Aphrodite assures him: "you have no reason to fear suffering evil from me, at least, or from the other blessed ones, since indeed you are dear (φίλος) to the gods" (194–195). Instead of becoming a man οὐ βιοθάλμιος "not blooming in life" (189), he will receive the θάλος "bloom" of their union, a son who will rule the Trojans, and, from him, perpetual progeny (196–197). The epiphany of Aphrodite unveiled and the revelation of her erotic deception end by elevating Anchises to erotic heroism, to the status of being the first mortal man to sleep with Aphrodite and to be related to the gods through the child of this intercourse. Not only will he sleep with the goddess without penalty, their "mixture" will make him the father of a race of rulers who will keep his seed alive past his own death. Having thus declared his unending fatherhood, Aphrodite now names their son.

In naming the child who brings victory to his father, her erotic victim, the victorious Aphrodite bespeaks her own sexual defeat:

τῷ δὲ καὶ Αἰνείας ὄνομ᾽ ἔσσεται οὕνεκά μ᾽ αἰνὸν

ἔσχεν <u>ἄχος</u> ἕνεκα[99] βροτοῦ ἀνέρος ἔμπεσον εὐνῇ.

And so indeed <u>Aeneas</u> will be his name because a <u>dread
grief</u> held me because I fell upon the bed of a mortal man.

Homeric Hymn to Aphrodite 198–199

As with the negated acknowledgment of Aphrodite's erotic power in the
mini-hymns to the virgin goddesses, so here the goddess's power of speech
is confirmed by its negative trope. On the one hand, it is an assumption of
authority unparalleled in early Greek literature for the mother to name the
child, and children named for maternal attributes are rare.[100] But, on the other,
that attribute is the "dread grief" of being degraded in her own sphere of
power. Aeneas becomes a living memorial to this degradation, but also, more
precisely, to the magnitude of the goddess's suffering over it, thus confirming
her majesty at the same time as he embodies the moment of its compromise.
Signifying origins as names do, the choice of "Aeneas" accurately indicates his
conception in an irresolvable ambiguity of power, subjection, and resistance
to subjection by a divine intensity of grief.

Aphrodite might have ended her prophecy at that. The flourishing future
of Anchises has been articulated. And with it, the desire of Zeus has been
accomplished, for it is now clear why Anchises is and must be "dear (φίλος)
to the gods," why he must be spared the death or impotence that might follow
intercourse with a goddess. If he dies then and there, or if he has no children,
there will be no sign of Zeus' subordination of Aphrodite, no ongoing αἰνὸν
ἄχος "dread grief" for the goddess, no "Aeneas." In this way, it is Zeus who
names Aeneas even through the goddess's own words. But the prophecy does
not end here. Somehow the intention of Aphrodite and the intention of Zeus
behind it are not yet fully articulated.

ii. Ganymede and Tithonus

Directly upon naming Aeneas, Aphrodite abruptly turns away from her pain to
praise the beauty of Trojan men: "But always most near to the gods (ἀγχίθεοι)
of all mortal men are those of your race in appearance and in stature" (200–
201).[101] She then recounts two signal instances, Anchises' ancestors, Ganymede
and Tithonus. Why does Aphrodite (and Zeus, and the hymnic voice) want
to introduce their stories? It would seem that her aim in this prophecy is
not simply to predict the future, but also to justify to Anchises her denial of
immortality.[102] For indeed, at this point, there is no reason to think that his
fruitful but mortal life is not her own wish. Her theodicy is based upon the

regular practice in early Greek thought of adducing analogical *exempla*, either positive or negative.[103] Here each story considers the fate of a Trojan abducted because of his beauty and then made immortal by his divine lover.[104] In each case, immortality results in everlasting loss of what is most valuable in a mortal man's life. In the homoerotic union of Ganymede and Zeus, the father-son bond is severed in both the past and future generations, as the father's mourning the loss of his son pre-figures Ganymede's never being able to have a son himself. For Tithonus, immortality without perpetual youth reduces the body to incorporeality, a voice alone, sounding forever (ἄσπετος, 237), but in perpetual solitary confinement with no one to hear or to answer (236). As illustrations of an immortal life worse than the necessity of death, especially in its forfeiture of fatherhood, these accounts seem aimed at proving that Anchises is better off with a son alone, and without Aphrodite as what she had pretended she would be, his wife.

But this interpretation of the stories is not without problems. With regard to Ganymede, the father is ultimately happy with the situation. For the joy of Tros upon receiving the immortal horses as recompense for the loss of his son is emphasized by the repetition, γεγήθει "he rejoiced," γηθόσυνος "rejoicing" (216–217), and will be repeated in Anchises' own joy at the sight of his son (γηθήσεις ὁρόων, 279).[105] Perhaps in this respect the story is meant to persuade by similarity rather than difference, with Tros' happiness at the immortal horses who replace the continuity that comes through a son (not his only son, however) acting as proleptic model of how Anchises should view the son who replaces immortality and brings continuity.[106]

The problematic implications of the case of Eos and Tithonus are harder to resolve. In relating this story to their present situation, Aphrodite reveals that she herself desires for Anchises the ageless youth he has been denied, the very denial her *exempla* would attempt to justify. Rather than proving the necessity of Anchises' mortality, then, why does Eos' omission not illustrate precisely what Aphrodite should do in order to assure undying happiness to her lover and herself?[107] Why does she not ask Zeus for the perpetual youth that Eos forgot? Could the son of Aphrodite and Anchises not, then, be immortal himself?

θάνατος "death" for Anchises

Aphrodite herself seems to raise this question by echoing the words with which Eos asked immortality but not agelessness of Zeus ("to be immortal and live for all days," 221), but then she avoids it altogether, as if ageless immortality for Anchises were out of the question:

οὐκ ἂν ἐγώ γε[108] σὲ τοῖον ἐν ἀθανάτοισιν ἑλοίμην
ἀθάνατόν τ' εἶναι καὶ ζώειν ἤματα πάντα.
ἀλλ' εἰ μὲν τοιοῦτος ἐὼν εἶδός τε δέμας τε
ζώοις ἡμέτερός τε πόσις κεκλημένος εἴης,
οὐκ ἂν ἔπειτά μ' ἄχος πυκινὰς φρένας ἀμφικαλύπτοι.
νῦν δέ σε μὲν τάχα γῆρας ὁμοίιον ἀμφικαλύψει
νηλειές, τό τ' ἔπειτα παρίσταται ἀνθρώποισιν,
οὐλόμενον, καματηρόν, ὅτε στυγέουσι θεοί περ.

I, to be sure, would not choose for you to be of such a sort
    among the immortals,
both to be immortal and live for all days.
But if, being such as you are both in appearance and in build
you might live, and you might be called my husband,
then grief would not veil my clever wits.[109]
But now quickly cruel old age will veil you,
pitiless, which then stands beside men,
destructive, wearing them down, which even the gods
    forever hate.

Homeric Hymn to Aphrodite 239–246

Why does she not ask Zeus for divinity without old age, when her own words point to such a possibility? On this question Aphrodite is simply silent, thus calling for interpretation. Can a god not get such a status for a mortal lover? Zeus did for Ganymede (214). Could not Aphrodite? Or could Zeus not at least be petitioned by Aphrodite, as he is by Thetis in the *Iliad*? Of course, he could not grant such a petition without changing the future of Anchises, fixed in epic tradition, but it is precisely the moments that determined the tradition – in narratological terms, the story – that the hymn repeats.[110] The narrative tradition here tells the story of its own formation, its own authorizing aetiology. To present Zeus giving immortality to Anchises would set the story against the tradition that purports to repeat it. But just such a disjunction between story and narration has seemed the inevitable consequence of having Aphrodite tell the tale of Eos without attempting to act in accord with its lesson. Smith explains that the poet wanted "to use myth to explore the value of mortality by juxtaposing it with examples showing one or another of its negative aspects arbitrarily removed . . . even though the juxtaposition can lead to nothing in the story."[111] The poet, the voice of epic tradition, seems to have achieved this goal in the narration even at the cost of verisimilitude in the story, where words are mimetic of a character's desire.

But is it true that Aphrodite's silence here has no mimetic import, that it indicates nothing about her desire or that of Zeus? Or, rather, is there no mimetic import in the fact that the hymnic voice is the representative of Zeus' will and the ultimate author of Aphrodite's words? In a brief but trenchant phrase, van der Ben points the way to such a mimetic reading, when he observes of Zeus' immortalization of Ganymede, "*quod licet Iovi non licet Veneri.*"[112] The text simply denies Aphrodite permission to try to fulfill the desire it puts into her mouth, that Anchises should be as "near to the gods" in beauty as he is today, the desire which, if fulfilled, would save her from grief. And when considered from Zeus' point of view, we can see the cosmic necessity for Aphrodite's silencing here. Were she allowed to gain immortal youth for Anchises, she would suffer no grief – the "dread grief" that signifies Zeus' appropriation of her power to instigate divine/human "mixtures." The original plan of Zeus would be turned against itself into a triumph for the goddess, whose pleasure in Anchises would be unmixed with the pain of his mortality.

And why does she not at least mention to Anchises the possibility of appealing to Zeus, if only to insist upon its futility? It is a question of the rhetoric of silence. Were she permitted to voice this possibility instead of confining the expression of her displeasure to the intensity of her grief, her subordination to the order of Zeus would be qualified. Within the either/or logic of the hymn's founding antagonism, the authority of Zeus is only so absolute and the distinctions of his order are only so stable and reliable as is their sign, the goddess's grief. By voicing no active resistance, by expressing, but then simply suppressing, her desire for Anchises' eternal youth and announcing his inevitable death, Aphrodite proves she accepts Zeus' will as ineluctable. He need no longer try to restrain her, since she accepts his absolute authority and restrains herself. Anything less than total silence would qualify her acceptance and thus the security of Zeus' victory.

But this *argumentum ex silentio* on the part of Aphrodite is no more conclusive than any other of its kind. Without the goddess's silence in the face of her own stated wish, without her failure to ask for what her own story implies she can and must ask for, Zeus cannot demonstrate absolute sovereignty over the goddess's desire. She must be allowed to voice her wish so that we can know what she wants. We must know from her own recollection of Eos' omission that she knows how to pursue her wish. (And she must give the example of Eos in the first place, so that Anchises will accept a son, who will embody Zeus' conquest.) Further, she must then fail to pursue her wish without a word about why. But her silent acquiescence leaves the actual state of her inner motivation and future intention an uncertainty. She does not voice any reasons of her own. The distinction between mortal and immortal has been sustained in this case only by the imposition of an ultimately ambiguous silence, disclosing the fact that Aphrodite can always pursue the option she omits now.

ὄνειδος "blame" for Aphrodite

The ultimate death of Anchises is not the only loss Aphrodite must accept as a result of her union with the mortal man. She must lose her prior powers of effecting divine/human unions through speech. Here, positioned at the center point of the goddess's prophecy, is the αἴτιον of the hymn and the heart of its generic ambivalence. In a bold *peripeteia* from her earlier power to "tame" (ἐδαμάσσατο, 3) gods, humans, and beasts, the goddess is made to voice in her own prophecy and in her own hymn – each a laudatory sign of her divinity – the "great blaming speech" of the other gods that now will silence her boasts. She is permitted to name the verbal and mental mechanisms of her repeated "mixing" in the past (note the frequentatives) only in predicting their discontinuation:

αὐτὰρ ἐμοὶ <u>μέγ</u>᾽ <u>ὄνειδος</u> ἐν ἀθανάτοισι θεοῖσιν
ἔσσεται ἤματα πάντα διαμπερὲς εἵνεκα σεῖο,
οἳ πρὶν ἐμοὺς <u>ὀάρους</u>[113] καὶ <u>μήτιας</u>, αἷς ποτε πάντας
ἀθανάτους συνέμιξα καταθνητῇσι γυναιξί,
<u>τάρβεσκον</u>· πάντας γὰρ ἐμὸν <u>δάμνασκε</u> νόημα.
νῦν δὲ δὴ οὐκέτι μοι στόμα χείσεται[114] <u>ἐξονομῆναι</u>
<u>τοῦτο</u> μετ᾽ ἀθανάτοισιν, ἐπεὶ μάλα πολλὸν ἀάσθην,
σχέτλιον, <u>οὐκ ὀνοταστόν</u>,[115] ἀπεπλάγχθην δὲ νόοιο,
παῖδα δ᾽ ὑπὸ ζώνῃ ἐθέμην βροτῷ εὐνηθεῖσα.

While for me there will be a <u>great blame</u> among the
    immortal gods
for all days, continually, because of you –
the gods, who before at my <u>amorous conversations</u> and <u>plots</u>,
by which I mixed gods with mortal women,
<u>again and again trembled</u>.[116] For my purpose <u>again and again</u>
    <u>tamed</u> them all.
But now indeed no longer will my mouth dare <u>to name</u>
<u>this</u> among the immortals, since I was very greatly deluded –
a wretched thing, <u>not to be made light of</u> – and I was driven out
    of my mind,

> and conceived a child under my girdle after going to bed with
> a mortal.

Homeric Hymn to Aphrodite 247–255

Yet the status of this ὄνειδος "blame" and the precise limitation upon the speech of Aphrodite in the future are not wholly clear.

There will be a great blame speech throughout all time to come among the gods, who used to tremble at the speech by which Aphrodite instigated demeaning liaisons among them. But will the gods ever actually utter this abuse? It is the interpretation of van der Ben that they will not, "since Aphrodite will be careful to avoid giving them any provocation." The goddess will cease, in other words, her "mixing" speech and thereby the unions it used to create. And this cessation is the very αἴτιον of the hymn.[117] Such an aetiology would accord ideally with the cosmic antagonism delineated in the opening of the hymn and with the justification via the previous *exempla* of breaking up mortal/immortal unions, and it is for that reason a virtually irresistible conclusion. For what could restore the order of Zeus more securely than preventing Aphrodite from ever again collapsing divine and human into one category subject to herself? And what could be a more perfect counterpart to Anchises' mortality than the restriction of Aphrodite to "mixings" that do not blur the boundary between humans and gods? Both man and goddess would then experience a loss – a sort of death – that paradoxically gains a cosmos of stable and meaningful difference between human and divine. But despite its appealing coherence, the certainty of this interpretation is undermined by two questions.

It would seem that there are two kinds of speech or at least two phases of speech mentioned by Aphrodite: that by which she creates god/woman unions (249–250) and that by which she speaks of these unions (ἐξονομῆναι τοῦτο "name this," 252–253) to the gods. Aphrodite admits that she can no longer "name this" among the gods – no longer boast, as she might have before (ἐπευξαμένη, 48), of causing such divine/human bonds – since they can make the same boast over against her. The first question is whether this silenced boasting entails cessation of the speeches by which Aphrodite brings about such couplings. Is the possibility not left open that she will continue them, but simply henceforth not boast of them?[118] Perhaps not. Maybe Aphrodite would not want to exercise the power to blur the divine/human distinction, were she unable to "boast" about it. For in early Greek the verb εὔχομαι means to utter proudly, not something false or pretentious, but the truth of one's nature.[119] To keep Aphrodite from boasting of the workings of her ὄαροι "amorous conversations" – designated in the *Theogony* (205) as part of her τίμη "sphere of honor"[120] – would be tantamount to forbidding a mortal to utter his own genealogy. Would Aphrodite continue to instigate such "mixing" speech without mentioning it? To this question the text provides no unequivocal answer, thus leaving its apparent aetiology uncertain and, at best, subject to Aphrodite's unstated desire.

The second question follows from the first. By ceasing her boasts or even indeed her "mixing" speech itself, can Aphrodite keep the μέγ' ὄνειδος "great blame" forever unexpressed? Will the gods refrain from disgracing the goddess for her intercourse with a mortal, if she no longer boasts or even if she no longer couples gods and women through gossips and schemes? Again, the text offers no definitive answer. But Aphrodite's curse of her liaison as οὐκ ὀνομαστόν "not to be named" seems virtually desiderative, and in this context suggests a possible *quid pro quo* by which in return for her no longer "naming this" (ἐξονομῆναι τοῦτο, 252–253), the gods would not mention her shame.[121] In the remainder of her prophecy, at any rate, the goddess appears to balance such a deal within the divine sphere by attempting to forestall this μέγ' ὄνειδος among men.

iii. Aeneas: Anchises' Boast vs. Aphrodite's Blame and Praise

After completing her description of the disgrace that parallels the death Anchises eventually will suffer, Aphrodite again might have ended her prophecy. Both the positive and the negative poles of Anchises' fate have been revealed. But again, the goddess's desire is not yet exhausted. What she still wants, in fact, turns out to be the silencing of another potential boasting (286) and naming (290) speech, that of Anchises. As in the realm of ἵμερος "sexual desire," she wants to exert over Anchises the power exerted over her by Zeus.

The mention of the child conceived in her unspeakable union with a mortal leads Aphrodite to an extended description of the nymphs who will nurse the infant apart from his mother (256–275). Through their own combination of divine and human properties, the nymphs embody Aeneas' double heritage and thus serve the hymn's characterization of him as the mediating figure that separates immortality from mortality.[122] This separation is fundamental to the cosmos of Zeus and the design of the hymnic voice. But if we ask why Aphrodite herself should expatiate upon these creatures, we find that both as signs of the divine/human cleavage and as alternative mothers of Aeneas, they figure importantly in the goddess's attempt to camouflage her ὄνειδος "blame."

In a final and apparently contradictory turn of her prophecy, Aphrodite makes promises that prove her motherhood of Aeneas and then prohibits Anchises from revealing it. She promises to assume the nurses' role long enough to present him to his father in person – hence the doublet where first the nymphs, then Aphrodite "bring" (ἄξουσιν, 275; ἄγουσα, 277) Aeneas to Anchises. And, recalling his earlier prayers for offspring (θαλερὸν γόνον, 104; οὐ βιοθάλμιος, 189), she calls the child his θάλος "shoot" (278) and assures Anchises of a joy like that of Tros, since the boy will be, if not immortal, at least a visual imitation of divinity, "for he will be very like to a god (θεοείκελος)" (279). And then she forbids Anchises to reveal that the child is hers. But the promise and the prohibition here are actually complementary. For if Anchises believes Aeneas is her child and is content with him as compensation for his own lost divinity, he may be persuaded – that is, successfully threatened – to keep the child's maternity secret.

In making her threat, she re-invokes the conventional fear of punishment for divine/human intercourse that she earlier assuaged:

> ἢν δέ τις εἴρηταί σε καταθνητῶν ἀνθρώπων,
> ἥ τις σοι φίλον υἱὸν ὑπὸ ζώνῃ θέτο μήτηρ,
> τῷ δὲ σὺ <u>μυθεῖσθαι</u> μεμνημένος, ὥς σε κελεύω:
> <u>φάσθαι</u>[123] τοι Νύμφης καλυκώπιδος ἔκγονον εἶναι,
> αἳ τόδε ναιετάουσιν ὄρος καταειμένον ὕλῃ.
> εἰ δέ κεν ἐξείπῃς καὶ <u>ἐπεύξεαι</u> ἄφρονι θυμῷ
> ἐν φιλότητι μιγῆναι ἐυστεφάνῳ Κυθερείῃ,
> Ζεύς σε χολωσάμενος βαλέει ψολόεντι κεραυνῷ.
> εἴρηταί τοι πάντα: σὺ δὲ φρεσὶ σῆσι νοήσας,
> ἴσχεο <u>μηδ</u>' <u>ὀνόμαινε</u>, <u>θεῶν</u> δ' ἐποπίζεο <u>μῆνιν</u>.

> And if ever someone of mortal men asks you
> who is the mother who conceived your dear child beneath
>   her girdle,
> do you <u>tell the story</u> to him, remembering what I order you.
> <u>Say</u> that he is the offspring of a nymph with a flowerlike face,
> one of those who dwell on this mountain clothed in forest.
> But if you ever speak out and <u>boast</u> with senseless heart
> that you mixed in love-making with well-crowned Cythereia,
> Zeus in his rage will smite you with a smoking thunderbolt.
> All has been said to you. Perceiving it in your mind,[124]
> restrain yourself and <u>do not name me</u>. Respect the <u>wrath</u>
>   <u>of the gods</u>.

Homeric Hymn to Aphrodite 281–290

For her threat to work, Anchises must really fear "the wrath of the gods." He must believe there is indeed a real difference between gods and men – one such as is illustrated by Aphrodite's shame at having slept with a mortal, by her separation from their half-human child, and by the intermediary creatures who will nurse Aeneas in her place. He must believe, too, that Zeus will punish the man who makes public his violation of this difference through boasting and naming the divine mother of his child.[125] And if he is to lie to avoid Zeus' retribution, he must be armed with a plausible subterfuge, one that can account for the child's godlike appearance. And so Aphrodite orders Anchises to name one of the child's godlike nurses as his mother.

Once again, then, Aphrodite attempts to control her erotic victim through her own speech. She wants to reduce Anchises to her own verbal position *vis-à-vis* the gods to whom she can no longer "boast of" or "name" her erotic conquests. Were the rhetoric of this final movement of her prophecy successful, were Anchises to keep her secret, she would rescue her long prophecy and her hymn itself from the generic subversion of voicing her own blame. But she would also – such is the tropology of her intention – succeed in preventing the first articulation of the very tradition that the hymnic voice now repeats. In saving her praise, she would silence herself. And in this she does not succeed.

For Anchises evidently did not keep his secret. He did not fear punishment from Zeus. He told the story and by that telling initiated, at the level of the story, the sequence of retellings that make up the hymnic tradition and now culminate in the narration of the *Homeric Hymn to Aphrodite* itself, in which Aphrodite is "quoted" telling the story herself. This fact of narrative tradition and rhetorical subordination is demonstrated by the brief, formal sign of epic convention that marks the close of Aphrodite's prophecy, a phrase as damaging here as it is usually innocuous: ὡς εἰποῦσ' "thus having spoken" (291). And after this marker of the narration, comes the sign of the narrating itself in the closing apostrophe, again a formality with more than its usual force – the hymnic voice addressing the divine victim of its now transcendent speech: χαῖρε θεὰ Κύπροιο ἐυκτιμένης μεδέουσα "Hail, goddess, reigning over well-founded Cyprus" (292).

VII. Epilogue

Ambiguous Aetiology

The *Homeric Hymn to Aphrodite*, like many erotic plots, ends with the future of the lovers – and thus its own ultra-textual meaning – partly clear and partly not. Why did Anchises reveal his secret? Did Zeus indeed blast him with a thunderbolt, as Aphrodite threatened and as later tradition maintained?[126] And was Aphrodite prevented from ever causing divine/human "mixtures" again or just from boasting of them? How securely established, in other words, is the aetiology of the hymn? The questions are interrelated.

In Anchises' revelation of his secret, we see again the ultimate authorship of Zeus. Were Anchises to obey Aphrodite, the whole meaning of "Aeneas" would be lost. He would no longer be the living sign of Zeus' humiliation of the goddess. His "name" would be changed. If Anchises did not tell the truth of Aeneas' parentage, Zeus himself would have to do so.[127]

But can Anchises be allowed to tell the world that he fathered the child of a goddess with impunity? Aphrodite's specific threat appears to allude to the tradition that Zeus did indeed punish Anchises for the very union he caused. Anchises does not suffer sterility or death for his love-making with the goddess, but neither does he escape entirely unscathed. Why would Zeus punish the man for what he made the goddess make the man do?

Here we have a hint about the future activity or the expected future activity of Aphrodite. If there are never again to be liaisons between mortals and immortals, if Aphrodite has been stopped from collapsing the cosmos of Zeus into her world of mixture, there is no need to validate the prohibition against divine/human intercourse with punishment of the mortal male. In his blasting of Anchises, Zeus himself proves that he must keep this prohibition alive and thus that the power of Aphrodite has not been completely subordinated to his order of meaningful distinctions. It is as if Zeus and the hymnic tradition itself realized the ambiguity in her failure to ask for ageless immortality for Anchises and feared its consequences. And so Aphrodite herself is made to allude to the mortal man's punishment, as a warning to other men she might "mix" with goddesses.

But could we perhaps at least say, by way of compensation, that the challenge posed to Anchises by the disguised Aphrodite is not an αἴτιον, not a "first cause" of an eternal verity, not a "first" but a "once" that will never occur again, that never again will a mortal man be confronted by Aphrodite pretending to be his virgin bride? With all the paradoxical force of an assertion of ambiguity, the hymn, by virtue of its intertextual connections with the traditions of Pandora, is unequivocal in this element of its aetiology, its proclamation that any virgin bride might be Aphrodite in disguise and that no man "seized by *eros*" for the bride can possibly know the difference. The *Homeric Hymn to Aphrodite* is the αἴτιον of how female sexuality (and sexuality as female) first came to present itself to the mortal male as an *eros* blinding him to its true nature, of how the epistemo-erotic dilemma of the human male first entered the Western world.

Notes

An earlier version of this essay appeared in *Classical Antiquity* 8 (1989) 1–40. It is my pleasure to thank David Blank, Carolyn Dewald, Bernard Frischer, Simon Goldhill, and Richard Janko for critical reading of that text. I am grateful also to Nicole Loraux and Marcel Detienne for the invitation to present the paper in their seminars in Paris in 1987 and for the many helpful comments of those attending, especially Françoise Frontisi-Ducroux, François Lissarrague, Giulia Sissa, and Jean-Pierre Vernant.

1. For the traditional themes and diction of praise and blame in early Greek poetry, see Nagy 1979 and Detienne 1967.

2. It is an analytical resource of aetiological myth to defy the exclusions of logic, to separate the integrated components of a synchronic system into a "before" and "after," and thereby to tell an αἴτιον: how something that has always existed first began. The *Homeric Hymn to Aphrodite* presents the "cause" of how "mixture" was once (is) integrated and subordinated (imperfectly, as we shall see) into a system in which meaning and value derive from hierarchical difference.

3. See Nagy 1976, esp. 223–224.

4. See Smith 1981a:33, who notes "so great a clarity of structure" in the introduction of the hymn. For other analyses of the structural function of word-repetitions in the introduction of the hymn, see Podbielski 1971:18–32; Porter 1949:251–254, 261–262; Pellizer 1978:119–123, who delineates the *"ripetizione a cornice"* that expresses the hymn's fundamental polarity between divine and human mediated by ἵμερος "sexual passion," wielded first by Aphrodite and then by Zeus against the goddess.

5. For such invocation as an optional feature in the corpus of Homeric hymns, and for other structural properties of the genre, see Janko 1981. For apostrophe in the hymns as establishing the poetic voice as able to make a divinity respond to invocation by presenting itself, see "Sacred Apostrophe: Re-Presentation and Imitation in *Homeric Hymn to Apollo* and *Homeric Hymn to Hermes*" in this collection. The apostrophe of the Muse here is a subtle but deliberate pointer toward the power of the narrating voice to represent the hymnic tradition of which the Muse is the voice. This self-reflection inaugurates the inclusion of the hymnist and the hymnic tradition within the thematics of the *Homeric Hymn to Aphrodite* itself.

6. According to Ruijgh (1971: paragraph 25), the use of epic τε with the aorist of acts by gods here and elsewhere is ambiguous, indicating either in the ordinary usage of the gnomic aorist a "permanent fact" or a "unique act of the far past and indeed close to the start of the world" – here, the moment when Aphrodite introduced love into the world – "but also an exemplary fact that implies a permanent fact," to wit, that the goddess concerns herself with love in all times, that is, a "mythic fact." He notes (paragraphs 746, 334) other instances of such usage in the hymn at lines 30, 36, 38 (see below, n. 21), and 261.

7. For the phrase ἔργα Ἀφροδίτης "works of Aphrodite" as a term for "sex," see the "tender-skinned virgin who does not yet know the ἔργα Ἀφροδίτης" (Hesiod *Works and Days* 521), and the periphrastic constructions, φιλοτήσια ἔργα "sexual intercourse" between Tyro and Poseidon, disguised as the river-god Enipeus (*Odyssey* xi 246), and ἱμερόεντα ἔργα γάμοιο "passionate acts of marriage" as the sphere of Aphrodite, in contrast to the ἔργα πολεμήια "acts of war" (*Iliad* V 428–429). See also Podbielski 1971:18–19.

8. See Smith 1981a:33.

9. See Rissman 1983:4. See also Janko 1994 on *Iliad* XIV 198.

10. See, for example, Vernant 1981 and Detienne 1972b = 1981.

11. For this proportional formulation, compare Aristotle *Nicomachean Ethics* 1131a30–32.

12. See Calame 1977:I.411–420.

13. Compare Aphrodite's claim later that her "purpose used to tame (δάμασκε) all the gods" (251).

14. In the *Theogony*, for example, it is through his mastery over mixture – both his matings with such older goddesses as Metis and his unions with mortal woman, such as that producing Heracles – that Zeus constructs a cosmos apparently stable and immune from the revolutions of the "succession myth." As the aetiology of such mastery, the *Homeric Hymn to Aphrodite* exposes both the necessity of mixture for meaning and the continual threat that derives precisely from that necessity. Compare the ambiguity inherent in the woman's necessary power of (dis)placement: she must be mobile in order to be exchanged by men in marriage, but that same mobility makes it possible for her not to stay put, not to maintain her position in the system of social meaning. For this spatial instability dramatized in the Herodotean "origin" of the Persian War, see "Language and the Female in Early Greek Thought," and in the "place" of Penelope, see "The (Re)Marriage of Penelope and Odysseus" in this collection.

15. See AHS:350.

16. Note also τέρψίν γλυκερήν "sweet delight," Hesiod *Theogony* 206, part of the τίμη "sphere of honor" of Aphrodite.

17. See AHS:350. In speculating upon the poet's purpose here, Smith (1981:34) notes that "a power to which the exceptions can easily be listed is made more impressive by the production of the list." It is in keeping with the hymn's qualified praise of Aphrodite that the force of such an indirect compliment is diminished by the antithetical structuring in which these three exceptions to the goddess's power in B (7–33) are paralleled with her subordination by Zeus in B′ (45–52).

18. See Podbielski 1971:19.

19. See below on the alpha-privative, παρθένῳ ἀδμήτῃ "untamed virgin" in line 82.

20. For the use of the neuter participle πεφυγμένον here, see AHS on 34, citing *Iliad* XXII 219. With the use of the verb φεύγω of the attempt to "flee, escape" Aphrodite, compare Sappho 1.21, 24 LP: καὶ γὰρ αἰ φεύγει, ταχέως διώξει . . . κωὐκ ἐθέλοισα "For indeed if she flees, quickly she will pursue . . . whether willing or not."

21. Ruijgh (1971: paragraph 746) notes that καί τε here "expresses the nuance of a climax."

22. The question of whether παρὲκ ἤγαγε and συνέμιξε here should be read as gnomic aorists (as they are usually translated), implying that Aphrodite continues to make Zeus mix with women, or as historical past tenses, implying an end to such unions, sums up the ultimate ambiguity in the apparent aetiology of the hymn. The problem is reflected in the textual tradition, since the manuscripts attest both a primary sequence subjunctive (ἐθέλῃ) read by Cassola 1975 and the secondary optative (ἐθέλοι) read by Allen 1961 [1946]; Smith 1981a; van Eck 1978; and van der Ben 1986. Van der Ben advocates taking the two aorists as different from one another (1986:4). Arguing (against Ruijgh) for the acceptability of the aorist rather than the imperfect after an optative, he claims that συνέμιξε is a "normal, historical past tense" with which καί τε indicates an act that is past, but exemplary of universal power. He further maintains that of the two verbs, συνέμιξε alone refers to unions with mortal women, since no such unions have been mentioned before παρὲκ ἤγαγε. The verb παρὲκ ἤγαγε then refers only to sexual intercourse in general, to which Zeus remains forever subject, and is therefore an instance of what Ruijgh terms a past but permanent "mythic fact." This interpretation does not wholly eliminate the ambiguity, however, since it assumes rather than proves the temporal distinction between the verbs. Unable to reproduce the ambiguity in English, I indicate the intention of Zeus and of the hymnic voice by translating the past tense.

23. In the rhetoric of its structure, the *Theogony* parallels the hymn as an attempt to establish the cosmos of Zeus over against all chaotic opposition. Compare Arthur 1982. With the τιμή "sphere of honor" of Zeus, compare that of Aphrodite at *Theogony* 205–206, which includes among her powers of attraction and pleasure, that kind of speech ὄαροι "amorous conversations" by which she mates gods and mortal women (249, see below, notes 113 and 120).

24. For this opposition at the level of ritual, the promiscuous sexuality permitted in the Adonia, honoring Aphrodite vs. the restriction of sexuality within legitimate marriage, celebrated in the Thesmophoria, honoring Demeter, see Detienne 1972a:187–226 = 1977b:99–122.

25. Breeding across the human/beast boundary is not alluded to here, but is acknowledged elsewhere in Greek mythic thought through such "monstrous" creatures as centaurs, silenoi, sirens, and sphinxes.

26. On the repetition of this phrase here and in 53 below, as marking the reversal from the situation in line 2, see Podbielski 1971:20.

27. Kamerbeek (1967:390) stresses the "vivacity" lent by the formulaic ὄφρα τάχιστα to the expression of Zeus' will.

28. Van der Ben (1986:6–7) astutely observes that the wording here can mean that after her intercourse with the mortal Anchises, Aphrodite can no longer speak about, but can continue to cause, such unions, whereas Zeus intends their complete cessation.

29. On the use of the subjunctive rather than the optative in clauses of negative purpose, see Goodwin *Syntax*:114§318, 321; Chantraine *GH* II.269§398, and Kühner-Gerth II.380: "the action of the main clause occurs in the past, but the purpose or the result itself must be represented as still continuing in the present time of the speaker." Aphrodite's boasting is to be silenced up to the time of the narrating of the poem.

30. For the formulation of metaphor as a proportion, see Aristotle *Poetics* 1457b7–30, *Rhetoric* 1411a33–b4.

31. For a similar relation between Zeus and a female power he would appropriate, compare the case of Metis in *Theogony* where Zeus succeeds in "swallowing" the goddess by conquering her with her own weapons (αἱμύλιοι λόγοι "wily words," 890), and thereby makes himself μητίετα "endowed with mêtis," even though he has been given this epithet before his conquest from the start of the poem (*Theogony* 56, 520). Zeus takes what he has always possessed, just as in the hymn he can, without any explanation of where or how he got it, wield the power of Aphrodite as "easily" as she made him breed with women. On this episode in *Theogony*, see "Language and the Female in Early Greek Thought" in this collection.

32. For *epos* as "speech in epic," see Koller 1972:16–24; Nagy 1979:30, 271–274, 299, 304.

33. Pellizer (1978:132–133) argues for the traditionality of this scene by comparing the toilette of Hera about to seduce Zeus at *Iliad* XIV 166–172 and of Aphrodite herself at *Odyssey* viii 362–366. For a detailed comparison between the preparations of Hera in the *Iliad* and Aphrodite in the hymn, see Janko 1994 on *Iliad* XIV 166–186. For an analysis of the similarities and differences between the whole epiphany and the traditional patterns of seduction scenes, see Sowa 1984:67–94. As we shall see, the *Homeric Hymn to Aphrodite* depends for its meaning upon such traditional connections.

34. On ἐπενήνοθεν, see Cassola 1975:547 on 62 with bibliography.

35. The term ἐδανῷ is sometimes read here in place of the manuscript's ἑανῷ on the basis of its use in *Iliad* XIV 171–174 of Hera's toilette:

> ἀλείψατο δὲ λίπ᾽ ἐλαίῳ
> ἀμβροσίῳ ἐδανῷ, τό ῥά οἱ τεθυωμένον ἦεν:
> τοῦ καὶ κινυμένοιο Διὸς κατὰ χαλκοβατὲς δῶ
> ἔμπης ἐς γαῖάν τε καὶ οὐρανὸν ἵκετ᾽ ἀϋτμή.

> And she anointed herself richly with oil,
> ambrosial, sweet, which had been perfumed for her.
> And when this is moved through the palace of Zeus with its bronze threshold,
> its fragrance reaches both earth and heaven alike.

Here in the *Iliad*, as with Aphrodite's perfume in Cyprus, the fragrance permeates its surrounding space. For the retaining of the manuscript's ἑανῷ, see Janko 1982:161 and for the interpretation of ἑανῷ as "dress," see also Janko 1994:174–175 on *Iliad* XIV 172–174, who maintains, following Hurst 1976, that the verb θυόω here refers to the boiling of oil to make perfume to scent clothes and cites *Cypria* 4 where the Graces and the Hours dip Aphrodite's garments "in spring flowers," so that she "wears perfumed [τεθυωμένα] dresses."

36. For perfume as Aphrodite's ambiguous instrument in promoting marriage, see Detienne 1972a:ix–x = 1977b: vi–vii.

37. Compare Pellizer (1978:123–124), who also notes the rhyming –οῦσα at the end of three alternating hemiepes: ἰδοῦσα (56), ἐλθοῦσα (58), εἰσελθοῦσα (60).

38. For Aphrodite's adornment, especially her golden necklaces, as a κόσμος, see *Homeric Hymn VI to Aphrodite* 11, 12, 15.

39. For the connection of Anchises with the pastoral activity of cattle herding, see *Homeric Hymn to Aphrodite* 55 and *Iliad* V 313.

40. For τέρπω as indicating the "delight" taken in poetry, see *Odyssey* i 346–347, 421–422; viii 45, 91, 367–368, 429; xii 52; xvii 385; xxii 330; *Iliad* IX 186–189; XVIII 603–604; *Homeric Hymn to Apollo* 169–170; Hesiod *Theogony* 36–37; Hesiod fr. 274 MW. For τέρπω as indicating the "delight" taken in sex, see Mimnermus 1.1.

41. In Greek hexameter poetry we find no instances of playing the lyre without singing, except when accompanying the song of others. For singing to the lyre in relative seclusion, compare Achilles' playing the phorminx and singing the κλέα ἀνδρῶν "famous deeds of men" (*Iliad* IX 186–189) during his withdrawal from the Achaean army. For the linkage of the lyre and song, see *Iliad* II 599–600 (where the poet Thamyris is termed a κιθαριστής "lyre-player"), XIII 731, and *Odyssey* i 159.

42. On ὁμοῖος as indistinguishably "similar" and "equal" in early Greek, see Pucci 1977:35n7.

43. Nagy (1983:35–55) shows how this verb denotes the recognition and interpretation of a sign, whether explicit or left implicit in context. Here the σῆμα "sign" is the ambiguous goddess in disguise.

44. The father-daughter relation between Zeus and Aphrodite is a subtle element in this story. As his daughter, Aphrodite belongs to Zeus to give to whomever he will. It is perhaps this patriarchal authority that permits Zeus in terms of sociological logic to assume the power of Aphrodite and exert it over the goddess herself.

45. See below, n. 92.

46. On the function of this alpha-privative form, see Puhvel 1953:14–25.

47. On the impersonal ἐλάμπετο, see AHS on 90 and van der Ben 1986:10. Janko 1994 on *Iliad* XIV 185–186 notes the traditionality of such a simile in toilette scenes.

48. Compare Pucci 1977:87–92 on *Works and Days* 61–63, and Janko 1982:161, 165–167. Loraux (1981:75–117) stresses the difference between the *Theogony* and the *Works and Days* with regard to Pandora as an imitation. Emphasizing the separation between men and gods rather than their mediation, the *Theogony* presents Pandora as an imitation not of goddesses but of a "respected virgin" – that is, of herself – and thus a wholly artificial creature, "the semblance of a copy without a model." Accordingly, it is the *Theogony* (575, 581, 584, 588) that insists in litany-like fashion upon Pandora as a θαῦμα "wonder."

49. Compare the effect of the κόσμος of Aphrodite upon the gods in *Homeric Hymn VI to Aphrodite* 18: εἶδος θαυμάζοντες "wondering at her appearance."

50. Pandora, too, wears ὅρμοι χρυσείοι "golden necklaces" (*Works and Days* 74). On the θαῦμα of Pandora in the *Theogony* as embodying that of Aphrodite, see Loraux 1981:85.

51. In being θαυμάσια, ζώοισιν ἐοικότα φωνήεσσιν "wonderful, like to living beings endowed with speech" (584), these well-wrought creatures act as a metonymic gloss upon the artificiality of the θαῦμα of Aphrodite and Pandora.

52. Loraux (1981:85n51) notes also that Pandora's robe is white, the color of wedding clothes.

53. For the ζώνη and the καλύπτρη of Pandora, see *Theogony* 573–575, where Athena "girded (ζῶσε) and ornamented her in silvery clothing" and "let down a veil (καλύπτρην) from her head," and Loraux 1981:87–88. For the ζώνη and καλύπτρη together on women in daily life, see *Odyssey* v 231–232 of Calypso and x 544–545 of Circe; for the ζώνη with a κρήδεμνον, see *Iliad* XIV 181–185 of Hera.

54. For "loosening of the ζώνη" as an expression of intercourse, see Smith 1981a:60.

55. As to what the κρήδεμνον or καλύπτρη looked like, the etymology (κράς + δέω) and usage of κρήδεμνον suggest a "head-binder" from which hangs fabric that can be held to cover the cheeks, as in the formula signaling Penelope's chastity and allure: ἄντα παρειάων σχομένη λιπαρὰ κρήδεμνα "holding the shining κρήδεμνα before her cheeks" (*Odyssey* i 334 = xvi 416, xviii 210, xxi 65; compare Nagler 1974:66ff., who cites the periphrasis of Apollonius of Rhodes *Argonautica* 3.445: λιπαρὴν σχομένη καλύπτρην). Since the text never mentions it overtly, we cannot be certain that Aphrodite is, in fact, wearing a veil here. Nagler's analysis (1974, esp. 45–86) of the veil as a marker of female chastity in hexameter poetry makes it clear that no marriageable female would appear unveiled before the man whose betrothed she pretends – as Aphrodite will pretend – to be. But if Aphrodite is lacking a material κρήδεμνον or καλύπτρη here, her disguise – both her visual costume and her verbal response to Anchises' *epos* – is nonetheless, as we shall see, an effective "veil," one that ultimately disables Anchises' powers of discernment, just as *eros* in the Iliadic counterparts to this scene φρένας ἀμφεκάλυψεν "veiled the wits" of Zeus and Paris. See below, n. 63.

56. Compare Pucci 1977:96–97. Such a mimesis is not inconsistent with the *Theogony*'s designation of Pandora as "like to a respected virgin," for it is as an "imitation virgin" that Aphrodite here presents herself to the human male. The circularity of all this leaves the female, in the terms of Deleuze (in *Logique du sens* [Paris 1969], quoted by Loraux [1981:87n60]), a "simulacrum" who "puts in question the very notions of copy . . . and model."

57. Podbielski 1971:42.

58. The phrase θαῦμα ἰδέσθαι, cited by Podbielski (1971:42) as evidence of Aphrodite's manifest divinity here, is, however, used also of Pandora's veil, *Theogony* 574–575.

59. Podbielski 1971:42–43.

60. Compare, by contrast, *Iliad* III 385–398, where Aphrodite disguises herself as an old woman to summon Helen to Paris, but leaves uncovered signs by which Helen recognizes (ἐνόησε) her identity: περικαλλέα δειρὴν, στήθεά θ' ἱμερόεντα καὶ ὄμματα μαρμαίροντα "exceedingly beautiful neck, alluring breasts, and sparkling eyes." Here, the success of Aphrodite's mission depends ultimately, not upon the maintenance of her disguise, but rather upon Helen's seeing that the old woman is indeed the goddess whose command may not be refused. Helen's reaction upon recognizing the goddess without having first been deceived – θάμβησεν "she marveled" (398) – may be compared with that of Anchises, τάρβησεν "he trembled" (182), each in line-initial position.

61. Pellizer 1978:115–144.

62. For parallels between the two scenes, see Reinhardt 1956:1–14.

63. The verb here, ἀμφικαλύπτω "veil, cover around," is cognate with καλύπτρη "veil, covering."

64. Compare Sowa (1984:84) and Podbielski (1971:43, 45), who describes Anchises' speech as a cult hymn, while acknowledging the inconsistency between such a response and the goddess's disguise.

65. Compare Odysseus to Nausicaa: σέβας μ' ἔχει εἰσορόωντα "reverential awe holds me, seeing you," *Odyssey* vi 161.

66. See Nagy 1979:234–241, who describes the αἶνος as "a discourse that aims at praising and honoring someone or something or at being ingratiating toward a person . . . that is in direct or indirect connection with a gift or a prize" (235) and as "an allusive tale containing an ulterior purpose" (237).

67. Sowa (1984:83–84) maintains that these deceptions differ in that Hera's purpose is "not to overcome Zeus's objections, but to fool him into thinking that he must overcome her objections," whereas Aphrodite must "overcome Anchises' fears of sleeping with her." As we shall see, however, Aphrodite's method is the same as Hera's: to make Anchises believe she is an "untamed virgin" whose objections to immediate love-making – "lead me untamed and inexperienced in love-making" (133) – he must overcome.

68. For the speech of the Muses, "we know how to say many false things like to real things, and we know, whenever we want, how to utter true things" (*Theogony* 27–28), see "Language and the Female in Early Greek Thought" in this collection.

69. Compare Barthes 1986.

70. Pellizer 1971:125 notes these repetitions.

71. For the Herodotean model of such exchange, see "Language and the Female in Early Greek Thought" in this collection.

72. For the concept of "festive conclusion" and its function in the *muthos* of comedy, see Frye 1965:72–76.

73. For modern and ancient Greek examples of maidens yielding to premarital sex, provided marriage is to follow, see Bickerman 1976:232–233.

74. I use the term "epistemology" here in its basic sense of a *logos* "speech, logical account" of *epistêmê* "knowledge." Its component of "speech" applies both to the *epos* "speech in epic" of Anchises and to the *muthos* "story" of the hymn that narrates it. The *epos* of Anchises reveals the limits of either/or logic in speech as a means of gaining knowledge of the object of *eros*. In narrating this *epos* and its equivocal consequences, the *muthos* of the hymn becomes a *logos*, an account of the knowledge of knowledge itself – a "mythical" epistemology and a prephilosophical critique of the logical epistemology advocated by philosophy and illustrated in its invention of the difference between *muthos* and *logos*. See Detienne 1986.

75. Compare Vidal-Naquet 1986a and b.

76. Compare Jenkins 1983:139, with bibliography.

77. Compare Smith 1981a:58–59.

78. Compare Smith 1981a:59, who notes that this proof of prowess helps to keep Anchises from seeming "a hopelessly weaker and inappropriate partner in the love-making which is to follow."

79. Richard Janko points out to me the revealing parallel of Medea, Jason, and the golden fleece.

80. Compare Sowa 1984:76.

81. Compare Janko 1994 on *Iliad* XIV 171 on how the poet "avoids giving too vivid a picture of the august Hera naked."

82. Smith (1981a:122n67) shows that οὐ σάφα εἰδώς here means not complete ignorance, but "incomplete knowledge, conjecture" – the emphasis being upon σάφα "clearly."

83. On the ἀνακαλυπτήρια, see Oakley 1982:113–118, with bibliography.

84. Line 64 from her dressing at Paphos is repeated in 172, except for the final εἵματα καλά, which comes at the end of the preceding 171. Note the repetition in 171–172 of χροΐ "skin," subtly emphasizing the body, both covered and revealed.

85. Smith (1981a:63n71) notes that the predicate genitive here in place of the dative emphasizes Aphrodite's unique possession of this beauty and renders it a "positive identifying mark" of the goddess in her "natural character when she is not disguised."

86. Smith (1981a:63) makes the sensitive observation that shedding sleep over Anchises prevents him from seeing her dress – prevents him, that is, from seeing her naked, after their love-making is complete. That the hymnic voice describes this dressing to its audience thus implies such a vision for itself.

87. Another privative compound: the negative particle ν- (with elongation of the subsequent vowel) plus the root ἔργε- (compare ἐγείρω "wake up").

88. See Smith 1981a:65, and Keaney 1981:261–264, on the diction of 184, 187–190.

89. On this term here, see Giacomelli 1980:13–19, and Segal 1986:43–44.

90. On the manifold intricacies of this scene and on epiphany elsewhere in Homer, see Pucci 1987.

91. The two passages display parallels of idea, diction, and word-order: σε . . . θεὰ . . . ἔγνων (*Homeric Hymn to Aphrodite* 185–186) / σε, τεά, γνῶναι (*Odyssey* xiii 312); σὺ δ' νημερτὲς ἔειπες (end of *Homeric Hymn to Aphrodite* 186) / σὲ γὰρ αὐτὴν παντὶ ἐίσκεις (end of *Odyssey* xiii 313).

92. See Giacomelli 1980:18–19; Smith 1981a:65 and n. 77.

93. Compare θαλερὸν γόνον, 104 with βιοθάλμιος, 189. See Smith 1981a:65–66.

94. Van der Ben 1986:20–21. This view is in opposition to that of Sowa (1984:51), who maintains that Anchises, on analogy with Odysseus in relation to Calypso, does not desire immortality. Her evidence, that Anchises asks first only for mortal goods (103–106), is qualified by the fact that this appeal is made before he knows he has already slept with the goddess. The intervening intimacy has, it would seem, expanded his view of the possibilities.

95. See especially Segal 1974:205–212; Pellizer 1978:121; Smith 1981a:67; van der Ben 1986:29–32.

96. Aphrodite: 137 out of 293 (47 percent) in *Homeric Hymn to Aphrodite*; Hermes: 106 (18 percent); Apollo: 150 (26 percent) out of 580 in *Homeric Hymn to Hermes*; Apollo: 78 out of 546 (14 percent) in *Homeric Hymn to Apollo*; Demeter: 75 out of 495 (15 percent) in *Homeric Hymn to Demeter*.

97. This analysis follows with some elaboration that of Smith (1981a:67, 91).

98. See Benveniste 1969:II.57–69.

99. On the irregular but not unprecedented use of ἕνεκα as a conjunction here, see Cassola on 199.

100. We find examples of the opposite, sons named by males (Odysseus by his maternal grandfather and at the suggestion of his nurse) and after their fathers' attributes (Telemachus, Astyanax, Neoptolemus). As instances of children named for maternal traits, there is Parthenopaeus, named after his mother's παρθενεία "virginity" and Cleopatra, wife of Meleager, "by-named" Alcyone after the action of her mother, who mourned her abduction by Apollo with a cry like that of the halcyon (*Iliad* IX 561–564).

101. For a possible pun here on the name of Anchises, now "near (ἄγχι) a god," see van der Ben 1986:24.

102. Smith (1981a:68) describes this portion of the goddess's prophecy as "a rhetorically constructed speech of persuasion."

103. Smith 1981a:69, 88.

104. For illuminating analyses of these stories and their thematic import in relation to the hymn as a whole, see Smith 1981a:71–86; Segal 1974:208–210; Segal 1986; King 1986.

105. The immortality of the horses is deduced from their being said to "carry the immortals" (211); note the tradition (*Iliad* V 265–272) that Anchises surreptitiously bred six horses from these gifts of Zeus, giving two to his son Aeneas.

106. For Tros' sons, see the useful genealogy in Smith 1981a:127.

107. Among commentators upon the hymn, Smith 1981a:87–90, confronts this question most directly. See also Sowa, who notes the problem (1984:49) but later seems to minimize it in claiming, despite Aphrodite's stated wish to give Anchises immortality, that she has already decided not to do so (1984:59).

108. See van der Ben (1986:29) for ἐγώ γε here as "I sc. as opposed to Eos."

109. Compare the use of this phrase in the traditional pattern of *eros* and *epos* to describe erotic captivation: the goddess's ἄχος "grief," the result of her *eros*, reduces her to the condition of Zeus at *Iliad* XIV 294 and of her protégé Paris at *Iliad* III 442, where ἔρως φρένας ἀμφεκάλυψε "*eros* veiled his wits."

110. For these terms of narratological analysis, see, for example, Genette 1980:25–32, *histoire* "story," *récit* "narrative," *narration* "narrating." In terms of early Greek epic, the story refers to the events told in the text; the narrative, to the oral tradition, as manifested in either a given text such as the *Odyssey* or the *Homeric Hymn to Aphrodite*; and the narrating to any performance of that tradition whether in speech or writing.

111. Smith 1981a:90.

112. Van der Ben 1986:25: "What is permissible for Zeus is not permissible for Aphrodite."

113. For this mode of speech as the "amorous conversation" that is the special province of "virgins," the object of Aphrodite's earlier imitation, see Loraux 1981:88n65.

114. See Cassola on 252 for στόμα τλήσεται in place of the στόμα χήσεται of the manuscripts with a review of other suggestions. See also van der Ben (1986:33), whose conjecture, γάμον ἔσσεται, depends upon his assumption that the gods will never express ὄνειδος of Aphrodite, since she will henceforth refrain from effecting divine/human liaisons.

115. For this reading see Kamerbeek 1967:393.

116. Compare Anchises' earlier "trembling" (182) and Aphrodite's earlier attempt to forestall it (83).

117. Van der Ben 1986:31.

118. For Aphrodite's coupling speech vs. her boasts, see above, notes 23 and 28.

119. See Muellner 1976:68–99.

120. See above, n. 23.

121. Indeed, the phraseological parallel ἐξονομῆναι τοῦτο supports the conjecture, οὐκ ὀνομαστόν.

122. Compare Pellizer 1978:126–129; Segal 1974; Segal 1986; Smith 1981a:92–95; van der Ben 1986:34–35.

123. Reading with Smith the infinitive φάσθαι, rather than the φασίν of the manuscripts, since reporting what others "say" seems inconsistent with directing Anchises to vouch himself for the child's maternity. For support of the manuscript, see AHS on 284.

124. Compare the command with which Apollo concludes the threat to the Cretans who are to become the priests of Delphi: "All has been said to you. Guard it in your mind" (*Homeric Hymn to Apollo* 544). Janko (1981:14) notes the tendency to end the myth-section of a hymn with the words of the god.

125. In Aphrodite's account, it is not their union *per se* that will elicit divine wrath – for Aeneas is its god-given issue – but rather, Anchises' publication of it.

126. Compare Rossbach 1894:cols. 2106–2109. For parallel instances, listed by Calypso for Hermes (*Odyssey* v 116–144), of mortal lovers of goddesses punished by Olympians, especially Iasion, lover of Demeter and killed by the thunderbolt of Zeus, see Sowa 1984:43, 58–59, esp. note 107.

127. Françoise Frontisi-Ducroux suggested at the presentation of this paper in Paris in 1987 that it was the Muses who revealed the truth. There is no indication of such a role for the Muses either in the hymn, unless it be the invocation of the Muse at the start (see above, n. 5), or in the extra-textual tradition. But it is nonetheless an arresting possibility. The question is whether the Muses could be conceived of as revealing such a fact apart from the will and knowledge of Zeus. Their parentage – they are daughters of Memory and Zeus (*Theogony* 53–55) – suggests for them the role of Zeus' *porte-parole*, and in that case their revelation would amount to the means by which Zeus himself told the truth. But it would be interesting to investigate whether the Muses ever reveal what all humans and gods involved in an event determine to keep secret. The Muses are theoretically capable of doing so, given their invocation at *Iliad* II 485: πάρεστέ τε, ἴστε τε πάντα "you are present at, and you know (have seen) everything." The problem in this situation would be to find a motive for the Muses' independent intervention.

WEAVING IN ARCHITECTURE
The Truth of Building

8

THE (RE)MARRIAGE OF PENELOPE AND ODYSSEUS

I N THE (RE)MARRIAGE OF ODYSSEUS AND PENELOPE, the *Odyssey* initiates a dialogue with the Western traditions of architecture, gender, and philosophy.[1] Although defined conceptually by discourses "invented" as different from mythology,[2] these three modes function actively in Archaic Greek culture and thought. As there was architecture before Vitruvius, gender before Freud or Lévi-Strauss, and philosophy before Plato, so in the *Odyssey* "para-theoretical" forms of architecture, gender, and philosophy mirror one another, creating what might be called an "Odyssean architectural theory."

In the *Odyssey*, architecture is the fabrication of material meaning, the transformation of nature into a material, mortal σῆμα "sign, tomb" – the tree supporting Odysseus' bed is the sign of immovability and unique identity, and Penelope weaves a shroud. Gender is a political instance of such architecture, insofar as it constructs the social significations of "natural" sexual difference. Odyssean gender makes difference a κίων "column" with roots in the earth. Its agent is philosophy, the knowing νόος "mind, intelligence" constructing and recognizing the σήματα "signs" of truth as unique identity.[3] Each of these three modes operates by means of *mêtis*, the working and work of "transformative intelligence" common to every τέχνη "craft."[4] In a continuous relay of reciprocal production, each can imitate the other's shape (or make the other imitate its shape) to win at the other's game. But as Zeus swallows the goddess Metis so that she "will devise evil and good in his interest alone," so Odyssean architectural theory confines this capacity within an ultimately uncertain "house arrest."

What do Penelope and Odysseus have to do with architecture? In the Western tradition, they are among its founding figures. By virtue of their *mêtis*, Odysseus and Penelope become each a myth of architectural mind and hand. *Mêtis* means both the working and the work of "transformative intelligence." It embraces both mental and manual prowess, both language and material.

215

Mêtis works by continual shape-shifting, turning the μορφή "shape" of defeat into victory's tool.[5] Its methods include the δόλος "trick, trap", the κέρδος "profit-gaining scheme", and the ability to seize the καιρός "opportunity". Each of these exploits the essential form of *mêtis*, the τρόπος "turning" that binds opposites, manifest in the reversal and the circle,[6] in weaving, twisting, and knotting, and in every joint. The mistress or master of *mêtis* knows how to manipulate "the circular reciprocity between what is bound and what is binding."[7] Etymologically, *mêtis* is derived from a verbal root meaning "to measure" with its implication of calculation and exact knowledge, preserved also in μέτρον "measurement".[8] A traditional connection between *mêtis* and the builder's skills is seen in the figure of Athena, daughter of the goddess Metis, who teaches τέκτονας ἄνδρας "builder men" to make (ποιῆσαι) elaborate war chariots and παρθενικάς "maidens" to weave (*Homeric Hymn to Aphrodite* 12–15),[9] and in the mythological architect, Trophonius.[10] The noun *mêtis* is the object of the verb of building itself in the phrase μῆτιν τεκτήναιτο "build a *mêtis*" (*Iliad* X 19).

The Greek mythology of *mêtis* dramatizes the mutual construction of architecture, gender, and philosophy under the sign of "father-ruled" marriage. Fashioned by Greek men and expressing their point of view, the myth casts *mêtis* as an undying female power that must be (re)appropriated through marriage by the political and philosophical power of the male. After her husband, the king Cronus, swallows her previous children to keep them from usurping his sovereignty, Rhea plots to protect her last-born, Zeus. To Cronus, she (or her mother Gaia) presents not the baby himself, but a *mêtis*.[11] Formally imitating his desire for another "swallowed" child, she gives him a stone wrapped in swaddling (that is, "swallowing") clothes.[12] Cronus "swallows the trick," thus enabling Zeus to grow up and to avenge himself by forcing his father to vomit the stone – which Zeus then "fastened down into the earth . . . to be a σῆμα 'sign' and θαῦμα 'marvel' to mortals" (*Theogony* 498–500). Now a political monument, the stone signifies Zeus' regime as the containment of *mêtis*, immobilized (like the rooted post of Odysseus' bed) in the ground.[13] To maintain this external, political fixation, Zeus matches it with an internal, domestic "incorporation" of *mêtis* in his marriage and ultimate "swallowing" of the goddess Metis herself (*Theogony* 886–900).

The marriage of Zeus and Metis is an "architectural contest" with her embodiment as the prize.[14] In the myth, the ultimate winner is never in doubt. In their struggle over entrance into her body, although Metis "turned into many forms to avoid being joined with him,"[15] Zeus "mixes" with her in sexual intercourse (his instrument, it would appear, is the same ἀνάγκη "force of necessity" that will compel the women in the *Odyssey*). Next they compete in body-making, matching their respective capacities for material and verbal transformation. Metis becomes pregnant and a prophecy reveals that she will bear a child who will usurp his father's rule. To bind the goddess within himself and thereby reverse the power of the pregnancy, Zeus "seduces her wits by a trick of wily words" and swallows her, "so that the goddess will devise evil and good in his interest alone" and he can give birth to the child himself from his own head. The proof of his victory is the goddess Athena, mistress of *mêtis* as swallowed by Zeus, who presides over the (re)marriage of Penelope and Odysseus.

In the (re)marriage of Penelope and Odysseus, the *Odyssey* tells a myth of architectural origins that prefigures and exceeds Vitruvius' aboriginal architects who build shelters by imitating the weaving and daubing of swallows' nests.[16] At a schematic level, the weaving of Penelope and the (re)marriage bed of Odysseus are emblems of the two basic elements of building: vertical space-enclosure and columns supporting a horizontal load.[17] Their collaboration constructs an ideal of architecture, gender, and philosophy in and as immovable (re)marriage. The partners in this collaboration, while mutually dependent, are not equal. Penelope is in charge of the (re)union. It is by virtue of her *mêtis* – her κέρδος "profit-gaining scheme" of secret, false speech, her δόλος "trick, trap" of weaving, and her trick to test for their secret σήματα "signs" – that Odysseus' *mêtis* of the bed can function as architect of his identity and hers. But Penelope's design serves a "program" – a system of social requirements and the power to enforce them – that she did not write. Itself an architecture, the program of Odyssean "father-rule" attempts ever to reconstruct its model of the female gender through the philosophic force of the *Odyssey* itself. The *Odyssey* divides the ambiguity (it posits as) essential to the female into an almost complete dichotomy of praise and blame.[18] It eulogizes the mind of the blameless wife, the best "Pandora" you can get.

In Praise of the Mind of Penelope

> "O blessed child of Laertes, Odysseus of many devices,
> surely you possessed a wife with great excellence (μεγάλη ἀρετῇ).
> How good were the wits (φρένες) in blameless Penelope,
> daughter of Icarius. How well she remembered Odysseus, her
>   wedded husband.
> Therefore his/her (oi) fame (κλέος) for her/his (ἧς) excellence
>   (ἀρετῆς)

will never perish, and the immortals will fashion for those upon
the earth
a song full of grace (ἀοιδὴν χαρίεσσαν) for prudent Penelope,
not as the daughter of Tyndareus devised (μήσατο) evil works,
when she murdered her wedded husband, and a hateful song
forever
will exist among men, and will forever bestow a harsh word
upon female women, even if there be one who does good."

Odyssey xxiv 192–202

Penelope is blameless because her wits are good. The text captures the virtue of her mind's devices in its own ambiguous expression of Penelope's ἀρετή "excellence," a quality attributed to no other female in Homeric epic: whether these pronouns – his/her (oi) fame for her/his (ἧς) excellence – refer to Odysseus or Penelope cannot be decided.[19] For it is precisely the ἀρετή of Penelope's mind – an exemplary *mêtis* in its tricky circularity of active and passive stances – to win κλέος for herself (*Odyssey* ii 125–126) by designing (re)marriage to the one in whom she locates all her ἀρετή:

"Stranger, truly my own excellence (ἐμὴν ἀρετὴν), both my
appearance and my build,
the gods destroyed, when the Argives embarked
for Ilium and my own husband Odysseus went with them.
If that man should come and tend this life of mine, my
own fame (κλέος ἐμὸν) would be both greater (μεῖζον) and more
beautiful (κάλλιον)."[20]

Odyssey xix 124–128

It is Penelope's *mêtis* to make her excellence and praise ultimately take the shape of her husband's, the shape of her husband as "her-self." She uses the mobility built into her gender to locate herself in and as his stable οἶκος "household," his unmoving, immovable place and space.

As foil for its praise of Penelope, the *Odyssey* blames Clytemnestra for using her *mêtis* (μήσατο) to "dys-locate" the place of her husband.[21] But in its drive to divide female *mêtis* into exclusive praise and blame, the text itself "dys-locates" the division. For it claims that the blame of Clytemnestra "will forever bestow a harsh word upon female women, even if there be one who does good" – even, that is, upon Penelope herself. With this censure of Clytemnestra, the *Odyssey* confesses the vulnerability of its architectural ideal to an independent female practice whose tropomorphic *mêtis* is forever reconstructed by the drive to contain it.

The *mêtis* of the Web

Praise, Blame, and the Ambiguity of a "Woman's Place"

> "High-speaking Telemachus, unrestrained in might, what sort
>   of thing
> have you said to shame us! You would like to fasten blame.
> But the suitors are not the cause or worthy of your blame
>   (αἴτιοι),
> but your dear mother, who beyond all others knows profit-
>   gaining schemes (κέρδεα)."

Odyssey ii 85–88

Casting the situation in the terms of praise and blame, the suitor Antinous defends himself to Telemachus. Penelope has superior knowledge of κέρδεα "profit-gaining schemes." She can make the other person look blameworthy, when it is actually she who is the αἴτιον "cause" and thus deserves the blame. The charge introduces the ambiguity of her situation.

Architecturally, Penelope's place as an αἴτιον "cause," locus of blame, is co-occupied by opposite but interdependent forces. For she does not change her position either in action, by returning to her father, or in word, by choosing one of the suitors or refusing to do so. In the terms of philosophical logic, A (force toward marriage as change of place) and *not*-A (force against marriage as change of place) occupy the same place at the same time. Here, as in buildings, the opposition of interdependent forces produces stability, but one that would arrest the Odyssean social system.

In receiving, but deflecting the suitors' petitions, Penelope would bring to a standstill the change of place that founds society. While she collects suitors, but does not move, Penelope "gains the profit" of praise in the medium of κλέος "fame."[22] Even the suitor Antinous' censure – by the "circular reciprocity" of praise and blame – functions here as indirect praise.[23] But if Penelope were never to move, what then? She would be forced to, as later "she finished the shroud, even though she was unwilling, compelled by force of necessity (ὑπ' ἀνάγκης)" (*Odyssey* ii 110). For the world of the *Odyssey* shares the system of father-rule charted by Lévi-Strauss in which men must exchange women in order to communicate with one another in networks of legitimate kinship and symbolic thought.[24] Men must move women from one οἶκος "household" to another in order to weave their social structure. A woman is moved from the οἶκος of her father and the status of an "Artemis" to the οἶκος of her husband and the sexual life of an "Aphrodite." From there she can be moved back to the father's house, if her husband dies, to be exchanged by her father again. Or, as in the case of Helen, she can be abducted from her husband's house by his rival. Such is the paradoxical architecture of marriage and of the female placement in it, a location built upon the necessity of dislocation.

But for now, Penelope maintains her position unmoved. By imitating the desires of her suitors in the twin strategies of secret, false messages and the treacherous (un)weaving of Laertes' shroud, she turns her adversaries into co-constructors of her ambiguous place.

The κέρδος "profit-making scheme" of Secret, False Speech

> "For it is now the third year, and quickly will be the fourth,
> that she has cheated the heart in the breasts of the Achaeans.
> To all she gives hope and promises each man,
> sending forth messages (ἀγγελίας). But her mind (νόος) designs
>   other things."

> *Odyssey* ii 89–92

Here is one of the κέρδεα "profit-making schemes" that Penelope knows beyond all others. She knows how to effect the emotions of others without moving herself. She is an "unmoved mover." This is her "gain." The mechanism of her unmoved movement is secret, false speech: *secret*, a message to each man individually, breaking up the many into several "ones,"[25] and *false*, a fictive exterior, when her interior mind designs other things.[26] This speech is not simply semiotic. It reflects and requires the operation of two architectural elements, *scale*: she analyzes a compound problem (the many suitors) into its constituent module (the individual suitor) and designs a solution at that level, and *space*: she constructs a division between outside and inside. This κέρδος of unmoved movement is an architecture of signs.

With their capacity to move bodies and minds, Penelope's secret messages illustrate the mistake in opposing speech to matter, an exclusion belied by writing, the "scandal of the talking body."[27] Like walls, signs divide and enclose. Their manipulation of scale and space is itself reproduced spatially in the "written" order of the text:

πάντας μέν ῥ᾽ ἔλπει, καὶ ὑπίσχεται ἀνδρὶ ἑκάστῳ.

to all she gives hope and promises each man.

Odyssey ii 91

Here ἔλπει "gives hope" and ὑπίσχεται "promises" divide πάντας "all" at line-beginning into ἀνδρὶ ἑκάστῳ "each man" at line-end.

If they followed regular Homeric practice, however, Penelope's ἀγγελίαι "messages" would not be conventional writings, but rather oral communications delivered by someone else.[28] For secret, false speech, such intangible messages would seem best. An "angelic" surrogate would allow Penelope the virtue of writing, the capacity to speak although absent. And as "winged words," the messages would leave no material trace of themselves. They would seem to escape the writing's vice of indiscriminate repetition. But the fact that Antinous can now recount Penelope's κέρδος "profit-making scheme" shows either that the messenger (or someone else) eventually revealed the message to all the suitors, telling the many what was meant for just one, or that the suitors told one another.[29] Once "written" on the mind, the message can be repeated. Intangible traces are thus no guarantee against iterability. Subdivision by architectural semiosis – as Penelope's scheme divides the suitors – entails its own instability.

Penelope's κέρδος "profit-making scheme" works only so long as the suitors do not speak the secret, false signs to one another. This collective silence depends upon moving each individual suitor to adopt an image of himself that matches the structure of the scheme. This is the *mêtis* of the κέρδος – to make each suitor act out his enemy's construction of him unawares. Each suitor must construe himself as a module divided between inside knowledge (what he knows from Penelope's message to him) and outside speech (what he says to the others). Penelope's *mêtis* of "unmoved movement" plays upon the pride of each man, upon the desire of each for unique identity as the only "chosen one" – and upon the force of that desire to displace and defer his even conceiving the possibility of another treated like himself.

The δόλος "trick, trap" of the Shroud

"And this is another trick (δόλον) she devised in her mind.
She set up a great loom in the halls and was weaving
a web both delicate and symmetrical. And then she said to us:
'Young men, my suitors, since shining Odysseus has died,

> wait, even though you are eager for my marriage, until I
> complete this mantle,
> lest my spinning be wasted and in vain,
> a shroud for the hero Laertes, for whenever
> the common doom of painful death brings him down,
> lest someone of the Achaean women in the community
> blame me,
> if he were to lie without a sheet to wind him, he who
> acquired much.'
> So she spoke, and the proud heart in us was persuaded."
>
> *Odyssey* ii 93–103

Why is Penelope's δόλος "trick, trap" persuasive? How does it make her worth waiting for? In displaying devotion to Odysseus' aged father, Penelope shows each suitor how she would act as his wife. She would not let either him or his father die without a shroud woven by the woman of his οἶκος "household."[30] This service to the father, enforced by the blame of other women, defers the suitors' sexual and social drive by tapping their fear of an ignominious death.

In the Homeric world death is a "common doom," erasing individual distinction. As a victor strips his victim's armor, so Pluto leaves only a bare corpse, despoiling even him who "acquired much." If the body is that of an old man like Laertes, it is κακόν "degraded, ugly, blameworthy" and αἰσχρόν "ugly, shameful."[31] Funeral rites cover the loss. Provided as a γέρας "gift of honor in compensation" for death (*Iliad* XVI 457, 675), burial and tombstone keep the corpse from becoming a forgotten "feast for dogs and birds" (*Iliad* I 4–5). Inside this outermost shield of the dead is another, ambiguous and architecturally more ambitious, materially distinct yet moulded to the body. Giving shape by screening, the shroud is the material surface of death itself.

Men depend on women for this covering. For in the Greek world only women weave shrouds. Penelope's δόλος "trick, trap"-speech persuades the suitors by promising to deploy this definitive mark of the female gender on behalf of the male over and against his mortality.

Why is it only women who weave shrouds? In Greek thought weaving is a mark of gender and race. Herodotus presents the men of Egypt as "virtual females" who "reverse the customs and laws of men" by weaving in the οἶκος "household," while their women trade in the ἀγορά "marketplace."[32] The aetiological myth of the female explains why weaving is her native art.

Weaving enters the human world with the woman and her *mêtis*, each as the αἴτιον "cause" of the other. It is Athena, daughter of the goddess Metis, who teaches weaving to Pandora, the first woman and model of all females, including the goddesses (like Athena and Metis) who preceded her.[33] Weaving and *mêtis*, too, are mutually originating. As the daughter of Metis teaches weaving, so one is said to "weave a *mêtis*."[34] In the logic of aetiological myth, such reciprocal origins represent the working of a system of jointly rein-forcing constructions. Weaving, *mêtis*, and Pandora: each is a tricky covering, an attractive outside that belies what is inside. Pandora is a work of plastic art, the ceramic likeness of a modest maiden, moulded by Hephaestus, the artisanal god.[35] Her modesty is a jar, an external verisimilitude. She is, like Penelope's web, a δόλος "trick, trap" against which men have no μηχανή "means of resistance,"[36] and, like the κέρδος of secret falsehoods, a partition of outside from inside. For, as Athena teaches her weaving, Aphrodite and Hermes constitute Pandora as a treacherous division between external, sexual power – "graceful beauty" that causes "painful yearning" and "limb-devouring sorrows" – and internal, mental power – the "mind of a bitch," the "character of a thief," "falsehoods," and that tool of *mêtis* wielded by Zeus against the goddess Metis, "wily words" (*Works and Days* 65–68, 78). [37] Pandora is an orna-mental screen. Her entire skin is covered by the κόσμος "order, ornament" that Athena as goddess of craft has "fastened together upon" (ἐφήρμοσε: ἐπί "upon" + ἁρμόζω "join, fit") it (*Works and Days* 76). In weaving, Pandora makes what she is, a covering of her (*mêtis*) inside.[38]

But why women alone are assigned the particular form of *mêtis* that is weaving, the myth of Pandora does not directly state. Its silence is understand-able psychoanalytically. For, lacking the inhibitions of Hesiodic theology, but ultimately derivative from its formulation of the female, it is a Freudian text that locates the reason this tradition sees weaving as women's invention – and in an area of maximum male anxiety:

> The effect of penis-envy has a share, further, in the physical vanity of women, since they are bound to value their charms more highly as a late compensation for their original sexual inferiority. Shame, which is considered to be a feminine characteristic *par excellence* but is far more a matter of convention than might be supposed, has as its purpose, we believe, concealment (*verdecken: Decke*, "cover, ceiling, roof, skin, envelope, coat, pretense, screen") of genital deficiency. We are not forgetting that at a later time, shame takes

on other functions. It seems that women have made few contributions to the discoveries (*Entdeckungen*) and inventions in the history of civilization; there is, however, one technique which they may have invented – that of plaiting and weaving. If that is so, we should be tempted to guess the unconscious motive for the achievement. Nature herself would seem to have given the model which this achievement imitates by causing the growth at maturity of the pubic hair that conceals the genitals. The step that remained to be taken lay in making the threads adhere to one another, while on the body they stick into the skin and are only matted together. If you reject this idea as fantastic and regard my belief in the influence of a lack of a penis on the configuration of femininity as an *idée fixe*, I am of course defenseless.[39]

Women invented weaving to conceal their genitals, the locus of their lack and envy of the male's (pro-)creative capacity and the place – indeed the *aition* – of castration, the "female" condition he fears for himself. From the Greek perspective, the covering of this place is praiseworthy, for all genitals are τὰ αἰδοῖα "the shameful parts." Veiling them, like wrapping a corpse, displays αἰδώς "shame" that "feminine characteristic *par excellence*."

Although based overtly upon women's "original sexual inferiority," Freud's aetiology of weaving repeats the Greek pattern of casting the male's creative capacity as originally female. For against its assumption of their lack and envy, Freud's text attributes to women an originary *mêtis*, whereby they invent "the step that remained to be taken . . . making the threads adhere to one another." This amounts to claiming that women use their inventiveness to cover their (lack of) genitals understood as their (lack of) inventiveness. And it is this very invention, weaving, that Greek men emulate in modes of creativity from which women in Greece are largely barred and thus might be thought to envy. For as Zeus appropriates the original Metis, so Greek men call their poetry, prophecy, and in Plato, even the art of the statesman himself, a "weaving."[40] But with weaving as figurative speech, and poetry, prophecy, and political philosophy as figurative web, each is the "non-original origin" and the "literal figure" of the other.[41] It is to overrule such reciprocal formation that Zeus fixes his *mêtis* stone in the ground, the σῆμα "sign" of the philosophical and political power to erect and enforce the hierarchy of figurative over literal, the "figurative" weaving for men and "literal" weaving for women.

The same arrested relay of emulative *mêtis* underlies Odyssean architectural theory. For in the female invention "of making the threads adhere to one another" is also the beginning of architecture. The Vitruvian myth of aboriginal architects "imitating" the weaving and daubing of birds' nests continues a widespread aetiology. The tradition reaches to the etymology of τεῖχος/ τοῖχος "wall" derived from a root with cognates in several Indo-European languages meaning "to mould a wall of mud"[42] and to the woven constructions that comparative architectural historian and theoretician, Gottfried Semper, adduces as the origin of vertical division between inner and outer space:

> . . . the beginning of building coincides with the beginning of textiles.

> The wall is that architectural element that formally represents and makes visible *the enclosed space as such*, absolutely, as it were, without reference to secondary concepts.

> We might recognize the *pen*, bound together from sticks and branches, and the interwoven *fence* as the earliest vertical spatial enclosure that man *invented.* . . .

> Whether these inventions gradually developed in this order or another matters little to us here, for it remains certain that the use of the crude weaving that started with the pen – as a means to make the "home," the *inner life* separated from the *outer life*, and as the formal creation of the idea of space – undoubtedly preceded the wall, even the most primitive one constructed out of stone or any other material.

> The structure that served to support, to secure, to carry this spatial enclosure was a requirement that had nothing directly to do with *space* and the *division of space.* . . .

> In this connection, it is of the greatest importance to note that wherever these secondary motives are not present, woven fabrics almost everywhere and especially in the southern and warm countries carry out their ancient, original function as conspicuous spatial dividers; even where solid walls become necessary they remain only the inner and unseen structure for the true and legitimate representatives of the spatial idea: namely, the more or less artificially woven and seamed-together, textile walls. . . .

> In all Germanic languages the word *Wand* (of the same root and same basic meaning as *Gewand*) directly recalls the old origin and

> type of the *visible* spatial enclosure. Likewise, *Decke, Bekleidung,*
> *Schranke, Zaun* (similar to *Saum*), and many other technical expres-
> sions are not somewhat late linguistic symbols applied to the
> building trade, but reliable indications of the textile origin of these
> building parts.⁴³

Given Semper's account of the "beginning of building," by marking weaving as
exclusively female, early Greek thought attributes to women the founding form
of architectural art. But the Odyssean system of praise and blame confines the
woman's architectural power to weaving its "walls." A praiseworthy "Pandora"
weaves to cover (herself as) shame – and blames women who do not.

Why do women enforce this confinement of their weaving? A "woman's
place" in the *Odyssey* is subject to male force – the ἀνάγκη "force of necessity"
that ultimately compels Penelope to finish the shroud (*Odyssey* ii 110). In this
position, women have neither security nor prestige unless they weave in the
interests – weave the "protection" – of the father-rule. It is the *mêtis* of the
Odyssean architecture of gender – *mêtis* as "swallowed" by the ἀνάγκη of Zeus'
regime – to elicit from women its double. Women restrict their architecture in
return for protection and praise.

Penelope's δόλος "trick, trap" of the shroud is persuasive because it
promises conformation with this ideal of female architecture. It is treacherous (an exemplary *mêtis*) because it both keeps and contravenes – indeed
it keeps by contravening – its promise. For as long as it operates, Penelope's
δόλος maintains the ambiguity of her position as αἴτιον "cause," a movement
without (re)location – toward the οἶκος "household" of her husband's rival as
she weaves by day, toward her husband's οἶκος as she unweaves at night. This
is not a static stand-off, for equal spending and saving here add up to a κέρδος
"profit" of praise. This scheme of rotating reversal is Penelope's solution to the
problem posed by the program of Odyssean architecture, gender, and philosophy: how to construct a praise-winning female place, when you do not know
whether your husband is alive or dead? If alive, keep his place alive (unweave
his father's shroud by night). If dead, make a new place for yourself (weave his
father's shroud by day). Thereby make your place simultaneously that of both
men and no man. Her strategy tropes the riddle of her situation with another:
when is the most blameworthy female action, refusing marriage exchange or
marrying a husband's rival, the most praiseworthy? Answer: when they are
done at the same time, just as Penelope is said to enter the room Ἀρτέμιδι
ἰκέλη ἠὲ χρυσῇ Ἀφροδίτῃ "like to Artemis or golden Aphrodite" (*Odyssey* xvii

37, xix 54). Hers is a *mêtis* of doing both, while doing neither, a "circular reciprocity" that binds the suitors and the system they represent.

But it binds Penelope, too. Time does not stand still. With repetition, ambiguity becomes architectural. Resisting the question of whose place she is weaving allows and even courts its occupation by the suitors. Their prolonged presence attracts the allegiance of women trained to exercise their *mêtis* on behalf of the man who occupies their οἶκος "household." Penelope's dislocating architecture provokes its "dys-location" in the figure of the servant woman who betrays her.

A treacherous double of Penelope's movement without changing place, the servant woman, like Clytemnestra, changes her place without movement. And like the ambiguity of Penelope's position, the servant's unmoved self-movement exploits the female role in marriage exchange. Although they are the passive σήματα "signs" of this system, exchanged so men can speak with each other, women are also, as Lévi-Strauss observes, active *"signes parlantes"* who can speak for themselves.[44] Women are thus like "linguistic shifters" (the pronouns "I" and "you," for example) whose meaning changes according to their "place" of utterance. But a woman can also – as in the case of Clytemnestra with Aegisthus or that of Odysseus' disloyal maidservants with the suitors – use her place or herself as place by designating its owner.

As Penelope's κέρδος "profit-making scheme" of secret speech works only so long as the many suitors are silent, so the δόλος "trick, trap" of her shroud succeeds only so long as the many women in the οἶκος "household" speak with a single voice. Such is the vulnerability of her "vertical space enclosures" to the perforation of speech. Now, with the breaking of the women's univocality, comes the τέλος "completion" of her weaving by ἀνάγκη "force of necessity" (*Odyssey* ii 110) and the order to return to her father (*Odyssey* ii 113–114) – and the arrival of a stranger in the οἶκος.[45] Henceforth Penelope's *mêtis* is devoted to the architectural philosophy of his identification.

The *mêtis* of the (Re)Marriage Bed

The Test for Architectural Signs

The *mêtis* of the (re)marriage bed begins with Penelope sleeping upon it, while Odysseus slaughters the suitors – sleeping more sweetly than ever before, since Odysseus left for Troy, so sweetly that she berates the nurse Eurycleia for awakening her with the news of his return (*Odyssey* xxiii 15–19).

Penelope refuses to believe the nurse. Eurycleia replies that Odysseus has returned "really" (ἔτυμον, *Odyssey* xxiii 26). Overjoyed, Penelope asks to hear "unerringly" (νημερτές, *Odyssey* xxiii 35), if he "really" (ἐτεόν, *Odyssey* xxiii 36) has returned, how he "although being only one," slaughtered the many (*Odyssey* xxiii 38). After listening to Eurycleia's account, she denies that it is a "true story" (μῦθος ἐτήτυμος, *Odyssey* xxiii 62) and initiates a test for the real identity of this "stranger" (ὁ ξεῖνος, *Odyssey* xxiii 28).

Earlier in the day she set up a contest to see who could string Odysseus' bow and hit a target through a row of twelve axes, promising to marry whoever succeeded.[46] The winner had to be at least a good copy, someone εἴκελος "like" or ὁμοῖος "same as, equal to" Odysseus – not false pretenders to his place like the suitors, but not necessarily the original man.[47] Now, in order to determine Odysseus' unique identity, Penelope designs a πεῖρα "penetration to the boundary, test" that is at once a work of architectural philosophy and of philosophic architecture.[48] Penelope's πεῖρα will define Odysseus by penetrating the space up to the πείρατα "boundaries" that enclose an individual, an inside distinct from all that is outside. These "boundaries" of Odysseus are architectural signs: the σῆμα "sign" of the scar engraved on his body and the σήματα "signs" of the bed he built. Qualified by Penelope as σήματα "which we two only know hidden from others" (*Odyssey* xxiii 110), the signs of the bed circumscribe an interior location, an exclusive mental place occupied by the two alone, another κέρδος "profit-making scheme" of secret, but this time not false, signification. In defining himself, Odysseus' architecture of the (re)marriage bed defines Penelope in and as the same place. And by the circular reciprocity of *mêtis*, Penelope's πεῖρα of Odysseus will prove her own identity as well. "Penelope" is just she who moves (herself as) the target so that it becomes something immovable and "Formal" – again, an "unmoved mover" – something only Odysseus in his "Formal" uniqueness can hit.

The σῆμα "sign, tomb" of the Scar

In keeping with the proper procedure in early Greek tradition of testing the identity of a "stranger," Penelope claims first that he is a god (*Odyssey* xxiii 63).[49] This assertion elicits from Eurycleia the σῆμα ἀριφραδές "very clear sign" (*Odyssey* xxiii 73) of Odysseus' scar, the one she had recognized as she bathed him the previous night. Her moment of recognition occasioned the text's extended reconstruction of the mark: it is the sign of the wound Odysseus received from a boar's tusk, while hunting on Parnassus with the sons of his mother's father Autolycus. It was Autolycus who gave him his name as an infant and promised to give him many possessions when he grew up. It was to collect this patrimony that Odysseus came to Parnassus and during the hunt that he received this initiatory sign of naming and manhood (*Odyssey* xix 386–475).

The σῆμα "sign, tomb" in Homer is most often a three-dimensional object entailing recognition, interpretation, and knowledge, in particular the grave marker.[50] Embedded in the body, a scar is a sort of grave marker *concave*, a trace of mortality in the living organism. It marks identity as born at the writing on the body of the body's death. It is the sign of name as incision.

After listening to Eurycleia's description of her discovery of the scar, a sign Penelope will have recognized as well as anyone, she leaves the bedchamber and goes down to see "the men, suitors, dead, and him who slew them" (*Odyssey* xxiii 84).

The σήματα "signs" of the Bed

The ultimate conversation of Penelope and Odysseus begins with the woman's uncertainty. She debates whether to question or to kiss him (*Odyssey* xxiii 85–87). The two sit apart, beside the architectural form associated with each, she by the wall, reminiscent of her weaving, and he beside the column, looking down and waiting (*Odyssey* xxiii 89–90). "At one time she looks him in the face and at another, she does not recognize (ἀγνώσασκε) him, wearing foul clothes on his skin" (*Odyssey* xxiii 94–95). When her son berates his mother for holding back, she insists:

> If really (ἐτεόν) indeed
> he is Odysseus and has come home, indeed we two especially
> shall know (γνωσόμεθ') each other even better. For we have
> signs (σήμαθ') which we two only know hidden from others.

> *Odyssey* xxiii 107–110

Apparently recognizing in these words an αἶνος, an "allusive speech" to test his knowledge of the secret signs,[51] Odysseus smiles and bids his son, "allow your mother to test me" (ἔασον πειράζειν ἐμέθεν). And quickly she will point things out to herself even better" (*Odyssey* xxiii 111, 113–114).

With this invitation to his wife, Odysseus sets the scene for a (re)marriage of the two. He directs the men and women to dress handsomely and the bard to sing the "wedding song" (expected after the contest of the axes to decide the bridegroom) so as to put off any rumor of the suitors' slaughter (*Odyssey* xxiii 130–151). Alleging his ragged clothes to be the reason his wife denies him, the bridegroom himself is bathed and beautified (*Odyssey* xxiii 115, 153–163).[52] Now "like (ὁμοῖος) to the immortals in build," he sits down again "opposite his wife" (*Odyssey* xxiii 163–165).

Accusing Penelope of a heart more stubborn than any woman's and answering her test of their private σήματα "signs" with an αἶνος "allusive speech" of his own, Odysseus asks the nurse to make him up a bed (*Odyssey* xxiii 166–172). His counter-αἶνος elicits from Penelope the final move of her πεῖρα "test." By way of "testing her husband" (πόσιος πειρωμένη, *Odyssey* xxiii 181), she orders Eurycleia to "make up a firm bed for him outside (ἐκτός) of the well-stabilized bedchamber he made himself (αὐτὸς ἐποίει).[53] Put his firm bed out there (ἔνθα οἱ ἐκθεῖσαι)" (*Odyssey* xxiii 177–179). Odysseus responds with the self-identifying sign of the bed he built so long ago.

He first stresses the unique resistance of the bed to the instability of both the οἶκος "household" and the female, lateral displacement. He demands to know who put his bed "in another place" (ἄλλοσε, *Odyssey* xxiii 184). Not a god himself could easily put it "in another place" (ἄλλῃ ἐνὶ χώρῃ, *Odyssey* xxiii 186). No mortal could "move it to the other side" (μετοχλίσσειεν, *Odyssey* xxiii 188), "since a great sign (μέγα σῆμα) has been built into the skillfully-wrought bed" (τέτυκται ἐν λέχει ἀσκητῷ, *Odyssey* xxiii 188-189). Metonymic of such fixity, Odysseus emphasizes his unique architectural authorship, "I myself wrought it with toil and no one else" (τὸ δ' ἐγὼ κάμον οὐδέ τις ἄλλος, *Odyssey* xxiii 189). Finally, he declares the details of his building, first of the bedchamber and its entrance, and then of the bed inside:

> A long-leafed trunk of an olive tree grew inside the enclosure,
> blooming to the topmost. Its thickness was like that of a column
>   (κίων).
> Surrounding this, I built the bedchamber until I finished it,
> with close-set stones, and I roofed it well down from above.
> I put upon it compacted doors, jointed closely.
> And then I cut off the foliage of the long-leafed olive,
> and trimming the trunk from the root up, I planed it around
>   with the bronze,
> well and with knowledge (ἐπισταμένως), and I made it straight
>   to a chalkline,
> thereby constructing a bed-post. I bored through it all over with
>   an auger.
> Beginning from this I kept carving my bed, until I finished it,
> decorating[54] it with gold and silver and ivory.

And I stretched inside the thong of an ox, shining with purple.
So I have articulated for you this sign (σῆμα). But I do not know
whether the bed is still in place (ἔμπεδον), woman, or whether
    now some other man
put it elsewhere (ἄλλοσε), by cutting under the stump of
    the tree.

Odyssey xxiii 190–204

This architecture is the secret σῆμα "sign" that Odysseus and Penelope know apart from others.

What is it a sign of? The bed is a sign of the Odyssean ideal of architecture, gender, and philosophy in and as immovable (re)marriage. The bed is a sign of support made immovable by transmuting organism and structure, model and copy. By planing off the bark, Odysseus removes the only part of the tree that is alive, its only source of growth either lateral or vertical. Now the tree will turn into the material of monumental building. Now surpassing even the stability of its model, a κίων "column," the tree is a copy with roots in the ground. It embodies the "Formal" ideal that all columnar forms imperfectly emulate.[55]

By its fixity, the bedpost signifies the ideal immovability of (re)marriage and, *a fortiori*, of the woman, once she is moved to weave the place of the bed. It is the σῆμα "sign" of female mobility limited to the movement of (re), of "again" within parentheses, of "again" within the walls of the οἶκος "household." Built by and for the man himself, the stationary bed betokens (re)marriage as his "swallowing" of the female's pharmacological movement, that movement whose *logos* shares the structure of the φάρμακον "cure, poison." A woman must be movable, so that men can communicate. She must enclose, so that he can support. But if the female can move, then her placement is unreliable. If she can weave, she can unweave space and place. What makes marriage possible makes its stability uncertain. So this constraint of the female architectural capacity – the containment of her movement and her weaving – is both health and harm, requiring its own architectural antidote, the immovable (re)marriage bed.

How can the bed guarantee the immovability of (re)marriage? Built into its roots is the μέγα σῆμα "great sign" of secret knowledge. Apparatus of gender and truth as exclusive difference, this secret sign divides inside from outside. By its secret structure and its structure as a secret, the bed frames the unity of a shared knowledge that cannot be replaced with a representative, an equivalent, or an imitation.[56] Designed so that disclosure and displacement

231

coincide, the knowledge and the location of the bed operate as *sumbola*, twin tokens of unique identity as unique relationship.[57] If he knows the bed, he is (her) Odysseus. Unless he has told the secret or she has, no one other than the actual man, not a pseudo-Odysseus but only the one "like to himself" (εἴκελος αὐτῷ) can speak its "hidden signs."[58] If she has not moved the bed, she remains (his) Penelope and their (re)marriage unmoved. But if it has been moved, then Penelope has castrated the marriage and, with it, her κλέος "fame" as female paragon.[59]

But the bed has not been moved. And Odysseus has spoken its "hidden signs." The text reiterates their architectural function:

> So he spoke, and right there her knees and her own heart were
>   released as she
> recognized (ἀναγνούσῃ) the fixed signs (σήματ' . . . ἔμπεδα) that
>   Odysseus spoke to her.
>
> *Odyssey* xxiii 205–206

The σήματα "signs" of the bed are ἔμπεδα "footed in" the ground, firmly standing, exclusively separating inside from out, the τέλος "completion" of Penelope's architectural and philosophic quest. Recognizing them brings ecstasy.

The *mêtis* of the Odyssean Architectural Ideal

In acknowledging her recognition, within the security of her immovable (re)marriage, Penelope inserts a parenthesis:

> But now, since you have now spoken signs easy to recognize
>   (σήματ' ἀριφραδέα)
> of our bed, that no other mortal man has seen,
> but only you and I – and only one handmaiden,
> Actoris, whom my father gave to me when I came here,
> who guarded the door of our firm chamber –
> you indeed persuade my spirit, though it is very unfeeling.
>
> *Odyssey* xxiii 225–230

Here – in the "parenthetical" person of the maid Actoris – is a potential gap in the σήματα ἀριφραδέα "signs easy to recognize" of Odyssean architecture, gender, and philosophy. Stationed in the liminal position of the female, mistress of passages, Actoris, "she who leads," could have told what she knew about the bed to others, just as Penelope's disloyal handmaids earlier revealed the *mêtis* of the web.

But what did Actoris know? In Greek "to know" is "to have seen." Did the sight of the bed reveal its foundation? And if Actoris did know and tell, who would be compromised? Only Penelope, since it would mean that someone other than Odysseus could speak the secret signs now or in the past. "We" know that either the present speaker is the true Odysseus or the *Odyssey* itself is a "Cretan lie." Penelope cannot. As for the past, if anyone has spoken these signs before, Penelope cannot take the present speaker for the unique Odysseus, unless she is hiding a past deception. Did a stranger melt her heart, as did Odysseus himself, with ψεύδεα ὁμοῖα ἐτύμοισιν "false things like to real things" (*Odyssey* xix 203–212)?[60] Did he speak signs with the same uncertain footing as the apparently σήματα ἔμπεδα "fixed signs" that were "recognized" by Penelope in Odysseus' description of his mantle and brooch?[61] Again, the authority of the *Odyssey* vouches for Penelope's fidelity. Odysseus cannot. If Actoris has told its secret, the bed fails as a construction of gender and philosophy, for it cannot maintain (re)marriage as immovable nor identity as unique.

Such a subversion of the system is a possibility that Odysseus overlooks. He weeps and holds the wife who is "jointed to his heart" (θυμαρέα, *Odyssey* xxiii 232). Against all its detractors – such as the Hesiodic account of Pandora that concludes: "Any man who marries and has a praiseworthy (κεδνήν) wife, one who is jointed to his mind (ἀρηρυῖαν πραπίδεσσι), for him evil matches itself against (ἀντιφερίζει) good forever" (*Theogony* 607–610) – with this consummate image of its ideal "joint," Odyssean architecture would close the door.[62]

Notes

An earlier version of this essay appeared in *The Ages of Homer*, edited by J. Carter and S. Morris, Austin, 1995:205-320. It is a pleasure to thank Jane Carter, Sarah Morris, and Laura Slatkin for helpful reading of that text. A modified version appeared in *Assemblage: A Critical Journal of Architecture and Design Culture* 21 (1993) 6-23.

1. The term "(re)marriage" is used to designate the renewal of an existing relationship, rather than a "remarriage" proper following either divorce or death.

2. For the foundation of history and philosophy via the "invention" of mythology as their differentiating "other," see Detienne 1986. For a psychoanalytic and an anthropological account of the relation between gender and what is understood as biological sex, see Mitchell and Rose 1982, and MacCormack and Strathern 1980. For a review of research on gender, see Laqueur 1990:1-24.

3. For νόος "mind" as the mental faculty of recognition and knowledge of the σῆμα "sign, tomb," see Nagy 1983.

4. For the essential work on *mêtis*, see Detienne and Vernant 1978. For the work and the intelligence of the artisan as *mêtis*, see Vidal-Naquet, "A Study in Ambiguity: Artisans in the Platonic City," in Vidal-Naquet 1986:224-245.

5. For classic examples, see Detienne and Vernant 1978:34, 37. The hunted fox reverses its direction and plays dead, lying in wait as a trap for the hunter. When caught, the fox-fish turns its body inside out, so that its interior becomes its exterior and the hook falls out.

6. See Detienne and Vernant 1978:46, "The ultimate expression of these qualities is the circle, the bond that is perfect because it completely turns back on itself, is closed in on itself, with neither beginning nor end, front nor rear, and which in rotation becomes both mobile and immobile, moving in both directions at once. . . . The circle unites within it several opposites, each one giving birth to its opposite; it appears as the strangest, most baffling thing in the world, *thaumasiotaton*, possessing a power which is beyond ordinary logic."

7. See Detienne and Vernant 1978:305.

8. See Chantraine 1999 *s.v.* μῆτις. Chantraine cites the cognate verbs μέδομαι and μήδομαι "devise, contrive" and the nouns, Sanskrit *mâti* "measure, exact knowledge" and Anglo-Saxon *mæd* "measure." See below on Clytemnestra's use of *mêtis* to "devise" (μήσατο) evil for her husband.

9. For the building of war machines as a part of the ancient architectural repertoire, see Vitruvius *De Architectura* 10.10-16. For the connection between weaving and architecture, see also Callimachus *Hymn to Apollo* 55-57: "Men follow Phoebus when they measure out cities. For Phoebus always delights in founding cities, and he himself weaves (ὑφαίνει) their foundations (θεμείλια)."

10. See Petrie 1979. For the ancient sources of the myth of Trophonius and its many variants in other cultures, see Frazer's note on Pausanias 9.37 (Frazer 1913:176–179). The activities of Trophonius and his brother Agamedes exemplify architectural *mêtis*. After building many monuments, including the temple of Apollo at Delphi, the pair design the treasury of a king who, like his divine counterpart, requires the products of *mêtis* to preserve his political "property." But rather than securing the king's gold, the architects build a secret passage through which to steal it gradually. Thus reversing the "proper" architectural function, the architects construct a means for exposure instead of enclosure and dispossess their client of the economic talisman of his political identity. Once he discovers their δόλος "trick," the king sets a trap of his own in which Agamedes is caught. The contest then continues as the brothers imitate the enemy to beat him at his own game. In an ironic assimilation of the king's loss of recognition, the two prevent the king from recognizing them by depriving themselves of identifiable form: Agamedes asks Trophonius to cut off his head, and after obliging his brother, Trophonius is swallowed up by the earth and becomes an oracular hero.

11. The trick of the stone is termed a *mêtis* at *Theogony* 471, when Rhea begs Gaia and Uranus to "devise together with her (συμφράσσασθαι) a *mêtis* by which she could make him forget that she bore her dear child." It is Gaia who takes the newborn Zeus to be raised secretly in the Cretan cave (*Theogony* 479–484) and she could be the subject of the phrase "having swaddled a great stone, she handed it to the son of Uranus" (*Theogony* 485), unless a change of subject back to Rhea is to be understood.

12. With the substitution of the swaddled stone for the real child, compare the Muses' capacity to substitute ψεύδεα ὁμοῖα ἐτύμοισιν "false things like to real things" and ἀληθέα "true things" εὖτ' ἐθέλωμεν "whenever we wish" (*Theogony* 27–28) in "Language and the Female in Early Greek Thought" in this collection. For the architectural significance of such swaddling, compare the *Bekleidung* "dressing, cladding" of a building in the theory of 19th century comparative architectural historian and theoretician Gottfried Semper (1989:24, 34, 36–40, 103–110, 240–243). On the relations between Semper's work and Karl Botticher's *Die Tektonik der Hellenen*, see Chapter 3, "Semper and the Archeologist Botticher," in Herrmann 1984.

13. This monolith would count among the examples of what Hegel calls "symbolic" architecture, the first stage in the progressive development toward the Classical and finally the Romantic/Gothic types. In contrast to the Classical, in which the elements must "display" (*zeigen*) their definitively architectural function, as a column, to take Hegel's prime example, demonstrates its load-bearing, the purpose of symbolic architecture is "the erection of something which is a unifying point for a nation." Its elements are often imitative of natural, organic forms and emphasize the unroofed enclosure of space rather than load-bearing support. See Hegel 1975:II.630–700. See also Payot 1982:29–50.

14. Aristotle's *Generation of Animals* presents a similar "battle of the sexes" as the sperm, a dynamic τέκτων "builder," attempts to master (κρατεῖν) the passive material of the menstrual fluid with the instrument of his "informing" soul (*Generation of Animals* 730b, 766b, 767b).

15. Apollodorus *Bibliotheca* 1.3.6. See also *Theogony* 886–900.

16. See Vitruvius *De Architectura* 2.1.2: "Therefore, since because of the invention of fire there was born at the beginning, a coming together among men and reasoning together and living together, and many came together into one place, by having from nature an advantage over other animals, so that they walked not with their head down but upright and gazed upon the magnificence of the world and the stars, and likewise with their hands and fingers they handled easily whatever they wished, they began in that joining together, some to make shelters (*tecta*) from a branch, others to dig caves under mountains, several by imitating (*imitantes*) the nests of swallows and their modes of constructing (*aedificationes*) to make places (*loca*) from mud and wattles which they might go under." For the view of Renaissance architect Leon Battista Alberti that it was "roof and walls" that first brought humans together in community, see Alberti 1988:3. On the Western tradition of myths of original architecture deriving from both Vitruvian and Biblical exemplars, see Rykwert 1972.

17. See Semper, "Structural Elements of Assyrian-Chaldean Architecture," Chapter 10 of "Comparative Building Theory" (*Vergleichende Baulehre* 1850) in Herrmann (1984:204) for these "two basic elements of building—the roof with the supporting columns, and the vertical enclosure later to become the wall of the living room." For these two elements as exemplary functions of the "Classical" and "Symbolic" stages respectively in Hegel's philosophy of architecture, see Hegel 1975:630–676.

18. For this ambiguity of the female, see "Language and the Female in Early Greek Thought" in this collection.

19. On this passage, see Nagy 1979:36–38, 255–256. Nagy interprets ἀρετή here as belonging to Odysseus, taking σὺν μεγάλῃ ἀρετῇ in 193 as instrumental with ἐκτήσω ("it is truly with great merit that you got a wife") and κλέος ἧς ἀρετῆς in 196–197 as "the *kleos* of his *aretê*," with the merit consisting in having won such a wife as Penelope. The ἀοιδὴ χαρίεσσα "song of grace" for Penelope in 197–198, clearly a gloss upon κλέος ἧς ἀρετῆς, is "part of the overall *kleos* of Odysseus."

20. See also *Odyssey* xviii 251–255.

21. For the relationship between μέδομαι and μῆτις, see Chantraine 1999 *s.v.* μῆτις.

22. See above on *Odyssey* ii 125.

23. For the circular relation of praise and blame, compare Pindar fr. 181 SM: ὁ γὰρ ἐξ οἴκου ποτὶ μῶμον ἔπαινος κίρναται "for by virtue of common origin (literally, 'from the household') praise is mixed with blame."

24. See Lévi-Strauss 1967:548–570 = 1969:478–497.

25. Compare Odysseus' ability to work as one against the many suitors.

26. Compare Achilles' condemnation of such a dichotomy at *Iliad* IX 312–313.

27. Compare Felman 1980.

28. Compare the case of Bellerophon, *Iliad* VI 155–202.

29. Was it the woman mentioned in *Odyssey* ii 108 who revealed the *mêtis* of the web to the suitors? It could also be a herald (Medon) or the domestic Dolion (*Odyssey* iv 735).

30. Antigone is a witness to the preeminent importance of proper death rites. For the role of women as leaders of funeral ritual, compare the mourning for Hector at the end of the *Iliad* and Alexiou 1974. For an analysis of the Homeric treatment of the corpse in terms of a cross-cultural account of the role of women in funerary rituals, see Bloch 1982:211–230.

31. Compare Priam's contrast between the corpse of a young man which retains its "beauty" (καλά) even in death and that of an old man, when "dogs disgrace (αἰσχύνωσι) the gray head and the gray beard and the shameful parts (αἰδῶ) (*Iliad* XXII 71–76) and the analysis of Vernant 1991:50–74.

32. See Herodotus 2.35. See also *Dissoi Logoi* [90] 2.17 DK.

33. See "Language and the Female in Early Greek Thought" with bibliography in this collection.

34. For "weave a *mêtis*," see *Iliad* VII 324, IX 93, *Odyssey* iv 678, 739, Hesiod *Shield* 28, for "weave a δόλος 'trick, trap,'" see *Iliad* VI 187, and for both as objects of "weave," see *Odyssey* ix 422.

35. Hesiod *Works and Days* 70–71 and *Theogony* 571–572: "Immediately from earth renowned Hephaestus moulded (πλάσσε) a likeness to a modest maiden."

36. Hesiod *Theogony* 588–589 of Pandora: "Marvel held both the immortal gods and mortal men, when they saw the sheer trap (δόλον αἰπύν), irresistible (ἀμήχανον) to men."

37. For γυιοβόρους "limb-devouring" vs. γυιοκόρους at 66, see West 1978.

38. As a construction enclosing her *mêtis*, Pandora is analogous to her jar containing hope. This jar, the body of Pandora, is also described as a house: "There in the unbreakable halls (δόμοισιν) hope alone was remaining inside under the lips of the jar, and it did not fly out from the door (θύραζε)" (Hesiod *Works and Days* 96–97). See Vernant 1989:77. As both body and house, the jar parallels Pandora with the οἶκος "household." The relation between the two is, however, hierarchical rather than equal. For the οἶκος is designed to work like the "swallowing" body of Zeus: to keep the female inside, able to use her *mêtis* for "weaving" only the walls of the οἶκος as an image and extension of the ideal wife. See "Female Fetish Urban Form" in this collection.

39. Freud 1933 [1932]: 132.

40. See Durante 1960. See also Schmitt 1967:299-301, Durante 1976:48,167-179, Snyder 1981, Scheid and Svenbro 1996, esp.111-130, Nagy 1996a:84-92, Nagy 1996b:63-74, Graziosi 2002:18-40, Nagy 2002:70-98. For the statesman's art as "weaving," see Plato *Politicus* 278e4–279c3. In the *Politicus*, weaving is appropriated as the paradigm of the statesman's ἐπιστήμη "knowledge," while the weaving τέχνη itself is degraded as a small, material, visible εἴδωλον "image" of one of τὰ ἀσώματα, κάλλιστα ὄντα καὶ μέγιστα "the immaterial things, being most beautiful and greatest" (*Politicus* 285d4–286b1). On the figure of weaving in Platonic thought, see Frère 1986.

41. For the philosophy of Plato and Aristotle as opposed to, while founded upon, metaphor, see Derrida 1972b = 1982.

42. See Chantraine 1999, *s.v.* τεῖχος "to fashion out of earth" (*façonner de la terre*), "make a wall out of earth" (*faire un mur de terre*). Cognates include Avestan *pairi-daêza* "enclosure, garden" and its Greek derivative *paradeisos* "garden, paradise." Compare also the architectural element of the "frieze" derived via French *frise* "border, fringe, ornament" from Latin *phrygium* (compare *Phrygiae vestes* "embroidered garments") and cognate with the verb "frieze" meaning "to cover with a nap" or "to embroider with gold." It is a pleasure to thank Richard Janko and Sarah Morris for suggesting these two etymological reflections of the processes of daubing and weaving respectively.

43. "The Textile Art" (Semper 1989:254–255, italics original); see also "The Four Elements of Architecture" (Semper 1989:102–103). Compare "Structural Elements of Assyrian-Chaldean Architecture," Chapter 10 of "Comparative Building Theory" (*Vergleichende Baulehre* 1850) in Herrmann 1984:205:

> It is well known that any wild tribe is familiar with the fence or a primitive hurdle as a means of enclosing space. Weaving the fence led to weaving movable walls of bast, reed, or willow twigs and later to weaving carpets of thinner animal or vegetable fiber....
>
> Using wickerwork for setting apart one's property and for floor mats and protection against heat and cold far preceded making even the roughest masonry. Wickerwork was the original motif of the wall. It retained this primary significance, actually or ideally, when the light hurdles and mattings were later transformed into brick or stone walls. The essence of the wall was wickerwork.

44. Lévi-Strauss 1967:548–570 = 1969:478–497.

45. See *Odyssey* xxiv 146–150, where the ghost of the suitor Amphimedon indicates that the finishing of the shroud directly precedes or is contemporaneous with the return of Odysseus.

46. Penelope uses the same instrument to construct her husband's identity as Clytemnestra uses to murder Agamemnon, the axe. The basic architectural function of incising material can either edify or destroy. I thank Sarah Morris for pointing out this contrasting use of the axe.

47. For the relation between Odysseus and the suitors as *simulacra* or "false pretenders" to his unique identity, see Deleuze 1969: "Platonism is the philosophical *Odyssey;* the Platonic dialectic is neither a dialectic of contradiction nor of contrariety, but a dialectic of rivalry (*amphisbetesis*), a dialectic of rivals and suitors (*prétendants*)" (293). "Copies are secondary possessors. They are well-founded 'suitors' (*prétendants*), guaranteed by resemblance; *simulacra* are like false 'suitors' (*prétendants*), built upon a dissimilarity, implying an essential perversion or a deviation. It is in this sense that Plato divides in two the domain of images-idols: on one hand there are *copies-icons*, on the other there are *simulacra*-phantasms" (296).

48. For the root **per* "go to the end point," in πείρω "penetrate, pierce," πεῖρα "penetration to the end, test," and πεῖραρ "boundary line, determinant," see Bergren 1975.

49. Compare the procedure of Anchises in "*Homeric Hymn to Aphrodite*: Tradition and Rhetoric, Praise and Blame" in this collection.

50. For the verbs of recognition, interpretation, and knowledge of the σῆμα – ἀναγιγνώσκω, νοέω, and γιγνώσκω – see Nagy 1983. Apropos of the σῆμα as a gravestone, see Vermeule 1979:45: "The classical *sêma* can be both the external sign of the invisible dead in the grave, and the substitute person, especially kept alive in memory when written upon." On the tomb as a signal instance of "symbolic architecture" in Hegelian philosophy, see Hegel 1975, esp. 650–654 on the pyramids and the Mausoleum.

51. For the αἶνος, see *Odyssey* xiv 462–506 and Nagy 1979:234–241. Compare the use of an αἶνος-mode of eliciting information and testing knowledge in "*Homeric Hymn to Aphrodite*: Tradition and Rhetoric, Praise and Blame" in this collection.

52. After his bath, Athena pours "great beauty" (πολὺ κάλλος) upon Odysseus so that his body looks bigger and thicker and lets down his hair in curls that are "like (ὁμοίας) to hyacinths" (*Odyssey* xxiii 156–158), a description that recalls the girth and locks of archaic *kouroi*. Compare Stewart 1990:2, plates 44–54, 57, 60, 132–135. The text then practices its own capacity to "liken" by comparing Athena's divine art to the work of a human sculptor: "And as when a man with knowledge (ἀνὴρ ἴδρις) pours gold around silver, one whom Hephaestus and Athena have taught every sort of art (τέχνην παντοίην) and he produces works of grace (χαρίεντα δὲ ἔργα τελείει), so did the goddess pour grace (χάριν) around his head and shoulders" (*Odyssey* xxiii 159–162). From Athena's sculpting (as assimilated to the human art that imitates her own) Odysseus emerges "like (ὁμοῖος) to the immortals in build" (*Odyssey* xxiii 163). In this context of poetic and sculptural "likening," the simile suggests a chiastic parallel between poet and sculptor made possible by (if it does not itself promote) anthropomorphic theology: as the poet fashions anthropomorphic divinities who imitate human sculptors, so the sculptor fashions humans who look like gods.

53. See Stanford 1973:2.378 on xxiii 178, citing van Leeuwen's collection of examples of the imperfect ἐποίει "he made" in artists' signatures on works of 6th century BCE art.

54. On the significance of the use of δαιδάλλων here, see Morris 1992:29–30.

55. For the κίων "column" as derived from the tree, being already rectilinear in its trunk and branches, and as exemplary of the beauty of Classical architecture, that is, the pure display of architectural purpose, see Hegel 1975:665–669.

56. Compare the relation of truth in the Platonic system as that of the ὅμοιον, the "like, same, equal to itself." For the Platonic idiom, "to be ὅμοιος 'like to' yourself," see *Symposium* 173d4, *Republic* 549e2. For the collocation of "like" and "true" as synonymous, see *Sophist* 252d1 and *Philebus* 65d2–3, as reciprocal, *Phaedrus* 273d2–6. The basis of this relation is the "likeness" or "sameness" of the sensible particular and the intelligible Form or paradigm; see, for example, *Timaeus* 28b–29d, *Republic* 472c9–d1, *Parmenides* 132d1–4 (where the participation of the particular in the paradigm is precisely the relation of likeness), and *Sophist* 264c–268d. The vulnerability of this mimetic conception of truth is registered in the Muses' speech, when they claim they can "say many false things (ψεύδεα) like (ὁμοῖα) to real things." See "Language and the Female in Early Greek Thought" in this collection.

57. On the early Greek *sumbolon*, see "Similes and Symbolization in *Odyssey* v" in this collection. Used as a means of identification, especially to secure contracts and treaties, the *sumbolon* designates an incomplete object, such as one half of a knucklebone, that must be brought together (*sumballein*) with the other half to prove the identity of the bearer. The term is also used of a single object related to individuals by their exclusive knowledge of it. In the case of the objects that identify Creusa and Ion as mother and son, for example, Creusa's description of the contents of Ion's cradle, before seeing them, works as her "half of the knucklebone" (Euripides *Ion* 1386–1442). In the same category belong the purple mantle and golden pin that the disguised Odysseus describes in response to Penelope's πεῖρα "test" of his claim to have been Odysseus' host in Crete (*Odyssey* xix 215–250). Penelope "recognizes" (ἀναγνούσῃ) them as "fixed signs" (σήματ' . . . ἔμπεδα) of their speaker's identity, when in fact they can signify either Odysseus, his host, or any other guest present at the time.

58. The phrase "like to himself" (εἴκελος αὐτῷ) is used at *Odyssey* xx 88 in a prefiguration of their recognition: Penelope awakes weeping from a dream in which Odysseus appeared "like to himself, such as he was when he went with the army. And my heart was rejoicing, since I said it was not a dream, but a waking vision," and Odysseus, perceiving her cry, "imagined she had already recognized him" (δόκησε δέ οἱ . . . ἤδη γινώσκουσα, *Odyssey* xx 93–94).

59. See *Odyssey* xix 109–114, where Odysseus appropriately likens Penelope's κλέος "fame" to that of the model male, a "blameless" king.

60. See *Odyssey* xiv 124–130 where Eumaeus, although insisting that Penelope cannot be persuaded by the report of a wanderer, describes needy vagabonds who "tell lies (ψεύδοντ') and are unwilling to say true things (ἀληθέα)" and admits that Penelope used to receive any wanderer who came to Ithaca, entertain him, question him, and mourn, "since this is the right conduct (θέμις) of a wife, whenever her husband has perished elsewhere."

61. See notes 57 and 60 above.

62. The argument of this paper finds a confirming supplement in the analysis offered *per litteras* by Deirdre von Dornum: "The story of Aphrodite and Hephaestus at *Odyssey* viii 266–366 is the thematic and architectural counterpart to the (re)marriage of Penelope and Odysseus." In contrast to "restrained" Penelope (ἐχέφρων, *Odyssey* iv 111), Aphrodite is "unrestrained" (οὐκ ἐχέθυμος, *Odyssey* viii 320), unstable, does move, and so endangers her marriage, leading to blame (*Odyssey* viii 309, 319). As Odysseus builds his bed as a σῆμα "sign" to keep his marriage immovable, Hephaestus constructs a δόλος "trick, trap" in the form of a bed (*Odyssey* viii 276, compare 281–282) in order to stop Aphrodite's shifting (at *Odyssey* viii 275 he makes her ἔμπεδον "fixed," compare Odysseus' bed as ἔμπεδον "fixed" and his σήματα ἔμπεδα "fixed signs" at *Odyssey* xxiii 203, 206). While Odysseus' bed permits mutual recognition of unique identity, Hephaestus' bed-trick forces Ares' and Aphrodite's recognition (γίγνωσκον) that they cannot shift (οὐκέτι φυκτὰ πέλοντο, *Odyssey* viii 299). By changing the symbol of his betrayal into the sign of his control, shifting the shape of the bed to keep Aphrodite from shifting (in) bed, Hephaestus "turns the μορφή 'shape' of defeat into victory's tool." His triumph is qualified, however, as Aphrodite receives mixed praise and blame (in contrast to Clytemnestra) and is able to shift again (*Odyssey* viii 337, 342), thanks to the mediation of Poseidon. Although a master builder, Hephaestus is outwitted by Aphrodite with the complicity of her society. Their bed scene represents the construction of failed marriage through impermanent, public architecture versus successful (re)marriage through permanent, private architecture.

9

ARCHITECTURE   GENDER   PHILOSOPHY

εἶς, δύο, τρεῖς·

One, two, three.

Timaeus 17a1

I BROACH THE TOPIC OF ARCHITECTURE AND GENDER AND PHILOSOPHY first because of an exchange that took place in the fall of 1987 in Chicago. During the meeting of the Associated Collegiate Schools of Architecture Forum on "Architecture and Deconstruction" Peter Eisenman described something of Jacques Derrida's attitude toward architecture in the course of their collaboration to design a section of the Parc La Villette in Paris. As the program for this collaboration – ultimately entitled *Choral Works* – Derrida supplied his essay on the *khôra* "place, space" of Plato's *Timaeus*.[1]

In the *Timaeus* architecture and philosophy sign a contract of mutual translation.[2] The terms of its model of building and of aesthetic excellence founded a tradition handed down via Vitruvius and Alberti as the "Bible" of Western architectural theory.[3] The mutual edification of philosophy and architecture in the *Timaeus* entails the construction of gender between them. Their "ground-as-support" requires their complicity in the stabilization of *khôra*. In deconstructing this cooperative "choral work" resides the potential for the dislocation of Platonic ontology as formulated in the *Timaeus* and of Platonically informed architecture.

Meanwhile, back in Chicago (to imitate the constructive practice of the *Timaeus*), of Derrida's reaction to the architectural process, Eisenman claimed:[4]

He wants architecture to stand still and be what he assumes it appropriately should be in order that philosophy can be free to move and speculate. In other words, that architecture is real, is grounded, is solid, doesn't move around – is precisely what Jacques

242

wants. And so when I made the first crack at a project we were doing together – which was a public garden in Paris – he said things to me that filled me with horror like, "How can it be a garden without plants?" or "Where are the trees?" or "Where are the benches for people to sit on?" This is what you philosophers want, you want to know where the benches are. . . . [T]he minute architecture begins to move away from its traditional role as the symbolization of use, is where philosophy starts to shake. Because it starts to question its philosophical underpinnings and starts to move it around and suggest that what is under philosophy may be architecture and something that isn't so nice. In other words, it's not so solid, it's not so firm, it's not so constructed.[5]

According to Eisenman, philosophy needs for its own stability and freedom to move, an architecture that does not move, an architecture that stays put and symbolizes nothing other than its use.

At the same conference, Catherine Ingraham presented a paper exploring the "rage" of architecture at the prospect of domination by language. She concluded:

It seems to me interesting that the plan of domination suppos- edly exercised by language over architecture is actually resonating architecture's own plan of domination. I have no proposals for the horror of architecture for philosophy. [But] it could be that philos- ophy recognizes in architecture its own most frightening realiza- tion, which is that in some way architecture is the aestheticization of the pornography of power.

These two remarks, Eisenman's and Ingraham's, seemed to me to be related in reflecting a "female" status of architecture *vis-à-vis* philosophy. I commented:

Apropos of "architecture as the aestheticization of the pornography of power" I asked myself whether power is or could be a *pornê* (prob- ably you all know that a *pornê* is a prostitute). And that reminded me of a thought I had in the morning when Peter was talking about the resistance of Derrida to the fact that your architecture won't stay put, once it is placed – that you want to move the idea of a garden. It reminds me of the whole problem of the female in general – that she must be mobile, she must be exchangeable in order for family and children and homes to take place. But the problem about her

243

is that she is not a "proper" wife for sure. Because by virtue of her movability, she also could move herself and she could be like a *pornê*. A *pornê* is the opposite of the proper wife – a *pornê* wouldn't stay put, once exchanged – this is Greek thinking about females. So the ambiguity with which architecture is treated is perhaps an essential and necessary one. Because you must be movable. Yet that is just what nobody can allow you – once you're placed, you have to stay put. I think it's the deconstructive activity that permits this kind of perception. So in a way deconstruction has made a contribution to you and you're perhaps the best example of it in that you show that architecture is a writing of power as a *pornê* – as a necessary, productive medium that must be mobile. And yet once put in place, the other can't allow the mobility. Plus, then, it also goes in the other direction. You seemed slightly angry at deconstruction for not providing a model and a foundation for you. So that there was a way in which you needed deconstruction and language to be a woman for you also.

After this comment in which I had, I thought, said something positive about Eisenman's dislocating architecture and about architecture as a *graphê* – which means both "writing" and "drawing" in Greek – a *graphê* of the power of the *pornê*, I was later complimented by an eminent architect present on having "wiped up the floor" with Eisenman. This interpretation of the female as a category of blame coheres with a second impulse toward exploring the relation among architecture and gender and philosophy.

There has been relatively little treatment of gender in the theoretical discourse – the "philosophy" – of architecture.[6] In architecture gender has been studied in the domains of history and form: what women have designed and built,[7] and what formal characteristics may be designated as intrinsically female.[8] But architectural theory does not meditate upon the gender of architectural activity itself. Architectural theory does not appear conscious of this issue as essential to its self-understanding, and thus germane to male or female, practitioner or theorist as well. This relative absence of theoretical reflection, together with the implication of gender in the remarks of Eisenman and Ingraham about architecture and philosophy, incites the present investigation. I begin by looking at gender in the mode of the symbolic, where it is constructed.

Psychoanalysis and anthropology have analyzed gender as the constellation of characteristics and values, the powers and the powerlessness, attached by a given social group to sexual difference.[9] As the sexes are different, the meaning of gender is differential. Gender is thus a machine for thinking the meaning of sexual difference. And, as if sexual difference were the very meaning of difference itself, gender functions universally as a machine for differentiation as such – the totem *par excellence*.[10]

Equally universal (so far) is the fact that gender difference is subjective in both senses of the term, and thereby rhetorical and political. The difference gender makes may be seen in a linguistic phenomenon of which gender is a chief example, if not the primary model and motivation. This is the phenomenon of marked vs. unmarked categories. It is the "pervasive tendency in human thinking" to take one of the members of an opposition as unmarked so that it represents either the entire oppositional group (the "zero-interpretation") or the opposite of the other, marked member (the "minus-interpretation") or in some contexts, even the marked category itself (the "plus-interpretation").[11] The classic example of the procedure is gender terminology itself. For example, in English the marked term "woman" indicates the presence of the "marked" property "female," while the unmarked term "man" is used to indicate both the "human being" in general (the "zero-interpretation"), the absence of "female" in the sense of "male human being" (the "minus-interpretation"),[12] and sometimes even "female human being" (the "plus-interpretation").[13] This mode of differentiation permeates both the linguistic and the non-linguistic spheres. For example, pants or trousers (in most Western cultures) are unmarked, skirts are marked. In logical symbolism, p is used ambiguously either as the proposition abstracted from its truth value or as the assertion of the truth of the proposition p. And it is the term "truth value" itself, derived from the unmarked member, not "falsity value," that designates the "over-all category which has truth and falsity as members."[14]

This marked vs. unmarked categorization results from and expresses a privileged point of view. Ethnography records many instances in which the tribal name is also used as the term for "human being," so that all other human groups become outside, "marked" members, who can be designated only by phrases in which the base term bears an adjectival modifier, the mark of the group's "something extra," its extra-normative condition.[15] The marked group has something excessive, something different – femininity or falsity, in the examples above – that makes it ambiguously more and less than human.[16]

Whether or not it is gender differentiation that provides the model for marked vs. unmarked thought, gender differentiation universally (so far) takes the form of a marked vs. unmarked distinction. By virtue of its subjectivity, however, this form of differentiation is not univocal. In the manner of linguistic shifters, a group may occupy both the marked and the unmarked condition, depending upon the other group with which it is being compared.[17] In English, for example, "female" may be marked in relation to "male," while "nurse" is unmarked, requiring the adjectival supplement in "male nurse" to designate a non-female.[18] Similarly, in the sphere of architecture – to turn back toward the subject at hand – architecture could be marked as "female" in relation to philosophy (and again, I do not intend "female" as a term of abuse or degradation), while architectural theory was marked in relation to practice, which in turn might function as marked "female" in relation to the economic and political power of the client. And, moreover, there is nothing essentially (or "ontologically") female about the biological sex to which the marked "female" position is assigned. Even in the case of grammatical gender, an especially pervasive instance in which the twin tools of gender and the marked/unmarked opposition coincide, we find one counter-instance to the otherwise universally unmarked status of the masculine: in the Iroquoian languages it is the feminine gender that is unmarked.[19] What is not yet attested in human society is a gender differentiation which does not take the marked/unmarked form.

Is this model of gender at work between the architecture and the philosophy of the *Choral Works*? To pursue this question I turn to what programs the program of the *Choral Works*, the female and the architect before philosophy and then in Platonic texts, culminating in the *khôra* of the *Timaeus*.

Female and Architect: Before Philosophy

The ancient Greek language records a culture dominated by the male. The term *anthrôpos* is unmarked, meaning both "human being" (zero-interpretation), "man" (minus-interpretation), and, with the addition of the female article, "woman" (plus-interpretation). Corresponding to the unmarking of the male, Greek myth ascribes to the female a marked relation to knowledge, speech, and graphic creativity by virtue of a similarly marked social (dis)placement.[20] It ascribes this markedness to the architect, too. These "para-philosophical" origins are critical to comprehending the gen(d)eric drama in the conceptual maneuvers of Platonic philosophy with regard to architecture and the female.

Early Greek epic attributes to the female in the figure of the Muses what will later become the object of philosophical desire – transcendent knowledge, grounded in presence and sight, that makes possible the speaking and the imitating of truth. The Muses are called upon to impart their truth to the male poet:

Speak to me now, Muses, with homes on Olympus, for you are
goddesses, you are present beside, you know (literally, "have
    seen") all things,
but we hear only the report and know nothing.

Iliad II 484–486

The Muses speak the truth, understood as the re-presentation in its totality
(here in *Iliad* II, the total catalogue of Greek ships) of a past presence and sight
in any present place. But because they know all, the Muses can speak not
only the truth, but also falsehood, as they reveal in handing over the staff of
inspiration to the male poet Hesiod:

We know how to say many false things (ψεύδεα) like to (ὁμοῖα)
    real things (ἐτύμοισιν),
and we know, whenever we want, how to utter true things
    (ἀληθέα).

Theogony 27–28

By virtue of their transcendent knowledge of the truth, the Muses can imitate
it perfectly. And since they can do so whenever they want to, who can tell
whether even this very instance of their speech is a case of the truth or of
its perfect imitation? Only those who know what the Muses "want" in this
situation – *Was will das Weib?* – can know for sure. The rhetorical status of the
Muses' speech cannot be determined by anyone outside themselves (or their
intention), since it depends upon a position of epistemological mastery and
individual desire that no man, not even the male "author" of the text, can
share.[21] This speech of the Muses remains an irresolvable ambiguity of truth
and its figuration.

    Greek myth derives this capacity to manipulate truth and imitation from
the woman's power to determine legitimacy and illegitimacy, the proper and
improper, in the area where it counts most in a system of "father-rule," the
reproduction of children. The woman can present a man with his own son or
with a supposititious child. True paternity only the woman knows for sure.
Rhea, the mother of Zeus, is a founding instance (*Theogony* 453–506). To her
husband, the king Cronus, who had swallowed all of her previous children
so that none could usurp his sovereign power, Rhea presents not the baby
himself, but a *mêtis*. This term forms a crucial link between the architect and
the female.[22]

    Mêtis means the power and the product of "transformative
intelligence" – the mental and material process common to every τέχνη "craft,"

247

to the work of every artisan.[23] It embraces both mind and hand, both language and material. *Mêtis* thus integrates powers and activities separated in aesthetic traditions that draw a sharp line between the verbal and the visual, between the linguistic and the plastic, the written text and the building. It means continual shape-shifting, imitating the form of your enemy and defeating him with your trick at his own game.[24] Formally, *mêtis* is the τρόπος "turning" that manifests itself in the complicity of putatively formal opposites. It is the reversal and the circle, each as the double of the other.[25] It is thus weaving and twisting and knotting. It is every joint. It is every instance of "the circular reciprocity between what is bound and what is binding."[26] *Mêtis* links the craft of weaving with builders and the builder's skills in the *Homeric Hymn to Aphrodite* (12–15), where Athena, daughter of the goddess Metis, teaches the construction (ποιῆσαι) of elaborate war chariots[27] to τέκτονας ἄνδρας "builder men" and weaving to παρθενικὰς "maidens."[28]

Meanwhile, back in the myth of Rhea, she presents to her husband Cronus not a baby, but a *mêtis* in the form of a stone wrapped in swaddling, that is, "swallowing" clothes – a morphological imitation of his desire for an inanimate child.[29] Cronus swallows the trick, literally (just as philosophy will later reappropriate the transcendental knowledge attributed to the Muses, and the creation by the Demiurge will surround the pre-cosmic *khôra* in the *Timaeus*). Later he is forced to vomit the stone, along with the rest of his children – forced by the true child, now grown into an avenger, the son he had thought dead within himself.

This son is Zeus. As "father of men and gods" and consummate ruler of the cosmos, Zeus pre-figures both the lawgiver of the *Laws* and the Demiurge of the *Timaeus.* His policy in relation to *mêtis* becomes a paradigm, a sort of Form, in which later philosophy and politics attempt to participate. Zeus' first act upon securing his kingship from his father is to turn the *mêtis* stone into a monument. In a "classic" instance of political sovereignty as architectural trope and of architecture as political symbolization, Zeus "sets up" the *mêtis* stone – the formal substitute for himself – "to be a σῆμα 'sign' and θαῦμα 'marvel' to mortals" (*Theogony* 500). The stone is a sign of Zeus and his rule as a working and work of *mêtis*, now fixed in the ground. His next move is to mirror that external fixation of *mêtis* by containing it within himself.

By an anachronism essential to the myth of valid sovereignty (one that is repeated in the institution of architecture in the *Timaeus*), Zeus now uses *mêtis* to acquire *mêtis*, as it were, for the first time.[30] The scene of his acquisition is marriage. For in early Greek *mêtis* is not just a common noun. It also designates a goddess, Metis, whom Zeus takes as his first wife. Their marriage is an architectural competition, pitting her *mêtis* against his in a contest of material and verbal transformation with her embodiment as the prize.[31] They first struggle over entrance into her body. Although "she turned into many forms to avoid being joined with him,"[32] Zeus manages to "mix" with her in sexual intercourse (a union we shall see paralleled in the "mixture" of the demiurgic intelligence and wandering necessity as causes in the *Timaeus*). Next they compete in body making. Metis becomes pregnant, and it is foretold that she will bear a son who will supplant his father. But before she can give birth to a child, he "utterly deceived her wits by a trick of cunning words" and swallows her, "so that the goddess might devise evil and good in his interest alone" (*Theogony* 889–890, 900). Having "incorporated" the power necessary for the maintenance of his regime, it is now Zeus himself who gives birth to her child, the goddess Athena, from his own head. On the divine level, at least, the unmarked "male" is now able to bear the "plus-interpretation" of a *mêtis*-man. This is the divine model, the Formal ideal. But the heads of the human household cannot contain their protean property so successfully.

The female's *mêtis* – her control over legitimacy, propriety, ownership, and the "own" itself – is a power of (dis)placement, a power of putting one child, both value and sign, in the place of the other. This power of place is gender-determined. It derives from the capacity and the necessity to change places imposed upon the female by marriage exchange. In order for men to communicate with one another in systems of kinship and symbolic thought, they must prohibit incest, that is, they must move women from one οἶκος "household" to another.[33] Once placed, however, the female is then (like a building and like Metis inside Zeus) supposed to stay put. She is supposed to become the sure foundation of the οἶκος "household" of her husband. But as Greek myth repeats, the placement of the female is unstable: if the female is able to move, the stability of her construction is uncertain. The legitimate wife can turn *pornê* "prostitute" and, like Helen, re-exchange or replace herself.[34] Diathetic ambiguity incarnate, "speaking sign" that she is, the female can control her own place, by moving it or by allowing an alien to enter it. Female mobility is a *mêtis*, a τρόπος "turning" that recoils like a φάρμακον "drug" – what makes marriage possible makes its certainty impossible.[35]

The φάρμακον-logic of female placement, like the ambiguity of the Muses' speech, is inherent as well in the graphic art of women, the work of *mêtis* par excellence – weaving – taught to women by Athena, the daughter of Metis herself (*Homeric Hymn to Aphrodite* 12–15). So prevalent and definitive is the association of weaving and the female that Freud calls it the one contribution of women to civilization and an imitation, in fact, of their own anatomical destiny, the woven threads emulating the pubic veil over their lack of the penis.[36] And indeed, in Greek culture, where women lack citizenship, the woman's web would seem to be supplemental, a silent substitute for (her lack of) phallo-political voice. But this is not a complete picture, for in Greek the utterance of poetry or prophecy – and in Plato, even the art of the statesman himself – is described as "weaving."[37] As Zeus appropriates *mêtis*, so Greek men call their product, in effect, a "metaphorical web." Weaving as figurative speech, and poetry, prophecy, and political philosophy as figurative web, each the "original" of the other (we shall find the same relation between architecture and philosophy in Plato).

Woman's weaving, her text, is thus a signal instance of the inebriated oscillation of truth and imitation, stability and mobility, sound and silence, speech and writing, and writing and drawing that constitutes for Greek the γραφή "drawing, writing."[38] The myth of Tereus, Procne, and Philomela is an eloquent example. When Tereus, husband of Procne, rapes her sister Philomela, he cuts out the woman's tongue to keep her silent – to keep her from telling her sister, his wife. Philomela responds with a *mêtis* that imitates her castrated voice. She "wove γράμματα 'pictures/writing' in a robe" which she sent to her sister.[39] In her power to defy physical constraints and to express what she knows through the silence of dumb material, the female remains the mistress of the graphic, of the constructed *mêtis*. This is the mark she shares with one Trophonius, mythological archetype of the architect.[40]

Trophonius occupies, along with other builders in Greek myth, an essentially marked, "female" position both above and below the male norm, in particular, the normative status of a citizen with political rights.[41] This double status is expressed mythologically by a duplication of the architect himself. Partnership consolidates the elements of architectual expertise then, as now. Trophonius works with his brother Agamedes, and Amphion, who raised the walls of Thebes by the sound of his lyre, with Zethos, who lugged the blocks of stone. The contrast between Amphion and Zethos is emblematic of two vectors of architectural skill. Amphion is the magician/musician, a *mêtis*–man who, like Prometheus or Odysseus, can foresee the end product and enchant the several stones into a single solid structure, a weaver of the many into one. Zethos is the manual laborer, a sort of Polyphemus, who exhausts his brute force hauling the elements of a Cyclopean wall. In the case of Trophonius and Agamedes, the doubling explicitly involves political and economic power and thereby points to the status of the architect in the ancient Greek *polis*.

After having built many monuments, including the temple of Apollo at Delphi, Trophonius and his brother Agamedes build the treasury of a king.

The king, like Zeus, requires the services of *mêtis* to control his political "property."[42] But like a woman who transgresses the boundaries of her οἶκος "household" or misappropriates the product of her womb, the pair of architects try to steal the king's gold little by little through a secret passage they construct in the treasure house. The architects thus invert the "regular" architectural function, building exposure instead of protection and dispossessing their client of his economic property, the talisman of political sovereignty. (It should be remembered that the *polis* is the sole commissioner of major architectural projects in Greece before the Hellenistic period.)[43]

The king, a *mêtis*–man, too, like his exemplar Zeus, retaliates by setting a trap of his own in which Agamedes is caught. Agamedes then asks his brother Trophonius to cut off his head to prevent his being recognized. After obliging his brother, Trophonius flees to a place where he is swallowed up by the earth and becomes an oracular hero. After decapitating his alter-ego so that his identity cannot be determined – a feminization by castration – the architect becomes, like the Muses, a voice of transcendent truth.

In both phases of their activity, as illegitimate competitor for political power and as a split figure "femininized" by emasculation and invested with the power of oracular speech, these mythological architects allude to the status of their historical counterpart. The architect in ancient Greece is one of the general category of artisan termed *dêmiourgos* "he who does the people's work."[44] The moral and social status of the *dêmiourgos* is of the same marked, ambiguous structure as that of the female: disdained for their manual and material labor, while magnified for their intellectual ingenuity. And although biologically male, the *dêmiourgos* shares the woman's specific attributes of *mêtis*, mobility (as an itinerant worker), and graphic art.[45] In terms of gender, the *dêmiourgos* is a virtual female.[46]

Among artisans, the architect rates relatively high by virtue of a particular closeness to the political function. The *dêmiourgos* is, to begin with, an ambiguous term in relation to political power. At Athens the word denotes a worker of low, non-land-owning status, whether slave or citizen,[47] while elsewhere in Greece, the term *dêmiourgos* is used for a political office, of high status and great antiquity.[48] But the architect in Athens combines both vectors of meaning, receiving the low pay of a carpenter, but being paid by the year like a magistrate and, unlike other artisans, building not private, but public works that symbolize the power of the *polis*.[49] The orders of the architect are obligatory, like those of the magistrate.[50] These orders refer to the "plans" as well as to the project itself. They are (like the woman's weaving) understood as a graphic entity and denoted by the term συγγραφή "a writing down, a contract."[51]

This homology between the female and the architect in early Greek thought is inherited by Platonic philosophy.

Female and Architect: Platonic Philosophy

As with the texts of Freud, what Plato says explicitly about women offers only a partial account of the place and function of the female gender in his philosophy. The overt strategy of the *Republic* is to expel the female through silence (a philosophizing of Tereus' tactic) and to minimize the marked valence of any women it finds necessary to retain. The holding of Guardian wives and children in common and the engineering of eugenic reproduction (under the guise of random coupling) advocated for the ideal state in the *Republic* attempts to eliminate marriage exchange and the father-ruled family, the very agents of the female's uncontrollable mobility and transcendent knowledge.[52] Such practice would collapse gender difference into gender singularity and leave women (Guardian women, at least) as unmarkedly male as possible,[53] a social homogenization radically in keeping with a system of thought in which the relation of truth is that of the ὅμοιον, the "like, same, equal to itself."[54] Both the force and the failure of this repression of the female mark are evident in the obscure but crucial *point de capiton*[55] where the Muses are invoked to utter the origin of the inevitable degeneration of the ideal state.[56] For it is these females with their transcendent knowledge in the sphere of reproduction who know the ἀρχή "origin" of why the ideal state will fall, and of why, therefore, the entire edifice of the *Republic* can never be maintained in the real world. Outside of such lapses, however, it is not in overt reference to the female, but in the figure of the *dêmiourgos* that Platonic philosophy appropriates the traditional structure and function of the female gender.

Just as the term can designate both artisan and magistrate in the social sphere, so in Plato the *dêmiourgos* presents a "study" in female-like "ambiguity"[57] – the statesman as weaver in the *Politicus*, the cosmic Demiurge of the *Timaeus*, and the status of the artisans in the *Laws*. The treatment of the *dêmiourgos* in Plato repeats the rhetoric of the female and the architect in pre-philosophical texts. Philosophy marks the "other" as the locus of transcendent knowledge, uncontrollable mobility, and graphic, material creativity and attempts to repossess these marked qualities, while either expelling or demoting the marked member. Weaving is marked as female, and while women are barred from politics, their characteristic art form is displaced "upwards" in the *Politicus* to become the paradigm of the statesman's τέχνη "craft," as it was of poetry and prophecy before.[58] We find a complex instance of the same process in the case of the *dêmiourgos*. In the *Timaeus* the figure is elevated and appropriated as the cosmic architect.

In the dialogue that bears his name, Timaeus, a politically and philosophically distinguished citizen of Locri near Sicily (*Timaeus* 20a1–5, 27a1–6), describes the construction of the universe. His can only be, he explains, a "likely story" (τὸν εἰκότα μῦθον, *Timaeus* 29d2, 59c6) or "likely account" (κατὰ λόγον τὸν εἰκότα, *Timaeus* 30b7). Because the universe is a sensibly perceptible, material εἰκών "likeness, image, copy" of an unchanging, intelligible παράδειγμα "model," it is describable only in "likely" terms.[59] This verbal likeness is itself a three-part construction (εἷς, δύο, τρεῖς):

Part I (*Timaeus* 29d7–47e2)
  τὰ διὰ νοῦ δεδημιουργήμενα "things built by the artisanship of intelligence"
Part II (*Timaeus* 47e2–69a5)
  τὰ δι᾽ ἀνάγκης γιγνόμενα "things coming into being through necessity"
Part III (*Timaeus* 69a6–92c9)
  συνυφανθῆναι "weaving together" of the two causes, intelligence and necessity.[60]

Part I (29d7–47e2): "things built by the artisanship of intelligence"

In Part I, the cosmos is created by a *dêmiourgos*, himself founded upon the repressed figures of the Muses and Metis (as swallowed by Zeus).[61] In his knowledge of the totality of the intelligible (*Timaeus* 30c2–31a1), this *dêmiourgos* is a philosopher.[62] He knows, that is, what the Muses know, and by virtue of that knowledge he is able to be a poet (ποιητής "maker," *Timaeus* 28c3) and to imitate the truth.[63] For he uses the eternal Forms as model (παράδειγμα)[64] in building (τεκταινόμενος, *Timaeus* 28c6)[65] the cosmos as visible, material likeness (εἰκών) of the intelligible[66] – and thereby as beautiful and good (καλόν).[67] Here is the architect as figurative philosopher and the philosopher as figurative architect, building "what he knows." Like Zeus, this *dêmiourgos* is a god (θεός, *Timaeus* 30a2). He, too, has "swallowed" Metis. For he is a con-structor (συνιστάς: συν- "together, with" + ἱστάς < ἵστημι "make stand, set up," *Timaeus* 29e1).[68] His construction is a harmony and a weaving.[69] And he is a πατήρ "father,"[70] who rejoices at the cosmos he has engendered without female consort (*Timaeus* 37c7).

His procreation is auto- and hom(m)o-erotic. Motivated by lack of envy, he creates an image of his own goodness,[71] a sphere of complete autarky (αὔταρκες):[72] auto-tropic (it turns around on itself, *Timaeus* 34a1-5),[73] auto-philic (φίλον ἱκανῶς αὐτὸν αὑτῷ "itself sufficiently a friend to itself" *Timaeus* 34b7-8), a "blessed god himself" (*Timaeus* 34b8-9). His mortal creations are unmarked *anthrôpoi*, human and male only, of whom the wicked will be reincarnated as women, and if still unregenerate, then as animals (*Timaeus* 42b5-c4, 90e6-91a1). The absence of divine females and the repression of mortal women would seem complete.

The mark of the female is born in the *Timaeus* by the male *dêmiourgos*, elevated to a figurehead for the philosophic god. And what of mortal artisans? Like goddesses, the *Timaeus* makes no mention of them. For the place of the human architect in the Platonic economy, it is necessary to look away from the *Timaeus* briefly to the *Laws* before returning to the *Timaeus* for Part II of its creation myth.

In the *Laws*, male artisans are marked as "female" in politico-economic status and in spatial placement. In the projected city of Magnesia all citizens are male landowners and no citizen is permitted to be a *dêmiourgos* (*Laws* 846d1-3). As in the myth of the architect Trophonius, therefore, the artisan is barred from acquiring the economic and political power of the male. The stationing of the artisans within the urban plan reflects their feminized role

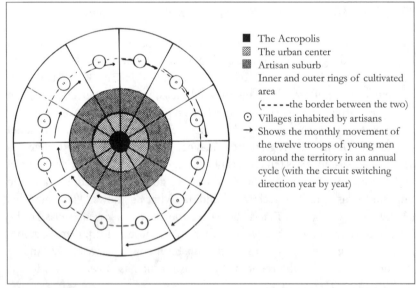

■ The Acropolis
▨ The urban center
▨ Artisan suburb
  Inner and outer rings of cultivated area
  (- - - -the border between the two)
⊙ Villages inhabited by artisans
→ Shows the monthly movement of the twelve troops of young men around the territory in an annual cycle (with the circuit switching direction year by year)

Figure 1. Plan of the city in Plato's *Laws*. Drawing after Pierre Vidal-Naquet, *The Black Hunter. Forms of Thought and Forms of Society in the Greek World* (Baltimore, MD: Johns Hopkins University Press, 1986), p. 225, fig. 3. Courtesy of Johns Hopkins University Press.

(*Laws* 848c7–849a2). In the plan as reconstructed by Pierre Vidal-Naquet, the *polis* is a circle divided into twelve sections, one for each tribe, with the center forming a thirteenth part, an Acropolis occupied by the gods.[74] [Figure 1. Plan of the city of Plato's *Laws*.] Each citizen owns a portion of the two concentric zones that form the city (the "urban center") and the surrounding country (the "rings of cultivated land"). The citizens live in the city, while the remaining territory is occupied by the artisans, segregated and divided into thirteen groups – one in a suburban periphery of the city, shaded in the plan, and the other twelve in villages located at the midpoint of each country district.[75] By this division and localization of the artisans, the plan attempts to control a spatial ambiguity parallel to that of the female in marriage exchange.[76] Like the woman, the *dêmiourgos* must be mobile, in the sense of being unlinked to any piece of land by ownership that would constitute citizenship.[77] But to be of regular and reliable use, he must also be put in a place and must stay put.

Read together with the *Timaeus*, this subordination of the "real" *dêmiourgos* of the *Laws* indicates that in the economy of Platonic thought, the making of philosophy architectural in the figure of the cosmic Demiurge results in the feminization of the artisan himself in the economic and political sphere. In the context of intellectual or political creativity, the unmarked male assumes the ambiguous "plus-interpretation" of signaling the female mark itself and thus requiring, in order to retain some diacritical difference, a re-marking of the female and of the male who creates not in mind or in law, but in matter. Each is re-marked with and as a female lack. In this negative incision, however, there re-appears in both the artisan of the *Laws* and the female principle of the *Timaeus* the imprint of the positive "female" mark.

Looking again at the urban plan of the *Laws*, the very fragmentation and spatial restriction of the artisans is a symptom of their transcendent knowledge and creativity. For like the gods and like the land itself – and unlike the male citizen – the artisans are divided into thirteen groups, with the "demiurgic suburb" echoing the divine Acropolis at the center of the city.[78] And of course it is as *dêmiourgos*, both architect and lawgiver, that the text itself constructs this spatial arrangement and the political structure it supports.[79]

The case of the female in the *Timaeus* is similar, but more complicated. In the *Timaeus* she returns as ἀνάγκη "necessity" and *khôra* "place, space" – each a principle of movement that must be controlled. These ontologically problematical powers are first described in Part II of the "likely story" of creation, when hetero-erotic rivalry supplements the hom(m)o-/auto-erotic procreation of the same. Part I of this creation myth, in which the demiurgic νοῦς "intelligence" fathered alone phenomenal replicas of intelligible forms (τὰ διὰ

255

νοῦ δεδημιουργήμενα "things built by the artisanship of intelligence) (*Timaeus* 47e4), concealed what we learn about in Part II, a concomitant family drama founded upon an uneasy intercourse. The architecture of pure paternity sheltered what was always already within the cosmic οἶκος "household" – an unstable erotic hierarchy with νοῦς on top.

Part II (47e2-69a5): "things coming into being through necessity"

Contrary to the impression created at the start of Part I, the world was not created with the Demiurgic νοῦς "intelligence" as its sole αἴτιον "cause" (*Timaeus* 28a4-5). Just as Zeus "mixed" in sexual intercourse with Metis in order to "incorporate" the power necessary to maintain his rule, so the cosmos was "born" as a "constructed mixture" of two causes – both νοῦς "intelligence" and ἀνάγκη "necessity":

> For the becoming (γένεσις) of this cosmos was engendered (ἐγεννήθη) by having been mixed (μεμειγμένη) from the construction (ἐξ συστάσεως) of both necessity (ἀνάγκης) and intelligence (νοῦ).
>
> *Timaeus* 47e5–48a2

Embodied in this edifying intercourse is a political hierarchy, itself supported by romance, as νοῦς "intelligence" is said to "rule" (ἄρχοντος) necessity by "persuasion" (τῷ πείθειν) (*Timaeus* 48a2) – the mark of successful rhetoric not only in political, but also in erotic contests.[80] This structure of conjugal subordination is the architectural principle and the principal architecture of the universe:[81]

> Through necessity (ἀνάγκης) subordinated (ἡττωμένης "made inferior")[82] by intelligent persuasion (πειθοῦς ἔμφρονος) this universe was thus constructed (συνίστατο) in the beginning.
>
> *Timaeus* 48a4–5

At stake in this containment of ἀνάγκη "necessity" within an οἶκος "household" of persuaded submission is the regulation of her movement. For ἀνάγκη "necessity" is the πλανωμένη αἰτία "wandering cause" – both the cause of wandering and the cause that wanders (*Timaeus* 48a7),[83] just as the body "wanders" in the six directions (*Timaeus* 43b4),[84] as symptoms "wander" in the body (*Timaeus* 47c3-4, 86e7, 88e2), as the woman's womb "wanders" (πλανώμενον) all over her body when left "fruitless" (ἄκαρπον) for a long time (*Timaeus* 91b7-c4), and as the sophists "wander" (πλανητόν, *Timaeus*

19e4-5) from city to city, without any home of their own. In their constructive intercourse, νοῦς "intelligence" governs this necessary movement, for he persuades ἀνάγκη "necessity" "to move (ἄγειν) most things (τὰ πλεῖστα) that come into being to what is best (ἐπὶ τὸ βέλτιστον)" (*Timaeus* 48a2-3).

To be "truly" true, any account of cosmic architecture must be an icon of this intermingling of causes, a narrative mixture of the cosmic mixture:

> If anyone, therefore, is going to say truly (ὄντως) how the world was born by these principles, it is necessary to mix (μεικτέον) also the category (εἶδος) of the wandering cause – in what way it is its nature (πέφυκεν) to cause movement (φέρειν).

> *Timaeus* 48a5-7

As the cosmic "mixture" (μεμειγμένη) results from the "con-struction" (ἐξ συστάσεως) – the "standing together" – of the two causes, "intelligence" and "necessity," so its narrative icon results from a textual juxtaposition of these two agencies: following "things built by the artisanship of intelligence" (τὰ διὰ νοῦ δεδημιουργήμενα), that is, Part I of Timaeus' account, "it is necessary to place beside in the story" (τῷ λόγῳ παραθέσθαι) "things that come into being through necessity" (τὰ δι' ἀνάγκης γιγνόμενα), that is, Part II (*Timaeus* 47e4-5). And as it is the nature of ἀνάγκη "necessity" to "cause movement," so its logical necessity entails a narratological displacement, the new beginning that creates Part II of the story:

> So therefore it is necessary to go back again (ἀναχωρητέον), and by taking again in turn (αὖθις αὖ) another suitable beginning (προσήκουσαν ἑτέραν ἀρχὴν) of these same things (αὐτῶν τούτων) – just as we did concerning things then, so now concerning these – we must begin (ἀρκτέον) back (πάλιν) from the beginning (ἀπ' ἀρχῆς).

> *Timaeus* 48a7-b3

In this ἑτέρα ἀρχή "other beginning" is the "necessity" of the "other," the ἀνάγκη that is *khôra*. For the ontological dyad of Part I, intelligible Forms and sensible images, cannot stand alone. It requires a "threesome" (εἷς, δύο, τρεῖς). The λόγος – both "logic" and "account" – of the construction of the cosmos as a building of the "same" entails the "necessity of trying to show forth in words a difficult and obscure form."[85] This is the τρίτον γένος "third kind, kindred, gender" – *khôra* (*Timaeus* 48e4, 52a8). The initial difficulty of this "difficult form" lies in the repeated necessity of putting her into words:

> What power (δύναμιν) and nature (φύσιν) must we suppose it to possess? Such as this especially: to be the receptacle (ὑποδοχὴν) itself of all becoming (γενέσεως) like a nurse (οἷον τιθήνην). This statement is true, but it is necessary to speak more clearly about it.

> *Timaeus* 49a4–7

> . . . It is necessary to be eager to speak again still more clearly about this.

> *Timaeus* 50a4–5[86]

Khôra

"To speak more clearly about it," the text continues its earlier verisimilitude: the language of human psychology and reproduction informed by and informing the language of building and plastic production.[87] "To speak again still more clearly about" the "power and nature" of *khôra* as "receptacle of all becoming like a nurse," *Timaeus* configures the moulding of figures and the begetting of children, each – like weaving and speech, and like architecture and philosophy – the "original" of the other. In this reciprocal information of semantic fields there appears: not only the return of the pre-Platonic homology between "graphic" art and reproductive (il)legitimacy, but also an attempt to regulate it. The iconological "buildup" here manifests a single drive – to present the power and nature of *khôra* as absolute impassivity. The threat of Rhea is past. This mother will not be able to "move" her offspring herself and present her husband with a supposititious "deFormation."

First deployed is the εἰκών "likeness, image" of sculpture.[88] As gold is moulded into various σχήματα "figures," but should always be called "gold," so the "nature (φύσεως) that receives all bodies" never "stands apart (ἐξίσταται) at all from its own power (δυνάμεως)" and must therefore always be "called the same."[89] Her δύναμις "power" as "receptacle of all becoming" consists in continuously "receiving" everything without ever "taking" any μορφή "shape" of her own, a passive movement (κινούμενον) of impermanent figuration (διασχηματιζόμενον) by entering and exiting agents.[90] The active members of this ontological intercourse are μιμήματα "copies" that have been "formed by impress" (τυπωθέντα) from the eternal Forms.[91] Then, in a trope on the word φύεται "is born" (*Timaeus* 50d2), the three parties to this cosmic sculpture "become" a family:

> And what is more (καὶ δὴ καί) it is fitting to liken (προσεικάσαι πρέπει) the one receiving (δεχόμενον) to a mother, the one from

which [supply from 50d1–2: "by being made like it, the one that becomes is born (φύεται)"] to a father, and the nature between these to an offspring (ἐκγόνῳ).

Timaeus 50d2–4

The εἰκών "likeness, image" is "appropriate" because – in this family – the relation between father and child is the same as that between a good copy and its paradigm. It is the relation that proves both the legitimacy of the son (it is, for example, his uncanny resemblance to Odysseus that makes Helen recognize Telemachus before she knows his name) and the "truth" of the copy: the reproduction of the same (ὅμοιον, the "like, same, equal to itself").[92] For the exactness of the replication is assured in this family by the function of *khôra*.

The ἔκγονος "offspring" in this ontological family is a perfect replica of the paternal Form because of the mother's absolute morphological neutrality.[93] If *khôra* presented any μορφή "shape" of its own, the copy would be vitiated.[94] The copying would be κακός "bad, ugly, low-class, worthy of blame," the epithet of aesthetic, social, and "natural" inferiority. Hence *khôra* must be without all fragrance, so that the copies may "become" perfume.[95] To receive the impression of the Formal σχήματα, she must be a *tabula rasa*, without any visible figure.[96] If the copies are to be καλός "good, beautiful, aristocratic, worthy of praise" (as they must be),[97] the "mother and receptacle" of material Becoming must be by her nature separate from all of its forms, and thus must not be called by the name of any of the four elements.[98]

> Rather, if we say that she is some form (εἶδος), invisible, without shape (ἄ-μορφον), and all-receiving (παν-δεχές), and that she participates (μεταλαμβάνον) in a most insoluble way (ἀπορώτατά)[99] in the intelligible (νοητοῦ) and is most hard to capture (δυσαλωτότατον),[100] we will not speak falsehood (ψευσόμεθα).

Timaeus 51a7–b2

This Platonic model of material (re)production makes architecture a fixed image and the architect the fixer. And what does it make *khôra*? The *sine qua non* of the entire tradition of Platonized architecture, the *genos* "kind, kindred, gender" that is a "necessity" for the mutual construction of Classical architecture and philosophy, not the program of its "dislocation." Back before the making of a cosmos out of the disordered universe, the *khôra* used to shake, in the manner of a winnowing basket, displacing the precursors of the four elements each to a different region of herself (*Timaeus* 52e5–53a7). But that movement was emphatically pre-architectural. Since the coming of the cosmic Demiurge, all material construction is "Typical" Becoming. But *khôra* cannot write or draw or imprint or build these "Types" (on) herself. The *khôra* is not auto-graphic. She is like Philomela with her hands (as well as her tongue) cut off,[101] a *pornê* without the means of γραφή "drawing, writing," a "pornography of power-less-ness." The copies entering *khôra* are themselves fixed by the immutability of the Forms they imitate, until they die away. By virtue of their Formal paternity, these images can do nothing more than "symbolize their use." To become works of "dislocating" architecture, they would have to have something of their mother active within them.

But an active *khôra* – an active, non-metaphysical, material event – is precluded even as it is revealed by the institution of Platonic philosophy as architectural. It would be the work of architecture outside of participation in the Forms, architecture outside of transcendental metaphysics, before the feminization of practical building in compensation for philosophical construction. It would be pre-architectural architecture, a building before building. As the city-plan of the *Laws* marks the artisan's power and its suppression in the same configuration, so the architect of the Platonic *khôra* builds architectural dislocation as the erection of its impossibility.

Khôra "after as before" the Demiurge

"Persuaded to move most things to what is best," Necessity moves to question the foundation of this impossibility.

The ambiguous movement of female and artisan in pre-Platonic thought makes it necessary to question the "passification" of *khôra*. If the Platonic architecture of philosophy is constructed upon a previously shaking and now impassive *khôra*, how firm can its foundation be? In this now Classic instance of a now classic move by which a constitutionally mobile female is *maintenant* supposed to stay put, can the Platonic text escape the φάρμακον "drug"-logic of female placement?

It is not only the pre-Platonic perspective that presses this question.

The text of the *Timaeus* calls itself an architecture. It is, in fact, a meta-architecture, pointing to its principles of construction at its constructed points. Its principles are those of Classical architecture and philosophy: spatial and temporal displacement of material (re)ordered and (re)joined in a "completion" (τελευτή, compare τέλος "end, completion") with the organic harmony of the human body.[102] At the juncture via recapitulation of Part III to

Part II of his story, Timaeus describes himself in terms which recall the pre-Platonic nexus of architecture and gender under the sign of *mêtis*. He calls himself a builder and a weaver and a fitter of textual joints:[103]

> Since then indeed now (τὰ νῦν) as material (ὕλη) for us builders (τέκτοσιν), the kinds (γένη) of causes lie beside (παράκειται) thoroughly separated, from which it is necessary to weave together (συνυφανθῆναι)[104] the remaining account (λόγον), let us go back (ἐπανέλθωμεν) again (πάλιν) to the beginning (ἀρχὴν) briefly and quickly proceed to the same place from which we have arrived here,[105] and let us try to put a completion (τελευτὴν) and head (κεφαλήν) upon the story (μύθῳ) that fits with (ἁρμόττουσαν, compare ἁρμονία "means of joining, fitting") the things before.

> *Timaeus* 69a6–b2

Then from this point in the present, Timaeus goes back to the time of disorder, and recapitulates the creation of the cosmos by the Demiurge in similarly tectonic terms (*Timaeus* 69b2–d6).[106] This recapitulation itself repeats the principle that regulates the composition of the *Timaeus* – including the placement of *khôra*.

The structure by which the architecture of the *Timaeus* places and displaces *khôra* is itself classic in the Greek (re)construction of meaning. It was known in antiquity as ὕστερον–πρότερον Ὁμηρικῶς "the later thing before the earlier thing as Homer does it."[107] It may be understood in the terms of contemporary narratology, which distinguishes three "levels" of a text:[108]

STORY (for example, the return of Odysseus)

NARRATIVE (for example, the text of the *Odyssey*)

NARRATION (for example, a poet reciting the *Odyssey*)

In ὕστερον–πρότερον, what is "later" (ὕστερον) in the STORY is "earlier" (πρότερον) in the NARRATIVE. By chiastic reversal, the historically later event is moved, as it were, and put in an earlier place in the narrative, there to be followed by what happened before it:

STORY:	earlier event	*later event*
NARRATIVE:	*later event* (ὕστερον)	earlier event (πρότερον)

A sort of narrative *mêtis*, the aim of this reversal is a circle, as the narration of the earlier event proceeds to the point of the later event again, thus producing an A – B – A circumstructure in which the "past" is framed within the "present" account:[109]

	A	B	A
NARRATIVE:	later event	earlier event	up to later event again
	ὕστερον	πρότερον	up to ὕστερον again
for example:	present	past	present

Anachronistic and metastatic, this ὕστερον–πρότερον "later before earlier" order defies as it defines a logic of identity, making the last first and the first last. It is a narrative instance of the fundamental tectonic power to displace an element from a temporal sequence and spatial location that might be called real, historical, or natural and to join it to another place. In the case of ὕστερον–πρότερον, the (re)placement erects an icon of truth as the (re)presentation of the same. When the "present" is stated before the "past" and then (re)occurs as previously described, the text acquires the veridical authority of accurate pre-dication. It becomes an εἰκών "likeness" of the Muses' transcendental memory and an εἰκὸς λόγος "likely account" of truth as that which (re)occurs as ὅμοιον "same, like, equal" to itself.[110] But truth so constructed depends upon construction for its truthfulness. The architectur-alization of philosophy is its deconstruction.

For Timaeus' "likely account" of *khôra* is built upon just such a ὕστερον–πρότερον "later before earlier" order. Part II of his creation myth is arranged in an A (ὕστερον: later event) B (πρότερον: earlier event) A (later event again) sequence. The creation of the cosmos by the Demiurge in the impassive *khôra* is moved out of chronological order and placed *before* the description of the pre-cosmic *khôra*,[111] which then continues with the creation of the cosmos by the Demiurge:

A	B	A
later event	earlier event	later event
(ὕστερον)	(πρότερον)	(again)
Demiurge creates	pre-cosmic	Demiurge creates
in *khôra*	*khôra*	in *khôra*
48c2–52d1	52d1–53a7	53b1–69a5

The text stresses the opposition between the two times – "at that time" (τότε, *Timaeus* 53a2), "even before" (πρὶν καὶ, *Timaeus* 53a7), "indeed, on one hand, to be sure, in the time before that" (καὶ τὸ μὲν δὴ πρὸ τούτου, *Timaeus* 53a7–8), "these indeed being then" (τότε, *Timaeus* 53b4), "for the first time" (πρῶτον,

Timaeus 53b4) – the more securely to exclude the movement of the pre-cosmic *khôra* from (the return in *Timaeus* 53b1-69a5 of) Platonic architectural order.[112]

The Demiurgic creation encases the pre-architectural *khôra* in the constitutive vocabulary of Classical architectural excellence.[113] Describing the condition of the elements "before the birth of heaven" are alpha-privative adjectives – ἄ-λογος "without rational account, logic" and ἄ-μετρος "without measure" – that present the absence of rational calculation and proportion as a temporary pre-condition.[114] Thus mathematics and measurement become instruments of the Demiurgic *kosmos* (κοσμεῖσθαι, *Timaeus* 53b1, compare κόσμος, *Timaeus* 24c1, 27a6, 28b3, 29a2, 29b2, 29e4, 30b7, 30d1, 32c1, 6, 42e9, 48a1).[115] For a *kosmos* is no mere aggregation of μορφαί "shapes, material appearances," but a particular σχῆμα "shape, figure" (διεσχηματίσατο, *Timaeus* 53b4, compare διασχηματιζόμενον, *Timaeus* 50c3 of *khôra* as an ἐκμαγεῖον "plastic medium" shaped by the entering μιμήματα "copies") made by means of εἴδη "forms" and ἀριθμοί "numbers" (*Timaeus* 53b5).[116] By this configuration, the Demiurge "constructs" (συν-ιστάναι, *Timaeus* 53b6) the four elements, before only the ἴχνη "footprints" of themselves, as representations of the divine beauty and virtue (κάλλιστα ἄριστά τε, *Timaeus* 53b5–6) they previously lacked.[117] For these material μιμήματα "copies" of Being to be born and die true to Type, they must enter and exit *khôra* without any threat of maternal (dis)placement to distort the resemblance. The pre-architectural condition of *khôra* must be absolutely past.

For "before the birth of heaven," *khôra* moved actively in a reciprocal mobilization of herself and the four pre-cosmic "kinds" (γένος "kind, kindred, gender"). Likened to a work of weaving and weaving herself with the diathetic ambiguity of the female (she displaces in being displaced), pre-architectural *khôra* figures a *mêtis*-like movement. Because the four "kinds" she contains are heterogeneous "powers" (δυνάμεων) of unequal weight, *khôra* lacks all equilibrium.[118] Her condition is one of complete and continuous ἀνωμαλία "lack of the same level, anomaly": she is "shaken" (σείεσθαι) and thereby "shakes" (σείειν) the elements.[119] Hers is the movement of elements ever differing and deferring. For the shaking of *khôra* (dis)locates the four "kinds" according to their weight and texture. Continuing the iconology of mother and nurse, Timaeus illustrates this process with a simile drawn from the sphere of Demeter, goddess of motherhood and agriculture: *khôra* is likened to a πλόκανον "woven winnowing basket" that winnows by shaking the corn from the chaff "so that the thick and heavy go in one direction, and the thin and light are carried into another place and settle there."[120] But "once (dis)placed" the elements do not "stay put." Quantitative differentiation (re)produces disequilibrium (re)produces quantitative differentiation. The "circular reciprocity" between what is shaken and what shakes is a perpetual weaving as unweaving, unweaving as weaving the four elemental "kinds."[121] All gen(d)eric resemblance – the condition of truth within the Platonic cosmos – is at once constructed and reversed without possibility of arrest. Here the working of gender is not constructed as a marked vs. unmarked opposition. Time and identity contradict without self-contradiction: the elements remain ἴχνη "footprints" of themselves, past results of future causes.[122] The pre-cosmic khôra programs a universe in the condition of the trace.

This is the "choral work" that must be "passified" within the circumstructure of the Demiurgic order. "Swallowing" this mêtis within itself, the "later before earlier" (ὕστερον–πρότερον) "Form" binds her architectural power of displacement within its (re)presentation of the passive khôra. Once the "later" and the "earlier" conditions of khôra are reversed, however, and once the "earlier" joins up with the "later" again, the circle must stay closed. The truth of Timaeus' ontology rests upon an architecture that excludes return to difference from the return of the same.

But once active and passive can be reversed, how irreversible can any "passification" be? Once there is displacement in and of time and space, no construction can escape its architecturality. There is no architectural law – and no law of an architectural ontology – to prevent B from coming again after A, to prevent khôra from shaking herself again. No ontology erected architecturally can be transcendental. This Platonic architecture (of A–B–A, with no return of B) cannot elude its foundation in "the circular reciprocity between what is binding and what is bound." It cannot certainly (re)occur as real and binding always. By its own criterion, it cannot be true.

The Platonic text does not fail to intimate this potential for dislocation within its ontological architecture. Over against the Demiurgic τάξις "ordering, arrangement" produced by causes that are "architects with the intelligence of the beautiful and the good" (μετὰ νοῦ καλῶν καὶ ἀγαθῶν δημιουργοί) work causes "devoid of reason that produce each time a happening without ordering" (τὸ τυχὸν ἄ-τακτον) (Timaeus 46e3–6)[123] – causes that (re)produce the pre-architectural ἀταξία "lack of ordering." Indeed, it is only "most" things that Necessity – whose "nature it is to cause movement" – can be "persuaded" to "move toward what is best" (Timaeus 48a2–3). Why only "most" things? Is it that to rule Necessity by rhetoric the Demiurgic νοῦς "intelligence" must speak like the Muses? Must the architectural mind be, like the Muses, able to construct ψεύδεα ὁμοῖα ἐτύμοισιν "false things like (ὁμοῖα 'like, equal, same') to real things" – a ὅμοιον "sameness" that does not distinguish between truth and falsehood?

In any case, it is in the supplementary relation between architectural truth and the necessity of movement[124] – in the imperfectly arrested capacity of *khôra* to shake again – that the program of a dislocating architecture may be read. The impassive, post-architectural *khôra* is not a "solicitation" of Platonism, but its illusion and its ideology of support. It can program only the repeated gesture of the Demiurge.

It is almost exclusively the post-architectural *khôra* that figures in the texts of the *Choral Works*.

Khôra "after as before" Choral Works

In the *Transcript* of their collaboration (as edited by Jeffrey Kipnis), both Eisenman and Derrida express the desire to dislocate the Classical institutions of architecture and philosophy by which each has been formed. Eisenman describes how his past work has attempted to "mount a critique of the systematic privileging of anthropocentric origins" in architectural Classicism, the tradition of "man" as the "measure of all things."[125] When Derrida apologizes for his "foreignness to architecture," Eisenman replies:

> Yes, but Jacques, you have to understand how unable I am *vis-à-vis* your work. My training, in its classical[126] extreme, probably means that I am less able to do the architecture of which we speak than you. My tendencies are all towards the anthropocentrism, aestheticism, and functionality which I am trying to critique. I gravitate towards them; they are in my bones. I must constantly work against this sensibility in order to do the architecture I am interested in. What is exciting in this circumstance is that you are going to provide the crutch for me to overcome certain resistant values that I constantly face. On the other hand, I could provide a corresponding crutch, in that I am familiar with operating in the realm of the sensible.[127]

As his initial contribution toward creating "the architecture of which we speak," Derrida offers the essay *"Chôra"* in which he criticizes the traditional attempt within Western philosophy to fit *khôra* into the framework of Classical oppositions.[128]

Despite the desire and the effort of each, Derrida and Eisenman emerge in *Choral Works* as names of institutions that remain undisturbed. As architectural program, the philosopher's *"Chôra"* became the "crutch" of a return in *Choral Works* of the "anthropocentrism" the architect desired to "overcome."

Why?

Among the forces determining the relative lack of architectural or philosophical dislocation in *Choral Works* is the treatment of gender in "*Chôra*." By dismissing the gender of *khôra* as neither Being nor Becoming and so outside all anthropomorphism, Derrida turns from the direction of analysis that might have led toward what there is in the Platonic rendition of *khôra* – the power of gender with all it implies of the ambiguities of movement and fixity in the construction of truth – that might program architectural dislocation. By confining his analysis within the problematics of Classical ontology, by maintaining, in effect, the truth of that ontology and accepting its foundation as an irreversible given, he misses the potential for its deconstruction in the pre-architectural *khôra* and her "passification."[129] In "*Chôra*" Derrida reconstructs the gender of *khôra* as a perpetual, non-anthropomorphic virginity. As such, gender lies between Eisenman and Derrida in *Choral Works*, supporting each in his reproduction of Classical philosophy and architecture.

Derrida's essay "*Chôra*" deconstructs the traditional readings of *khôra* in Western philosophy. This tradition centers upon the problem of whether *khôra* belongs to the category of *muthos* or serious *logos*, to the metaphorical or the philosophical proper. Derrida argues that *khôra* as the third ontological γένος "kind, kindred, gender" cannot belong to either member of any opposition (including that of gender, "female" vs. "male"), since oppositions belong to the other two ontological kinds, Being and Becoming. For *khôra* as "place" of inscription "gives place" to intelligible and sensible oppositions, but is herself always outside of them.[130] She bears no property of Being or Becoming. Nothing can be predicated of *khôra*. Thus anything said of *khôra* should be put under some form of erasure, enclosing it in quotation marks or overmarking it with a slash-sign /, for example. No pronouns or definite articles, whether feminine or neuter, are appropriate to "her/it."[131]

For Derrida, this function of *khôra* as the third ontological kind has implications for her temporality and for her gender. These two categories are connected: because she is outside all the temporal distinctions of the realms of Being and Becoming, *khôra* lacks all intelligible or sensible properties, including those of "anthropomorphic" gender. To make this argument Derrida must suspend it in each category once. Apropos of time: to be outside all spatio-temporal positions, *khôra* must occupy the one irreversible moment of her "passification." Apropos of gender: while denying *khôra* all properties, those of receptivity and plastic impression are admitted as explanatory of her temporality and its "structural law."

Temporality

Khôra "is" the space of all temporal and spatial divisions, while remaining outside their horizon. Hence, the temporality of *khôra* is anachronism.

All interpretations of *khôra* (including that of the Platonic text itself) share her anachronistic structure, one that makes them what Derrida calls "retrospective projections." All these interpretations (like everything else in the sensible realm) come into being in a *khôra* that "receives" all their "forms" without ever being permanently "informed" by them. Because they all share this condition, every interpretation of *khôra* "casts forth ahead of time" (projection) all the interpretations to come, which themselves "look back" (retrospective) on all that have come before. Such anachrony is an inevitable result of what Derrida calls "the structural law of *khôra*." The *khôra* "is" the structural law by which all "being" is anachronized, that is, comes "after as before" itself.[132]

But this law of *khôra* can be valid, only if and after it is invalid once. For *khôra* may be said to "be" outside the horizon of temporal oppositions only after the institution of the Demiurgic cosmos and only if *khôra* herself never moves again "after as before" Platonic architecture. *Khôra* "is" outside all attribution – temporal and otherwise – only if "she" or "it" bears the attribute of this single, original, unanachronizable moment.[133]

Gender

"She" or "it"? Neither "is" ontologically true. But each is a "necessity" of Platonic architecture and (as) philosophy in language.

Attempting "to speak still more clearly" about *khôra*, Plato configures the language of gender with the language of building, sculpture, and inscription to describe an ontological family whose members reflect the unmarked vs. marked construction of gender in Greek culture: father Being and his child Becoming share the unmarked attribute of real existence over against mother *khôra*'s marked lack of any property of her own. In his treatment of the gender of *khôra*, Derrida constructs, in effect, a similar unmarked vs. marked opposition between the two iconologies used to describe her.

Derrida is not uninterested in the function of γένος "kind, kindred, gender" in the *Timaeus*. He analyzes masterfully Socrates' ambiguous status inside and outside the *genera* of politicians and sophists.[134] Of the gender of *khôra*, however, Derrida confines his analysis to its "radical rebellion against anthropomorphism."[135] He is aware that this limitation may elicit objection. About using the term *khôra* without a definite article and thus creating (in French, that is) a proper noun, he says:

> Does that not aggravate the risks of anthropomorphism against which we would like to guard? Are these risks not run by Plato himself when he seems to "compare," as one says, *chôra* to a mother or a nurse? Is the value of a receptacle not also associated, like passive and *virgin* matter, with the feminine element, and precisely in Greek culture? These objections are not without value. [Emphasis added]

But in answer to these objections he only reiterates *khôra*'s non-existence:

> But if *chôra* indeed presents certain characteristics of the word as proper noun, if only by its apparent reference to something unique [*à de l'unique*] (and there is in the *Timaeus*, more rigorously in a certain passage of the *Timaeus* which we will approach later, *only one chôra*), the referent of that reference does not exist.[136]

Dismissing the gender of *khôra* as ontologically non-existent (besides resting on the truth of the ontology) fails to account for why her gender is in the text at all, why it is emphasized as part of a family whose other, male members are not non-existent. It leaves unanalyzed, as if its politics had no philosophical import, Plato's "risk" in systematically gendering the whole cosmic drama, not only *khôra*, but the *dêmiourgos* as father, the gods as obedient children, Being as father, Becoming as son. But it is not just for what it omits that Derrida's treatment of the gender of *khôra* is open to criticism.

Derrida's overriding concern is to establish that the structural law of *khôra* removes her from all existential properties and attributes, making this "third *genre* . . . only the moment of a detour in order to signal a *genre* beyond *genre*."[137] But Derrida deduces this very structural law from language no less anthropomorphic, no less iconic, no less improper to her than that of gender.[138] *Khôra* lacks the properties of gender by the same ontological law and to the same degree that she or it lacks the properties of the receptacle, the amorphous gold that receives σχήματα "shapes, figures," the plastic medium of typographic information, or any other of the attributes that "she" does not really possess, all the improper properties from which Derrida deduces "her" function. Derrida's analysis effectively marks the language of gender as solely a lack, leaving the language of plastic modeling alone as unmarked indication of how *khôra* works. Ostracized as anthropomorphic from the field of relevance, gender returns under the alias of this marked vs. unmarked division of choral iconology. Stipulating its ontological illegitimacy cannot exclude gender from the *genre* of *khôra*.

Indeed Derrida himself, while privileging the language of impression, cannot – or at least, does not – exclude the language of gender completely. For he does admit into his analysis one presumably female term:[139]

> The hermeneutical *types* are not able to inform, are not able to give form to *chôra* except to the degree to which, inaccessible, impassive, "amorphous" (*amorphon*, 51a) and always virginal, with a virginity radically rebellious against anthropomorphism, she/it *appears to receive* these types and *to give place* to them.[140]

This version of the gender of *khôra* as a "virginity radically rebellious against anthropomorphism" stages a revolt of its own against the Platonic text. Where Derrida assumes exclusive separation of the ontological genres, Plato poses a more enigmatic relation. For according to Plato, *khôra* is not simply divorced from Being and Becoming *tout court*, but rather "participates in a most insoluble way in the intelligible."[141] And as for the gender term itself, Derrida chooses a sexual and social category of the female, perpetual virginity, not only absent from the Greek text, but indeed radically divergent from its emphasis on the roles of mother and nurse within a full family constellation. As it divided the plasticity from the gender of *khôra*, so here the marked vs. unmarked structure divides the gender of *khôra* itself, between the exclusively female functions of the *Timaeus* and Derrida's more ambiguous, almost androgynous (for a virgin need not, of course, be female) creature, as devoid of marked female powers as are the Guardian women of the *Republic*. This reconstruction of the gender of *khôra* raises the question of why Derrida, after such careful effort to eliminate anthropomorphism, would choose a term he must qualify as non-anthropomorphic, why does he – must he – have recourse to the language of gender at all? Why must he reconstruct (female) gender to say what he means?

By what philosophical and architectural ἀνάγκη "necessity" must the mark of the female return? Perhaps it is because all discourse on *khôra* is a construction *maintenant*, a "now" that "maintains,"[142] a "projective retrospection" that must reinscribe the Classical philosophy and architecture of gender. All Platonic "choral work" maintains the mark of *thinking*: of the ontological category as a γένος, a *genre*, a naturally reproducing kind (contrast the term "class," for example, which does not entail the model of generation and sexual differ-ence) and of *constructing*: gen(d)eric difference as unmarked-vs.-marked oppo-sition. If the ontological category is a γένος, (its) gender must return.

Eisenman's ultimate response to Derrida's "*Chôra*" is a project – a version of his trademark "scaling" schemes – whose anthropocentrism and Classical totalizations were recognized acutely by the participants, who tried "after as before" to "overcome" them.

It was nearly otherwise.

By the necessity of Platonic architecture and (as) philosophy in language, in his essay "*Chôra*" Derrida makes use of the metaphorical representation of *khôra*, even as he condemns its ontological illegitimacy. But in the collabora-tion of the *Choral Works*, Derrida refuses architecture the comparable license of material embodiment. While admitting the "metaphor of impression or printing" in the philosophy of "*Chôra*," in the *Transcript* Derrida avers of architecture:

> Of course, *chôra* cannot be *represented in any form, in any architecture.* That is why it should not give place to an architecture – that is why it is interesting. What is interesting is that the *non-representable space* could give the receiver, the visitor, the possibility of *thinking about architecture.* [Emphasis added][143]

Here philosophy recreates the Platonic text's treatment of the "real" female and artisan: while appropriating the architectural mark of constructing *khôra* in metaphorical form, philosophy relegates architecture to architectural lack. Reconstructing its Classical subordination of formal representation to thought, philosophy requires architecture to do what it does, "thinking about architecture," but denies her "representation in any form, in any architecture" by which to do so.[144] As the Freudian female is condemned to hopeless envy of the logo-phallus, architecture here must emulate philosophy with her tongue cut out.

Despite this stricture, later in the collaboration, but before the formu-lation of his own "scaling" scheme, Eisenman ventures a materialization of *khôra*, almost a cognate of the pre-architectural ἀνωμαλία "lack of the same level, anomaly" in its "circular reciprocity" of formant and trace :

> I am describing an analogy of the receptacle and the object. The object is formed by the receptacle and the traces of the receptacle are left on the object. At the same time, the object forms the receptacle and leaves traces on it. It is a reverberating, displacing activity.[145]

But Derrida refuses this "physical analogue" of a receptacle as being an "inadequate metaphor" along with "figure/ground," even as he admits the unavoidability of both metaphors and buildings:

> JD: This is more difficult. The receptacle does not receive anything. Everything is inscribed in it, but, at the same time, the receptacle remains virgin.[146] ... The problem is that there is no physical analogue. Plato uses many metaphors to describe something for which metaphors are essentially inadequate. Receptacle is a metaphor. ...
>
> PE: But why, then, isn't a receptacle a ground?
>
> JD: Because it [i.e., *khôra*] is nothing. ... It is not a being.
>
> PE: ... We are constrained to make being in architecture.
>
> JD: Of course. That is the trouble. We have to make being out of something which is not being. ... What is being? The paradigm, the intelligible paradigm, the sensible emanation, these are beings. The intelligible is more being than the sensible, but they are both beings, the mother[147] and the copy. But *chôra* ... is nothing. ... So we have the use only of bad metaphors; indeed the concept of metaphor itself is "bad," it has no pertinence. So, for instance, to get rid of figure/ground is very good. ...
>
> PE: And metaphor/metonymy also?
>
> JD: Also. But we cannot avoid metaphors. We know they are inadequate but we cannot simply avoid them, just as we cannot avoid buildings.[148]

At this point, Eisenman does not resist the impasse or pursue his intimation of choral anomaly.

Later, instead, architecture reverses its Classical feminization by philosophy. Eisenman re-appropriates the unavoidable license of building to produce a model of what Derrida in *"Chôra"* terms the "absent support" or "absence as support" – the "binary or dialectical determination" – into which *khôra*, while "provoking and resisting" it, cannot be "translated."[149]

What Eisenman makes of Derrida's *"Chôra"* is a version of the "scaling" method of design that he has practiced in previous projects. This design process is devoted to avoiding the anthropocentrism of architectural Classicism, in which "man" functions – as in the meta-architecture of the *Timaeus* – as the original measure or scale of all things.[150] Instead, the parts of

271

the project are measured or "scaled" to non-anthropomorphic elements of the site, such as topographic features (the bend of a river, the grid of the streets) or previous buildings (the course of a wall, the foundations of a slaughterhouse, the plan of an unbuilt hospital) or narratives, whether historical or fictional (the traditions of Romeo and Juliet), for example.[151]

In *Choral Works* the "scaling" method is devoted to figuring the permutations of the complex relationship between Eisenman and Bernard Tschumi. As supervising architect of the whole Parc La Villette, it was Bernard Tschumi who invited Eisenman and Derrida to collaborate on a portion of the project. Tschumi is thus Eisenman's client. He is also a fellow architect, having designed a portion of the park himself, a design Eisenman saw as recalling an earlier one of his own. Eisenman explains to Derrida at their first meeting:

> This situation is very strange for me, because Bernard Tschumi's La Villette project is, I believe, related to an earlier one of mine. The grid in particular is reminiscent of a project that I did some years ago for Cannareggio in Venice; many of my colleagues have also made this association. Bernard's invitation to work with you on a small project for La Villette therefore creates an opportunity for a misreading of a misreading – a displacement of a certain irony.[152]

This "misreading" takes the form of a "scaling" that involves the two sites, Parc La Villette in Paris and Cannareggio in Venice, and the two projects, Tschumi's at La Villette and Eisenman's earlier one at Cannareggio. These two sites and projects are correlated by: time (present, past, future), space (present, absent), scale (full scale, half scale), materiality (solid, void), and what might be called the ontological status of these factors (real, fictional).

Eisenman's "scaling" scheme for *Choral Works* derives from manipulating these parameters of relationship. The scheme is described by Eisenman's associate, Thomas Lesser, at the fifth meeting of the team:

> What I did was to set up a scheme with four elements – the site of La Villette, Tschumi's project [there], the site of Cannareggio in Venice, and Peter's project there. I then arranged these four elements vertically, one on top of the other, and elaborated them through their four possible permutations. By letting each horizontal level represent a different time as well as a different condition of solid and void, form and receptacle, a system was created in which each element is related to the others in various conditions of past, present, and future, absence and presence, and materiality: solid or void.[153]

Referring to a diagram like this one:

1. Tschumi's project at La Villette
2. site of La Villette in Paris
3. site of Cannareggio in Venice
4. Eisenman's project at Cannareggio in Venice

		REAL	FICTIONAL			
		I	II	III	IV	
	[half scale]	*1*	4	3	2	*Future*
SOLID present						
	[full scale]	*2*	1	4	3	
GROUND		———	———	———	———	*Present*
	[full scale]	*3*	2	1	4	
VOID absent						
	[half scale]	*4*	3	2	1	*Past*

Lesser continues:

> As you can see, the first column of the diagram, which shows Tschumi's scheme and La Villette as presences and Peter's scheme and Venice as absences, represents facts as they exist relative to the site. So, we will not build that column, but the other three, "fictional" columns. For example, in the next condition Venice [4] as a future for Bernard's project [1] and La Villette [2] as the present for Peter's Cannareggio scheme [3]. So in this permutation, Bernard's scheme is the influence on Peter's scheme. Each column contains a different fiction, created by different ordering of the four elements in the horizontal conditions of presence and absence, solid and void.[154]

In the model of the scheme [Figure 2. Model of *Choral Works.*], in which fictional version II is worked out, "present solids" appear as vertical extrusions of the ground, those of the "future" reaching higher than those of the "present." "Absent voids" appear as negative depressions, those of the "past" dug deepest into the ground. In the three "fictional" transformations of the "real" condition, elements are scaled up or down from their original dimensions, whichever is necessary, in order for the "future" and "past" to be superimposed at "half scale" upon the "present" rendered at "full scale." Lesser explains:

Which way to scale, up or down, comes from the relations of the schemes. So, in the fourth column [the third fictional scheme] in which Peter's project [4] and Venice [3] are at real scale, Paris [2] is scaled to, that is, superimposed with Peter's project [4] and Bernard's project [1] is superimposed with Venice [2]. So, Paris [2] must be scaled down and Bernard's [1] scaled up.[155]

While producing a "reversal of reality and meaning,"[156] the scheme is not satisfying either to Eisenman or Derrida.

Both architect and philosopher recognize in the proposal Classical limitations. While neither points overtly to the obvious "anthropocentrism" of making Eisenman's and Tschumi's rivalry the "original measure" of the scheme, the features each does choose to criticize and the measures he takes to correct them are not arbitrary. In them, the materials, matters, and forces co-constructing Classical architecture, gender, and philosophy reconverge.

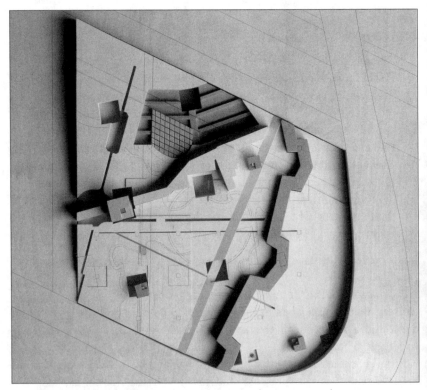

Figure 2. Model of *Choral Works*. Photo, Eisenman Architects, New York.

The final movement of *Choral Works* replays the architecture of the *Timaeus* as the Demiurge again "passifies" the pre-architecture *khôra*.

For Eisenman, the problem with the project concerns the hierarchy of "whole" over "hole." His scheme does not, he believes, sufficiently reverse its subordination to Tschumi's larger design. Speaking of the "three [fictional] sites" he proposes to build in relation to the "entire park," he explains:

> PE: I see the whole project as a continuous fabric, with the three sites as holes within it. So, what I would like to see is a notation of a larger scale which erases these other scales at each site. That's what I think is missing from this project at the moment. . . . Let's say the three sites are like holes in a fabric and that the entire park is also a hole in the same fabric. Therefore, what we do on these three sites makes Bernard's project as a whole an aspect of the same fabric and the three sites part of a scheme underlying the whole thing. Thus the elements in each of the three sites would not only relate to each other at various scales and times, but also to the scale of the fabric. . . . As it stands now, everything is in the same scale relative to a human being. What we need somewhere is a notation of one of the schematic elements, say one of the Tschumi/Eisenman squares, that would be larger, at real scale relative to the actual park. This would break the boundary of the scheme and relate it and the park to a larger fabric.[157]

In Eisenman's own terms, the "whole project" of the Parc La Villette is a "continuous fabric" with his three sites as smaller-scale "holes within it." Because they are scaled in relation to Tschumi's larger design, these three smaller "holes" become "part of a scheme underlying the whole thing" and "make Bernard's project as a whole an aspect of the same fabric." But currently every element in the three smaller sites is "in the same scale relative to a human being." The "hole" is still subordinate to Tschumi's "whole." To reverse the relegation, Eisenman wishes to scale up an element of his smaller sites to "real scale relative to the actual park," thus extending the "boundary of his scheme" to that of a "larger fabric" that would encompass both "it and the park." In this vision, the Parc La Villette becomes a woven allomorph of *khôra*, one that rival Platonic architects, *mêtis*-endowed masters of the weaving art, compete to contain as and by a (w)hole.

For Derrida, the problem is a version of (w)holeness that he terms "totalization." By including all the possible permutations that retain the original relations of project and site (Peter at Venice and Bernard at Paris), the three "fictional" sites theoretically offer visitors all the data needed to reconstruct the "real" situation. So the project needs, says Derrida, "something which prevents them from closing the circle" (as Platonic architecture encloses the pre-cosmic *khôra*), "something temporal perhaps . . . something which should not only prevent you from totalizing but also motivate an infinite desire to start again."[158] "What is needed here is some heterogeneity. Something impossible to integrate into the scheme. . . . We might call this a 'lateral focus' because, since it is totally heterogeneous, it could become *the* focus."[159] Derrida's call for "total heterogeneity" initiates the final turn in the gen(d)eric contest of *Choral Works*.

As he could not complete his description of *khôra* without reconstructing her gender, so Derrida cannot leave *Choral Works* "without gender." Derrida asks for radical difference, a totally "other (*heteron*) gender (*genos*)" within Eisenman's male-only scheme. Eisenman concurs, ominously reciting what he expels. He proposes that Derrida himself provide what will prevent "closing the circle" and "totalizing," so that it will be "totally heterogeneous" and will bring "closure" to the project:

> PE: I'll tell you what we could do – we could have Jacques put what feels right to him. Then it would be *totally* heterogeneous. It will bring the final *closure* to the project, in the sense that we started with your program, *chôra*. We took it and developed it, and now you add the heterogeneous element. It will be terrific. . . . That finally *closes* the thing from the *totally* heterogeneous to the *totally* rational. If you think of the text that we are making together as some sort of narrative, then we began with the program, then we drew and had discussions and various attempts at this, and the last thing is M. le Philosophe draws the piece. I think it is perfect. It gives us no responsibility.[160] [Emphasis added]

Apparently ready to share, if not concede, its "responsibility," architecture asks philosophy to "draw" its "other gender."

Derrida's drawing almost returns the pre-architectural *khôra* to *Choral Works*. Enjoined to play architect, the philosopher gamely supplements his programmatic "*Chôra*." [Figure 3. Derrida's Drawing.] Now availing himself lavishly of philosophic iconology, the representation in material form that he refused architecture and the anthropomorphism he refused himself before, Derrida not only draws Plato's metaphor of the pre-architectural *khôra*, the πλόκανον "woven winnowing basket," but assimilates it to a lyre, thereby configuring a graphic title for the entire collaboration:

JD: I drew a lyre, which is also a sieve. In Plato's text, *chôra* is compared to a sieve which separates things into the world of the sensible and intelligible.[161] So this is both sieve and lyre, for what we did together was like a musical event. We call it choral work – music.[162]

The "difference" between architecture and philosophy blurs, as the philosopher has drawn his "other gender." Confronted with this pro-gram of Classical dislocation, this γραφή "drawing, writing" of the "universe in the condition of the trace," what does the architect do?

A true avatar of the Demiurge, Eisenman at once locates and stabilizes this "other" *khôra*, indeed as the very centerpiece of the *Choral Works*. [Figure 2. Model of *Choral Works*.] As Zeus would swallow *mêtis*, as the οἶκος "household" would contain female mobility, as Platonic architecture would enclose the pre-cosmic *khôra*, and as Derrida refused Eisenman's "physical analogue" of choral ἀνωμαλία "lack of the same level, anomaly," so Eisenman makes Derrida's "other gender" into a radically non-anthropomorphic, perpetually virgin "hole" in the middle of his "ground."

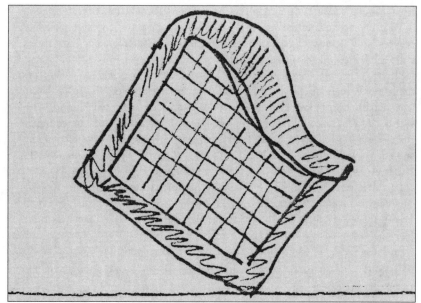

Figure 3. Jacques Derrida (1930-2004), drawing for *Choral Works*. Detail from a letter to Peter Eisenman of May 30, 1986. Photo, Collection Centre Canadien d'Architecture / Canadian Centre for Architecture, Montréal.

Notes

An earlier version of this essay appeared in *Innovations of Antiquity*, edited by R. Hexter and D. Selden, New York, 1992:253–305 and *Strategies in Architectural Thinking*, edited by R. Burdett, J. Kipnis, and J. Whiteman, Cambridge, Mass., 1992:8-46. This essay was originally written for the Conference on Architectural Theory at the Chicago Institute for Architecture and Urbanism, Skidmore, Owings, and Merrill Foundation, Chicago, Illinois, September 9–11, 1988. An expanded version was presented to the departments of Classics and Architecture at the University of California, Berkeley and the Peter Eisenman office in New York in 1989. The paper was completed with the support of a Fellowship in 1989-1990 from the Chicago Institute for Architecture and Urbanism, helpful reading by Andrew Dyck and Sarah Morris, invaluable discussion of the *Timaeus* with David Blank, the constructive criticism of Peter Eisenman, the inspiration of Daniel Selden, and the abiding solicitation of Jeffrey Kipnis. The reading of John Whiteman saw it through.

1. The noun *khôra* "place, space" is transliterated as *chôra* in Derrida's essay and in other texts cited below. Derrida's essay *"Chôra"* was first published in a volume honoring the Classicist Jean-Pierre Vernant, *Poikilia: Études offertes à Jean-Pierre Vernant* (Paris, 1987:265–295), cited below as Derrida *"Chôra"* 1987a. Its epigraph is a quote from Vernant's *"Raisons du mythe"* in Vernant 1974:195–244 = 1980:186–242, in which Vernant distinguishes the logic of *muthos*, of ambiguity, equivocality, and polarity, from that of the *logos*, the philosophical logic of non-contradiction. Derrida presents to Vernant, as scholar of the opposition *muthos/logos* and of the "incessant inversion of poles," the "homage of a question" with regard to the Platonic *khôra*: "how are we to think that which, while exceeding the regularity of *logos*, its law, its natural or legitimate genealogy, does not, however, belong, *stricto sensu*, to *muthos*?" (266). For the thought of Vernant on the *muthos/logos* opposition, Derrida refers also to Vernant 1978 (266). English translations here of Derrida's essay are mine. The French text of *"Chôra"* with an English translation by Ian McCloud is included in a volume documenting the collaboration, *Choral Works: Jacques Derrida and Peter Eisenman*, edited by Jeffrey Kipnis and Thomas Leeser (New York, 1997:15–32, 190–207), cited below as *Choral Works* 1997. This book contains transcripts edited by Jeffrey Kipnis of the tape-recorded meetings of Derrida, Eisenman, and other members of the design team as well as an extensive commentary on both Derrida's essay and the design process of the project by Kipnis, "Twisting the Separatrix" (137–160). Jacques Derrida writes of the collaboration in *"Pourquoi Peter Eisenman écrit de si bons livres"* (Derrida 1987b:495–508). This text with an English translation by Sarah Whiting is included in *Choral Works* (95–101, 173–179).

2. For the mutual construction of philosophy and architecture, see Wigley 1989:7–21, esp. 11–12:

> Metaphysics produces the architectural object as the paradigm of ground-as-support in order to ground its own ungrounded condition. Philosophy represents itself as architecture, it translates itself as architecture producing

itself in translation. The limits of architecture are established by the metaphorical status of architecture. . . . Philosophy describes itself in terms of that thing which it subordinates. . . . It produces an architecture of grounded structure which it then uses for support, leaning on it, resting within it. The edifice is constructed to make theory possible, then subordinated as a metaphor in order to defer to some higher, non-material truth. Architecture is constructed as a material reality in order to liberate some higher domain. As material, it is but a metaphor. The most material condition is used to establish the most ideal order, which is then bound to reject it as merely metaphorical.

3. For the "archeology," see Wittkower 1988, esp. 32, 38–39, 104–137. Wittkower notes that the Renaissance knew the principles of Greek Classicism from texts such as the *Timaeus* rather than from temples (41).

4. The following quotations are excerpted from my tape recordings of the sessions.

5. Compare the remarks of Eisenman (PE) and Derrida (JD) in *Transcript* One, 17 September 1985 (*Choral Works* 1997:13):

> PE: What I would suggest is that we try to find a mechanism which, in a sense, initially destabilizes the work we produce from a traditional architectural reading. It is also possible to destabilize its traditional functionality. We could, for example, make part of it inaccessible.
>
> JD: In La Villette you cannot make it inaccessible.
>
> PE: But you can make part of it inaccessible.
>
> JD: The concept of the garden is something that contains access, the product of the garden is the pleasure of walking.

and *Transcript Four*, 3 April 1986 (*Choral Works* 1997:70):

> PE: Ordinary Parisians . . . should feel dislocated. That is the important thing – the dislocation from the ordinary expectation of what is a garden. It should be like reading *Finnegan's Wake* for the first time.

Derrida argues for the *maintenant* of architecture – the "now" that "maintains" – in "*Point de Folie – Maintenant l'Architecture*" (Derrida 1986 = 1987b:477–494).

6. For consideration of gender at the Conference on Architectural Theory, see the comments by Mark Wigley following his paper and the papers of Beatriz Colomina and her respondent Silvia Kolbowski, Jennifer Bloomer and her respondent Durham Crout, Robert Segrest, and Robert McAnulty. The proceedings of the conference are published by the Chicago Institute for Architecture and Urbanism in a volume entitled *Strategies in Architectural Thinking*, edited by Burdett, Kipnis, and Whiteman 1992.

7. See, for example, Favro 1989, published in *Architecture: A Place of Women*, a collection of articles grouped under the categories of I. "Researching the Past," II.

"Recounting Personal Involvement," III. "Suggesting Various Possibilities," and IV. "Envisioning Future Roles." See also Hayden 1981, 1984; Torre, ed. 1977 and 1981.

8. See, for example, Erlemann 1985:125–134.

9. For the relation between gender and what is understood as biological sex, as articulated by psychoanalysis and anthropology, see Mitchell and Rose, eds. 1982 and MacCormack and Strathern, eds. 1980. For a review of the research on gender, see Laqueur 1990:1–24.

10. A pervasive example is the classification of nouns by gender. This mode of classification is ambiguous in what linguists term "motivation": in some languages, the total of feminine nouns contains nearly all feminine living beings and correspondingly for the masculine, while in other languages the genders have "no discernible semantic core" (Greenberg 1966:39). Ambiguity of motivation is one of the characteristics of semiotic "marking" – as it is defined below – and thus makes gender itself a "marked" category. This marking of gender implies the existence of an unmarked, gender-neutral condition – a condition repressed by the universality of differentiation by gender.

11. See Greenberg 1966:25 and Waugh 1982:302–303. Waugh (1982:300) quotes Jakobson in a letter to Trubetzkoy: "It seems to me that it [the marked/unmarked opposition] has a significance not only for linguistics but also for ethnology and the history of culture, and that such historico-cultural correlations as life ~ death, liberty ~ non-liberty, sin ~ virtue, holidays ~ working days, etc., are always confined to relations a ~ non-a, and that it is important to find out for any epoch, group, nation, etc., what the marked element is. For instance, Majakovskij viewed life as a marked element realizable only when motivated; for him not death but life required a motivation." Waugh then notes that Majakovskij committed suicide.

12. "Male human being" or as Gregory Nagy used to say, "male man."

13. Man = human bears the "zero-interpretation" (zero degree of x), man = not-female bears the "minus-interpretation" (minus x). It is the context alone that determines the "plus-interpretation," thus imposing special effort upon the interpreter (compare Greenberg 1966:28, 51, who designates this usage "facultative"). Waugh (1982:305) gives an example of the plus-interpretation of man: "everyone in New York State is entitled to an abortion if he wants it." We shall see a plus-interpretation of "man" below in the figure of the Greek male appropriating powers his language has marked as "female."

14. See Greenberg 1966:26 and 52–53 for other such pairs of adjectives. Compare Waugh 1982:308–309 on "speech" vs. "writing" as an illustration that markedness is hierarchical rather than derivational, since writing is marked in relation to speech, despite possessing its own properties and structure.

15. See Greenberg 1966:26.

16. Waugh (1982:309) notes the marked vs. unmarked pairs: barrenness/fertility, homosexuality/heterosexuality, black person/white person.

As in the example of "barrenness," the "something different" possessed by the marked member may be conceived as a "lack." In the Aristotelian construction of gender, for example, females are marked as members of the same *genos* (defined by Aristotle in *Metaphysics* 1024a: γένος λέγεται τὸ μὲν ἐὰν ᾖ ἡ γένεσις συνεχὴς τῶν τὸ εἶδος ἐχόντων τὸ αὐτό "the term *genos* is used whenever there is a continuous *genesis* 'generation' of those entities having the same *eidos* 'visible or intelligible form'") as males, but lacking sperm (defined by Aristotle as the sole principle of movement, form, and soul in human reproduction; see, for example, *Generation of Animals* 730a–b, 736a–737a). Aristotle maintains this marking, despite the difference in the *eidos* "visible form" of male and female genitals and despite the regular Greek usage, followed by Aristotle himself in *Rhetoric* 1407b, of *genos* to designate the masculine, feminine, and inanimate grammatical "genders." Sissa (1991:58–100) unfolds this "sexual politics" in Aristotle's philosophy of gender.

Another example from ancient Greek is the term *barbaroi* from which European languages inherit the notion of the "barbarian." So greatly do the ancient Greeks privilege their language that ethnic, local, national, and cultural differences are subsumed under the linguistic. As females lack sperm, so non-Greeks are marked by their lack of the Greek language, for *barbaroi* are those who cannot speak Greek, but only "bar-bar-bar." In this "linguo-centric" reduction, "race" is constructed as language. The unmarked vs. marked division between Greeks and barbarians is criticized in Plato *Politicus* 262c10–263a1, where it is claimed that the correct division of racial *genera* should take the "separate but equal" form of an odd vs. even or female vs. male split; see below, n. 58.

17. Compare Jakobson to Trubetzkoy (quoted in Waugh 1982:300–301): "I'm convinced that many ethnographic phenomena, ideologies, etc. which at first glance seem to be identical, often differ only in the fact that what for one system is a marked term may be evaluated by the other precisely as the absence of the mark."

18. See Greenberg 1966:66.

19. See Greenberg 1966:39, 79–80. See also Waugh 1982:309–310 on some instances of the reversal of the markedness relation over time.

20. For the details of the material sketched below, see "Language and the Female in Early Greek Thought" in this collection.

21. Compare the dilemma of the male as represented by Jacques Lacan in relation to the knowledge and the desire of the female in "God and the *Jouissance* of The Woman," in Mitchell and Rose 1982:137–149.

22. For the work and the intelligence of the artisan as *mêtis*, see Vidal-Naquet 1986d:224–245.

23. The essential work on *mêtis* is Detienne and Vernant 1974 = 1978.

24. See Detienne and Vernant 1978:34, 37 for examples from the animal world: the hunted fox reverses itself, plays dead, and turns into a trap for the hunter; the fox-fish on the hook turns its body inside out, so that its interior becomes its exterior, and the hook falls out.

25. See Detienne and Vernant 1978:46: "The ultimate expression of these qualities is the circle, the bond that is perfect because it completely turns back on itself, is closed in on itself, with neither beginning nor end, front nor rear, and which in rotation becomes both mobile and immobile, moving in both directions at once. . . . The circle unites within it several opposites, each one giving birth to its opposite, it appears as the strangest, most baffling thing in the world, *thaumasiôtaton*, possessing a power which is beyond ordinary logic."

26. See Detienne and Vernant 1978:305.

27. For the construction of war machines as a part of the ancient architectural repertoire, see Vitruvius *De Architectura* 10.10–16, the climax of his treatise.

28. For the connection between weaving and architecture, Daniel Selden refers me to Callimachus *Hymn to Apollo* 55–57: "Men follow Phoebus when they measure out cities. For Phoebus always delights in founding cities, and he himself weaves (ὑφαίνει) their foundations (θεμείλια)."

29. The trick of the stone is termed a *mêtis* at *Theogony* 471 when Rhea begs Gaia and Uranus to "devise together with her (συμφράσσασθαι) a *mêtis* by which she could make him forget that she bore her dear child." It is Gaia who takes the newborn Zeus to be raised secretly in the Cretan cave (*Theogony* 479–484) and she could be the subject of "having swaddled a great stone, she handed it to the son of Uranus" (*Theogony* 485), unless a change of subject back to Rhea is to be understood. For the architectural significance of such swaddling, compare the *Bekleidung* "dressing, cladding" of a building in the theory of 19th century comparative architectural historian and theoretician Gottfried Semper (1989:24, 34, 36–40, 103–110, 240–243).

30. As Detienne and Vernant observe (1978:57–130, esp. 67–68, 109), Zeus "attacks Metis with her own weapons" and the text of the *Theogony* calls him μητίετα Ζεύς "Zeus endowed with *mêtis*" even *before* his defeat of the goddess. The anachronism is central to the goal of the text, the validation of Zeus' rule: Zeus is able to acquire *mêtis* and the "right to rule" it brings because he has already always possessed it. The ruler takes what has always been inherently his own.

31. Compare the architectural "battle of the sexes" between the sperm as dynamic τέκτων "builder" endowed with informing soul and the menstrual fluid as passive ὕλη "material, matter" in the embryology of Aristotle's *Generation of Animals*: "The sperm of the male differs, because it possesses a principle (ἀρχήν) in itself of such a kind as to cause movement (κινεῖν) and to concoct thoroughly the ultimate nourishment, but the [sperm] of the female contains matter (ὕλην) only. If [the male sperm] gains mastery (κρατῆσαν), it brings [the matter] into itself, but if it is mastered (κρατηθέν), it changes

into its opposite or is destroyed" (*Generation of Animals* 766b12–16). See also *Generation of Animals* 730b, 736a, 737a, 765b, 767b.

32. Apollodorus *Bibliotheca* 1.3.6.

33. See Lévi-Strauss 1967:548–570 = 1969:478–497.

34. For Helen as the figure of such female placement, see "Language and the Female in Early Greek Thought" and "Helen's 'Good Drug'" in this collection.

35. For the attempt to resolve this ambiguity of female movement via the Odyssean architectural ideal of immovable (re)marriage, see "The (Re)Marriage of Penelope and Odysseus" in this collection.

36. Freud 1933 [1932]:132:

> It seems that women have made few contributions to the discoveries and inventions in the history of civilization; there is, however, one technique which they may have invented – that of plaiting and weaving. If that is so, we should be tempted to guess the unconscious motive for the achievement. Nature herself would seem to have given the model which this achievement imitates by causing the growth at maturity of the pubic hair that conceals the genitals. The step that remained to be taken lay in making the threads adhere to one another, while on the body they stick into the skin and are only matted together. If you reject this idea as fantastic and regard my belief in the influence of a lack of a penis on the configuration of femininity as an *idée fixe*, I am of course defenseless.

In a nice stroke of irony, Freud hits upon a certain truth in the aetiology of architecture, namely the lack – lack of shelter, protection, beauty, meaning, value – that it attempts to supplement. And in naming that lack, the female lack of a penis, Freud repeats, against the will of his text (which would downplay the woman's construction), the Greek attribution of a female gender to *mêtis* and thus to architecture.

Compare Gottfried Semper's theory of weaving as the origin of architecture as vertical space enclosure. See, for example, "Structural Elements of Assyrian-Chaldean Architecture" = chapter 10 of "Comparative Building Theory" (*"Vergleichende Baulehre,"* 1950), in Herrmann 1984:204–218, especially 205–206:

> It is well known that any wild tribe is familiar with the fence or a primitive hurdle as a means of enclosing space. Weaving the fence led to weaving movable walls. . . . Using wickerwork for setting apart one's property and for floor mats and protection against heat and cold far preceded making even the roughest masonry. Wickerwork was the original motif of the wall. It retained this primary significance, actually or ideally, when the light hurdles and mattings were later transformed into brick or stone walls. The essence of the wall was wickerwork. Hanging carpets remained the true walls; they were the visible boundaries of a room. The often solid walls behind them

were necessary for reasons that had nothing to do with the creation of space; they were needed for protection, for supporting a load, for their permanence, etc. . . . Even where solid walls became necessary, they were only the invisible structure hidden behind the true representatives of the wall, the colorful carpets that the walls served to hold and support.

37. See Durante 1960:231–249. See also Schmitt 1967:299–301, Durante 1976:48, 167–179, Snyder 1981, Scheid and Svenbro 1996, esp. 111–130, Nagy 1996a:84–92, Nagy 1996b:63–74, Graziosi 2002:18–40, Nagy 2002:70–98.

38. The ambiguity of the γραφή "drawing, writing" is obscured in languages that attempt a clean break between the graphic and the linguistic, between building as "dumb object" and language: for example, English "draw" vs. "write" (though "draw" means "write" in "draw a contract"), French *dessiner* vs. *écrire*, German *zeichnen* vs. *schreiben*, Italian *disegnare* vs. *scrivere*. On the glossary of drawing, see Derrida 1978 = 1987c. For painting (ζωγραφία "writing/drawing living things") as a special case of writing (γραφή "drawing, writing"), since in both cases, the graphic object remains silent when questioned, see Plato *Phaedrus* 275d.

39. The root of γράμμα "drawing, written character" is γραφ- (as in γραφή "drawing, writing"): γραφ + μα > γράμμα. For the text, see Apollodorus *Bibliotheca* 3.14.8.

40. For the details of the summary below, see Petrie 1979. For the ancient sources of the myth of Trophonius and its many variants in other cultures, see the note on Pausanias 9.37 in Frazer 1913:176–179. Together these stories reveal a complex and pervasive account within traditional thought of the relationship between architectural and politico-economic power.

41. On the problematic status of the architect in the Greek *polis*, its local and historical variations, and the lack of scholarly consensus on the evidence, see Coulton 1977:23–29.

42. Political power in archaic Greek thought is dependent upon the products of *mêtis*. In addition to Metis herself, Zeus' sovereignty depends upon acquiring his characteristic weapon, the thunderbolt, a work of *mêtis* by the Cyclopes. See Detienne and Vernant 1978:57–105.

43. See Petrie 1979:24.

44. See Austin and Vidal-Naquet 1977:12.

45. In the Homeric world, *dêmiourgoi* were "travelling specialists who offered their services to the community (*dêmos*)" (Austin and Vidal-Naquet 1977:45–46; see also 201). Compare *Odyssey* xvii 383–386: ". . .those who are *dêmiourgoi* - the prophet, the healer of sicknesses, the builder with beams (τέκτονα δούρων), or the inspired bard, who delights by his singing - for these are the mortals invited from place to place upon the limitless earth."

46. Compare Vidal-Naquet 1986d:240: "In likening artisans to women I am not indulging in a simplistic comparison."

47. Aristotle records that in some city-states, before the institution of radical democracy, the *dêmiourgos* was excluded from political office (*Politics* 1277b1–3). Compare also the ancient practice of admiring the work without mentioning the artist and of denigrating those who attain a professional level of skill in any performing art (Austin and Vidal-Naquet 1977:177–178).

48. Austin and Vidal-Naquet 1977:12, 190–193, 246–248, and Brisson 1974:92.

49. The salary of Archilochus, architect of the Erechtheum, was 1 drachma per day, comparable to that of a carpenter (Petrie 19779:24). Greek legendary history preserves accounts of architects vying with the political power of the client for the "paternity" of the building. For example, the architect of the lighthouse of Alexandria builds his authority into the structure's future, its deterioration through time: he covers his construction with a coating of plaster bearing the king's name – which falls away after a few years to reveal his own (Petrie 1979:29).

50. Inscriptions record the name of the architect just after that of the magistrate and a repeated phrase indicating the architect's authority: "however the architect orders . . ." (Petrie 1979:26–27).

51. The συγγραφή was not a prefiguration of the project, but rather a detailed description of the phases of execution and of their cost – the ancient architect was a writer and a contractor – and it was as such that his orders carried obligatory force (Petrie 1979:27). Compare the διαγράμματα "diagrams" by "Daedalus or some other *dêmiourgos* or painter," Plato *Republic* 529e1–3.

52. For eugenic marriage and communal child-rearing, see *Republic* Book V. For an alternate vision in Platonic thought of how to regulate marriage, see *Laws* 771d5–772a4 and for another eugenic scheme, *Politicus* 310b–e. For the effort in the *Republic* to eliminate the "mark" of the female, see Rosenstock 1994.

53. Compare the résumé of an argument like that of the *Republic* at the start of the *Timaeus*, where the assimilation of female to male is described as an architectural construction – a "harmonization:"

And indeed we also made mention of women, how it would be necessary to fit together (συναρμοστέον < ἁρμόζω "fit, join" of carpentry, compare ἁρμονία "fitting together, harmony") their natures so that they are nearly beside (παραπλησίας: παρά "beside, nearly" + πλησίος "beside, near") men (*Timaeus* 18c 1–2).

Compare the desire of the Demiurge that the cosmos be "as nearly like (παραπλήσια) himself as possible" (*Timaeus* 29e2–3). For the verb συναρμόζω "fit together" of the Demiurgic architecture, see *Timaeus* 32b3, 35a8, 53e7–8, 56c7, 74c7, 81d5.

Contrast this universalization of unmarkedness in the zero-interpretation, whereby all human beings become male, with the gender-neutral unmarkedness entailed by the marking of gender *per se* (see above, n. 10) in which neither gender would differentiate.

54. In Platonic idiom to be "true to yourself" is to be "like" or "the same;" see, for example, *Symposium* 173d4, *Republic* 549e2. For the collocation of "like" and "true" as synonymous, see *Sophist* 252d1 and *Philebus* 65d2–3, as reciprocal, *Phaedrus* 273d1–6. The basis of this relation is the "likeness" or "sameness" of the sensible particular and the intelligible Form or paradigm; see *Republic* 472c4–d1, *Parmenides* 132d1–4 (where the participation of the particular in the paradigm is precisely the relation of likeness). The vulnerability of this mimetic conception of truth is registered in the Muses' speech, when they claim they can "say many false things (ψεύδεα) like (ὁμοῖα 'like, equal, same') to real things."

55. For the *points de capiton* "upholstery buttons" as the anchoring or nodal points that bind together associative material of the unconscious in the "knotted" structure of the symptom, see Lacan 1966:260 = 1977:154 and Muller and Richardson 1982:113.

56. The Muses "speak to us in a tragic manner, as to children, playing and bantering, as though speaking with seriousness in lofty language," articulating a perfect number for the divine creature and for the human creature, in ignorance of which the Guardians will mate couples at the wrong time and thus cause the birth of unworthy offspring – who will display their degeneracy first of all in the neglect of the Muses, "considering the arts less important than is required" (Plato *Republic* 545e, 546d). Grube (1974:197) expresses the ambiguity with which this pivotal passage is viewed: "The mock heroic invocation to the Muses and their talking in tragic language should warn us not to take the mathematical myth which follows too seriously or too literally. It is perhaps the most obscure and controversial passage in the whole of Plato's works." He translates:

> For a divine creature which is born there is a cycle contained in a perfect number; for man it is the first number in which are found root and square increases, taking three dimensions and four limits, of the numbers that make things like and unlike, cause them to increase and decrease and which make all things correspond and rational in relation to one another. Of these the lowest numbers in the ratio of four to three, married to five, give two harmonies when multiplied three times, the one a square, so many times a hundred, the other of equal length one way, but oblong, the one side a hundred numbers obtained from the rational diameters of five, each reduced by one, or from the irrational diameters reduced by two, the other side being a hundred cubes of three.

> *Republic* 546b–c

But the numbers themselves are, in fact, calculable and significant, the human one being apparently the sum of the cubes of the numbers of the "right triangle" (3, 4,

5), that is, 216, the shortest period of human gestation in days, plus the Pythagorean marriage number, 6. See Grube 1974:197n6.

57. See Vidal-Naquet (1986d:240) who concludes his essay "A Study in Ambiguity: Artisans in the Platonic City" by citing Plato *Republic* 620c1–2, where the soul of Epeius, architect of the Trojan horse, "enters the nature of a female skilled in τέχνη 'craft'."

58. See *Politicus* 278e4–279c3. Although posing a "separate but equal" division of the genders at 262c10–263a1 (see above, n. 16), the text returns the unmarked vs. marked hierarchy: the female mark of weaving is adopted as the paradigm of the Statesman's ἐπιστήμη "knowledge" (while the weaving τέχνη "craft" itself is belittled as a small, material, visible εἴδωλον "image" of one of τὰ ἀσώματα, κάλλιστα ὄντα καὶ μέγιστα "the immaterial things, being most beautiful and greatest" 285d8–286b1) and in the dialogue's creation myth the male *dêmiourgos* governs cosmic cycles that move back and forth like the woven thread (268d8–274e4). See also Vidal-Naquet 1986d:227. On the figure of weaving in Platonic thought, see Frère 1986.

59. See *Timaeus* 28b–29d, esp. 29b3–c2:

> So therefore concerning an εἰκών "likeness, image, copy" and its παράδειγμα "model" it is necessary to draw a distinction (διοριστέον): that accounts (λόγους) are cognate (συγγενεῖς) with those things of which they are the interpreters (ἐξηγηταί). So of what is abiding and stable and clearly seen with the intelligence (μετὰ νοῦ), the accounts are abiding and unchanging – to the degree it is possible and appropriate for accounts to be irrefutable and invincible, they must lack nothing of this. But of what is likened (ἀπεικασθέντος) to that [the intelligible] and is a likeness (εἰκόνος), the accounts are likenesses (εἰκότας) and in analogical relation with the former accounts: as being (οὐσία) is to becoming (γένεσιν), so truth (ἀλήθεια) is to belief (πίστιν). If then, Socrates, in many respects concerning many things – the gods and the becoming (γενέσεως) of the universe – we are not able to render accounts that are everywhere entirely consistent with themselves and accurate, do not be amazed. But if we present accounts no less likely than any other, we must be content, remembering how I who speak and you who are the judges possess human nature, so that it is fitting for us to receive a likely tale (εἰκότα μῦθον) concerning these things and to seek nothing beyond this.

Timaeus frequently reiterates the iconological status of his narrative (*Timaeus* 34c2–4, 44c7–d1, 48c1, d2, 49b6, 53d5–6, 55d5, 56a1, 56c8–d1, 57d6, 72d5–8, 90e8) and at *Timaeus* 59c5–d2 defends it (on which passage, see Derrida 1987a:282). See also *Timaeus* 49a6–50a4 where Timaeus insists that terminology should match ontological status, so that no perpetually changing element should be called a "this," as if it possessed permanent being, but rather a thing "of such a quality always recurring as the same" – for example, not "fire," but "something with the quality of fire that always recurs with the same quality." On the metonymic relation between the kinds of being and the kinds of discourse in the *Timaeus*, see Derrida 1987a:266–267.

60. For these divisions, see the translation and commentary of Cornford 1937:32–39, 159, 279.

61. The term *dêmiourgos* is appropriate for the creator of the cosmos insofar as it covers the whole world of construction and production, both concrete (for example, shoes, *Gorgias* 447d1–3, *Theaetetus* 146d1; beds, *Republic* 597d9–11; images of animals and houses, *Republic* 401b1–7; women's κόσμος "ornament," *Republic* 373b8–c1; musical instruments, *Republic* 399c10–d1; Silenus-statues, *Symposium* 215a6–215b3; brass-ware, clay pots, cooked meat, *Euthydemus* 301c3–9; Pheidias' Parthenon sculptures, *Hippias Major* 290a5–9; refined gold, *Politicus* 303d10–e5) and figurative (for example, justice, *Protagoras* 327c7; moderation, justice, and virtue, *Republic* 500d4–8; crimes, *Republic* 552d3-6; freedom, *Republic* 395c1; love between gods and men, *Symposium* 188d1; painted images in the soul, *Philebus* 39b3–7; names, *Cratylus* 431e1; noble deeds, *Laws* 829d1–4; beautiful εἰκόνες "likenesses" in speech, *Laws* 898b3). The particular craft of architecture is indicated here in the *Timaeus* by the use with *dêmiourgos* of verbs of building: τεκταίνομαι (compare τέκτων "builder" and ἀρχιτέκτων "architect") and construction: σύν "together, with" + ἵστημι "make stand, set up." The *Timaeus* is not the only dialogue in which a *dêmiourgos* figures as architect of the cosmos: see also *Republic* 530a4–7, *Politicus* 270a5, 273b1–2, and *Republic* 507c6–8 for the *dêmiourgos* as fabricator of the "lavish power of seeing and being seen."

62. For the *dêmiourgos* as characterized by special knowledge, see also *Republic* 360e7–361a1, *Sophist* 232d5–8.

63. For the linking of *dêmiourgos* and ποιητής "maker, poet," see also *Republic* 599d2–e1, *Symposium* 205b8–c2, 209a3–5.

64. See also *Timaeus* 31a4, 37c8–d1 (for the cosmos as ὅμοιον "like" its paradigm), *Timaeus* 38b6–c3 (for time as ὁμοιότατος "most like" its paradigm of eternal nature), *Timaeus* 39e2–7 (for the cosmos as wrought εἰς ὁμοιότητα "in the likeness of" and ἀποτυπούμενος "typed from" its paradigm), *Timaeus* 48e4–49a1.

65. For the verbs τεκταίνομαι "build" and συντεκταίνομαι "build together" of the Demiurge and the gods as his deputies, see *Timaeus* 33b1, 36e1, 68e5, 70e3, 91a2, and 30b5, 45b3.

66. See *Timaeus* 29b1–2, 37d5–7, 52c2, 92c7 (for the cosmos as εἰκὼν τοῦ νοητοῦ "likeness of the intelligible").

67. See *Timaeus* 28a6–b1:

> Whenever the *dêmiourgos*, by looking always toward what is the same and using something of this sort as model (παραδείγματι), produces the visible form (ἰδέαν) and power of his work, by necessity everything he accomplishes in this way must be beautiful and good (καλόν).

68. See also *Timaeus* 30b4–5:

> Having constructed (συνιστάς) intelligence (νοῦν) in the soul and the soul in the body, he built together (συνετεκταίνετο) the totality (τὸ πᾶν).

See also *Timaeus* 30c3, 32c7. The verb συνίστημι is used of the *dêmiourgos* constructing the heavens (συνεστάναι τῷ τοῦ οὐρανοῦ δημιουργῷ) at *Republic* 530a6.

69. See *Timaeus* 36d8–e2:

> And when the whole construction (σύστασις) of the soul had come into being according to the intelligence (κατὰ νοῦν) of the constructor (συνιστάντι), then he built (ἐτεκταίνετο) within it all that is corporeal, and bringing them together, middle to middle, he fit them together (προσήρμοττεν: compare ἁρμονία "fitting together"). And the soul was interwoven (διαπλακεῖσα) everywhere from the middle to the outermost heaven.

70. See *Timaeus* 28c3, 41a7, 42e6–7.

71. As the plot of the *Iliad* represents the βουλή "wish, plan" of Zeus (*Iliad* I 5), so the ἀρχή "origin" (*Timaeus* 29e4) of the cosmos is located in the psychological condition – the goodness (ἀγαθός), the lack of envy (φθόνος), the wish (ἐβουλήθη, βουληθείς), the considered judgment (ἡγησάμενος) – of its anthropomorphic creator (*Timaeus* 29e1–30a6).

72. See *Timaeus* 33d2, 68e3.

73. See also *Laws* 898a8–b3.

74. See Vidal-Naquet 1986d.

75. Vidal-Naquet 1986d:229–232. Compare the segregation of the artisans and the farmers from the elite Guardian class in the *Republic* 415a–c, 466a8–b2, 468a1–7.

76. Vidal-Naquet (1986d:238) notes the closest thing in all of Greek history to "a collective action with political goals" mounted by artisans: the plan of Cinadon in the 4th century BCE to overthrow the Spartan constitution, leading a group whose weapons were the tools of the artisans (Xenophon *Hellenica* 3.3.7). Lacking any independent political identity, the artisans are regulated by the city, rather than participating as a group in its governance.

77. Note also the linkage between the artisans and ξένοι "guests, foreigners," *Laws* 848a3–4, 849d4–5.

78. In addition, it is the two tutelary deities of the artisans, Athena and Hephaestus, who preside over the city in the *Timaeus* and the *Critias*. And like the gods, the artisans have a right to be paid and to collect interest if it is late, a practice usually forbidden in the *Laws* (921a–d). See Vidal-Naquet 1986d:231, 233.

79. See Morrow 1954:5–23.

80. For πειθώ "persuasion" (and ἀπάτη "deception") as the powers of Aphrodite, see the *Homeric Hymn to Aphrodite* 7, 33. With the Sophists' ability to "make the worse

argument seem the better" compare the Muses' ability to speak "false things (ψεύδεα) like (ὁμοῖα) to real things" (*Theogony* 27–28). For the linkage of rhetorical and erotic persuasion in the rhetorician Gorgias' *Praise of Helen*, see "Language and the Female in Early Greek Thought" in this collection. For rhetoric as the *dêmiourgos* of persuasion, see Plato *Gorgias* 453a2, 454a4–5, 454e9–455a1. On the relation between "necessity" and "persuasion" in the *Timaeus*, see Morrow 1965.

81. Compare *Timaeus* 68e4–5, where the *dêmiourgos* is said to use necessary (as opposed to divine) causes as ὑπηρετούσαις "subordinates, ministers" in his "building (τεκταινόμενος) of the good in all things that come into being."

82. Compare the use of this verb in Aristotle's embryological contest between the sexes: "whenever the [male] principle (ἀρχή) does not gain mastery (κρατῇ) and through lack of heat is unable to concoct and lead [the matter] into its own proper form (εἶδος), but in this it is subordinated (ἡττηθῇ 'made inferior'), it must change into its opposite. The female is opposite of the male, and [it is so] in that by which one is male, and the other female" (*Generation of Animals* 766a18–22). See also above, n. 31.

83. On Necessity as a divine power and principle of irregular and unpredictable movement, see Cornford 1937:163–177. On the homelessness of the Sophists, see Derrida "*Chôra*" 1987a:278–279.

84. To endow the circular cosmos with the motions proper to νοῦς "intelligence" and φρόνησις "thought," the Demiurge removes these six-directional movements and makes the cosmic "body" ἀπλανὲς "free from wandering" (*Timaeus* 34a1–5).

85. See *Timaeus* 48e2–49a4:

So let the new beginning (ἀρχή) of the universe be divided more than the one before: for then we distinguished two forms (εἴδη), but now we must disclose another, third kind (τρίτον γένος). For the two were sufficient for what was said before: one form supposed (ὑποτεθέν) as that of the model (παραδείγματος), intelligible and always being the same; and the second, as the copy (μίμημα) of the model, possessing becoming (γένεσιν) and visible. Then we did not distinguish a third, considering that the two would be sufficient. But now the account (λόγος) seems to introduce the necessity (εἰσαναγκάζειν) of trying to show forth in words (λόγοις ἐμφανίσαι) a difficult and obscure form (εἶδος).

86. Between the two assertions of the necessity of speaking more clearly, Timaeus links the problem of speaking about *khôra* with that of how to speak of the four elements: terms like "this" or "that" denoting perdurable being should be used not of the four elements (fire, earth, air, and water), since these are ever-changing qualities, but only of "that in which (ἐν ᾧ . . . ἐκεῖνο) each of these things always coming into being appears and then vanishes from there again" (*Timaeus* 49e7–50a1).

87. The νοῦς as "father," "demiurge" (δημιουργὸς πατήρ τε ἔργων, *Timaeus* 41a7), and "poet" (*Timaeus* 28c3), the gods as his "children" (*Timaeus* 42e6–8), Being as a "model," Becoming as a "copy" (*Timaeus* 48e3–49a1).

88. The prejudicial assimilation of architecture to sculpture in Western philosophy is founded here – the stone σῆμα "sign" of Zeus being lost under the rubric of "mythology" to the tradition of philosophy and architectural theory. See Kipnis "Twisting the Separatrix" in *Choral Works* 1997:137–160 for the Hegelian hierarchy of architecture as unsublimated sculpture and its influence on Derrida's contributions to *Choral Works*.

89. See *Timaeus* 50a5–b8:

> For if someone should mould all figures (σχήματα) out of gold and not cease moulding each of them into all the rest, and if someone should point to one of them and ask what it is then, it is by far most secure in relation to truth to say that it is gold, and – of the triangle and as many other figures as have come into being – never to speak of these as *being*, which indeed are changing even while someone asserts their *being*. Instead we should be content if ever they are willing to receive even the description "what is of such a quality" with any security. Indeed the same account (λόγος) applies also to the nature (φύσεως) that receives (δεχομένης) all bodies (σώματα). It must itself always be called the same (ταὐτὸν . . . προσρητέον). For it never stands apart (ἐξ-ίσταται) at all from its own power (δυνάμεως).

90. See *Timaeus* 50b8–c4:

> For it both always receives (δέχεται) all things and never in any way whatsoever has it taken on (εἴληφεν) any shape (μορφὴν) like (ὁμοίαν) to any of those going in. For by nature (φύσει) it is there for everything as a plastic medium (ἐκμαγεῖον "that which wipes off, that in or on which an impression is made"), moved (κινούμενον) and figured (διασχηματιζόμενον) by those going in, and through those it appears (φαίνεται) to be of different qualities at different times.

91. See *Timaeus* 50c4–6:

> The things going in (εἰσιόντα) and going out (ἐξιόντα) are copies (μιμήματα) of the eternal things, impressions (τυπωθέντα "things formed by impress, moulded, typed") from them in a certain way that is hard to explain and marvelous, which we will pursue again.

92. See *Odyssey* iv 140–146. Compare *Works and Days* 182, where the evils of the Iron Age of humankind include a father who is not ὁμοίιος "like" his children, and *Works and Days* 235, where justice in the city is manifested by women giving birth to children who are ἐοικότα "like" their parents (on both usages, see West 1978:215–216 on 235 and Aristotle *Generation of Animals* 767b6, where any child who is not ἐοικὼς "like" its parents is a τέρας "monstrosity").

291

93. See *Timaeus* 50d4–e1:

> And it is necessary to understand that if the impression (ἐκτυπώματος "that which is modeled out") is going to be visually varied with every diversity, the thing itself in which (τοῦτ' αὐτὸ ἐν ᾧ) it stands modeled out (ἐκτυπούμενον) would in no way be well prepared except by being without the shape (ἄμορφον) of all the forms it is going to receive (δέχεσθαι) from elsewhere (πόθεν).

94. See *Timaeus* 50e1–4:

> For if it were like (ὅμοιον) any of those going in, whenever those of an opposite or wholly other nature came, in receiving them it would copy (ἀφομοιοῖ "make like"; compare ἀφομοιούμενον *Timaeus* 50d1) them badly (κακῶς) by making its own aspect appear besides (παρεμφαῖνον).

95. See *Timaeus* 50e4–8:

> Therefore it is necessary that what is going to receive all the kinds (γένη) in itself must be free from (ἐκτὸς "outside") all the forms (εἰδῶν), just as in the case of unguents – as many as they contrive by skill to make sweet-smelling – they create this condition first: that the waters about to receive the scents are completely without smell.

96. See *Timaeus* 50e8–51a1:

> And as many as try to take impressions (ἀπομάττειν "wipe off"; compare ἐκμαγεῖον, *Timaeus* 50c2) of figures (σχήματα) in any of the soft substances allow absolutely no figure (σχῆμα) to be visible, but by leveling it first they make it as smooth as possible.

97. The copies that constitute γένεσις "becoming" must be καλός, for the Demiurge who created the universe of becoming is himself ἄριστος "most good, well-born, brave," and it is not θέμις "what is put or placed as law" for anyone who is ἄριστος to do anything except the κάλλιστον "what is most καλός" (*Timaeus* 30a6–7). For the Demiurgic construction as κάλλιστα, see also *Republic* 530a5.

98. See *Timaeus* 51a1–6:

> So, in the same way, to that which is going to receive beautifully (καλῶς) many times over the entirety of itself the copies (ἀφ-ομοιώματα "that which is made like") of all the eternal things it belongs also to be by nature (πεφυκέναι) free from all the forms (εἰδῶν). For this reason, then, the mother (μητέρα) and receptacle (ὑποδοχὴν) of what has become visible and in every way perceptible we must not call earth or air or fire or water nor any of their compounds or components.

99. On this passage, see Brisson 1974:197–208. In his analysis of the "*connaissance du milieu spatial*" Brisson argues that *khôra* "participates in the intelligible" insofar as she, like Being, is forever imperishable and thus knowledge of her can be certain, but "most

insolubly" because she is without an intelligible Form (ἄ-μορφον). The description of *khôra* as "third kind" specifies her condition as eternal and indestructible:

> And then there is the third kind, being that of the eternal *khôra* (ὂν τὸ τῆς χώρας ἀεί), not admitting destruction (φθορὰν οὐ προσδεχόμενον) but providing a seat for all things, as many as have becoming (γένεσιν).

> *Timaeus* 52a8–b1

The description continues with a critical account of how this "third kind" is known:

> And it [is] graspable (ἁπτὸν) without sense-perception (μετ' ἀναισθησίας) by a certain bastard logic (λογισμῷ τινι νόθῳ), hardly an object of belief (μόγις πιστόν), toward which indeed looking we also dream (πρὸς ὃ δὴ καὶ ὀνειροπολοῦμεν βλέποντες).

> *Timaeus* 52b1–3

Brisson understands λογισμῷ τινι νόθῳ "by a certain bastard logic" as employing the image of a numerical calculation (λογισμός) made illegitimate (νόθος) by the fact that it ends up in a number that does not exist, so as to indicate a logical calculation leading to the impossible fact that the *khôra* "participates in the intelligible" although there is no Form in which as a "father" she may participate. With regard to this interpretation it should be noted that the Greek term νόθος "bastard" describes not a child without a known father, but one whose parents are not married and who is thus deprived of citizenship and possibly of inheritance. The Greek "bastard" is a child deprived of the "father function" as a social construction. The logic leading to *khôra* ends in a form (εἶδος, *Timaeus* 51a7) that is not a Form. The text goes on to explain this "bastard logic." Reinforcing μετ' ἀναισθησίας "without sense-perception," μόγις πιστόν "hardly an object of belief" reiterates that *khôra* does not belong to the realm of Becoming of which knowledge can be only variable "belief." Rather, our illegitimate reasoning about *khôra* takes the form of a dream. The phrase πρὸς ὃ δὴ καὶ ὀνειροπολοῦμεν βλέποντες "toward which indeed looking we also dream" does not mean, as the phrase is understood by Brisson ("the representation that we make for ourselves of it is related to a dream," 201–202) and Derrida ("here is how one catches a glimpse of *chôra* . . . as in a dream," "*Chôra*" 1987a:272), that we see *khôra* as in a dream, that is, that the dream is the cognitive mode proper to *khôra*. Rather, the dream is here, as elsewhere in Plato, a mode of cognitive error, specifically, a failure to distinguish copy from model, semblance from true Form (see, for example, *Republic* 414d5, 476c2–d3, 533b1–c5, 534c6–7, *Theaetetus* 158b1–d4). The image of the dream continues, as the mistaken understanding of *khôra* is specified:

> toward which indeed looking we also dream (πρὸς ὃ δὴ καὶ ὀνειροπολοῦμεν βλέποντες) and say that everything that exists (τὸ ὂν ἅπαν) must somehow be in some place (τόπῳ) and possess a certain *khôra*, and that what is neither in the earth nor somewhere in heaven does not exist. Because of this dreaming we are not able, even when awakened, to speak the truth by making all the

following distinctions indeed and others cognate with them even concerning the sleepless and truly existing nature: namely that, for a likeness (εἰκόνι), since the thing itself on the basis of which it has come into being is not its own and it is moved always as the semblance (φάντασμα) of something else, for these reasons it is proper to come into being in something else, by clinging in some way to existence, or be itself in no way at all; but for what is really existing, the accurately true account is an ally: as long as the two [the εἰκών "likeness, copy" and its model] are distinct, neither ever will come into being in the other and become at once one and the same thing, and two.

Timaeus 52b3–d1

The point is that we apprehend *khôra* by supposing that every Being must be somewhere, but it is in fact only the εἰκών "likeness, copy" of Being that requires *khôra* in which to be born. We dream in mistaking the copy's need for that of its model.

100. The term intimates a link between *khôra* and *mêtis* via hunting, in which nets, traps, and reversals, both material and mental, enact the "circular reciprocity" between the hunter and the hunted. See Detienne and Vernant 1978:27–54 and Brisson 1974:199. For the "hunting" of the sophist as master of rhetorical feints and shape-shifting, see Plato *Sophist* 218d–223b.

101. Thus precluding the *main-tenant* of architecture. See above, n. 5.

102. Compare the Aristotelian teleology in the Vitruvian ideal of the temple as reproducing the proportions of the body of a *hominis bene figurati* "well-shaped man" at *De Architectura* 3.1.5, where the body parts providing the crucial dimensions are said to have been grouped by the Greeks into the "perfect number which the Greeks call *teleon*."

103. Derrida closes *"Chôra"* (1987a:293) by quoting this passage from the *Timaeus*, having observed:

> Homology or analogy at least formal, one more time: in order to think *chôra*, it is necessary to return to a beginning more ancient than the beginning, namely, the birth of the cosmos, just as the origin of the Athenians must be recalled to them from beyond their own memory. In that which it has of the formal, precisely, the analogy is declared: a concern for composition that is architectural, textual (histological) and even organic is presented as such a little further on.

This observation of the textual architecture of the *Timaeus* is not mentioned in the transcripts or discussed by Kipnis in "Twisting the Separatrix" in *Choral Works* 1997: 137–160. Nor does Derrida return to it in *"Pourquoi Peter Eisenman écrit de si bons livres"* (1987b).

104. Compare the gods' creation of mortals by "weaving together (προσυφαίνοντες) mortal with immortal" (*Timaeus* 41d1–2) and the Demiurge as weaver at *Timaeus* 36d8–e2.

105. To gloss "the same place from which we have arrived here" Cornford (1937:280n2) writes: "The 'same position' is sensation and sense-perception, which we reached at the end of the first part (45b–47e), and have now reached again in the concluding paragraphs of the second part." The résumé, in other words, is meant to cover only Part I of the account. It does include, however, elements from Part II: the disorder of the pre-cosmic chaos and the terminology of the cosmic order. See the translation below.

106. The passage is replete with architectural language:

> For just as was said also at the beginning (κατ' ἀρχὰς), because these things were in disorder (ἀτάκτως), in each itself in relation both to itself and to the others, the god created (ἐνεποίησεν) symmetries (συμμετρίας), both as many as and in whatever way it was possible for them to be analogous (ἀνάλογα) and symmetrical (σύμμετρα). For then (τότε) they had no share of these, except insofar as it happened by chance, and there was nothing at all of those things now named worthy of the name – like fire and water and the rest. But all these he put in order (διεκόσμησεν) for the first time, then from them constructed (συνεστήσατο) this totality, one living thing having all living things in itself both mortal and immortal. And of the divine things he himself was the artisan (δημιουργός), while the generation of mortal things he commanded his own offspring to fabricate (δημιουργεῖν). They, imitating him, took an immortal principle (ἀρχὴν) of soul, next framed (περιετόρνευσαν "turn as in a lathe") a mortal body around it and gave the whole body as a vehicle and in this built in addition (προσῳκοδόμουν) another form (εἶδος) of soul, the mortal.

> *Timaeus* 69b2–c8

107. For the operation of this structure in the composition of the *Odyssey*, see "Odyssean Temporality: Many (Re)Turns" in this collection.

108. For these categories of narratological analysis, see Genette 1980:25–32, whose original French terms are: *histoire* "story," *récit* "narrative," and *narration* "narration, narrating instance."

109. This structure produces the "abyss" of narrative "encasings" (*enchâssement*) examined by Derrida to show how the multi-layered, chronological containments in the prologue of the *Timaeus* prefigure *khôra* as "receptacle of all becoming" ("*Chôra*" 1987a:282–290). Derrida enumerates: F1 (the whole dialogue entitled *Timaeus*) is a "receptacle" containing F2 (a dialogue yesterday, *Timaeus* 17a2), which contained F3 (the fictive model of an ideal city, *Timaeus* 17c1–3) – "a structure of inclusion makes of the *included* fiction the theme in some way of the prior fiction which is its *including* form, its capable container, let us say, its receptacle" (286) – and F4 (the young Critias mentioned an ancient story yesterday, *Timaeus* 20d1) containing F5 (the story told to the young Critias by his grandfather Critias – who heard it from Dropides, *Timaeus*

20e1–4, a layer not counted by Derrida) containing F6 (the story told to Dropides by Solon) containing F7 (the story told Solon by the Egyptian priest of the "amazing achievements" of Athens as recorded in Egyptian writings, *Timaeus* 20e5, 21d4–25d6). Derrida observes that "the whole of the *Timaeus* is thus scanned by these returns backward" (291), but does not observe the "return backward" that contains the pre-cosmic *khôra*.

110. Compare the Muses' capacity to (re)present in its totality a past presence and sight in any present place.

111. The description of the pre-cosmic *khôra* follows a mini-recapitulation of the three ontological kinds and the assertion of their existence as "three in three ways" (τρία τριχῇ) "even before the birth of heaven" (*Timaeus* 52d2–4). The repetition of triadic form in the *Timaeus* is insistent. Timaeus himself is called the "third companion" (*Timaeus* 20d4). With the three sides of the Nile's "Delta" (called *khôra*, *Timaeus* 22e2) – the inverted "delta" being a frequent symbol for the female genital in antiquity and later – compare Wittkower (1988:104–107) on the significance of the number "three" in Renaissance architectural theory with its Christian as well as Classical resonances.

112. It is important to note that while the λόγος "account, logic" makes it necessary to introduce *khôra* into the cosmology, there is no "logical" necessity for describing the prior condition of *khôra*. The necessity, rather, is architectural: to *establish* a temporal and qualitative difference between the two conditions.

113. See *Timaeus* 53a7–b7:

> Indeed, on one hand, to be sure, in the time before this (καὶ τὸ μὲν δὴ πρὸ τούτου), all these were irrational (ἀ-λόγως "without rational account, logic") and disproportionate (ἀ-μέτρως "without measure"). But when he took it in hand to order (κοσμεῖσθαι) the whole, fire first and water and earth and air – having some traces (ἴχνη "tracks") of themselves, but in every way disposed as it is likely (εἰκὸς) that anything is, whenever the god is absent from it – these indeed being then (τότε) by nature in this condition, he for the first time (πρῶτον) shaped them (διεσχηματίσατο) by both forms (εἴδεσί) and numbers (ἀριθμοῖς). That the god constructed (συν-ιστάναι) them with the greatest possible beauty and excellence (κάλλιστα ἄριστά τε) out of what is not thus, beyond all else let this stand as asserted by us always.

114. Compare Vitruvius' list of the elements of architecture (*De Architectura* 1.2.1): "Now architecture consists of ordering (*ordinatio*) which in Greek is called τάξις, of design (*dispositio*) which the Greeks name διάθεσις, and of proportion (*euruthmia*) and symmetry (*summetria*) and correctness (*decor*) and allocation (*distributio*) which in Greek is called οἰκονομία." On the meaning of these terms, see Rowland 1999:24–26, 143–151. Compare also the first of these elements, *ordinatio* or τάξις, with the description of the pre-cosmic condition by the alpha-privatives ἀ-τάκτως "without

ordering" and ἀ-ταξία "lack of ordering" (*Timaeus* 30a5). For the aesthetic and moral power of τάξις "ordering, arrangement" and κόσμος "order" and ἀταξία "lack of ordering" in the work of all *dêmiourgoi,* including architects, see *Gorgias* 503d6–504a9:

> Socrates: The good man, who aims toward speaking the best in whatever he speaks, will he speak not at random anything else, but looking toward something? Just like all other *dêmiourgoi* as well, looking toward their own work – each selects and brings forth the things he brings forth for that work of his not at random, but so that this thing which he is working on may have its certain form. For example, if you wish to look at painters, house-builders, ship-builders, and all other *dêmiourgoi,* any one of them you wish, how each places each thing he places in a certain arrangement (τάξιν) and compels the one to be fitting and to harmonize with the other, until he has constructed (συστήσηται < σύν + ἵστημι "make stand together") a whole thing both arranged (τεταγμένον, compare τάξις) and ordered (κεκοσμημένον, compare κόσμος). And also indeed the other *dêmiourgoi* and those whom we were just now mentioning, those concerning the body, both the trainers and the doctors, they too bring order (κοσμοῦσί) somehow and arrangement (συντάττουσιν) to the body. Do we agree that this is so or not?
>
> Callias: Let this be as you say.
>
> Socrates: If a house should achieve arrangement (τάξεως) and order (κόσμου), it would be good (χρηστὴ "useful, honest, beneficent"), but if lack of arrangement (ἀταξίας), then bad (μοχθηρά "wretched, unsafe, wicked").
>
> Callias: Right.

For the pre-architectural *khôra* as an alpha-privative condition of ἀν-ωμαλία "lack of the same level, anomaly," see below, n. 119.

115. For mathematics in architectural training, see Vitruvius *De Architectura* 1.1.4.

116. For example, the εἶδος "form" of a triangle has a certain ἀριθμός "number" of sides.

117. For such representation as the philosophical paradigm of architecture, compare Wigley 1989:12:

> The eventual status of architecture as a discipline began to be negotiated by the first texts of architectural theory, which drew on the canons of the philosophical tradition to identify the proper concern of the newly constituted figure of the architect with drawing (*disegno*) that mediates between the idea and the building, the formal and the material, the soul and the body, the theoretical and the practical.

118. See *Timaeus* 52d4–e3:

> Indeed the nurse of becoming, being made wet and fiery and receiving (δεχομένην) the shapes (μορφὰς) of both earth and air, and experiencing

all the other conditions that accompany these, appeared by sight to be of every sort. And because of being filled with powers (δυνάμεων) neither alike (ὁμοίων) nor of equal balance (ἰσορρόπων), in no part of herself was she equally balanced (ἰσορροπεῖν).

Contrast the ideal of symmetrical balance in Classical proportions.

119. See *Timaeus* 52e3–5:

But swaying unevenly everywhere (ἀνωμάλως πάντῃ ταλαντουμένην) she herself was shaken (σείεσθαι) by these powers, and by being moved (κινουμένην) she shook them (σείειν) again in turn (αὖ πάλιν).

Compare *Timaeus* 57e1–58a1 for motion as requiring a lack of ὁμαλότης "evenness" between mover and moved. By the term ἀνώμαλος, *khôra* is again described by an alpha-privative: ἀ(ν)- "not" + ὁμαλός "even, level." Both ὁμαλός and ὅμοιος "same, equal, like" derive from the root ὁμο- "one and the same." The ἀνωμαλία of *khôra* precludes concomitant spatial and temporal "sameness" and thus Platonic truth.

120. See *Timaeus* 52e5–53a6:

Because of being moved (κινούμενα), they were continually separated and carried in different directions – just as when things are shaken (σειόμενα) and winnowed (ἀνικμώμενα) by baskets (πλοκάνων "woven winnowing basket") and tools (ὀργάνων) for the cleaning of corn, the thick and heavy go in one direction, and the thin and light are carried into another place and settle there. At that time (τότε) in the same way the four kinds (γένη, that is, pre-cosmic water, fire, earth, and air) were shaken (σειόμενα) by her who received them, with herself being moved like a tool producing (παρέχοντος) a shaking, so as to separate (ὁρίζειν) the most unlike (ἀν-ομοιότατα) kinds farthest from one another and to thrust the most alike (ὁμοιότατα) close together into the same place.

On the πλόκανον "woven winnowing basket" and its relation to the cult of Demeter, see Cornford 1937:199–202.

121. Compare Vlastos 1965:395–396.

122. The criticism by Vlastos (1965:390) of the usage of ἴχνη "footprints" as "self-contradictory" misses the (attempted) differentiation between a cosmos in which the putative stability of opposites makes contradiction possible and the "anomaly" of pre-cosmic "choral work."

123. Compare Vlastos 1965:395n2.

124. Compare Derrida "*Chôra*" 1987a:292:

The strange (*insolite*) difficulty of this whole text derives from (*tient à*) the distinction between these two modalities: the true and the necessary.

125. *Transcript One*, New York, September 17, 1985, *Choral Works* 1997:7:

> In my own work I have been mounting a critique of the systematic privileging
> of anthropocentric origins. As well as looking at questions of scale, I have
> regulated the concept of function as origin in the traditions of architectural
> aesthetics, which reinforce the status of anthropocentric origins such as
> scale and function. . . . Traditional architectural aesthetics takes for granted
> hierarchy, closure, symmetry and regularity, thus foreclosing the possibility
> of dissonance, non-closure, non-hierarchy, and so on. For me, this is no longer
> tenable.

126. The editor prints "classical" rather than "Classical" in the proofs of *Transcript*,
but the tradition in which Eisenman is trained and which he critiques is that of
Western Classicism and thus the capitalized form would best render his meaning
graphically.

127. *Transcript One*, New York, September 17, 1985, *Choral Works* 1997:9.

128. *Transcript One*, New York, September 17, 1985, *Choral Works* 1997:9:

> So, let me go very quickly to the single idea I have. When Tschumi asked me
> to participate in this project, I was excited, but at the same time, I was totally,
> totally empty. I mean, I had no ideas at all. I was in the midst of writing a text
> in homage to the philosopher Jean-Pierre Vernant, which had to do with
> something I taught twelve years ago concerning a very enigmatic passage in
> the *Timaeus*, a passage which has amazed generations of philosophers. In it,
> Plato discusses a certain place. The name for this singularly unique place is
> *chôra*.

129. Compare Kipnis' aim in analyzing *khôra*, "Twisting the Separatrix" in *Choral
Works* 1997:153:

> Deconstruction is not destruction, it does not pursue the separatrix to
> destroy it and the laws it enables; it does not seek the *chaos* which would
> result from the destruction of either the separatrix or *chôra*. It seeks, instead,
> to expose the hidden agenda behind an untenable reification of the order
> that the separatrix imposes. Deconstruction questions the repressions of the
> instability that the separatrix, like *chôra*, reflects into order, making order
> possible. Deconstruction, returning to Nietzsche's question, "What if truth
> were a woman?" respects the mark for what it/she is.

My deconstruction of the institution of *khôra* does not destroy her, but exposes the
valorization of Platonic order made possible by the maintenance of choral stability and
the repression of choral instability in "respecting the mark for what it/she is."

130. Derrida "*Chôra*" 1987a:268:

> While giving place to oppositions, she herself would never submit herself
> to any reversal. And that, another consequence, not because she would
> be inalterably *herself* but because in going beyond the polarity of meaning

(metaphorical or proper), she would no longer belong to the horizon of meaning, nor of meaning as the meaning of being.

131. Derrida *"Chôra"* 1987a:270–271.

132. Compare Derrida *"Chôra"* 1987a:268–269, especially:

> It would be a question of a structure and not of some essence of the *chôra*, the question of essence no longer having any meaning on the subject of her. The *chôra*, we will say, is *anachronic*, she "is" the anachrony in being – better – the anachrony of being. She anachronizes being.

133. Kipnis ("Twisting the Separatrix" in *Choral Works* 1997:152) notes the "absolute anteriority" of *khôra*, but does not deconstruct the institution of a moment when "all true movement begins":

> ... *chôra* is neither word nor concept, neither proper noun nor common noun, and it is a condition of absolute anteriority. Moreover, though Derrida treats of it only in passing, *chôra* shakes, shakes the whole, separating before the separation; it is movement before movement begins, since in the *Timaeus* all true movement begins with the world-soul and comes after the Demiurge does his work. Yet *chôra* shakes and orders even the chaos.

Similarly, Kipnis' account of the relation between *khôra* and the Demiurgic inscription – "*Chôra* has no existence, no pure being anterior to and free from inscription, outside of rhetoric and trope: it is, though it is only and always in the text as before it" (152) – is not contradicted by the choral "movement before movement begins" only if "existence" and "pure being" begin with that inscription.

134. Derrida *"Chôra"* 1987a:278–279.

135. Derrida *"Chôra"* 1987a:269.

136. Derrida *"Chôra"* 1987a:271.

137. Derrida *"Chôra"* 1987a:266.

138. Derrida reiterates the metaphorical status of *both* categories of language, but privileges that of "impression or printing." See, for example, *Transcript* One, New York, September 17, 1985, *Choral Works* 1997:9–10:

> To discuss this, he has to use what generations of philosophers have called "metaphors," though I do not think they are metaphors. These are the mother, the matrix or the nurse. You can compare, he says, the paradigm with the father, the sensible world with the child or the infant, and *chôra*, this place of inscription, with the mother or nurse. But these are only metaphors, because they are borrowed from the sensible world. So *chôra* is not the mother, nor the nurse who nurtures infants.

Derrida continues a moment later (10):

> *Chôra* is the spacing which is the condition for everything to take place, for everything to be inscribed. The metaphor of impression or printing is

very strong and recognizable in this text. It is the place where everything is received as an imprint.

139. The quality of "virginity" can, of course, be male: compare the Greek noun παρθένος indicating either a male or female virgin, depending upon the gender of the article used with it. But in apposition with "inaccessible" and "impassive," "virginity" appears, as in the passage cited above ("Is the value of a receptacle not also associated, like passive and virgin matter, with the feminine element, and precisely in Greek culture"), to be intended as female here.

140. See Derrida "*Chôra*" 1987a:269. See also Derrida's use of the term "virgin" in *Transcript One*, New York, September 17, 1985, *Choral Works* 1997:10:

> What interests me is that since *chôra* is irreducible to the two positions, the sensible and the intelligible, which have dominated the entire tradition of Western thought, it is irreducible to all the values to which we are accustomed – values of origin, anthropomorphism, and so on. I insist on the fact of this non-anthropomorphism of *chôra*. Why? Because *chôra* looks as though it were giving something, "giving" place . . . yet Plato insists that in fact it has to be a virgin place, and that it has to be totally foreign, totally exterior to anything that it receives. Since it is absolutely blank, everything that is printed on it is automatically effaced. . . . Everything inscribed in it erases itself immediately, while remaining in it.

141. See *Timaeus* 51a7–b2, translated above.

142. For *maintenant* as a virtual "technical term" in Derrida's philosophy of architecture, see above, n. 5.

143. *Transcript Two*, Paris, November 8, 1985, *Choral Works* 1997:35. See also *Transcript Four*, New York, April 3, 1986 (71):

> PE: As Thomas will tell you, La Villette is a killer project. The theoretical paradigms which you set up are so difficult to make.
>
> JD: Do not worry; it is an impossible program for architecture. It is the challenge in itself that is important.

144. It should be noted that material works of architecture always achieve the goal set here by philosophy – they always "give the receiver, the visitor, the possibility of thinking about architecture." And indeed, in its manipulations of scale, ground, and solid and void, in relation to time, place, and authorship, the project designed by Eisenman, described below, like many of his works, stimulates the pondering of architectural verities.

145. *Transcript Four*, New York, April 3, 1986, *Choral Works* 1997:70.

146. With Derrida's use of the term "virgin" here, compare above, n. 140.

147. Derrida's "feminine slip" here, printed in the original transcript of the meeting, is corrected by the editor to "paradigm" in the published text of *Transcript Four*.

148. *Transcript Four*, New York, April 3, 1986, *Choral Works* 1997:70.

149. Derrida *"Chôra"* 1987a:273:

Simply that excess is nothing, nothing which may be or be said ontologically. That absence of support, that one cannot translate into absent support or into absence as support, provokes and resists every binary or dialectic determination, any examination [*arraisonnement*] of a philosophical type, let us say more rigorously, of an *ontological* type.

150. For the *locus classicus* in Vitruvius, see *De Architectura* 3.1.5.

151. For *Choral Works* as an instance of Eisenman's "scaling" method, as practiced in the "Romeo and Juliet" and "Long Beach Museum" projects, and for a defense of this design process as "avoid[ing] the trap of architectural totalization (not literary totalization) by replacing the universalizing discourse which drives traditional design with a local fiction," see Kipnis, "Twisting the Separatrix" in *Choral Works* 1997:140–144.

152. *Transcript One*, September 17, 1985, *Choral Works* 1997:7.

153. *Transcript Five*, New Haven, April 21, 1986, *Choral Works* 1997:77.

154. *Transcript Five*, New Haven, April 21, 1986, *Choral Works* 1997:77.

155. *Transcript Five*, New Haven, April 21, 1986, *Choral Works* 1997:77. Lesser also explains fictional site one / column 2 (78):

Let's look at site one (column 2). Venice, which appears at the top, is scaled up, is solid, and is the highest. It is the future plan. The only part of Venice which you will see is the canal of Venice as a wall, three or four metres high. Bernard's scheme, the second element in the column, is at full scale, since it is in the present, and solid, but it only comes a little bit out of the ground. . . . La Villette, the third element in the column, is also in the present, but as a small void. It is a receptacle, as in its superposition it is both the wall of Paris and the canal. Peter's scheme, the bottom element in the column, is the past, and is a deeper void.

156. Lesser and Eisenman observe (*Transcript Five*, New Haven, April 21, 1986, *Choral Works* 1997:78):

TL: For [fictional] site two (column 3) . . . If you look at this diagram in which La Villette [2] is scaled down to make the squares in Bernard's project [1] the same size as those in Peter's [4], the Parisian abattoirs seem to be at the right scale, but they aren't. The Parisian abattoirs are so much bigger than the ones in Venice, that when you scale Paris down, the abattoirs appear to be at the same scale.

PE: Which is nice.

TL: Yes, it is a reversal of reality and meaning.

PE: You get this terribly strange play of scale and reality, as if half is always at the same scale and half not, as if something terrible has happened.

157. *Transcript Five*, New Haven, April 21, 1986, *Choral Works* 1997:78.

158. *Transcript Five*, New Haven, April 21, 1986, *Choral Works* 1997:79.

JD: To put it in an abstract way, I would be interested in a way of opening the dimension of either the future or the past in such a way that they could never be integrated into the totality as present-future or present-past. In that way, the relationship to the future could be totally open; this could motivate the visitor to stop and read, and even gain a virtual perception of the whole.

Eisenman describes "virtual perception of the whole" as a feature of Classical architecture:

PE: Traditional architecture provides a virtual perception of the whole. When you walk through a Palladian plan, you schematize it in your mind – you don't have to walk through the whole building to understand its symmetries. The somatic memory puts these things together. Classical architecture always provided parts in different places to allow the whole scheme to be put together. What Jacques is saying is that maybe there could be something in each piece that would provide an aperture, a kind of opening to nowhere.

TL: That breaks the circle.

159. *Transcript Five*, New Haven, April 21, 1986, *Choral Works* 1997:80.

160. *Transcript Five*, New Haven, April 21, 1986, *Choral Works* 1997:80.

161. Note that in Plato's text, no analogue of the pre-Platonic *khôra*, neither the baskets (πλοκάνων) nor the tools (ὀργάνων) for the cleaning of corn, "separates things into the world of the sensible and intelligible."

162. See *Transcript Six*, New York, January 10, 1987, *Choral Works* 1997:92.

10

FEMALE FETISH URBAN FORM

I. Introduction

EMALE, FETISH, AND URBAN FORM are mutually fashioned in Aristophanes' comedy *Ecclesiazusae*, in which the women of Athens, under the leadership of their new στρατηγός "general" Praxagora, disguise themselves as men in order to infiltrate the ἐκκλησία, the male-only "legislative assembly," where they vote in a new order, one that abolishes the institutions of phallocracy – private property, individual father-ruled households, law courts – and institutes instead, a communistic gynocracy.[1] By this new regime, the women successfully mount a rebellion against the Classical architecture of the house and city. Through their revolution, the play poses the question: What form of city will a woman build, if left to her own devices? To this question, the play answers: If a female designs urban form, she will show phallocracy to be architectural, subject to construction and deconstruction – the phallus subject to cutting, the fundamental architectural act, the detail that joins.[2] She will expose the "reign of the phallus" as the rule of the fetish.[3]

What is a fetish? The psychoanalytic fetish is an architecture, a perverse construction driven by fear of what the male sees in the female genital – the existence and the possibility of castration. It manifests itself in two apparently contradictory forms – both a supplement to and a mutilation of the female genital – that employ the two basic techniques of architectural construction, joining (in the case of the supplement) and cutting (in the case of mutilation). These two forms of the fetish are like the two faces of Janus, the Roman god of doorways, for they share a single goal, to disavow, while simultaneously maintaining, the difference, as the male perceives it, between the female's genital and his own.

Fetish as "Pseudo-Phallic" Joint

In Freud's theory, the fetish is created as a reaction to the boy's vision of his mother's penis-free genital.[4] Assuming that all human beings begin as anatomically the same, the boy interprets his mother's penis-free condition as castration, that is, the loss of the penis she must have originally possessed.[5] In fear of such castration as the punishment he would receive from his father, were his Oedipal desire for his mother to be fulfilled, the boy creates the fetish as a supplement to the female genital, a *Penisersatz* "substitute penis" that serves simultaneously to affirm (yes, she is lacking and needs a penis) and to deny (no, she is not lacking, she has a penis) his sight of female lack.[6]

> It is not true that, after the child has made his observation of the woman, he has preserved unaltered his belief that women have a phallus. He has retained that belief, but he has also given it up. In the conflict between the weight of the unwelcome perception and the force of his counter-wish, a compromise has been reached, as is only possible under the dominance of the unconscious laws of thought – the primary processes. Yes, in his mind the woman *has* got a penis, in spite of everything; but this penis is no longer the same as it was before. Something else has taken its place, has been appointed its substitute (*Ersatz*), as it were, and now inherits the interest which was formerly directed to its predecessor. But this interest suffers an extraordinary increase as well, because the horror of castration has set up a memorial to itself (*gesetzt ein Denkmal* 'monument, memorial') in the creation (*Schaffung* 'production, creation, making') of this substitute. Furthermore, an aversion, which is never absent in any fetishist, to the real female genitals remains a *stigma indelebile* of the repression that has taken place. We can see now what the fetish achieves and what it is that maintains it. It remains a token of triumph (*Zeichen Triumphes*) over the threat of castration and a protection against it.[7]

What is the form of this pseudo-phallic supplement? What governs the choice of "organs or objects" to serve this function? Not solely their apparent symbolism of the penis. Rather, says Freud, often

> the last impression before the uncanny and traumatic one is retained as a fetish. Thus the foot or shoe owes its preference as a

fetish – or a part of it – to the circumstance that the inquisitive boy peered at the woman's genitals from below, from her legs up; fur and velvet – as has long been suspected – are a fixation of the sight of the pubic hair, which should have been followed by the longed-for sight of the female member.[8]

This focus upon the pubic hair motivates the other face of the fetish, the cutting of the female's hair.

Fetish as "Cutting of the Female's Hair"

In addition to supplementing it, the goal of assuaging the male's castration anxiety can be achieved – paradoxically, it may seem – by the cutting of the hair of the female genital. Here, too, as in the case of the pseudo-phallic supplement, the starting point is the boy's perception of the female's lack of a penis as proof of the possibility of castration and his subsequent need both to acknowledge and to disavow this perception. This "divided attitude" can manifest itself in cuttings that re-enact, even as they deny, the female's lack:

> To point out that he [the fetishist] reveres his fetish is not the whole story; in many cases he treats it in a way which is obviously equivalent to a representation of castration. This happens particularly if he has developed a strong identification with his father and plays the part of the latter; for it is to him that as a child he ascribed the woman's castration. Affection and hostility in the treatment of the fetish – which run parallel with the disavowal and the acknowledgement of castration – are mixed in unequal proportions in different cases, so that the one or the other is more clearly recognizable. We seem here to approach an understanding, even if a distant one, of the behavior of the '*coupeur de nattes*' ["cutter of hair"]. In him the need to carry out the castration which he disavows has come to the front. His action contains in itself the two mutually incompatible assertions: 'the woman has still got a penis' and 'my father has castrated the woman.'[9]

Like its apparent opposite, the augmentation of her genital by a phallic supplement, this cutting of the female's pubic hair aims to tame terror by rendering its source ambiguous: the female may both lack and not lack a penis and thus the female may both be and not be a male.

The Fetishized Female as "Para-Male"

Whether in supplementing her genital with a penis that simultaneously affirms and denies her castration or in reproducing the same contradictory condition by cutting her pubic hair, the male makes of the female what we may call a "para-male." The Greek preposition *para* is useful in capturing the architectural force of Freud's "language of indecidability" here,[10] for it expresses the ambivalence of the "beside" – the position that is at once different, deviating from an origin (as in the use of *para* in nouns such as "para-normal" or "para-dox") and also the same as, at one with, an origin (as in the use of the preposition *para* with the genitive case of a noun in Greek to mean, like French *chez*, "at the home of"). A "para-male" is indecidably different from (that is, castrated) and the same as (that is, not castrated) the male. In constructing the fetishized female, the male makes a "para-male," a parodic version of himself – ironically parodic, perhaps, since parody in literature is so often formed as a critique of the original.[11]

As we will see her in the *Ecclesiazusae*, the female is just such a "para-male." Turning away from time to time to other texts that the play calls to mind – the myth of Pandora, the first female who is also a male-molded jar and a house, in Hesiod, the training of the wife in Xenophon's *Oeconomicus*, and the wife's manipulation of that training in Lysias' *On the Murder of Eratosthenes* – we will see the Classical οἶκος "house" as the female's architectural school. There she is taught to devote her architectural capacity, her *mêtis* "transformative intelligence," to the formation of herself in both modes of the fetish, both the pseudo-phallic supplementation and the "cutting of the female's hair" – the first, by imitating male roles, a "general," a "guardian of the laws," a "garrison commander," and the second, by depilating her pubic hair.

It is not by counteracting, but rather by continuing to design just as the οἶκος "house" has taught her that Praxagora will overturn its "power structure." This is the play's ultimate irony – that the female's mode of deconstruction is built into her construction as fetish. In creating their new urban form, the women of Athens – now unfettered by, released from their own "formation" by the οἶκος "house" – in creating this new urban form that abolishes the father-ruled city, what is their source? what are the tools of their design? where did they learn to build in this way? Their school was the very οἶκος "house" in which we, the men, the architects of the phallocratic tradition, formed them in the image of ourselves. In designing as she does, left to "her own devices," the female will not be exercising some new female identity, some new difference – but she will design and build exactly as we have trained her to do.

The female's urban form in the *Ecclesiazusae* is thus an ironic reflection of the phallocracy that formed her. In "cutting off" the structures of phallic power from the city, in the institution of communistic gynocracy in place of phallocracy, Praxagora will reveal these phallic power structures as "fetishes" – indecidable supplements, yes, but just by being supplements, subject to "decision." She will detach each structure of phallic power from "mother earth" and by this detachment, dispel any illusion that it grows there naturally. In this revelation of the architecture of their construction, she will also destroy it. By separating phallic power structures from the city, she will reveal each as able-to-be-separated, and thus not a natural phallus, a corporeal growth, but a fetish – a "pseudo-phallic supplement" to the female body, indecidably masking and affirming that body's phallic lack. So long as this indecidability remains intact, the fetish can work as designed: it can assuage the male's fear of what he sees in the female genital, the cutting-off-of-the-penis, castration. But to cut off the fetish from the female body is to expose it as de-cidable, "cut-off-able" – the spell of simultaneous affirmation and denial is broken and with that breaking of indecidability is broken the efficacy of the fetish itself. Once the secret of the fetish is told, it can no longer work as designed.

II. The οἶκος "house" as the Female's Architectural School

Invoking the Ceramic Lamp as the Female's Sign

The *Ecclesiazusae* opens in the predawn as the leader of the women's plot, Praxagora, invokes a ceramic lamp, explaining why it is the right sign by which to signal the other women to assemble. [Figure 1. Ceramic lamp from the Athenian agora.]

Ὦ λαμπρὸν ὄμμα τοῦ τροχηλάτου λύχνου
κάλλιστ' ἐν εὐστόχοισιν ἐξηυρημένον
γονάς τε γὰρ σὰς καὶ τύχας δηλώσομεν·
τροχῷ γὰρ ἐλαθεὶς κεραμικῆς ῥύμης ὕπο
μυκτῆρσι λαμπρὰς ἡλίου τιμὰς ἔχεις·
ὅρμα φλογὸς σημεῖα τὰ ξυγκείμενα.
σοὶ γὰρ μόνῳ δηλοῦμεν εἰκότως, ἐπεὶ
κἀν τοῖσι δωματίοισιν Ἀφροδίτης τρόπων
πειρωμέναισι πλησίον παραστατεῖς,
λορδουμένων τε σωμάτων ἐπιστάτην
ὀφθαλμὸν οὐδεὶς τὸν σὸν ἐξείργει δόμων.

μόνος δὲ μηρῶν εἰς ἀπορρήτους μυχοὺς
λάμπεις ἀφεύων τὴν ἐπανθοῦσαν τρίχα·
στοάς τε καρποῦ Βακχίου τε νάματος
πλήρεις ὑποιγνύσαισι συμπαραστατεῖς·
καὶ ταῦτα συνδρῶν οὐ λαλεῖς τοῖς πλησίον.
ἀνθ' ὧν συνείσει καὶ τὰ νῦν βουλεύματα
ὅσα Σκίροις ἔδοξε ταῖς ἐμαῖς φίλαις.

O shining eye of the wheel-driven lamp,
among clever men a discovery most noble and fair –
we shall disclose both your birth and your fortunes:
for driven by the wheel and born from the potter's thrust,
you hold in your nostrils the shining honors of the sun –
rouse up the agreed-upon signs of light.
For by you alone do we fittingly reveal our secrets, since
indeed in our bedrooms, as we make heroic trial
of the tropes of Aphrodite, you stand near beside,
and of our bodies curved with our heads thrown back
no one bars from the house your eye as superintendent.
Alone into the unspeakable recesses of our thighs
you shine as you singe off the flowering hair.
And with us as we furtively open the full storehouses
of grain and flowing wine you stand beside.
And although you do these things with us, you don't babble to
    those who are near.
Because of all these things, you will be a witness of our present
    plans as well,
as many as were ratified by my women friends at the ritual of
    the Skira.

Aristophanes Ecclesiazusae 1–18

This lamp is crucial to understanding the architectural meaning of the play, for it embodies the ideal, institutionalized relation in Greek thought between architecture and the female body.[12] In being a molded clay vessel and an instrument of depilation ("Alone into the unspeakable recesses of our thighs you shine as you singe off the flowering hair"), the lamp will show, indeed, why and how architecture in its Classical foundation is a matter, both for men and for women, of forming the female body. As a work of the potter's wheel, the lamp evokes the fundamental analogy, figured in the myth of Pandora, between the female body, the ceramic jar, and the οἶκος "house." This analogy is an ideological construction, designed to mold women who will mold themselves according to the architecture of father-rule.[13] The most intimate physical instance of this self-formation is the Greek woman's depilation of her pubic hair. As a tool of such "auto-architecture," the lamp displays women who act as properly male-formed architects by using their form-making power first and foremost to fashion themselves, so that the man will least fear and take most pleasure from the feminine *sexe*.[14] By giving us this glimpse of how the architecture of the οἶκος "house" normally regulates the female, Praxagora's apostrophe of the lamp also predicts, in effect, how the women will rebel against it: the women's strategies for resisting male constructions are themselves built into the original structure of the household. With this prefabrication in mind, let us examine more closely the function of the lamp as ceramic jar and as instrument of depilation.

Female Body as Ceramic Jar and οἶκος "house"

Tracing the implications of the lamp as "driven by the wheel and born from the potter's thrust" leads us outside the play to the myth of Pandora, which establishes the analogy between the female body, the ceramic jar, and the

Figure 1. Ceramic lamp, found in the Athenian Agora. Photo courtesy of the American School of Classical Studies at Athens, in Judith Perlzweig, *Lamps from the Athenian Agora* (Princeton, NJ: ASCSA, 1963), fig.18.

οἶκος "house," and from there, to Xenophon's *Oeconomicus*, which details the ways in which the household works as the woman's architectural school.

Pandora, the first woman and founding model of all the rest, is molded by the craft-god Hephaestus out of earth and water. In describing how "hope" remains within Pandora, Hesiod presents her as simultaneously a body, a ceramic jar, and a house, with lips as door:

μούνη δ' αὐτόθι Ἐλπὶς <u>ἐν</u> <u>ἀρρήκτοισι</u> <u>δόμοισιν</u>
ἔνδον ἔμεινε <u>πίθου</u> <u>ὑπὸ</u> <u>χείλεσιν</u> οὐδὲ <u>θύραζε</u>
ἐξέπτη.

Hope alone there <u>in the</u> <u>unbreakable</u> <u>halls</u>
was remaining within <u>under the lips of the jar</u> nor <u>from the door</u>
did it fly out.

Hesiod *Works and Days* 96–98

As a male-molded jar, Pandora mediates between and thereby links the female as male-molded body and the female as male-molded house. This identification of body and house is embedded in the word for "own" itself, οἰκεῖος, an adjectival form of οἶκος "house." Your "own" thing is the thing of your house, and your house is your "ownership" – your "ownness" itself – a unity that will be crucial to Praxagora's urban form, when her operation upon the οἶκος "house" demolishes the distinction between "own" and "other's."

The analogy posed by the myth of Pandora is not a simple assimilation of separate and equal male-molded containers. Within their relation of mutual likeness is the hierarchy of original over copy and container over contained with the jar as mediator. The female is modeled upon the jar, being herself ceramic only in metaphor, and she is subordinated to the house that encloses her, molding her as an image of itself, a domestic container like the jar.[15] [Figure 2. Pandora as "mermaid" of female and jar.] What the woman (as contained by the house) is supposed to contain is the female's architectural power, her *mêtis* "transformative intelligence."[16] If the architecture of the οἶκος "house" works, the female will imitate it. She will, like Penelope, confine her "shape-shifting" to the edification of her husband, limiting her material production to the weaving of his walls and her sexual reproduction to the bearing of his legitimate children. Such is the lesson of Xenophon's *Oeconomicus*, in which the husband Ischomachus tells Socrates how he taught his bride, who comes to him knowing nothing except how to weave, everything else she needs to know.

The husband's first lesson is the coincident aetiology of marriage and architecture itself.[17] Not simply to produce children or to care for the aged, the ζεῦγος "joining" that is marriage derives from what makes humans different from animals: the need for shelter instead of living in the open air.

> 'The gods, O wife,' he said that he had said, 'seem with great discernment to have put together this joining (ζεῦγος) which is called female and male chiefly so that it might be most beneficial to itself with regard to commonality (εἰς τὴν κοινωνίαν). For first, so that the races of living creatures may not die out, this joining is established for the making of children with one another; then for human beings at least it is given from this joining to possess supporters in old age; and then also the way of life for human beings is not as it is for cattle, in the open air, but clearly it needs roofed shelters (στεγῶν).'

Xenophon *Oeconomicus* 7.18–19

Figure 2. Campanian red-figure neck-amphora: Pandora as "mermaid" of female and jar. Attributed to the Owl-Pillar Group, ca. late 5th century BC. British Museum, inv. no. F 147. Photo © Copyright, Trustees of the British Museum.

Humans need the joint that divides – or the division that joins – inside and outside, and with it, the divisive ζεῦγος of female and male. But in order to have something to bring inside the shelter, so the husband reasons, the man must go outside to work in the open air, while the woman remains within, devoting her *mêtis* to transforming what he brings in – sperm into children, grain into bread, and wool into woven cloth.

> 'It is necessary, however, if the human beings are going to have something to bring inside the shelter, that someone work at the open air occupations. For indeed ploughing, sowing, planting, and herding – all these are works of the open air. And from these come the things that are needed. But again, when these things have been brought inside the shelter, it is necessary that someone preserve them (τοῦ σώσοντος ταῦτα) and work at the tasks that require shelters (στεγνῶν). Shelters are necessary for the rearing of newborn children, shelters are necessary for the making of bread from the fruit of the earth, and likewise for the manufacture of clothing from wool. And since both of these, the things inside and the things outside, require work and attentive care, the god from the first prepared the nature of the woman, it seems to me, for the works and the concerns of the inside and that of the man for those of the outside.'

Xenophon Oeconomicus 7.20–22

All physical and psychological differences between male and female were created by "the god himself" as "architect" of this marital "joint" to fit the sexes for this basic spatial division (Xenophon *Oeconomicus* 7.23–28).

The sexual spaces of marriage, however, are far from "separate, but equal."[18] For it is the male outside who functions as architect, teacher, and model of the female and the οἶκος "house" inside. And, paradoxically, the male's design to maintain the female's architectural difference – indeed, to maintain the female as architectural difference – does not make her different. Rather, in anticipation of the function of the psychoanalytic fetish, the male's design of female differences makes her a parodic imitation of himself.

The Female Formed as "Para-Male"

In the *Oeconomicus* the husband constructs the woman's realm – from the innermost recesses of her mind and body to the organization of the οἶκος "house" itself – as a microcosm of the roles, institutions, and ideals of the exterior, male world. In the manner of a Socratic teacher, the husband illustrates his wife's role by an analogy, comparing it to that of ἡ τῶν μελιττῶν ἡγεμών "a female general of the bees." While remaining herself strictly within the οἶκος "house," the wife is to regulate the passage of goods and workers between inside and outside by copying the administrative authority and strategic deployments of a military leader.

> 'In what way,' she said, 'are the works of the general of the bees (ἡ τῶν μελιττῶν ἡγεμών) like those it is necessary for me to do?' 'Because,' I replied, 'she remains in the hive and does not allow the bees to be idle, but those who must work outside she sends to the work and whatever each of them brings in, she both knows and receives and preserves these things until the time it is necessary to use them. And when the time comes to use them, she distributes a just portion to each.'

Xenophon Oeconomicus 7.32–33

Under the command of this ἡγεμών "general," the hive becomes more than a model house. The bees' οἶκος "house" is rather a miniature πόλις "city," indeed a metropolis, for the bee-ruler dispatches the products of her weaving, just as a city-ruler sends out citizens to form a colony.[19]

> 'And she stands in charge of the weaving of the cells inside, so that they may be beautifully and quickly woven, and when the offspring is born, she is concerned with how it is nourished. And once it is nourished and the young are fit for work, she sends them out as a colony (ἀποικίζει) with one as general.'

Xenophon Oeconomicus 7.34

In like manner, as commander of her own domestic "mother-city," the wife is to send workers outside, receive and distribute what is brought inside, and make sure that clothes are woven from wool for all those who need them (Xenophon *Oeconomicus* 7.36). To fail in this function is to saddle the husband with a faulty "Pandora," a ceramic container that fails to contain.

> 'My bringing things in would appear laughable, if there were no one to preserve them. Do you not see,' I said, 'how they are to be pitied who are said to "draw water into a leaking jar (τὸν τετρημένον πίθον)" because they labor in vain?'

Xenophon Oeconomicus 7.40

Lest she become such a leaking πίθος "jar," the wife must emulate in the οἶκος "house," in her body, and in her deepest beliefs, the consummate architectural virtue of order – expressed here by the nouns τάξις and κόσμος. Within the οἶκος "house" such order is crucial to the household's chief purpose, maximum economic profit. For it is order that maximizes both spatial efficiency, human productivity, and the coincidence of aesthetic and moral value that constitutes beauty. "There is nothing, O wife," says her husband, "so useful (εὔχρηστον) or so beautiful (καλὸν) for humans as order (τάξις)" (Xenophon *Oeconomicus* 8.3). If she cannot give her husband whatever he asks for instantly, the fault is his, he says, "since I handed things over to you without giving you orders (οὐ τάξας) as to where they must be placed so that you would know where to put them and from where to take them again" (Xenophon *Oeconomicus* 8.2). The design of the house is the husband's, an architecture he must teach her continually to reconstruct.

To teach his wife the power of order, the husband again uses examples from the male world: a chorus in drama, a deployed army, and a Phoenician ship (Xenophon *Oeconomicus* 8.3–17).[20] While random and capricious actions of men in a chorus produce confusion and a lack of pleasure (ἀτερπές), by their ordered movement (τεταγμένως), the same men are worth seeing and hearing. While a disordered (ἄτακτος) army is similarly a source of confusion and an easy prey, an ordered (τεταγμένη) army – echoing the aesthetics of Sappho 16 – is "the most beautiful thing" (κάλλιστον) for friends and "most intractable" for enemies. And the sight of a trireme is similarly fearful to enemies and welcome to friends, just because its sailors – in an anaphora echoing the crew's concerted, repeated movements – "are seated in order (ἐν τάξει), lean forward in order (ἐν τάξει), fall back in order (ἐν τάξει), and embark and disembark in order (ἐν τάξει)." When the interior of the οἶκος "house" emulates such exterior orders, when by means of such τάξις the greatest number of objects are most easily accessible in the smallest amount of space, not only can the wife give her husband whatever he asks for instantly, but "place" itself becomes a working person, since "the place itself," the husband explains, "will miss the thing that is not there" (Xenophon *Oeconomicus* 8.10). Such is the radical *mêtis* of architectural order, the power to personify place.

Climaxing this panegyric of the economic dividends and aesthetic power of Classical order, the husband claims that κόσμος can create beauty out of the most ordinarily ugly things. Again, the text simulates its message, here by the stately reiteration – as if the word were itself one of the ordered objects – of καλόν "beautiful."

'How beautiful (ὡς δὲ καλὸν) is the sight of all sorts of shoes, provided they are in sequence, beautiful (καλὸν) is the sight of all sorts of clothes, when they are separated, beautiful (καλὸν) are bedcovers, beautiful (καλὸν) are bronze kettles, beautiful (καλὸν) is tableware, and beautiful (καλὸν) is also what of all things would be most laughable, not to the serious but to the comic man – namely, the fact that I say even cooking pots (χύτρας) appear with good rhythm (εὔρυθμον φαίνεσθαι) provided they are distinctly arranged (εὐκρινῶς κειμένας).'

Xenophon *Oeconomicus* 8.19

Countering the traditional Greek liaison of the ugly and the impure, the husband declares:

'All the other things look more beautiful (καλλίω) when they are placed according to order (κατὰ κόσμον κείμενα). Each group appears as a chorus of implements (χορὸς σκευῶν), even the space in the middle appears beautiful (καλὸν), because each thing lies outside it – just as a circular chorus is not only a beautiful sight (καλὸν θέαμα) itself, but also the space in the middle of it appears beautiful and pure (καλὸν καὶ καθαρὸν).'

Xenophon *Oeconomicus* 8.20

Here articulated for the first time in Western thought is an idea at the heart not only of architecture, but also of sculptural and graphic design – that of space as a distinct aesthetic phenomenon, a relation between solid and void creatable by the deliberate placement and serial repetition of any material object.

It is as a microcosm of such exterior, male κόσμος "order" that the husband has designed the domestic world. The overall aim of his architecture is beauty in and as the form of maximum economic efficiency. Accordingly "cosmetic" adornments are subordinated to the coordination of form and function.

'For the house has not been adorned (κεκόσμηται) with many ornaments, but the rooms have been planned (ἐσκεμμένα) and built toward this very end, that they might be the most advantageous receptacles possible for what they will contain.'

Xenophon *Oeconomicus* 9.2

Hence, a secure location for the storeroom of valuables, a dry covered place for grain, coolness for wine, good light for those jobs and implements that require it, and for human activity, a southern exposure providing cool shade in summer and warm sunshine in winter (Xenophon *Oeconomicus* 9.3-4). And finally, to regulate the human source of the household's profit, sexual reproduction, the husband turns to architecture's founding act, the building of spatial division.

To control its output of children, the husband subdivides the space of the οἶκος "house," already contained by its exterior walls, into two subsidiary containers, the commerce between the two being controlled by the device that moves architecture from its beginnings as neutral space enclosure to political force, the lockable/unlockable door.

> 'Then I showed her the women's quarters, divided (ὡρισμένην, compare ὁρισμός "marking by boundaries, definition") from the men's by a bolted door, so that nothing may be taken out from there that should not be and that servants may not breed children without our knowledge.'
>
> Xenophon *Oeconomicus* 9.5

Such "social engineering" pervades the house, as all its portable goods are divided "according to tribes" and each "tribe" then taken to its proper place, thereby making an analogue in miniature of political organization (Xenophon *Oeconomicus* 9.6-9).

To maintain this in-house parody of political τάξις "order," the wife must become an equally parodic allomorph of male rulers in the outside world. After having taught her how cities with good laws always choose "guardians of the laws" who oversee their application, the husband enjoins his wife to assume this position within the household and to augment it with other, equally male forms of authority.[21]

> 'Therefore,' he said, 'I charged my wife to consider herself, too, a guardian of the laws in the household, and to inspect our equipment, whenever it seems right to her, just as a garrison commander inspects his guards, and to test whether each thing is in good condition, just as the Council (βουλὴ) tests horses and horsemen.'
>
> Xenophon *Oeconomicus* 9.14-15

By itself, however, the wife's copying of male models in her behavior is not quite enough to assure the husband's architectural order. In the grand finale

317

to her schooling, the husband explains how and why the wife must mold her body.

This phase of his teaching is triggered when Socrates exclaims, "'By Hera, Ischomachus,' I said, 'you show that the mind of your wife is indeed that of a man (ἀνδρικήν γε ἐπιδεικνύεις τὴν διάνοιαν τῆς γυναικός).'" When Ischomachus answers by offering to recount another instance of his wife's immediate obedience, Socrates eagerly accepts.

> 'Speak, for to me it is much more pleasant to learn thoroughly the virtue (ἀρετὴν) of a living woman than if Zeuxis were to display a beautiful woman by making a likeness of her in painting (καλὴν εἰκάσας γραφῆι γυναῖκα).'
>
> Xenophon *Oeconomicus* 10.1

This philosophical preference for living truth over material artifice takes the form of an architectural construction, a doctrine of female "auto-architecture" that begins with a wall.

In teaching the wife correct self-fashioning, the Classical οἶκος "house" erects a barrier between the pure and natural beauty of male-designed κόσμος "order" and the women who imitate it, on one hand, and female "cosmetic" deception, on the other. For once, when the husband caught his wife with white lead and rouge on her face (makeup we will see figure in the conclusion to the *Ecclesiazusae*) and wearing high heels, he was able to correct her instantly by explaining: just as she would not like him to present counterfeit money, fake gold, or fading purple instead of the real thing, or a body smeared with vermilion and flesh color under the eyes instead of one ruddy from natural exercise, so she must present him with a pure body (σῶμα καθαρὸν), free of cosmetic deceit (ἀπάτη) (Xenophon *Oeconomicus* 10.2–8). And when the wife asks how she might make her body as truly – and not merely apparently – beautiful as possible, the husband recommends exercise through household duties, especially those specialties of *mêtis*, weaving and bread-baking, because they produce a physique more healthy and "with better color in truth (εὐχρωτέραν τῇ ἀληθείᾳ)" (Xenophon *Oeconomicus* 10.9–11). To neglect these domestic jobs leaves the woman, ironically, as sexually unattractive as when she employs cosmetic deceits and thereby vulnerable to sexual supplantation. For she will, says her husband, defeat the maid (her ever-present sexual rival) if she is more pure and properly dressed – and if she gratifies him willingly (in comparison with the compulsory submission of the maid). But if she were to eschew her domestic exercise and become one of those "'women who always sit solemnly," she would open herself "for comparison with those who use cosmetics and deceits (τὰς κεκοσμημένας καὶ ἐξαπατώσας)'" (Xenophon *Oeconomicus* 10.12–13).

This doctrine of the female "auto-architecture" necessary to win the man's sexual approval returns us to the *Ecclesiazusae* and to Praxagora's invocation of the lamp as a tool of depilation.

Depilation as Female "Auto-Architecture"

In requiring women to depilate their genital hair, the architecture of father-rule reaches into the female body's "unspeakable recesses" (ἀπορρήτους μυχοὺς) as Praxagora puts it in her prologue (Aristophanes *Ecclesiazusae* 12), using the term μυχός that refers to the innermost part of a landscape or a house. [Figure 3. Ceramic lamp as instrument of pubic depilation.][22] At the site of these "unspeakable recesses" is the female's pubic hair. Here is the sight and the site that provokes the Freudian fetish, the pseudo-phallic prosthesis that supplements or the cutting that worships by mutilating the female genital, simultaneously denying and affirming her castration, her "sameness" with men. It is here that the woman's architectural power is born. For it is on the model of the matted pubic hair that covers her lack of a penis that the female invented weaving, according to Freud, and it is weaving, according to Semper, that is the origin of architecture as vertical space enclosure, and it is cutting, we may add, together with weaving, that constitutes the primary architectural mechanism, the "detail."[23]

In the detail of pubic depilation, the twin strategies of the fetish and the father-ruled house coincide. Each has the same mission: to form the female by cutting her sexuality – her manifest sexual difference – short.[24] Without such "cosmetic surgery," female sexuality knows no natural bounds. For in the oppositional categories of Greek thought, the male is dry and limited and the female is unlimited and wet, the two categories being closely connected architecturally. As Aristotle puts it:

> The wet is that which is not bounded (ἀ + όριστον, compare "horizon") by any boundary of its own (οἰκείῳ ὅρῳ) while being easily bounded (εὐ + όριστον) and the dry is that which is easily bounded (τὸ εὐόριστον) by its own boundary (οἰκείῳ ὅρῳ), but with difficulty bounded (δυσ + όριστον).

> Aristotle *On Coming-to-Be and Passing Away* 329b29–31

Figure 3a-b. Attic red-figure cup: tondo, woman performing pubic depilation with ceramic lamp. Attributed to the Onesimos Painter, ca. 500-450 BC. University of Mississippi Art Museums, Robinson Collection, 77.3.112. Photo courtesy of University of Mississippi Art Museums. Drawing after Friedrich Hauser, "Aristophanes und Vasenbilder," *Jahreshefte des Österreichischen Archäologischen Institutes in Wien* 12 (1909), p. 86.

Because the female's wetness – the sign, like the male's erection, of her sexual capacity – knows no intrinsic limit, it must be bound by a formative force outside itself, the institution of father-ruled marriage and its material embodiment in the οἶκος "house."[25] The trimming of her pubic hair signals the woman's willingness to draw this horizon, to conform herself to Classical κόσμος "order." As she devotes her architectural *mêtis* to weaving the walls that mold the οἶκος "house" and the clothes that veil her body, so the woman trims her genital hair into a particular schema – for example, the delta, one of the two types of triangles described by Plato in the *Timaeus* as the elementary geometrical forms of the cosmos itself.[26]

At every level of her architectural formation, the female is imbued with a single ideal: to devote her *mêtis* exclusively to making herself – her mind, her body, and her house – a parodic imitation of male design and desire. Her architectural imperative is thus to fetishize herself – to make herself a quasi-phallic construction and a depilated deconstruction. Ironically, but perhaps inevitably, this very indoctrination programs the methods and forms of the architectural rebellion staged in the *Ecclesiazusae*. Both in her plot to take over the government and in her new urban form, Praxagora combines two basic architectural operations, sectional inversion and extension in plan, that for all their revolutionary ingenuity are, nevertheless, applications of her in-house training to emulate the male's design.[27] Sectionally, she maintains the traditional structure of hierarchy, but inverts gender, putting the woman on top, where, true to the self-fetishizing imperative, she can "play the man."[28] In plan, Praxagora extends the household horizontally, turning the πόλις "city" into one big οἶκος "house," where women will continue to perform their parodically male role.[29]

In Praxagora's urban form the female innovates, in effect, by archaizing – by applying just what is traditionally taken to be her founding architectural capacity. For the mechanism common to both her sectional inversion and her horizontal extension is the tropic character of *mêtis* itself.[30] In its basic constitution as "the circular reciprocity of what is bound and what is binding," *mêtis* characterizes those conditions that turn around on themselves, procedures that retreat by advancing, and advance via retreat.[31] In the world of humans and animals, creatures of *mêtis* imitate their enemies to beat them at their own game.[32] As a mistress of *mêtis* the female will win not by countering, but by extending her construction by the Classical οἶκος "house" to the point where it, like a drug, recoils upon its practitioner. Such is the insight of a domestic parallel for the technique of Praxagora's urban revolution, one found among the texts of the Athenian law court. So before turning to the details of Praxagora's plot and plan, let us again depart briefly from the play itself to pursue this precedent.

Inverting the "Power Structure" of the Classical οἶκος *"house"*

In Lysias' *On the Murder of Eratosthenes*, a husband defends his killing of the man he caught in adultery with his wife. In the course of his exculpation, he provides a brief, but vivid vignette of the potential for tropic manipulation within the Classical architecture of the οἶκος "house." By adhering to the tenets of her architectural education, the wife is able to turn the "power structures" of the household, both the material constructions and the freedom of movement that goes with them, upside down. By appearing to conform completely to the correct use of her *mêtis*, she reverses the vectors of the husband's design, down to its very details.

The dynamics of her plot, as they are described by the husband himself, confirm the coincidence of marriage and architecture taught in the *Oeconomicus*. For here violation occurs via successive breaches of that union's containing walls. Just as the structure common to marriage and shelter in the *Oeconomicus* is the division of inside from outside and the containment of the wife within, so the husband's account of the adulterer's crime culminates in the act that was first in time, but ultimate in seriousness, mere entrance into the house.

> I believe, gentlemen of the jury, I must show this: that Eratosthenes committed adultery with my wife, that he corrupted her and shamed my children and committed outrage against me myself (ἐμὲ αὐτὸν ὕβρισεν) by entering into my house (εἰς τὴν οἰκίαν τὴν ἐμὴν εἰσιών).

Lysias *On the Murder of Eratosthenes* 4

How was such an infraction ever possible? The husband starts at the beginning, with his wife's own entry into the household as bride. At first, he says, I was wary and watchful, aiming neither to restrict her painfully nor allow her too much freedom to do as she pleased. But when she appeared to be devoting her *mêtis* solely to the augmentation of her husband's οἶκος "house," his policy toward her changed.

> But when a child was born to me, I began to trust her and I gave over all that was mine into her hands, because I believed that this was the greatest intimacy (οἰκειότητα "being οἰκεῖος 'own' to one another, belonging to the same οἶκος").

Lysias *On the Murder of Eratosthenes* 6

And indeed his trust seems initially well-placed, as the wife fulfills her traditionally "economic" role superbly, distinguishing herself as clever, frugal, and "arranging all things in the οἶκος impeccably" (ἀκριβῶς πάντα διοικοῦσα, Lysias *On the Murder of Eratosthenes* 7). At the funeral of his mother, however, one of those religious occasions when wives are permitted to leave the house, the wife is seen and thence seduced by Eratosthenes, through the go-between of the maid (Lysias *On the Murder of Eratosthenes* 7–8). Once the "wall" of her mind is thus penetrated, the wife herself applies her *mêtis* to inverting the function of the walls in her husband-designed house.

To explain how his wife succeeded in admitting the adulterer into the house, the husband begins by describing its basic vertical hierarchy: "My dwelling is on two floors, the upper equal to the lower, with the women's quarters above and the men's below" (Lysias *On the Murder of Eratosthenes* 9). With apparently no other exit than through the main floor, the house sets the men's quarters as a barrier to the women's mobility, confining them upstairs. It is the working of this "power structure" that the wife inverts. She effects a voluntary exchange of places. Devoting herself, like a good "general bee," to the care and nurture of her husband's offspring, she plays upon her husband's desire for the safety of mother and child. A true mistress of *mêtis,* she so imitates her husband's desire that he defeats himself.

> When the child was born, the mother suckled it, and in order that she might not run a risk by having to go down the ladder, whenever the child needed to be washed, I myself began to live above, and the women below. And by then it became so customary that often my wife would go away from me downstairs to sleep beside the child, so she could give it her breast and it would not cry.

Lysias *On the Murder of Eratosthenes* 9–10

Not by redesign, but by replacement – a spatial reversal, the wife has transformed the οἶκος "house." Before on top, but subordinated, now the woman is below, but in terms of architectural power, she is "on top." It is now the woman who controls access to her house and to her body, and in this position, she stages a scenario, one that again depends for its success upon her *mêtis*, "imitating the enemy to beat him at his own game."

Again, the husband gives the details of the plot. Once he returned home unexpectedly from the country and later that night, when the child began crying (having been prodded by the maid, the wife's co-conspirator), he urged his wife to go down and nurse him, in order to stop the noise.

323

> At first she was not willing, as though delighted to see me come home after a long time. And when I started to get angry and was ordering her to go away, she said, "Yes, so that you can have a try here at the little maid. Once before, you pulled her around, when you were drunk." At that I myself began laughing, while she stood up, went out, and closed the door, pretending to be playing, and turned the key in the lock. And I, thinking nothing of these things, nor suspecting anything, went to sleep happy at having returned from the country.

Lysias *On the Murder of Eratosthenes* 11–13

Like the fox who plays dead to lure his victim, the wife feigns defeat at the hands of the maid, her ever-present sexual rival (as we saw in the *Oeconomicus*). In her testimony to her husband's earlier conquest is the tool of her own triumph. In her beguiling words, he relives his drunken indulgence. By her cosmetic jealousy, by her pretence of erotic play, she casts him as the object of a domestic triangle. Seduced by the pleasure of the role, he takes it to be true. He laughs and goes back to sleep. By devoting her "auto-architecture" to the impersonation of a wife correctly formed by the architecture of the οἶκος "house," the woman inverts that architecture in its essential joint, the bolt that locks the female under male control. It is by a similar imitation of traditional female *mêtis* that Praxagora achieves a similar inversion of hierarchy in both city and house. And just as the husband is moved to become himself the ironic agent of his wife's removal from her place of subordination, so Praxagora's plot moves the men of Athens to vote in their own removal from the places of urban power.

III. Praxagora's Plot

Praxagora's plot has two phases, first visual and then verbal, and in both the women work as masked men. Taking the architectural imperative of the Classical οἶκος "house" to its logical extreme, the women make themselves parodic copies of male models of political action and thought. In order to infiltrate the male-only legislative Assembly and vote in a new regime, the women disguise themselves as men. Thus accoutered, Praxagora will win the votes of the male Assembly by imitating male speech about women. She will cite women's traditional role – that is, what men traditionally say about women – as the grounds for her proposed gynocracy.

Visual Costume: Female as Fetish

In response to the signal light from Praxagora's lamp, the women come together for a pre-dawn review of their masquerade. To become pseudo-males, they have decked themselves out in typical fetishes – pseudo-phallic supplements – stolen from their sleeping husbands, their platform shoes, their cloaks, and their walking sticks (Aristophanes *Ecclesiazusae* 26–27, 40, 47, 73–75).[33] This theft reverses the clothing of sexual difference, as we see later, when Praxagora's husband Blepyrus emerges from his house, complaining that he has only his wife's clothes to wear (Aristophanes *Ecclesiazusae* 311–326). This sartorial reversal triggers the vertical dimension of Praxagora's plan, inversion of sexual hierarchy, an inversion achieved not by countering, but by applying the injunction to emulate the male.

Moving inward from its exterior envelope to the "auto-architecture" of the body, the women violate the law of the οἶκος "house" by extending its basic principle – extending it to the point where it turns upon itself. By a *reductio ad absurdum* of the logic of the Classical οἶκος and of the psychoanalytic fetish, if it is good to form your body in the image of male desire, how much better, then, to form it in the image of the male himself. Thus does the architecture of erotically subordinated difference become the building of the same. For the women have now defied the original construction of the οἶκος "house" as a wall to confine them and their *mêtis* inside. As if their education has given them the ability to analyze the architectural possibilities of any given design, they have taken advantage of the definitive characteristic of the male in the Classical construction of the household, the fact that he goes outside, leaving her alone within.

> Whenever my husband would go to the marketplace, I would rub oil
> over my whole body and throughout the day I would color my skin
> by standing in the sun.

Aristophanes *Ecclesiazusae* 62–64

If not as irrevocable as a tattoo or scar, this tinting of the skin is still an on-going witness in the material of the body to the woman's troping of architectural confinement. This "circular reciprocity between what is bound and what is binding" reaches to the woman's most intimate "auto-architectural" containment, the restriction of her hair.

In the treatment of their hair, the women pursue their imitation of the male to the point of counteracting traditional female depilation. Rather than reduce their body hair through the details of aesthetic cutting, the women try instead to augment it, working both by nature and by artifice. During her days of suntanning, one woman refrains from shaving, so that now, she says, "I have armpits more shaggy than a thicket, just as was agreed." "Me too," says another, "I first threw my razor out of the house, so that I could be rough and hairy all over and no longer resemble a woman" (Aristophanes *Ecclesiazusae* 60–61, 65–67).[34] Anti-depilation alone, however, cannot reach the face, where the presence or absence of hair most immediately reveals the identity of the genitals below.

To mask their lack of facial hair, the women apply their *mêtis* to the making of a classical Freudian fetish, a work of artificial maleness *par excellence*. As women invent weaving, according to Freud, by interlacing their pubic hair to cover their lack of the penis, so the women here sew beards to cover their smooth facial cheeks.[35] As if they are replacing the shame Freud says women feel about their deficient genitals,[36] the women here admire the beauty of their ἐρραμμένους πώγωνας "stitched beards." One woman exclaims, "By Hecate, this one here that I have is beautiful indeed (καλόν γ')," while another, pitting her creation against a real man's beard, proudly insists, "Mine is much more beautiful (καλλίονα) than that of Epicrates" (Aristophanes *Ecclesiazusae* 24–25, 70–71). And finally, Praxagora explicitly correlates these factitious face-extensions with the women's "beards" below. For when one woman displays the wool she intends to card during the Assembly, a task often conducted with one foot propped up and the clothes pulled above the knees, Praxagora objects:[37]

ἰδού γέ σε ξαίνουσαν, ἣν τοῦ σώματος
οὐδὲν παραφῆναι τοῖς καθημένοις ἔδει.
οὐκοῦν καλά γ' ἂν πάθοιμεν, εἰ πλήρης τύχοι
ὁ δῆμος ὢν κἄπειθ' ὑπερβαίνουσά τις
ἀναβαλλομένη δείξειε τὸν Φορμίσιον.
ἢν δ' ἐγκαθεζώμεσθα πρότεραι, λήσομεν
ξυστειλάμεναι θαἰμάτια· τὸν πώγονά τε
ὅταν καθῶμεν ὃν περιδησόμεσθ' ἐκεῖ,
τίς οὐκ ἂν ἡμᾶς ἄνδρας ἡγήσαιθ' ὁρῶν;
Ἀγύρριος γοῦν τὸν Προνόμου πώγων' ἔχων
λέληθε· καίτοι πρότερον ἦν οὗτος γυνή.

Just imagine you carding! You who must display
no part of your body to the men sitting down.
We would fare beautifully indeed, if the Assembly
should happen to be full and then one of us by stepping over

and raising up her cloak should display her "Phormision."[38]
But if we sit down first, we will escape notice
by wrapping our cloaks around us. And the beard,
whenever we let fall the one we will bind around there,
what man seeing us would not think we are men?

Figure 4. Rene Magritte (1898-1967), *The Rape*, 1934. Oil on canvas, 28.5 × 21 in.
Houston, TX, Menil Collection. Photo, Banque d'Images, ADAGP / Art Resource, NY.

Agyrrhius, after all, by having Pronomus' beard
has escaped notice. And yet before this man was a woman.

Aristophanes *Ecclesiazusae* 93–103

If the women completely obscure their pubic hair below, its artificial
counterpart above will effectively replace it. [Figure 4. René Magritte. *The
Rape.* 1934. A Surrealist assimilation of pubic and facial hair.] All it takes to be
taken for a man is a beautiful beard. By hair alone is sex recognized.

Verbal Rehearsal: Pseudo-Phallic Political Speech

Having reviewed the visual elements of their disguise, the women now stage a
rehearsal of the speech by which Praxagora will persuade the Assembly to vote
for her plan.[39] Like the accoutrements of the women's costume, her speech
and her plan, by following the way she was taught to use her *mêtis*, pursue
this "party line" to the point where it turns into a circle, a figural ouroboros
devouring its own tail. By imitating male thought, Praxagora overturns male
power. She takes the Athenian male's habit of perpetual political innovation
to the point where it turns into female-rule, that being the only action not yet
tried.[40] By an apparent inconsistency with the Athenian penchant for novelty,
Praxagora argues for the innovation of gynocracy by adducing women's lack
of innovation. She catalogues those manifestations of traditional female *mêtis*
that never change. But in this assertion of an unchanging female essence,
Praxagora acts as a ventriloquist of the husband in the *Oeconomicus.*

Adopting the voice of an Athenian male, Praxagora argues, in effect, we
must put women in power in the πόλις "city," because they will always do what
we have trained them to do in the οἶκος "house."[41]

> ταῖς γὰρ γυναιξὶ φημὶ χρῆναι τὴν πόλιν
> ἡμᾶς παραδοῦναι. καὶ γὰρ ἐν ταῖς οἰκίαις
> ταύταις ἐπιτρόποις καὶ ταμίαισι χρώμεθα.

> For I declare we must hand over the
> city to the women. For indeed in our households
> we use these as overseers and managers.

Aristophanes *Ecclesiazusae* 210–212

Women, she insists, are τοὺς τρόπους βελτίονες "better in their habits"
than "we" men, because they act – as in the case of dyeing wool in hot

water – κατὰ τὸν ἀρχαῖον νόμον "according to ancient custom." They never change how they use their power to make changes. Yes, their works of *mêtis* "transformative intelligence" are many, but they never exceed the "wall" of women's formation by the οἶκος "house." Yes, women are "Pandoras," but as jars wholly conforming to their domestic containers. To prove its predictability, Praxagora catalogues nine instances of typical female behavior – roasting corn sitting down, carrying things on their heads, keeping the Thesmophoria rituals, baking cakes, irritating their husbands, admitting adulterers into the house, buying extra food, loving strong wine, enjoying intercourse – capping each with the refrain ὥσπερ καὶ πρὸ τοῦ "just as also before." Above all, she argues, it is by embodying the ideal of the *Oeconomicus*, the maximizing of productive and reproductive good, that women deserve to rule. For being the mothers of the soldiers, they will send them extra supplies to assure their safety, and "when it comes to providing money, a woman is the most resourceful thing" (Aristophanes *Ecclesiazusae* 214–236). And in the final twist of her argument, Praxagora turns what most defines the female as an artificial creation who must be confined by the οἶκος "house," that is, her capacity for ἀπάτη "deception," into the ultimate reason she should rule in the πόλις "city."[42]

> ἄρχουσά τ' οὐκ ἂν ἐξαπατηθείη ποτέ·
> αὐταὶ γάρ εἰσιν ἐξαπατᾶν εἰθισμέναι.

> Were she to rule, she would never be deceived.
> For they themselves are accustomed to deceive.

Aristophanes *Ecclesiazusae* 237–238

Female deception detects deception, leaving nothing but political truth. Such are the paradoxical dynamics of Praxagora's whole plot. For having completed its dress-rehearsal, Praxagora now turns her cohort toward their performance, reiterating the elements of their male costume – short tunics, Laconian shoes, the all-important beards, the cloaks, and the staffs, and directing their exit toward the Assembly singing an old man's song (Aristophanes *Ecclesiazusae* 268–278). But by neither dimension of the women's political theater, neither their physical disguise nor Praxagora's parody of an Athenian male's political reasoning, is her audience in fact deceived. Indeed, the plan she persuades them to ratify produces precisely what her imitation-male speech has promised – women ruling a city as one big house.

IV. Praxagora's Urban Form

Once the Assembly, packed by the disguised women, votes in Praxagora's new regime, Athens becomes, in effect, a naked female body stripped of all fetishes, all the quasi-phallic supports of the father-ruled city: private property, marriage, political and judicial institutions, along with the oppositions and hierarchies upon which they stand. This status of the fetish in Praxagora's city emerges from measuring her plan against the model with which it shares the revolutionary domestic and political tenets of communistic economics, the abolition of patriarchal marriage, and women with political power, that is, the organization of the Guardians in Plato's *Republic*. Comparing the two systems with regard to political power, economic ownership, sexual selection, and urban architectural form reveals key provisions of the Platonic system that preserve the rule of the phallus intact.[43]

Political Power

In its political structure, Praxagora's Athens preserves hierarchy, while Socrates advocates a near-equality. As in Orwell's *Animal Farm,* in which "all pigs are equal, but some are more equal than others," Guardian women may share rule with men – except to the degree that they are physically weaker (Plato *Republic* 451d–e). Equal education allows these women to become as nearly like men as possible.[44] And marking a subtle, but crucial opposition to arguments like Praxagora's that women's essential nature makes them especially fit for political rule, Socrates proves to his interlocutor's satisfaction ὅτι οὐδέν ἐστιν ἐπιτήδευμα ἴδιον γυναικὶ πρὸς διοίκησιν πόλεως "'that there is no pursuit with regard to the management of the city that is particular to a woman'" (Plato *Republic* 455b).[45] After describing the marks of natural ability – that the mind learns quickly, discovers new things independently, and is well served by the resources of the body – Socrates asks:

> Οἶσθά τι οὖν ὑπὸ ἀνθρώπων μελετώμενον, ἐν ᾧ οὐ πάντα ταῦτα
> τὸ τῶν ἀνδρῶν γένος διαφερόντως ἔχει ἢ τὸ τῶν γυναικῶν; ἢ
> μακρολογῶμεν τήν τε ὑφαντικὴν λέγοντες καὶ τὴν τῶν ποπάνων
> τε καὶ ἑψημάτων θεραπείαν, ἐν οἷς δή τι δοκεῖ τὸ γυναικεῖον γένος
> εἶναι, οὗ καὶ καταγελαστότατόν ἐστι πάντων ἡττώμενον;

> 'Do you know any occupation practiced by humankind in which the race of men is not superior to that of women in all these respects?

Or should we lengthen the argument by speaking of the weaving art
and the care of pancakes and vegetables, in which, to be sure, the
race of women seems to be distinguished, and it is most laughable of
all for it to be inferior to the race of men?'

Plato *Republic* 455c–d

No typical acts of female *mêtis* equip women for political rule. Rather, '"woman
participates in all pursuits according to nature, and man in all, but in all of
them woman is weaker (ἀσθενέστερον) than man"' (Plato *Republic* 455d–e). In
Plato's ideal city, women are enabled to emulate the male as best they can.[46]

In contrast to this almost perfect, male-modeled equality, Praxagora's
plan applies at the scale of the πόλις "city" the sectional strategy of the
wife in *On the Murder of Eratosthenes*. As the wife exchanges places with her
husband, leaving him locked upstairs and herself in charge of access to the
outside, so Praxagora maintains political hierarchy, but puts herself on top.
Now men are to remain inside, while women alone go outside into the city to
rule. Like the plot that produced it, the play presents this role reversal theatri-
cally. If the Guardian women of the *Republic* are permitted, in effect, to "wear
pants" like men, the men in the *Ecclesiazusae* are limited to a woman's "dress."
As the double of its dress-rehearsal with women dressed as men comes the
mise-en-scène of Praxagora's legislative coup, when her husband Blepyrus and
his neighbor, the drama's first real men, emerge from their houses wearing
their women's clothes (Aristophanes *Ecclesiazusae* 317–319, 331–347, 374).
Their costume is no merely temporary travesty, as the men now hear. For
with "all the duties that used to be the concern of male citizens now assigned
to the women," men are now confined to the female's role, enclosed within
the household and subject to compulsory sex by force in order to be given
food – "it's the most terrible thing," laments Blepyrus, "to do it by force" (τὸ
πρὸς βίαν δεινότατον) (Aristophanes *Ecclesiazusae* 458–471). As the wife in the
Oeconomicus was trained to imitate the male, so now the husband must play
the parodic female, subordinated to real women's rule.

Economic Ownership

Under Praxagora's gynocracy, just as she promised in her rehearsal, the
women will extend the economics of the οἶκος "house" and their role within it
to the border of the πόλις "city."[47] As marriage in the *Oeconomicus* is said to be
constructed by the gods as a beneficial κοινωνία "commonality" (Xenophon
Oeconomicus 7.18–19), so Praxagora's plan now decrees the city and all of

its contents a grand "common possession," from which women distribute resources as the "general bee" of the now city-wide household.

> τὴν γῆν πρώτιστα ποιήσω
> <u>κοινὴν</u> πάντων καὶ τἀργύριον καὶ τἆλλ', ὁπόσ' ἐστὶν ἑκάστῳ.
> εἶτ' ἀπὸ τούτων <u>κοινῶν</u> ὄντων ἡμεῖς βοσκήσομεν ὑμᾶς
> ταμιευόμεναι καὶ φειδόμεναι καὶ τὴν γνώμην προσέχουσαι.

> In the first place, I will make the earth
> the <u>common</u> <u>possession</u> of all, and both the money and the
> other things, as many as each owns.
> Then from these <u>common</u> <u>resources</u> we will feed you
> by dispensing as manager and thriftily conserving and applying
> our intelligence.

> Aristophanes *Ecclesiazusae* 597–600

And just as in the *Oeconomicus*, economic order is taught by the husband to his wife, so now the new economic order is presented in a scene of spousal instruction. But since she now rules as the city's new στρατηγός "general" (Aristophanes *Ecclesiazusae* 491), Praxagora will play with Blepyrus the teacher's role.

This pedagogical reversal is triggered by an ironic dialogue which turns Praxagora from feigning ignorance to undertaking the proof of her plan's benefits. After defending her early-morning departure, wearing Blepyrus' clothes, and thus forcing him to miss the Assembly, Praxagora pretends to know nothing of the new legislation. So her husband reports what he has heard from his neighbor, "They say the city has been handed over to you women!" Then ironically echoing her own earlier rationale in the Assembly for the transfer – that women would rule by performing their traditional role, Praxagora asks, τί δρᾶν; ὑφαίνειν; "To do what with? To weave?" Equally ironic is Blepyrus' reply, οὐ μὰ Δί' ἀλλ' ἄρχειν "No by Zeus, but to rule," for the women will now rule precisely by applying their weaving art on an urban scale.[48] At this declaration of gynocracy, Praxagora exclaims, νὴ τὴν Ἀφροδίτην μακαρία γ' ἄρ' ἡ πόλις ἔσται τὸ λοιπόν "By Aphrodite, blessed indeed then will the city be for the rest of time" (Aristophanes *Ecclesiazusae* 555–559). In retrospect, this exclamation, too, is ironic, for just as the wife's training in the *Oeconomicus* moves from walls to clothes to body and mind, so Praxagora's economic law will reach finally into Aphrodite's domain, where it will seem later, to a young Athenian male at least, not a blessing, but a phantasmagorical curse. But for now, Praxagora takes up the challenge to "teach the benefits" (χρηστὰ διδάξω) of her plan (Aristophanes *Ecclesiazusae* 569–570, 583).[49]

Like Lysistrata, who proposes the uniting of Athens' various constituencies by weaving a cloak for the people (τῷ δήμῳ χλαῖναν ὑφῆναι),[50] Praxagora announces an interweaving of rich and poor.

> κοινωνεῖν γὰρ πάντας φήσω χρῆναι πάντων μετέχοντας
> κἀκ ταὐτοῦ ζῆν, καὶ μὴ τὸν μὲν πλουτεῖν, τὸν δ' ἄθλιον εἶναι.

> For I declare that all people must share all things in common
> and live from the same store, and that no one should be rich
>   and another wretched.

Aristophanes Ecclesiazusae 590–591

To abolish economic disparity, she eliminates private property: ἀλλ' ἕνα ποιῶ κοινὸν πᾶσιν βίοτον, καὶ τοῦτον ὅμοιον "I will make one means of life, common to all, and this will be equal" (Aristophanes *Ecclesiazusae* 594). Erasing the difference between "own" and "other's" is also the goal of the Guardians' communism. Identifying the city's good as unity based in common feelings of pleasure and pain, Socrates insists:

> Ἡ δέ γε τῶν τοιούτων ἰδίωσις διαλύει, ὅταν οἱ μὲν περιαλγεῖς, οἱ δὲ περιχαρεῖς γίγνωνται ἐπὶ τοῖς αὐτοῖς παθήμασι τῆς πόλεώς τε καὶ τῶν ἐν τῇ πόλει;

> 'But indeed does the individualization of such feelings dissolve the city, when some grieve exceedingly and others rejoice exceedingly at the same experiences both of the city and of those in the city?'

Plato Republic 462b–c

And regarding the cause of such disintegration, Socrates asks:

> Ἆρ' οὖν ἐκ τοῦδε τὸ τοιόνδε γίγνεται, ὅταν μὴ ἅμα φθέγγωνται ἐν τῇ πόλει τὰ τοιάδε ῥήματα, τό τε ἐμὸν καὶ τὸ οὐκ ἐμόν; καὶ περὶ τοῦ ἀλλοτρίου κατὰ ταὐτά;

> 'So, then, does such a condition not derive from this condition: when they do utter such sayings as these, both "my own" and "not my own," at the same time in the city? And in the same way, with regard to 'somebody else's'?"

Plato Republic 462c

But a crucial limitation in the Platonic system preserves male privilege. It occurs at the point where economic communism comes up against the dynamics – and, indeed, becomes the basis – of the range and the freedom of erotic choice.

Sexual Selection

With regard to sexual selection, both Praxagora and Plato abolish father-ruled marriage, thereby dissolving the distinction between legitimate and bastard children – that is, between "own" and "other's" at the level of reproductive wealth, where economic and sexual profit coincide in the term τόκος, meaning both "child" and "interest on a loan."[51] In each system, the parental function is spread out over the space of a generation with all older men regarded as "fathers" in the *Ecclesiazusae* and in the *Republic* all children born seven to ten months after a man's marriage called "sons" and "daughters."[52] But among Plato's Guardians, communism is constrained by the presiding model of the male as ideal.

Guardian men hold both women and children in common, but no such common ownership of men is accorded to Guardian women. The system is always described from the male position as, for example, when it is introduced in Book V as "'the common ownership for our Guardians of wives and children'" (ἡ κοινωνία τοῖς φύλαξιν ἡμῖν παίδων τε πέρι καὶ γυναικῶν, Plato *Republic* 450c). As with their access to political rule, the sexual status of Guardian men and women is almost perfectly equal. Both men and women are joined in eugenically arranged marriages, but it is male Guardians only who are rewarded for military prowess with extra sex. He who distinguishes himself in battle is to be crowned by the right "to kiss (φιλῆσαί)" and "to be kissed (φιληθῆναι)" by every man and child in the army and "'no one he wants to kiss (φιλεῖν)' is permitted to refuse, so that if he happens to be in love with someone, whether male or female, he will be more eager to carry away the prize of victory'" and "'for him, because he is a good man, more marriages will be provided than for the other men and he will have choices for that sort of thing more often than the others'" (Plato *Republic* 468b–c). No such erotic benefit is offered to female Guardians. The possibility that they might display extraordinary valor and be given additional opportunities for intercourse with men is not even conceived.[53]

In Praxagora's city, by contrast, not only women and children but men as well become common property.[54] Her goal is radical equality, and thus wholly equal access to sexual pleasure, despite all physical disparities. To create uncompromised freedom of erotic choice, Praxagora upends traditional aesthetic value: in order to enjoy someone young and beautiful, if you are young and beautiful, you must satisfy someone old and ugly first. Under this new law, erotic freedom and economic communism are mutually dependent. Indeed, the issue of sexual access emerges from a question about the continued usefulness of money. When challenged to say what a man would gain by refusing to submit all his resources, including money, to a common store, Blepyrus adduces the example of sexual commerce: "If ever he sees a young girl and desires her, and wants to dig into her, he will be able to take some of his money to give her, and have a share of things 'communistically' by sleeping with her in bed." "But," objects Praxagora, "he will be able to sleep with her *gratis*. And these women, too, I make common property (κοινὰς), for any man who wishes, to have sex with and make children." To such "free love," Blepyrus raises the obvious objection, "How then will not all men go to the most young and attractive of them and try to press them hard?" Praxagora assuages his anxiety spatially, putting a man's choices side by side: "The cheapest (φαυλότεραι) women and the most snub-nosed (σιμότεραι) will sit beside those who are worthy of respect (σεμνὰς). And if ever he desires this one, he will give the ugly one a knock first." And similarly, for women, "they will not be allowed to sleep with beautiful men before they please ugly and short ones" (Aristophanes *Ecclesiazusae* 611–618, 629–630). Here in the sphere of sexual power, as in its political and economic dimensions, Praxagora's plan joins vertical inversion with horizontal expansion. The space of equal erotic rights is now extended to include women and traditional erotic hierarchy is turned upside down. No phallic priority remains.

With the tenets of her gynocratic communism now delineated, Praxagora's teaching might come to an end, leaving its overtly architectural implications implicit, as they are in Plato's ideal city. In the *Ecclesiazusae*, however, the architecture of Praxagora's revolution is explicit – indeed, the culminating topic in her instruction of her husband.

Urban Form

To support her new structure of social, economic, and political power, Praxagora reconstructs the material structure of the city. By applying her traditional training in "home-making" to both domestic and public space, she transforms the πόλις "city" into one big οἶκος "house."

In being taught to devote their *mêtis* to weaving the walls of the οἶκος, women learn, like Penelope, how to unweave them, when the preservation of the household demands. In its treatment of the οἶκος "house," Praxagora's urban plan is just such a constructive undoing. Near the end of their dialogue in which he probes the specifics of the new order, Blepyrus asks his wife for a description of its general character, τὴν δὲ δίαιταν τίνα ποιήσεις; "What way of life will you make?" His wife's answer might not be expected. For to this request for a summation of a life-style, Praxagora responds with an architecture.

> κοινὴν πᾶσιν. τὸ γὰρ ἄστυ
> μίαν οἴκησίν φημι ποιήσειν συρρήξας' εἰς ἓν ἅπαντα,
> ὥστε βαδίζειν ὡς ἀλλήλους.

> [A way of life] common to all. For I
> declare I will make the city
> one household by uniting-through-breaking [*sun* "together" +
> *rhêgnumi* "break"] all things into one,
> so that as a result everyone walks toward one another.

> Aristophanes *Ecclesiazusae* 673–675

All of the walls that divide the city into separate households will be unwoven, leaving only a single οἶκος "house," surrounded by the city's walls alone. By this (de)construction, the Classical architecture of single-family father-rule is demolished.

The result of Praxagora's primary move of uniting-through-breaking makes room for a second architectural process, that of re-programming. Now that the city is a single house, its public spaces are large rooms. And as the wife is taught to maintain the program of indoor, domestic spaces, so Praxagora knows how to re-program outdoor spaces – now wholly domestic – so that they serve the function of the ἀνδρών, the "men's dining room" in the οἶκος "house," namely, the male-only symposium.[55] With this final phase of her urban form, Praxagora overturns every revered institution of phallic political and economic power, for she deprives each of its foundation, the space and place to act.[56] In answer to Blepyrus' question of where dinner will be served, his wife explains, "I will make all the law courts and the colonnades into men's dining rooms (ἀνδρῶνας)." And what, he asks, will be the function of the βῆμα, the "speaker's platform" – the material pedestal without which the essential, yet non-material element of Athenian democracy, the voice of the individual citizen, is silent? Eradicating this democratic role, Praxagora answers, "To put the mixing-bowls and the water-jars on." And what of the urns of lots used to designate judicial assignments by lot, the definitive instrument of egalitarian democracy? They will now be placed in the Agora, beside the statue of Harmodius, the tyrant-killer symbolic of democratic virtue, but from this

Figure 5. Engraving by Charles Eisen (1720-1778), *The Devil of Pope-Fig Island,* in Jean de la Fontaine, *Tales and Novels in Verse* (London: Privately Printed for the Society of English Bibliophilists, 1896). Photo courtesy of The Library of Congress.

vessel of political equality will issue now not the chance to serve on a jury, but a letter designating a place to eat.[57] "The herald will announce that those with Beta should follow her to dine at the Basileus Colonnade, the Thetas to the one next to it, and the Kappas to the Cornmarket Colonnade" (Aristophanes *Ecclesiazusae* 675–686).

With this vision of democratic spaces turned into megalo-domestic dining rooms, Praxagora completes her husband's indoctrination. Now he knows the details of her communistic gynocracy, and now to the question with which we began – "What will a woman build, if left to her own devices?" – the play has provided an answer, "She will build as we have taught her." She will turn the city into one big house with herself in power and sexually uncontained. She will expose the land as a female genital stripped of every pseudo-phallic stand-in. Female urban form means the end of the "phallus" as architect of all these oppositions – inside versus outside, own versus other's, legitimate versus bastard – and all those hierarchies – male over female, youth over age, beauty over ugliness – upon which Classical value and meaning depend. Female urban form means the death of architecture as phallic differentiation.

What is one to see in this vision of the unadorned, unconfined, uncovered, unfetishized female genital? That depends on how you look at it, indeed, upon who you are who is looking. For with an ambiguity true to the fetish's simultaneous affirmation and denial of loss, the final two scenes of the play present two kinds – two genders, we might say – of response. In the first, the sight is horrible, as when the Devil himself is put to flight by the female's *anasurma* "lifting of the skirts" [Figure 5. A female puts the Devil to flight by exposing her genitals]. In the second, we find a counterpart to the laughter of Demeter, as she gazes upon the naked genitals of Baubo [Figure 6. Terracotta figurine of Baubo with a torch. Priene. 4th century BCE].[58]

Female Urban Form as Phallic Loss

In its penultimate scene, the play displays the impact of Praxagora's law upon the body of a young man. Here the female is still assimilated, like Pandora, to the man-made containers of ceramic jar and house, but with her openings now free of phallic regulation. In dramatizing what the young man suffers from this unfettered vagina, the scene becomes, in effect, a defense of the fetish and a demand for its return. For the loss of phallic power breeds fear of incest not only in the young man, but also in the woman who fears she might be his mother. Attempting to avail herself of the new sexual order, an ugly old hag competes with a beautiful young girl for the young man's sexual service, each woman stationing herself in an orifice of the house, one at the window and the other at the door, to hurl abuse at the other (Aristophanes *Ecclesiazusae* 877–889). The young man, Epigenes, too, insults the hag. Loaded down, as she is, with white lead and rouge on her face, he likens her to a certain type of ceramic jar, the *lêkuthos*, a one-handled jug with narrow neck and deep mouth used for athlete's oil, unguents, makeup, and as an offering for the dead.[59] He charges that her lover is that master pot-painter, Death himself, who makes such a *lêkuthos* of and for us all.

> Epigenes: But, dear lady, I'm concerned about your lover.
>
> Hag: Who is that?
>
> Epigenes: The best of painters.
>
> Hag: And who is that?
>
> Epigenes: He who paints *lêkuthoi* for corpses. So go away, lest he
>   see you at the door. [60]

Aristophanes Ecclesiazusae 994–997

These insults alone do not dissuade the hag. But when threatened with the flip-side of eliminating father-ruled marriage-exchange, namely, the violation of the incest-taboo – as if all these hyphenated terms were somehow essential to her safety – the hag turns and runs. As she is about to drag the young man across her threshold, thus inverting the roles of regular marriage, she is put to flight, when the young girl warns: "You would be more like a mother to him than a wife. If you establish this law, you will fill the whole earth with Oedipuses!" (Aristophanes *Ecclesiazusae* 1040–1042).

The hag's reaction might seem anomalous. Why does she care whether or not the young man is her son? While her plan provided for an inter-generational father-son recognition in order to prevent patricide, Praxagora's conversation with Blepyrus produced no comparable questioning of how to avoid incest. To some commentators, this silence indicates that Praxagora is not concerned with preventing mothers' recognition of their children.[61] Another conclusion is that Aristophanes has left a loop-hole in Praxagora's plan – one which he now exploits. By leaving this gap in the overt defense of her plan – namely, the failure to address the problem of preventing incest – Aristophanes leaves Praxagora's law vulnerable to this apparent internal contradiction. If erotic equality requires that the young have sex with the old before the young, and if "father" and "mother" now designate the whole of an older generation, how can the system avert the threat of incest? If the system, as Aristophanes has permitted Praxagora to formulate it, is to achieve wholly communistic *eros*, its rationale must penetrate – as was the goal of the husband in the *Oeconomicus* – the body and the mind, there to eradicate fear of incestuous sex. But when the hag is confronted with the possibility of mother-son union, fear overrides the new sexual right. Ironically recalling Jocasta, who retreats into the house at the realization of her incest,

Figure 6. Terracotta figurine: Baubo, with a torch. From Priene, ca. 4th century BC. Antikenmuseum Berlin, Staatliche Museen Preussischer Kulturbesitz, TC 8612. Photo, Bildarchiv Preussischer Kulturbesitz / Art Resource, NY.

the hag runs into the house, figurally re-submitting herself to its sexual law.[62] But no sooner is this hag expelled than she proliferates – another arrives, one uglier than the first, and then a third arrives, the ugliest of all.

Caught in a physical tug-of-war between these two new hags, each trying to drag him into the door of her house, Epigenes must now submit to sex with a woman who might be his mother. His vision of the union contains every dimension of castration anxiety, every fear that motivates the creation of the fetish. He bewails his fate in and as a synesthesia of intercourse, castration, and death, and he caps it with a chimera of compensatory revenge:

> O three-times damned, if I must screw a
> putrid woman the whole night and day, and then,
> whenever I escape from this one, again have to screw
> a toad (φρύνην)[63] who has a funeral *lêkuthos* on her jaws.
> Am I not damned? Indeed, I am deeply damned,
> by Zeus the savior, a man indeed ill-fated,
> who will be shut up inside with such wild beasts.
> But still, if – as is very likely – I suffer something,[64]
> as I sail hither into the harbor under these whores as pilots,
> bury me upon the mouth itself of the entrance,
> and this woman above, on top of the tomb (σήματος),
> tar her down alive, then pour lead
> on her feet in a circle around her ankles,
> and put her on top above me as a substitute (πρόφασιν) for
>   a *lêkuthos*.[65]

Aristophanes *Ecclesiazusae* 1098–1111

In this phantasmagorical vision, entities bear multiple, simultaneous meanings. Intercourse with the female-as-ceramic-embodiment-of-death means imprisonment in her body-as-a-house and being devoured there by the "wild beasts" of her castrating *vagina dentata*. This diabolical confinement of the man inverts Zeus' swallowing of Metis and the household's containment of the wife. And just as the wife before tried to emulate a "ship-shape" κόσμος "order," so the female is now the pilot of the male, himself a ship, sailing into the harbor of her voracious genital mouth, upon which he will be buried – but not without his revenge. For in his final words, Epigenes envisions a return of the female fetish – that "monument" (*Denkmal*), in Freud's terms, "to the horror of castration" feared as punishment for incest – and with the fetish, a return of the "phallus" as architectural support. Tarred alive and welded to his

341

tomb by her feet, those perennial objects of the fetishist's sadistic adoration, female *mêtis* stands now wholly immobilized, a reduction of the constricting drive of the οἶκος "house" to its ultimate logical absurdity. The female as ceramic Pandora is now the parodic *lêkuthos*, a pseudo-phallic memorial upon the grave of male glory.

Female Urban Form as Baubo

And then suddenly, as if this fantasy of violent Oedipal transgression had never occurred, the play turns into a "festive conclusion," comedy's normative end.[66] We, its audience – especially its judges – are invited to see in Praxagora's new regime what Demeter saw when Baubo lifted her skirts.

When her daughter Persephone is raped by Death, Demeter, goddess of marriage, childbirth, and chthonic fertility, suspends her powers and wanders the now sterile earth disguised as an old woman. Arriving at Eleusis, she is received by the queen, Baubo, who offers her food and drink. When the mourning goddess refuses this traditional hospitality, Baubo responds by lifting her skirts and exposing her naked genitals. At this sight, the goddess laughs. She eats and drinks, and with her resumption of human social exchange, the fertility of women and the earth returns.[67]

In its final scene, the *Ecclesiazusae* aims at the tropic power of Baubo's display. Rather than a system of sterile intercourse with women too old to bear children, rather than requiring a young man's rape, it offers Praxagora's city as a source of sexual luxury and gargantuan nourishment for all. It hopes to turn horror into happiness and fear into laughter, thereby to win the comic prize. On the heels of Epigenes' sexual damnation, a maidservant enters proclaiming this compound benediction:

> O blessed is the people, and happy am I myself,
> and my mistress herself is most blessed,
> and all of you women, as many as stand beside here upon the
> doors,
> and all our neighbors and all the fellow-demesmen,
> and I, in addition to these, the maidservant.

Aristophanes Ecclesiazusae 1112–1116

The source of her bliss is a profusion of "good perfumes" on her head – perfume being a powerful tool of sexual attraction,[68] and of Thasian wine, whose effect within her head lasts a whole night long (Aristophanes *Ecclesiazusae* 1116–

1124). She has come not just to extol her pleasure, however, but rather to share it, as she asks the chorus where her master, that is, the husband of her mistress, is. Here he comes on his way to dinner, answers the chorus leader, as a man enters with a couple of μείρακας "young girls." Whether or not he is to be identified as Blepyrus, the new "first husband," he is "blessed and three-times happy," being assured of sexual pleasure in the persons of the "chicks" on his arm and of a sumptuous feast. [69] For his wife has sent the maidservant to bring him and his girlfriends to dinner, where, although he is the last of the 30,000 male citizens, there is still Chian wine and other "good things" left for him (Aristophanes *Ecclesiazusae* 1125–1140).

Indeed, in Praxagora's grand provision of sex and food, there is enough left for all men, as the invitation to dinner expands to dissolve the "fourth wall" and solicit the audience's favor. Turning from her master to the audience, the maidservant says:

> And of the spectators, if anyone happens to be well-disposed,
> and of the judges, if anyone is not looking in the other direction,
> come with us. For we will provide all things.

Aristophanes *Ecclesiazusae* 1141–1143

In return for your approbation, you may cross the theatrical threshold and come with us to the feast. But then, urges her master, why not "speak nobly" and "freely invite the old man, the young man, and the boy?" For such is the extent of the gynocratic largess that "there is a dinner prepared for each and every one of them, too, if they return home" (Aristophanes *Ecclesiazusae* 1144–1148) – not a disinterested offer, of course, since the *Ecclesiazusae* is the first play in the day's competition and departure at this point would mean missing the others (Aristophanes *Ecclesiazusae* 1158–1159).[70] Rather, the point of the extended invitation is that Praxagora's new city transcends the space of the theater to encompass the totality of households in Athens itself. All citizens may share its wealth of unlimited pleasure, if only they, like this morning's Assembly, vote for it. For, as the maidservant and her master then leave for dinner, the chorus-leader appeals to the judges:

> τοῖς σοφοῖς μὲν τῶν σοφῶν μεμνημένοις κρίνειν ἐμέ,
> τοῖς γελῶσι δ' ἡδέως διὰ τὸν γέλων κρίνειν ἐμέ·
> σχεδὸν ἅπαντας οὖν κελεύω δηλαδὴ κρίνειν ἐμέ.

> to those who are clever, remember the clever things and vote
>   for me;

> to those who laugh with pleasure, on account of laughter, vote
> for me:
> virtually all men, therefore, I clearly order to vote for me.
>
> Aristophanes *Ecclesiazusae* 1155–1157

Does the manifold σοφία of Praxagora's plot and plan resonate with your own? When you gaze at her urban form, do you see Baubo and laugh?

In case you hesitate – in case your hunger is not quite strong enough to scotomize what Epigenes sees in the unadorned female genital – Aristophanes ends the *Ecclesiazusae* with the promise of an irresistibly huge piece of food, named in "the longest word ever known to have been created in the Greek language, comprising (subject to textual uncertainties) 170 letters and 79 syllables, and describing a gargantuan dish consisting mainly of fish (1169–1170) and birds (1172–1174), plus hare (1174), well sauced and seasoned (1170–1171, 1174)."[71] Who could resist this gigantic offering? Who, now, could withhold his vote? With this sign of the city's new power to satisfy human hunger, no matter how immense, Aristophanes would seem to have brought us all to the point of ratifying his creation of female urban form. Here, it seems, he brings the turns and returns of comic *mêtis* finally to a close.

But maybe here it is the goddess Metis herself who has the final word. Maybe the tropology of *mêtis* exceeds the mastery even of him who created this play's ingenious play. For if we vote in favor of Praxagora's gynocratic communism, we have not escaped the effects of the Freudian fetish. If we see ourselves as one of the men treated by the new system to endless sex and food, we have not excluded from our society the young man who sees the unadorned female genital as the site of castration. If we take his fears for fantasy, if we assure ourselves that within the walls of the Hag's "house," he will find nothing ultimately more lethal than intercourse – if we, indeed, find ourselves laughing a bit at the groundlessness of his panic and more than a bit indignant at the extremity of his hoped-for revenge, we have not thereby excluded from our society all that continues to result from the force of his fear.

Notes

An earlier version of this essay appeared in *The Sex of Architecture*, edited by
D. Agrest, P. Conway, and L. Weisman, New York, 1996:73–92. It is a pleasure to thank
Bruce Rosenstock and Giulia Sissa for critical reading of this current version.

1. For editions of and commentaries on the *Ecclesiazusae,* see Ussher 1973 and
Sommerstein 1998. For the historical context and a comprehensive interpretation of
the play from the perspective of political philosophy, see Ober 1998. For a penetrating
reading of the play's critical force, see Saïd 1979 and 1996.

2. The architectural term "detail" is derived from the French verb *détailler* "to cut in
pieces."

3. For the "reign of the phallus" in Classical Athens, see Kuels 1985.

4. For the Freudian account of the fetish, see Freud 1905, 1910 (esp. 96–97), 1927,
1940 [1938]a (esp. 202–204), 1940 [1938]b. The fetish enters Freudian theory in 1905
in the first of the "Three Essays on the Theory of Sexuality," namely, "The Sexual
Aberrations," as a "perversion," one among the "deviations in respect of the sexual
aim." As that "aim" is limited to heterosexual, genital intercourse, "perversion" from
this point of view includes such common practices as the "overvaluation of the sexual
object," the "sexual use of the mucous membrane of the lips and mouth," the "sexual
use of the anal orifice," and the "significance of other regions of the body" (Freud
1905:150–153; see also Freud 1917 [1916–1917]:305–306). In the concluding section
of that essay, Freud reflects upon the relation between perversion and what is to be
considered normal: "the extraordinarily wide dissemination of the perversions forces
us to suppose that the disposition to perversions is itself of no great rarity but must
form a part of what passes as the normal constitution. . . . The conclusion now presents
itself to us that there is indeed something innate lying behind the perversions but that
it is something innate in everyone, though as a disposition it may vary in its intensity
and may be increased by influences of actual life" (Freud 1905:171).

5. On the assumed universality of the penis as the foundation for the construction
of the fetish, see Bernheimer 1991:2: "The purpose of the fetish is to preserve
the fantasy that all humans have a penis – the childhood theory of anatomical
sameness – and simultaneously to represent a recognition that women lack this
organ."

6. Freud 1927:155:

> An investigation of fetishism is strongly recommended to anyone who still
> doubts the existence of the castration complex or who can still believe that
> fright at the sight of the female genital has some other ground.

7. Freud 1927:154 = "Fetishismus," 313.

8. Freud 1927:155. As "the last impression before the uncanny and traumatic one," the fetish functions as what Freud calls a "screen memory." For the detailed parallels in Freud's texts between the fetish and the screen memory, see Bergren 1992:138–139.

9. Freud 1927:157. See also Freud 1910:96:

> The erotic attraction that comes from his mother soon culminates in a longing for her genital organ, which he takes to be a penis. With the discovery, which is not made till later, that women do not have a penis, this longing often turns into its opposite and gives place to a feeling of disgust which in the years of puberty can become the cause of psychical impotence, misogyny, and permanent homosexuality. But fixation on the object that was once strongly desired, the woman's penis, leaves indelible traces on the mental life of the child, who has pursued that portion of his infantile sexual researches with particular thoroughness. Fetishistic reverence for a woman's foot and shoe appears to take the foot merely as a substitutive symbol for the woman's penis which was once revered and later missed; without knowing it, 'coupeurs de nattes' [cutters of hair] play the part of people who carry out an act of castration on the female genital organ.

10. Apter 1991:13.

11. While obvious differences obtain – those of gender and race, in particular – it may be instructive to compare the fetishized female as "para-male" with Homi Bhahba's description of the "mimicry" imposed upon the colonized male (Bhahba 1994).

12. For this lamp as symbolic of the play's didactic aim – μόνος δὲ μηρῶν εἰς ἀπορρήτους μυχοὺς λάμπεις "alone into the unspeakable recesses of our thighs you shine," see Ober 1998:126n10 and for its illumination of the traditional features of women's life within the οἶκος "house," see Saïd 1979:40.

13. In light of this analogy, the Vitruvian ideal of the building as male body appears to be less an original principle than a secondary compensation for the primary Classical correlation between architecture and the body, namely, that between the female and the house.

14. Arguing against the claim that Greek males assuaged a fear of the female genital by requiring its complete depilation, Kilmer 1982 shows that the evidence in comedy and vase painting indicates (1) that depilation was partial and not complete, the aim being a particular shape – for example, a halo of hair surrounding an exposed vulva (plate Ib) – and (2) that the goal of the depilation was to enhance erotic attractiveness. From the psychoanalytic point of view, however, requiring women to cut their pubic hair into particular forms is not inconsistent with male fear of the female genital.

15. Compare this complex circulation of likeness and hierarchy with the depiction of Pandora in Figure 2 as a "mermaid"-like combination of female on the top and *pithos* on the bottom.

16. For *mêtis* as the female's architectural power, see "The (Re)Marriage of Penelope and Odysseus" and "Architecture Gender Philosophy" in this collection.

17. Xenophon *Oeconomicus* 7.18–36.

18. Note the subtle distinction in how the text rates violations by women and men of their proper spatial assignment: "for a woman it is more praiseworthy (κάλλιον) to remain inside than to go outside, but for a man it is more blameworthy (αἴσχιον) to remain inside than to concern himself with things outside" (Xenophon *Oeconomicus* 7.30).

19. For the analogy of οἶκος "house" and πόλις "city," see also Xenophon *Oeconomicus* 8.22, where the husband compares the house with the *agora*, where anything may be found because it is in a fixed place.

20. Compare Saïd 1979:47–48.

21. Note that the wife's authority remains subordinate to the husband's orders: "'In addition,' he said, 'I taught her that she would not be justly angry, if I gave her more orders with regard to our possessions than to the servants'" (Xenophon *Oeconomicus* 9.16).

22. For the object in Figure 3 as a lamp for depilation, see Hauser 1909.

23. For women's invention of weaving, see Freud 1933 [1932]:132:

> The effect of penis-envy has a share, further, in the physical vanity of women, since they are bound to value their charms more highly as a late compensation for their original sexual inferiority. Shame, which is considered to be a feminine characteristic *par excellence* but is far more a matter of convention than might be supposed, has as its purpose, we believe, concealment [*verdecken: Decke* "cover, ceiling, roof, skin, envelope, coat, pretense, screen"] of genital deficiency. We are not forgetting that at a later time, shame takes on other functions. It seems that women have made few contributions to the discoveries [*Entdeckungen*] and inventions in the history of civilization; there is, however, one technique which they may have invented – that of plaiting and weaving. If that is so, we should be tempted to guess the unconscious motive for the achievement. Nature herself would seem to have given the model which this achievement imitates by causing the growth at maturity of the pubic hair that conceals their genitals. *The step that remained to be taken lay in making the threads adhere to one another* while on the body they stick into the skin and are only matted together. If you reject this idea as fantastic and regard my belief in the influence of a lack of a penis on the configuration of femininity as an *idée fixe*, I am of course defenseless. [Emphasis added]

For weaving as the origin of architecture, see Semper 1989, "The Textile Art," 254–255:

The beginning of building coincides with the beginning of textiles. The wall is that architectural element that formally represents and makes visible *the enclosed space as such*, absolutely, as it were, without reference to secondary concepts. We might recognize the *pen*, bound together from sticks and branches, and the interwoven *fence* as the earliest vertical spatial enclosure that man invented. . . . Whether these inventions gradually developed in this order or another matters little to us here, for it remains certain that the use of crude weaving that started with the pen – as a means to make the "home," the *inner life* separated from the *outer life*, and as the formal creation of the idea of space – undoubtedly preceded the wall, even the most primitive one constructed out of stone or any other material. The structure that served to support, to secure, to carry this spatial enclosure was a requirement that had nothing directly to do with *space* and the *division of space*. . . . In this connection, it is of the greatest importance to note that wherever these secondary motives are not present, woven fabrics almost everywhere and especially in the southern and warm countries carry out their ancient, original function as conspicuous spatial dividers; even where solid walls become necessary they remain only the inner and unseen structure for the true and legitimate representatives of the spatial idea: namely, the more or less artificially woven and seamed-together, textile walls. . . . In all Germanic languages the word *Wand* (of the same root and same basic meaning as *Gewand*) directly recalls the old origin and type of the *visible* spatial enclosure. Likewise, *Decke, Bekleidung, Schranke, Zaun* (similar to *Saum*), and many other technical expressions are not somewhat late linguistic symbols applied to the building trade, but reliable indications of the textile origin of these building parts. [Emphasis added]

See also Semper, "The Four Elements of Architecture," 102–103, and compare "Structural Elements of Assyrian-Chaldean Architecture" in Herrmann 1984:205–206:

It is well known that any wild tribe is familiar with the fence or a primitive hurdle as a means of enclosing space. Weaving the fence led to weaving movable walls of bast, reed, or willow twigs and later to weaving carpets of thinner animal or vegetable fiber. . . . Using wickerwork for setting apart one's property and for floor mats and protection against heat and cold far preceded making even the roughest masonry. Wickerwork was the original motif of the wall. It retained this primary significance, actually or ideally, when the light hurdles and mattings were later transformed into brick or stone walls. The essence of the wall was wickerwork. Hanging carpets remained the true walls; they were the visible boundaries of a room. The often solid walls behind them were necessary for reasons that had nothing to do with the creation of space; they were needed for protection, for supporting a load, for their permanence, etc. Wherever the need for these secondary functions did not arise, carpets remained the only means for separating space. Even where solid walls became necessary, they were only the invisible structure hidden behind the true representatives of the wall, the colorful carpets that the walls served to hold and support. It was therefore the covering of the wall that was primarily and essentially of spatial and architectural significance; the wall itself was secondary.

For the role of women's weaving in the architectural theory of the *Odyssey*, see "The (Re)Marriage of Penelope and Odysseus" in this collection.

24. Charles Platter "Depilation in Old Comedy," typescript, 3–4: "The matrix of depilation described by our sources is fundamentally associated with . . . the attempt to control the women of the household whose extravagant sexuality, symbolized by tangled hair, represents a threat to the solid edifice of the family and the social status of the man."

25. Compare Carson 1990 and Platter "Depilation," 9: "Thus, the male gender, by virtue of its dryness, lends itself to definition and self-ordering. The female, by contrast, has no mechanism for self-limitation, and like water, spreads out until exhausted – like the sleeping *Bacchae* of Euripides and the sexually voracious women who appear in Old Comedy, or until stopped by some limit imposed from the outside."

26. For δέλτα παρατετιλμέναι "plucked in the form of a delta" at Aristophanes *Lysistrata* 151 as a pubic hair style, see Kilmer 1982:106n10 and compare the "pubic triangle" of his plate Id. For equilateral triangles as cosmic building-blocks, see Plato *Timaeus* 53c–55c and Cornford 1937:210–219.

27. On the role of extension in Praxagora's plan, see Ober 1998:127: "the humor of the plot derives from a comic extension (albeit extreme) of the democratic-egalitarian ethos" and "the means by which Aristophanes' characters effect this comic extension of the democratic ethos is the institutional machinery of the democratic state and its associated ideologies." For gynocracy as an extension of democratic logic, see also Saïd 1979:35–36, 51–52.

28. Ober (1998) argues that Praxagora's "proposals for communalization of property and equalized sexual relations stretched the existing reality, without inverting it" (149–150) and that theirs is "the egalitarian logic of the democratic polis taken to extremes, not set on its head" (153). Yet Ober also notes that "[t]his 'private world of men versus public world of women' inverts the Athenians' ordinary assumption that the private realm is the appropriate domain of women, while the public realm is for men only" (132). Ober's point seems to be that while Praxagora's plan inverts gender roles, it extends the egalitarianism of democracy without overturning it. What Ober terms the play's "hyperegalitarianism" (129 n16, 134) is, of course, limited by the fact that it is not women and men together, but women only who rule. Men and women citizens share goods, sex, and children equally, but not political power. On the reduction of the males under Praxagora's plan to the condition of wholly passive consumers of food and sex – veritable "stomachs" – see Saïd 1979:54.

29. For Praxagora's plan as turning the πόλις "city" into a single οἶκος "house" with the distinction between inside and outside abolished, see Saïd 1979:46–47.

30. Bly (1982) shows how the phases of Praxagora's plot manifest the semantic field of *mêtis*, the mode of intelligence that permits the women to defeat their husbands despite their relative physical weakness.

31. See Detienne and Vernant 1978:305.

32. See Detienne and Vernant 1978, esp. 34 and 37.

33. Because all parts in Greek drama are played by men, we have here males playing females playing males. Taaffe (1993:9–10, 112, 116, 130 and 1991:96–97) shows that among comic actors depicted on vase paintings, the "illusion of gender disguise" was often imperfect: they wear female dresses or masks, but with their beards intact or with the ithyphallic appendages worn by comic actors showing underneath their gowns. Taaffe observes: "There is no way to determine the actual nature of the costumes for *Ecclesiazusae*, but if the actors wore pads and the *phallos* protruded from these supposedly feminine bodies once in a while, the comic and metatheatrical effects would be hilarious" (1991:99, see also 1993:104–105, 113). In this context, however, of supposed females decked out in actual male attire, the question might arise: which is the artificial male accoutrement? Such ambiguity is precisely that of the fetish – and indeed, is embodied by the actors, whether or not their prosthetic *phalloi* were evident. For the "illusion of gender disguise" here is manifestly imperfect, as the supposed females repeatedly reveal their underlying female nature both visually and verbally. For example, despite tanning, their skin remains relatively light, so that Chremes describes the man who persuaded the Assembly to vote in the new order as a "good-looking, white-faced young man" (427–428); the women's beards are clearly artificial, carried by the women as they arrive (24–25, 68–72) and put on in front of the audience (118–127, 272–274); and during the rehearsal of their impersonation of male speech, one woman slips and swears by the "Two Goddesses" (155–156), another addresses the Assembly as "ladies" (165–166), and they refer to themselves using female gender forms (μεμνημένας, ἡμᾶς) when reminding themselves to call each other "men" (285–287); on these and other examples, see Taaffe 1993:112–114, 116–119. It is this ambiguity that qualifies the women's disguise as a fetish: their accoutrements both affirm and deny their male identity. Their transvestitism is detectable, but also sufficient to persuade the rest of the male Assembly – possibly, as Saïd (1979:35–36) maintains, because popular male political orators were already held to be effeminate (101–104). The women's costume is pseudo-phallic, a "*phallos* that is not one."

34. For the women's suspension of underarm depilation and suntanning of their skin as evidence that femininity is not "a simple fact of nature," but "an artifact of voluntary human action," see Ober 1998:136 with bibliography. As another instance of the construction of sexual appearance in Greek literature, Ober cites the report of Plutarch (*Life of Theseus* 23) that Theseus disguised two young men as women by having them take warm baths, stay out of the sun, smooth their skin with unguents,

adopt women's hairdos, and imitate women's speech, clothes, and walk, and then successfully substituted these pseudo-females in the group of maidens he took to Crete – a ruse commemorated in the festival of the Oschophoria, named for the vine-branches the men carried when they returned to Athens. Thus the women's imitation of the opposite sex in order to infiltrate its exclusive group is itself an emulation of a male exemplar. For the relation between the Oschophoria and the women-only festival of the Skira, where Praxagora and her cohorts hatched their plot, see Vidal-Naquet 1986a:114–117, 1986c:211, 217–218 and Saïd 1976:37.

35. See above, n. 23.

36. See above, n. 23.

37. See Sommerstein 1998:147 on 90.

38. For the explanation of the "Phormision" here, see Sommerstein 1998:147 on 97. See also Ober 1998:136 and Taaffe 1993:110.

39. Ober 1998:138–139 shows how Praxagora's "felicitous performance[s] of a speech act in the Assembly" – both in rehearsal and as recounted later by Chremes – are "models of sophisticated rhetoric."

40. See Aristophanes *Ecclesiazusae* 455–457:
Blepyrus: So what was finally decided?
Chremes: To hand the city over to these women. For it seemed that this only had not been done before in the city.
Compare Saïd 1979:35.

41. On the relation between Praxagora's plan and what women are taught in the *Oeconomicus*, see Foley 1982:3–6, 16–17. On her speech as reflecting a "traditional male point of view," see Taaffe 1993:120.

42. Compare Saïd 1979:41.

43. For other differences between Praxagora's plan and the Platonic utopia, see Saïd 1979:61.

44. Compare "Architecture   Gender   Philosophy" in this collection and Rosenstock 1994:370, 372.

45. Compare Saïd 1979:45.

46. Compare Rosenstock 1994:381: "When Plato insists that women be trained as guardians, he hopes to undo the 'beautiful evil' ([Hesiod *Theogony*] 585) that enters the world with Pandora. He is recreating Woman, this time with as close a resemblance to Man as possible, a masculinized woman." See also Saïd (1979:36), who describes the nature of female power in Plato's city as a "virilization of women" in contrast with the "feminization of power" under Praxagora's regime.

47. On Praxagora's plan as "domestic utopia" and a "symbolic extension of the household," see Foley 1982:15n33.

48. In addition to the metaphorical weaving of rich and poor and beautiful and ugly, Praxagora's gynocracy provides that women continue their literal weaving of men's cloaks. See Aristophanes *Ecclesiazusae* 653–654.

49. See Slater 1997:108–109.

50. Aristophanes *Lysistrata* 586.

51. Compare Aristophanes *Ecclesiazusae* 614–615:

καὶ ταύτας γὰρ κοινὰς ποιῶ τοῖς ἀνδράσι συγκατακεῖσθαι
καὶ παιδοποιεῖν τῷ βουλομένῳ.

For I make these women too common property for men to sleep with
and for the man who wishes to, to make children.

with the law regarding the Guardians (Plato *Republic* 457c–d):

τὰς γυναῖκας ταύτας τῶν ἀνδρῶν τούτων πάντων πάσας εἶναι κοινάς, ἰδίᾳ
δὲ μηδενὶ μηδεμίαν συνοικεῖν· καὶ τοὺς παῖδας αὖ κοινούς, καὶ μήτε γονέα
ἔκγονον εἰδέναι τὸν αὑτοῦ μήτε παῖδα γονέα.

'that these women are to be common to all men, and no one of them is to live privately with any man, and the children, moreover, are common, and no parent is to know his own offspring and no child, his parent.'

52. Compare Aristophanes *Ecclesiazusae* 635–637:

Blepyrus: How, then, if we live in this way, will each man be able to distinguish
    his own children?

Praxagora: Why is this necessary? For they will regard as fathers all men who
    are older than they are in time.

with Plato *Republic* 461c–d:

'How are they to recognize their fathers and daughters and the other relationships you mention?' 'They will have no way,' I said, 'except that all offspring born in the tenth and in the seventh month after he became a bridegroom a man will call his sons, if they are male, and daughters, if they are female.'

See also Rosenstock 1994:371 on how Plato's transformation of the terms "father" and "mother" from signifying kinship to defining a generational group promotes the model of mono-gendered autochthony by "effacing his culture's most significant factor in gender role differentiation, namely, reproduction." Saïd (1979:58) calls attention to the difference between the *Ecclesiazusae* and the *Republic* with regard to the origin of the parent-child bond: under Praxagora's system, the children create the bond by regarding the men of the older generation as "fathers," while in the Platonic system, it is the citizens old enough to be fathers who create the bond by means of naming the children as "sons" and "daughters." She notes that this second mode is the same as that employed in Athens, where it is the father who "creates" his son by giving him his name on the tenth day after birth, by attaching him to his οἶκος "house" via the ritual of the Amphidromia and to the πόλις "city" by enrolling him in the registry of his phratry. This parallel with Athenian practice reflects the maintenance of the rule of the phallus in the Platonic city.

53. Compare Rosenstock 1994:381: "The possibility that a woman might exercise sexual power over a male is unthinkable, whereas a man's sexual power over women and, in some instances, over other men, seems utterly natural to Plato."

54. See Saïd 1979:33

55. For the plan and program of the Classical οἶκος "house," see Walker 1983.

56. On Praxagora's abolition of Athenian political and judicial institutions through the re-programming of the πόλις "city" as domestic space, see Saïd 1979:47–48.

57. For the assignment of jury duty by letter, see Sommerstein 1998:199 on 683.

58. These two responses to the unadorned female genital parallel the two poles of interpretation the *Ecclesiazusae* has evoked: for the play as critical satire, see Saïd 1979 and Strauss 1966:263–282; for the play as a testimony to the transformative power of the comic spirit, see Slater 1997:119–123 with bibliography. Acknowledging both positions, Foley (1982) analyzes the criticism of the Athenian males as a potentially constructive call to renewed commitment to the public good, and Reckford (1987:353) concludes that the "final revelry, I think, conveys a spirit of vitality that goes beyond weariness, and hope that goes beyond disillusionment." See also Ober 1998:134 with n28.

59. For her makeup, see Aristophanes *Ecclesiazusae* 878–879, 929. On the question of whether the *lêkuthos* was used for cosmetic paint, see Quincey 1949:38.

60. Slater (1989) sees this passage as a play upon the fact that both funerary *lêkuthoi* and the hag's mask were colored white. Funerary *lêkuthoi* were placed around the bier at the *prothesis* of the dead body and used to carry unguent to the tomb; see Oakley 2004:4–5, 86, 234n43, n44, n45.

61. See Sommerstein 1998:228 on 1042.

62. Ussher 1973:219–220 on 1041–1042 makes the comparison with Jocasta.

63. On the scholiast's interpretation of Greek *phrunê* "toad" as the nickname of prostitutes, see Ussher 1973:225–226 on 1098–1101.

64. On this expression as a euphemism for "to die," and on κασαλβάδοιν "whores" to be taken "as pilots" with ἐσπλέων, see Ussher 1973:226 on 1105–1106.

65. Slater (1989:50–51) argues that the *lêkuthos* referred to here is no longer a white ground ceramic vase, but a white marble vessel of the sort customarily placed as a grave monument: the greater size of the marble vase would motivate the reference to the molten lead poured around the "ankles" to affix this *lêkuthos* to a stone base.

66. For Northrop Frye's concept of the "festive conclusion" in comedy, see Frye 1965:75-76, 103–104, 115, 128–130.

67. On the figure of Baubo, see Olender 1990, Gsell 2001:31–47, and Freud 1916.

68. For perfume as an aphrodisiac that is necessary to attract marriage partners to one another, but also potentially threatening to the ongoing stability of the union, see Detienne 1972a:ix–x = 1977b: vi–vii.

69. The appearance of Blepyrus here, not having eaten and not having come from the Agora, has appeared to be inconsistent with 727, when he followed Praxagora to the Agora, where the communal dinners were to be provided. For discussion of the various attempts to solve the difficulty, see Sommerstein (1998:233 on 1113), who concludes that the inconsistency is unavoidable. See also Ussher 1973:xxxii–xxxiv.

70. See Slater 1997:98. See also Saïd 1979:55.

71. Sommerstein 1998:238 on 1169–1175. See also Saïd (1979:55), who notes that the audience is here given literally a word to eat.

BIBLIOGRAPHY

AHS = Allen, T. W., W. R. Halliday and E. E. Sykes, eds. 1936. *The Homeric Hymns*. Oxford.

Alberti, Leon Battista. 1988. *On the Art of Building*. Translated by J. Rykwert, N. Leach, and R. Tavernor. Cambridge, Mass.

Alexiou, M. 1974. *The Ritual Lament in Greek Tradition*. Cambridge.

Allen, D. C. 1970. *Mysteriously Meant: The Rediscovery of Pagan Symbolism and Allegorical Interpretation in the Renaissance*. Baltimore.

Ameis, K. F. and C. Hentze, eds. 1877. *Anhang zu Homers Ilias*. Leipzig.

Andersen, Ø. 1977. "Odysseus and the Wooden Horse." *Symbolae Osloenses* 52:5–18.

Anderson, W. S. 1958. "Calypso and Elysium." *Classical Journal* 54:2–11.

Apter, E. 1991. *Feminizing the Fetish: Psychoanalysis and Narrative Obsession in Turn-of-the-Century France*. Ithaca and London.

Arthur, M. B. 1982. "Cultural Strategies in Hesiod's *Theogony*: Law, Family Society." *Arethusa* 15 (American Classical Studies in Honor of J.-P. Vernant):63–82.

———. 1983. "The Dream of a World Without Women: Poetics and the Circles of Order in the *Theogony* Prooemium." *Arethusa* 15:97–114.

Auerbach, E. 1973 [1953]. *Mimesis: The Representation of Reality in Western Literature*. Translated by W. R. Trask. Princeton.

Austin, M. M. and P. Vidal-Naquet. 1977. *Economic and Social History of Ancient Greece: An Introduction*. Translated and revised by M. M. Austin. Berkeley.

Austin, N. 1972. "Name Magic in the *Odyssey*." *California Studies in Classical Antiquity* 5:1–19.

———. 1975. *Archery at the Dark of the Moon: Poetic Problems in Homer's Odyssey*. Berkeley.

Barber, E. W. 1994. *Women's Work: the First 20,000 Years: Women, Cloth, and Society in Early Times*. New York.

Barthes, R. 1968. "L'effet de réel." *Communications* 11:84–89. Available in English translation as Barthes 1986.

——. 1986. "The Reality Effect." In *The Rustle of Signs*. Translated by
   R. Howard:141-149. New York.

Bassett, S. E. 1920. "ΥΣΤΕΡΟΝ ΠΡΟΤΕΡΟΝ ῾ΟΜΕΡΙΚΩΣ (Cicero, *Att.* 1, 16, 1)."
   Harvard Studies in Classical Philology 31:39-62.

Benveniste, E. 1969. *Le vocabulaire des institutions indo-européenes*. 2 vols. Paris.

Bergren, A. L. T. 1975. *The Etymology and Usage of PEIRAR in Early Greek Poetry:
   A Study in the Interrelation of Metrics, Linguistics and Poetics*. American
   Classical Studies 2. New York.

——. 1992. "MOUSEION. VENICE, CA. Memory and the Fetish in the Murals
   and Buildings of Venice, Ca." in *Fetish. The Princeton Architectural Journal*
   4:130-157.

Bernheimer, C. 1991. "'Castration' as Fetish," *Paragraph* 14:1-9.

Bhabha, H. 1994. "Of Mimicry and Man." In *The Location of Culture*:85-92.
   London and New York.

Bickerman, E. J. 1976. "Love Story in the *Homeric Hymn to Aphrodite*."
   Athenaeum 54:229-254.

Bloch, M. 1982. "Death, Women, and Power." In *Death and the Regeneration
   of Life*. Edited by M. Bloch and J. Parry:211-230. Cambridge.

Boedeker, D. 1974. *Aphrodite's Entry into Greek Epic*. Leiden.

Bowra, C. M. 1930. *Tradition and Design in the Iliad*. Oxford.

Brisson, L. 1974. *Le même et l'autre dans la structure ontologique du Timée de
   Platon*. Paris.

Brown, C. S. 1966. "Odysseus and Polyphemus: The Name and the Curse."
   CompLit 18:193-202.

Buffière, F. 1956. *Les mythes d' Homère et la pensée grecque*. Paris.

Burdett, R., J. Kipnis, and J. Whiteman, eds. 1992. *Strategies in Architectural
   Thinking*. Cambridge, Mass.

Burnyeat, M. F. 1976. "Protagoras and Self-Refutation in Later Greek
   Philosophy." *The Philosophical Review* 85.1:44-69.

Buschor, E. 1944. *Die Musen des Jenseits*. Munich.

Byl, S. 1982. "La mètis des femmes dans l'Assemblée des femmes
   d'Aristophane." *Revue Belge de Philologie et d'Histoire* 60:33-40.

Calame, C. 1977. *Les choeurs de jeunes filles en Grèce archaique*. 2 vols. Rome.

Carson, A. 1990. "Putting Her in Her Place: Women, Dirt, and Desire." In *Before
   Sexuality: The Construction of Erotic Experience in the Ancient World*. Edited by
   D. M. Halpern, J. J. Winkler, and F. I. Zeitlin:135-169. Princeton.

Cassola, F., ed. 1975. *Inni Omerici*. Milan.

Chantraine P. 1958-1963. *Grammaire homérique*. 2 vols. Paris.

Chantraine *DELG* = Chantraine, P. 1968–1980. *Dictionnaire étymologique de la langue grecque.* Paris.

Clader, L. L. 1976. *Helen: The Evolution from Divine to Heroic in Greek Epic Tradition.* Leiden.

Clifford, G. 1974. *The Transformations of Allegory.* London.

Cornford, F. M. 1937. *Plato's Cosmology: The Timaeus of Plato Translated with a Running Commentary.* New York.

Coulton, J. 1977. *Ancient Greek Architects at Work: Problems of Structure and Design.* Ithaca.

Culler, J. 1975. *Structuralist Poetics.* Ithaca.

———. 1977. "Apostrophe." *Diacritics* 7:59–69.

DK = Diels, H. and W. Kranz, eds. 1964. *Die Fragmente der Vorsokratiker, griechisch und deutsch.* 3 vols. Zurich and Berlin.

Davreux, J. 1942. *La légende de la prophétesse Cassandre d'après les textes et les monuments.* Paris, Zurich, and Berlin.

Deleuze, G. 1969. "Simulacre et philosophie antique." In *Logique du sens*:292-324. Paris. Available in English translation as Deleuze 1990.

———. 1990. "The Simulacrum and Ancient Philosophy." *The Logic of Sense.* Translated by M. Lester:253-279. New York.

De Luca, K. M. 2005. *Aristophanes' Male and Female Revolutions. A Reading of Aristophanes' Knights and Assemblywomen.* Lantham, Md.

de Man, P. 1969. "The Rhetoric of Temporality." In *Interpretation: Theory and Practice.* Edited by C. S. Singleton:174-177. Baltimore.

———. 1979. *Allegories of Reading: Figural Language in Rousseau, Nietzsche, Rilke, and Proust.* New Haven.

de Romilly, J. 1973. "Gorgias et le pouvoir de la poésie." *Journal of Hellenic Studies* 93:155-162.

Derrida, J. 1967. *De la grammatologie.* Paris. Available in English translation as Derrida 1976.

———. 1972a. "La pharmacie de Platon." In *La dissémination*:71-197. Paris. Available in English translation as Derrida 1981.

———. 1972b. "La mythologie blanche." In *Marges de la philosophie*:247-324. Paris. Available in English translation as Derrida 1982.

———. 1976. *Of Grammatology.* Translated by G. Spivak. Baltimore.

———. 1978. "Cartouches." In *La Vérité en peinture*:211-290. Paris. Available in English translation as Derrida 1987c.

———. 1981. "Plato's Pharmacy." In *Dissemination*:60-171. Translated by B. Johnson. Chicago.

———. 1982. "White Mythology: Metaphor in the Text of Philosophy." *Margins of Philosophy.* Translated by A. Bass:207-271. Chicago.

———. 1986. "Point de Folie—Maintenant l'Architecture." *AA Files-Folio VIII, La Case Vide,* with English translation by K. Linker:4–19. Original French text republished as Derrida 1987d:477-494.

———. 1987a. "*Chôra.*" In *Poikilia: Études offertes à Jean-Pierre Vernant*:265–295. Paris.

———. 1987b. "Pourquoi Peter Eisenman écrit de si bons livres." In *Psyché: Inventions de l'autre*:495–508. Paris. Available in English translation by S. Whiting in Kipnis and Leeser, eds. 1997:95-101.

———. 1987c. "Cartouches." In *The Truth in Painting.* Translated by G. Bennington and I. McLeod:185-253. Chicago.

———. 1987d. "Point de Folie—Maintenant l'Architecture." In *Psyché: Inventions de l'autre*:477–494. Paris.

Detienne, M. 1967. *Les maîtres de vérité dans la Grèce archaïque.* Paris. Available in English translation as Detienne 1996.

———. 1972a. *Les jardins d' Adonis.* Paris. Available in English translation as Detienne 1977b.

———. 1972b. "Entre bêtes et dieux." *Nouvelle revue de psychanalyse* 6:231–246. Available in English translation as Detienne 1981.

———. 1977a. *Dionysos mis à mort.* Paris.

———. 1977b. *The Gardens of Adonis: Spices in Greek Mythology.* Translated by J. Lloyd. Atlantic Highlands, N.J.

———. 1981. "Between Beasts and Gods." Translated by M. and L. Muellner, revised by R. L. Gordon. In Gordon, ed. 1981:215-228.

———. 1986. *The Creation of Mythology.* Translated by M. Cook. Chicago.

———. 1996. *The Masters of Truth in Archaic Greece.* Translated by J. Lloyd. Cambridge, Mass.

Detienne, M. and J.-P. Vernant. 1974. *Les ruses de l'intelligence: la mètis des grecs.* Paris. Available in English translation as Detienne and Vernant 1978.

———. 1978. *Cunning Intelligence in Greek Culture and Society.* Translated by J. Lloyd. Atlantic Highlands, N.J.

Detienne, M. and J.-P. Vernant, eds. 1989. *The Cuisine of Sacrifice Among the Greeks.* Translated by P. Wissing. Chicago.

Dimock Jr., G. E. 1956. "The Name of Odysseus." *Hudson Review* 9:52-70.

Dupont-Roc, R. and A. Le Boulluec. 1976. "Le charme du récit (*Odyssée* iv 218–289)." In *Écriture et théorie poétiques: lectures d'Homère, Eschyle, Platon, Aristote*:30-39. Paris.

Durante, M. 1960. "Ricerche sulla preistoria della lingua poetica greca. La terminologia relativa alla creazione poetica." *Atti della Academia Nazionale dei Lincei. Classe di scienze morali, storiche, critiche e filologiche* 15:231–249.

———. 1976. *Sulla preistoria della tradizione poetic greca. Parte seconda: Risultanze della comparazione indoeuropea.* Rome.

Edmonds, S., P. Jones, and G. Nagy. 2004. *Text and Textile: An Introduction to Wool-Working for Readers of Greek and Latin.* DVD by A. Marek. New Brunswick, N.J.

Erlemann, C. 1985. "What is Feminist Architecture?" In *Feminist Aesthetics.* Translated by H. Anderson, edited by G. Ecker:125–134. London.

Erbse, H., ed. 1969-1988. *Scholia Graeca in Homeri Iliadem.* 7 vols. Berlin.

Eustathius. 1960. *Commentarii ad Homeri Odysseam.* Edited by G. Stallbaum. Hildesheim.

Eustathius. 1971-1987. *Commentarii ad Homeri Iliadem.* Edited by M. van der Valk. Leiden.

Faesi, J. U. 1888. *Homers Iliade.* Berlin.

Farnell, L. R. 1971 [1896–1909]. *The Cults of the Greek States.* 5 vols. Chicago.

Favro, D. 1989. "Ad-Architects: Women Professionals in Magazine Ads." In *Architecture: A Place of Women.* Edited by E. P. Berkeley and M. McQuaid:187–200. Washington, D.C.

Fehling, D. 1979. "Zwei Lehrstücke über Pseudo-Nachrichten." *Rheinisches Museum* n.s. 122:193–210.

Felman, S. 1980. *Le Scandale du corps parlant.* Paris.

Fenik, B. C. 1968. *Typical Battle Scenes in the Iliad.* Wiesbaden.

———. ed. 1978. *Homer, Tradition and Invention.* Leiden.

Fineman, J. 1980. "The Structure of Allegorical Desire." *October* 12:48–66.

Finley Jr., J. H. 1978. *Homer's Odyssey.* Cambridge, Mass.

Fletcher, A. 1964. *Allegory: The Theory of a Symbolic Mode.* Ithaca.

Foley, H. 1978. "'Reverse Similes' and Sex Roles in the *Odyssey*." *Arethusa* 11:7–26.

———. 1982. "The 'Female Intruder' Reconsidered: Women in Aristophanes' *Lysistrata* and *Ecclesiazusae*." *Classical Philology* 77:1-21.

Foucault, M. 1971a. *L'ordre du discours.* Paris.

———. 1971b. *Les mots et les choses.* Paris.

Frame, D. 1978. *The Myth of Return in Early Greek Epic.* New Haven.

Frazer, J. 1913. *Pausanias's Description of Greece.* Translated with commentary. London.

Freccero, J. 1966. "Dante's Prologue Scene." *Dante Studies* 84:1–26.

Frère. J. 1986. "La Liaison et le tissu. De la *sumplokê* platonicienne." *Revue internationale de philosophie* 156/157:157–181.

Freud, S. 1953-1974. *The Standard Edition of the Complete Psychological Works of Sigmund Freud.* Edited and translated by J. Strachey. 24 vols. London.

———. 1905. "Overvaluation of the Sexual Object," "Sexual Use of the Mucous Membrane of the Lips and Mouth," "Sexual Use of the Anal Orifice," "Unsuitable Substitutes for the Sexual Object – Fetishism," and "Intimation of the Infantile Character of Sexuality" in *Three Essays on Sexuality. Essay I. The Sexual Aberrations,* vol. 7:150-155 and 171-172.

———. 1910. "Leonardo Da Vinci and a Memory of His Childhood," vol. 11:63- 137.

———. 1916. "A Mythological Parallel to a Visual Obsession," vol. 14:337-338.

———. 1917 [1916-1917]. "The Sexual Life of Human Beings," in *Introductory Lectures on Psycho-analysis, Part III. General Theory of the Neuroses,* vol. 16:303-319.

———. 1927. "Fetishism," vol. 21:149-157. Available in German as Freud 1948.

———. 1933 [1932]. "Femininity" in *New Introductory Lectures on Psycho-analysis,* vol.22:112-135. Available in German as Freud 1940c.

———. 1940 [1938]a. "The Psychical Apparatus and the External World" in *An Outline of Psycho-analysis,* vol 23:195-204.

———. 1940 [1938]b. "Splitting of the Ego in the Process of Defence," vol. 23:275-278.

———. 1940c. "Die Weiblichkeit" in "Neue Folge der Vorlesungen zur Einfürung in die Psychoanalyse," *Gesammelte Werke. Chronologisch geordnet.* Frankfurt-am-Main. vol. 15:119-145.

———. 1948. "Fetishismus" in *Gesammelte Werke. Chronologisch geordnet.* Frankfurt-am-Main. vol. 14:311-317.

Frontisi-Ducroux, F. 1975. *Dedale, mythologie de l'artisan en Grèce ancienne.* Paris.

———. 1976. "Homère et le temps retrouvé." *Critique* 32:538–548.

Frye, N. 1965. *A Natural Perspective: The Development of Shakespearean Comedy and Romance.* New York.

Garcia, L. 2007. *Homeric Temporalities: Simultaneity, Sequence, and Durability in the Iliad.* PhD Thesis, Classics. University of California, Los Angeles.

Gauthier, P. 1972. *Symbola: Les étrangers et la justice dans les cités grecques.* Nancy.

Genette, G. 1969. *Figures II.* Paris.

———. 1972. "Discours du récit." In *Figures III:*67-282. Paris. Available in English translation as Gerard 1980.

———. 1980. *Narrative Discourse: An Essay in Method.* Translated by J. E. Lewin. Ithaca.

Giacomelli, A. C. 1980. "Aphrodite and After." *Phoenix* 34:1–19.

Goodwin *Syntax* = Goodwin, W. W. 1889. *Syntax of the Moods and Tenses of the Greek Verb.* London.

Gordon, R. L., ed. 1981. *Myth, Religion and Society: Structuralist Essays by M. Detienne, L. Gernet, J.-P. Vernant and P. Vidal-Naquet.* Cambridge and New York.

Graziosi, B. 2002. *Inventing Homer: The Early Reception of Epic.* Cambridge.

Greenberg, J. H. 1966. *Language Universals.* The Hague.

Greene, W. C. 1951. "The Spoken and the Written Word." *Harvard Studies in Classical Philology* 60: 23–59.

Grube, G. M. A. 1974. *Plato's Republic.* Translation with commentary. Indianapolis.

Gsell, M. 2001. *Die Bedeutung der Baubo: kulturgeschichtliche Studien zur Repräsentation des weiblichen Genitales.* Frankfurt.

Guillen, C. 1971. *Literature as System.* Princeton.

Güntert, H. 1919. *Kalypso. Bedeutungsgeschichtliche Untersuchungen auf dem Gebiet der indogermanischen Sprachen.* Halle.

Harrison, J. E. 1960. [1922]. *Prolegomena to the Study of Greek Religion.* New York.

Haslam, M. 1976. "Homeric Words and Homeric Meter: Two Doublets Examined (*leibo/eibo, gaia/aia*)." *Glotta* 54:201–11.

——. 1978. "The Versification of the New Stesichorus (P. Lille 76abc)." *Greek, Roman and Byzantine Studies* 19:80–100.

Hauser, F. 1909. "Aristophanes und Vasenbilder." *Jahreshefte des Österreichischen Archäologischen Institutes in Wien* 12:80–100, 215–218.

Hayden, D. 1981. *The Grand Domestic Revolution: A History of Feminist Designs for American Homes, Neighborhoods, and Cities.* Cambridge, Mass.

——. 1984. *Redesigning the American Dream: The Future of Housing, Work, and Family Life.* New York.

Hegel, G. F. W. 1975. *Aesthetics: Lectures on Fine Art.* Translated by T. Knox. Oxford.

Herrmann, W. 1984. *Gottfried Semper: In Search of Architecture.* Cambridge, Mass.

Hocart, A. 1970 [1963]. *Kings and Councilors.* Chicago.

Holtsmark, E. B. 1966. "Spiritual Rebirth of the Hero: *Odyssey 5.*" *Classical Journal* 61:206–210.

Hurst, A. 1976. "L'Huile d' Aphrodite." *Ziva Antika* 26:23–25.

Heyne, C. G., ed. 1834. *Homeri Ilias.* Oxford.

Ian, M. 1993. *Remembering the Phallic Mother.* Ithaca and London.

Jakobson, R. 1971 [1962]. "Why 'Mama' and 'Papa'?" In *Selected Writings* I:538–545. The Hague.

Janko, R. 1981. "The Structure of the Homeric Hymns: A Study in Genre."
    Hermes 109:9–24.

———. 1982. *Homer, Hesiod and the Hymns.* Cambridge.

———. 1994. *The Iliad: A Commentary. Volume IV: Books 13–16.* Cambridge.

Jenkins, I. 1983. "Is There Life after Marriage? A Study of the Abduction Motif
    in Vase Paintings of the Athenian Wedding Ceremony." *Bulletin of the
    Institute of Classical Studies of the University of London* 30:137–145.

Kahn, L. 1978. *Hermès passe: ou, Les ambiguïtés de la communication.* Paris.

———. 1980. "Ulysse, ou la ruse et la mort." *Critique* 393:116–134.

Kakridis, J. Th. 1971. *Homer Revisited.* Lund.

Kamerbeek, J. C. 1967. "Remarques sur l'*Hymne à Aphrodite.*" *Mnemosyne*
    20:385–395.

Kannicht. R. 1969. *Euripides, Helena.* 2 vols. Heidelberg.

Keaney, J. J. 1981. "*Hymn. Ven.* 140 and the Use of ἄποινα." *American Journal
    of Philology* 102:261–264.

Keuls, E. C. 1985. *The Reign of the Phallus: Sexual Politics in Ancient Athens.*
    New York.

Kilmer, M. 1982. "Genital Phobia and Depilation." *Journal of Hellenic Studies*
    102:104–112.

King, H. 1986. "Tithonos and the Tettix." *Arethusa* 19:15–35.

Kipnis, J. and T. Leeser, eds. 1997. *Choral Works: Jacques Derrida and Peter
    Eisenman.* New York.

Kirk, G. S. 1978. "The Formal Duels in Books 3 and 7 of the *Iliad.*" In Fenik, ed.
    1978:18–40.

Klein, T. M. 1980. "Myth, Song, and Theft in the *Homeric Hymn to Hermes.*" In
    Classical Mythology in Twentieth Century Thought and Literature. Edited by
    W. M. Aycock and T. Klein:125–144. Lubbock.

Klinz, A. 1933. *Hieros Gamos.* Halle.

Kofman, S. 1986 [1979]. "Baubô: Perversion théologique et fétichisme."
    In *Nietzsche et la scène philosophique*:225-260. Paris. Available in English
    translation as Kofman 1988.

———. 1988. "Baubô: Theological Perversion and Fetishism." In *Nietzsche's New
    Seas: Explorations in Philosophy, Aesthetics, and Politics.* Edited by
    M. A. Gillespie and T. B. Strong:175-202. Chicago and London.

Koller, H. 1956. "Das kitharodische Prooimion." *Philologus* 100:159–206.

———. 1972. "Epos." *Glotta* 50:16–24.

Kühner-Gerth = R. Kühner, F. Blass, B. Gerth. 1904. *Ausführliche Grammatik der Griechischen Sprache*. 3 vols. (Teil I, Bd. 1: R. Kühner, F. Blass. *Ausführliche Grammatik der Griechischen Sprache. Elementar- und Formenlehre des Nomens und Pronomens*; Teil II, Bd. 1: R. Kühner, B. Gerth. *Ausführliche Grammatik der griechischen Sprache. Satzlehre: Syntaxe des einfachen Satzes*; Teil II, Bd. 2: R. Kühner, B. Gerth. *Ausführliche Grammatik der griechischen Sprache. Satzlehre: Syntaxe des zusammengesetzten Satzes*). Edited by I. Ibraguimov. Hannover.

LP = Lobel, E. and D. Page, eds. 1955. *Poetarum Lesbiorum fragmenta*. Oxford.

Lacan, J. and W. Granoff. 1956. "Fetishism: The Symbolic, the Imaginary, and the Real." In *Perversions: Psychodynamics and Therapy*. Edited by S. Lorand and M. Balint:265-276. New York.

Lacan, J. 1966. "L'instance de la lettre dans l'inconscient ou la raison depuis Freud." In *Écrits*:249-289. Paris. Available in English translation as Lacan 1977.

——. 1977. "Agency of the Letter in the Unconscious or Reason Since Freud." In *Écrits: A Selection*. Translated by A. Sheridan:146-178. New York.

Laqueur, T. 1990. *Making Sex: Body and Gender from the Greeks to Freud*. Cambridge.

Leaf, W. 1892. *A Companion to the Iliad*. London.

Lendle, O. 1957. *Die "Pandorasage" bei Hesiod. Textkritische und motivgeschichtliche Untersuchungen*. Würzburg.

Lévi-Strauss, C. 1967. *Les structures élementaires de la parenté*. Paris. Available in English translation as Lévi-Strauss 1969.

——. 1969. *The Elementary Structures of Kinship*. Translated by Bell, von Sturmer, and Needham. Boston.

Lloyd, G. E. R. 1971. *Polarity and Analogy: Two Types of Argumentation in Early Greek Thought*. Cambridge.

Loraux, N. 1981. *Les enfants d'Athéna: Idées athéniennes sur la citoyenneté et la division des sexes*. Paris.

MW = Merkelbach, R. and M. L. West, eds. 1967. *Fragmenta Hesiodea*. Oxford.

MacCormack, C. and M. Strathern, eds. 1980. *Nature, Culture, and Gender*. Cambridge.

Mactoux, M.-M. 1975. *Pénélope: Légende et Mythe. Annales Littéraires de l' Université de Besançon 175*. Paris.

Mazon, P. 1948. *Introduction à l' Iliade*. Paris.

Miller, A. 1979. "The 'Address to the Delian Maidens' in the *Homeric Hymn to Apollo*: Epilogue or Transition?" *Transactions of the American Philological Association* 109:173–86.

Mitchell, J. and J. Rose, eds. 1982. *Feminine Sexuality. Jacques Lacan and the école freudienne.* New York.

Monro, D. B. and T. W. Allen, eds. 1969-1974 [1920-1946]. *Homeri Opera: recognovervnt breviqve adnotatione critica instrvxervnt,* vols. 1-2: *Ilias*; vols. 3-4: *Odyssea*; vol. 5: *Hymni, Cyclus, Fragmenta, Margites, Batrachomyomachia, Vitae.* Oxford.

Morris, S. 1992. *Daidalos and the Origins of Greek Art.* Princeton.

Morrow, G. 1954. "The Demiurge in Politics: The *Timaeus* and the *Laws*." *Proceedings and Addresses of the American Philosophical Association* 27:5–23.

———. 1965. "Necessity and Persuasion in Plato's *Timaeus*." In *Studies in Plato's Metaphysics.* Edited by R. E. Allen:421–437. London.

Moulton, C. 1977. *Similes in the Homeric Poems.* Göttingen.

Muellner, L. 1976. *The Meaning of Homeric* εὔχομαι *Through Its Formulas.* Innsbruck.

Muller, J. and W. Richardson. 1982. *Lacan and Language: A Reader's Guide to Écrits.* New York.

Murrin, M. 1969. *The Veil of Allegory: Some Notes Toward a Theory of Allegorical Rhetoric in the English Renaissance.* Chicago.

Naegelsbach, C. F. 1864. *Anmerkungen zur Ilias.* Nürnberg.

Nagler, M. 1974. *Spontaneity and Tradition: A Study in the Oral Art of Homer.* Berkeley.

———. 1977. "Dread Goddess Endowed with Speech." *Archaeological News* 6:77–85.

Nagy, G. 1974. *Comparative Studies in Greek and Indic Meter.* Cambridge, Mass.

———. 1979. *The Best of the Achaeans.* Baltimore.

———. 1982. "Hesiod." *Ancient Writers.* Edited by T. J. Luce:43–73. New York.

———. 1983. "*Sêma* and *Noêsis*: Some Illustrations." *Arethusa* 16 (Semiotics and Classical Studies):35–55.

———. 1996a. *Homeric Questions.* Austin, Texas.

———. 1996b. *Poetry as Performance: Homer and Beyond.* Cambridge.

———. 2002. *Plato's Rhapsody and Homer's Music.* Cambridge, Mass. and London.

Neitzel, H. 1980. "Hesiod und die lügenden Musen." *Hermes* 108:387–401.

Niles, J. 1979. "On the Design of the *Hymn to Delian Apollo*." *Classical Journal* 75: 36–39.

Oakley, J. H. 1982. "The *Anakalupteria*." *Archäologischer Anzeiger* 8a:113–118.

———. 2004. *Picturing Death in Classical Athens: The Evidence of the White Lekythoi.* Cambridge.

Ober, J. 1998. *Political Dissent in Democratic Athens: Intellectual Critics of Popular Rule.* Princeton.

Olender, M. 1990. "Aspects of Baubo: Ancient Texts and Contexts." In *Before Sexuality: The Construction of Erotic Experience in the Ancient World*. Edited by D. M. Halperin, J. J. Winkler, and F. Zeitlin:83-113. Princeton.

Otto, W. F. 1965. *Dionysus: Myth and Cult*. Translated by R. B. Palmer. Bloomington.

Owen, E. T. 1966 [1946]. *The Story of the Iliad*. Ann Arbor.

Page, D. 1955a. *Sappho and Alcaeus. An Introduction to the Study of Ancient Lesbian Poetry*. Oxford.

——. 1955b. *History and the Homeric Epic*. Oxford.

Parry, A. 1973. "Language and Characterization in Homer." *Harvard Studies in Classical Philology* 77:1-21.

Parry, M. 1971. *The Making of Homeric Verse*. Edited by A. Parry. Oxford.

Payot, D. 1982. *Le philosophe et l'architecte*. Paris.

Pellizer, E. 1978. "Tecnica compositiva e struttura genealogica nell' *Inno omerico ad Afrodite*." *Quaderni Urbinati di Cultura Classica* 27:115-144.

Pépin, J. 1958. *Mythe et allégorie: Les origines grecques et les contestations judeo-crétiennes*. Aubier.

Peradotto, J. 1974. "*Odyssey* viii 564-71: Verisimilitude, Narrative Analysis and Bricolage." *Texas Studies in Literature and Language* 15:803-832.

——. 1980. "Prophecy Degree Zero: Teiresias and the End of the *Odyssey*." In *Oralità: cultura, letteratura, discorso: Atti del Convegno internazionale (Urbino 21-25 Iuglio 1980)*. Edited by B. Gentili and G. Paioni:429-455. Urbino.

Petrie, Z. 1979. "Trophonius ou l'architecte. À propos du statut des techniciens dans la cité grecque." *Studii Classice* 19:23-37.

PMG = Page, D., ed. 1962. *Poetae Melici Graeci*. Oxford.

Podbielski, H. 1971. *La structure de l'hymne homérique à Aphrodite*. Wroclaw.

Podlecki, A. 1961. "Guest-Gifts and Nobodies." *Phoenix* 15:125-133.

Pollard, J. 1952. "Muses and Sirens." *The Classical Review* 2:60-63.

Porter, H. N. 1949. "Repetition in the *Homeric Hymn to Aphrodite*." *American Journal of Philology* 70: 249-272.

Pucci, P. 1977. *Hesiod and the Language of Poetry*. Baltimore.

——. 1979. "The Song of the Sirens." *Arethusa* 12:121-132.

——. 1982. "The Proem of the *Odyssey*." *Arethusa* 15 (American Classical Studies in Honor of J.-P. Vernant):39-62.

——. 1987. *Odysseus Polutropos: Intertextual Readings in the Odyssey and the Iliad*. Ithaca.

Puhvel, J. 1953. "Indo-European Negative Compounds." *Language* 29:14-25.

Quincey, J. H. 1949. "The Metaphorical Sense of ΛΗΚΥΘΟΣ and *AMPULLA*." *Classical Quarterly* 43:32-44.

Reckford, K. J. 1964. "Helen in the *Iliad*." *Greek, Roman, and Byzantine Studies* 5:5–20.

——. 1987. "Utopia Limited: *Ecclesiazusae*." In *Aristophanes' Old-and-New Comedy*:344-353. Chapel Hill and London.

Redfield, J. 1975. *Nature and Culture in the Iliad: The Tragedy of Hector*. Chicago.

Reinhardt, K. 1956. "Zum homerischen Aphroditehymnus." In *Festschrift Bruno Snell*:1–14. Munich.

Richardson, N. 1981. "The Contest of Homer and Hesiod and Alcidamas' *Museion*." *Classical Quarterly* 31:1–10.

Riezler, K. 1936. "Das homerische Gleichnis und der Anfang der Philosophie." *Antike* 12:253–271.

Rissman, L. 1983. *Love as War: Homeric Allusion in the Poetry of Sappho*. Beitrage zur klassischen Philologie 157. Königstein.

Rose, V., ed. 1886. *Fragmenta Aristotelis*. Leipzig.

Rosenmeyer, T. 1955. "Gorgias, Aeschylus and *Apatê*." *American Journal of Philology* 76:225–260.

Rosenstock, B. 1994. "Athena's Cloak. Plato's Critique of the Democratic City in the *Republic*." *Political Theory* 22:363-390.

Rossbach, O. 1894. "Anchises." In *Paulys Real-Encyclopädie der classischen Altertumswissenichaft*, Volume I: cols. 2106–2109. Stuttgart.

Rowland, I. 1999. *Vitruvius. Ten Books on Architecture*. Translation with commentary and illustrations by T. Howe. Cambridge.

Ruijgh, C. J. 1971. *Autour de "Te Épique."* Amsterdam.

Rykwert, J. 1972. *On Adam's House in Paradise: The Idea of the Primitive Hut in Architectural History*. New York.

Saïd, S. 1979. "*L'Assemblée des femmes*: Les femmes, l'économie et la politique." In *Aristophane, les femmes et la cité*. Edited by J. Bonnamour and H. Delavault. *Les Cahiers de Fontenay* (Fontenay-aux-Roses) 17:33-69. Available in an abridged English translation as Saïd 1996.

——. 1996. "*The Assemblywomen*: Women, Economy, and Politics." In *Oxford Readings in Aristophanes*. Edited by E. Segal:282-313. Oxford and New York.

Sandoz, C. 1971. *Les noms grecs de la forme: étude linguistique*. Université de Neuchâtel.

Scheid, J. and Svenbro, J. 1996. *The Crafts of Zeus: Myths of Weaving and Fabric*. Cambridge, Mass. and London.

Scheinberg, S. 1979. "The Bee Maidens of the *Homeric Hymn to Hermes*." *Harvard Studies in Classical Philology* 83:1–28.

Schmitt, R. 1967. *Dichtung und Dichtersprache in indogermanischer Zeit*. Wiesbaden.

Segal, C. 1962a. "Gorgias and the Psychology of the *Logos.*" *Harvard Studies in Classical Philology* 66:99–155.

——. 1962b. "The Phaeacians and the Symbolism of Odysseus' Return." *Arion* 1:17–64.

——. 1967. "Transition and Ritual in Odysseus' Return." *La Parola del passato: Rivista di studi antichi* 116:321–342.

——. 1974a. "The Raw and the Cooked in Greek Literature." *Classical Journal* 69:289–308.

——. 1974b. "The *Homeric Hymn to Aphrodite*: A Structuralist Approach." *Classical World* 67:205–212.

——. 1986. "Tithonus and the *Homeric Hymn to Aphrodite*: A Comment." *Arethusa* 19:37–47.

Semper, G. 1989. *The Four Elements of Architecture and Other Writings.* Translated by H. Mallgrave and W. Herrmann. Cambridge.

Shannon, R. 1975. *The Arms of Achilles and Homeric Compositional Technique.* Leiden.

Singleton, C. S., ed. 1970. *Dante Alighieri, The Divine Comedy. Translated with a Commentary. vol. 1. Inferno.* 2 vols. Princeton.

Sissa, G. 1991. "Philosophes du genre: Platon, Aristote et la différence des sexes." In *Histoire des femmes.* Edited by M. Perrot and G. Duby:58–100. Paris.

Slater, N. W. 1989. "Lekythoi in Aristophanes' *Ecclesiazusae.*" *Lexis* 3:43–51.

——. 1997. "Waiting in the Wings: Aristophanes' *Ecclesiazusae.*" *Arion* 3rd series, 5.1:97–129.

Slater, P. 1971. *The Glory of Hera: Greek Mythology and the Greek Family.* Boston.

Smith, P. M. 1981a. *Nursling of Mortality: A Study of the Homeric Hymn to Aphrodite.* Frankfurt.

——. 1981b. "Aineiadai as Patrons of *Iliad* XX and the *Homeric Hymn to Aphrodite.*" *Harvard Studies in Classical Philology* 85:17–58.

Snyder, J. 1981. "The Web of Song: Weaving Imagery in Homer and the Lyric Poets." *The Classical Journal* 76.3:193–196.

Sowa, C. A. 1984. *Traditional Themes and the Homeric Hymns.* Chicago.

Stanford, W. B, ed. 1961. *The Odyssey of Homer.* 2 vols. London.

——. 1972 [1939]. *Ambiguity in Greek Literature: Studies in Theory and Practice.* New York.

Stewart, A. 1990. *Greek Sculpture: An Exploration.* 2 vols. New Haven.

Stewart, D. 1976. *The Disguised Guest: Rank, Role, and Identity in the Odyssey.* Lewisburg, Pa.

Strauss, L. 1966. *Socrates and Aristophanes.* Chicago and London.

Stroh, W. 1976. "Hesiods lügende Musen." In *Studien zum antiken Epos*. Edited by H. Görgemanns and E. Schmidt:85–112. Meisenheim.

Svenbro, J. 1976. *La parole et le marbre: Aux origines de la poétique grecque*. Lund.

Taaffe, L. K. 1991. "The Illusion of Gender Disguise in Aristophanes' *Ecclesiazusae*." *Helios* 18:91-107.

———. 1993. *Aristophanes and Women*. London and New York.

Thompson, D. 1974. *Dante's Epic Journeys*. Baltimore.

Thompson, G. 1966. *Aeschylus and Athens*. London.

Todorov, T. 1977. *Théories du symbole*. Paris.

Torre, S., ed. 1977. *Women in American Architecture: A Historic and Contemporary Perspective*. New York.

Torre, S., et al. (Heresies Editorial Collective), eds. 1981. *Making Room: Women and Architecture*. Heresies 11. New York.

Toubeau, H. 1972. "Le *pharmakon* et les aromates." *Critique* 28:681–715.

Treu, M. 1959. *Archilochus*. Munich.

Trubetzkoy, N. S. 1969. *Principles of Phonology*. Translated by C. A. M. Baltaxe. Berkeley.

Ussher, R. G., ed. 1973. *Ecclesiazusae*. Oxford.

van der Ben, N. 1981. "De Homerische Aphrodite-hymne 2: Den interpretatie van het gedicht." *Lampas* 14:67–107.

———. 1986. "*Hymn to Aphrodite* 36-291: Notes on the *Pars Epica* of the *Homeric Hymn to Aphrodite*." *Mnemosyne* 39:1–41.

van der Valk, M. 1976. "On the Arrangement of the Homeric Hymns." *Acta Classica* 45:419–445.

van Eck, J. 1978. *The Homeric Hymn to Aphrodite: Introduction, Commentary and Appendices*. PhD Thesis, Classics, Utrecht.

Vermeule, E. 1979. *Aspects of Death in Early Greek Art and Poetry*. Berkeley.

Vernant, J.-P. 1972. "Les Troupeaux du soleil et la table du soleil." *Revue des études grecques* 85:xiv–xvii.

———. 1974 [1965]. "Le mythe hésiodique des races, essai d'analyse structurale." In *Mythe et pensée chez les Grecs*:1.13–41. 2 vols. Paris. Available in English translation as Vernant 2006.

———. 1974. *Mythe et société en Grèce Ancienne*. Paris. Available in English translation as Vernant 1980.

———. 1975. "Image et apparence dans la théorie platonicienne de la mimesis." *Journal de psychologie* 2:133–60.

———. 1975-1976. "Étude comparée des religions antiques." *L'Annuaire du College de France* 76:367–376.

——. 1976. "Grèce ancienne et étude comparée des religions." *Archives de Sciences Sociales des Religions* 41:5–24.

——. 1977-1978. "Étude comparée des religions antiques." *L'Annuaire du Collège de France* 78:451–466.

——. 1978. "Ambiguity and Reversal: The Enigmatic Structure of the *Oedipus Rex*." *New Literary History* 9:475–501.

——. 1980. *Myth and Society in Ancient Greece*. Translated by J. Lloyd. Atlantic Highlands, N.J.

——. 1981. "Sacrificial and Alimentary Codes in Hesiod's Myth of Prometheus." In Gordon, ed. 1981:57–79.

——. 1989. "At Man's Table: Hesiod's Foundation Myth of Sacrifice." In Detienne and Vernant, eds. 1989: 21–86.

——. 1991. *Mortals and Immortals*. Translated and edited by F. I. Zeitlin. Princeton.

——. 2006. "Hesiod's Myth of the Races: An Essay in Structural Analysis." In *Myth and Thought Among the Greeks*:25-51. New York.

Vidal-Naquet, P. 1970. "Valeurs religieuses et mythiques de la terre et du sacrifice dans l'*Odyssée*." *Annales Économies-Sociétés-Civilizations* 25:1278–1297.

——. 1986a. "The Black Hunter and the Origin of the Athenian *Ephebia*." In *The Black Hunter: Forms of Thought and Forms of Society in the Greek World*. Translated by A. Szegedy-Maszak:106–128. Baltimore.

——. 1986b. "Recipes for Greek Adolescence." In *The Black Hunter: Forms of Thought and Forms of Society in the Greek World*. Translated by A. Szegedy-Maszak:129-156. Baltimore.

——. 1986c. "Slavery and the Rule of Women in Tradition, Myth, and Utopia." In *The Black Hunter: Forms of Thought and Forms of Society in the Greek World*. Translated by A. Szegedy-Maszak:205-223. Baltimore.

——. 1986d. "A Study in Ambiguity: Artisans in the Platonic City." In *The Black Hunter: Forms of Thought and Forms of Society in the Greek World*. Translated by A. Szegedy-Maszak:224-245. Baltimore.

Vivante, P. 1970. *The Homeric Imagination*. Bloomington.

Vlastos, G. 1965. "The Disorderly Motion in the '*Timaeus*'." In *Studies in Plato's Metaphysics*. Edited by R. E. Allen:379–399. London.

Wade-Gery, H. T. 1967 [1936]. "Kynaithos." In *Greek Poetry and Life*:56–78. Oxford.

Walker, S. 1983. "Women and Housing in Classical Greece: The Archaeological Evidence." In *Images of Women in Antiquity*. Edited by A. Cameron and A. Kuhrt:81-91. Detroit.

Watkins, C. 1971. "Studies in Indo-European Legal Language, Institutions and Mythology." In *Indo-European and Indo-Europeans*. Edited by G. Cardona, H. Hoenigswald, and A. Senn:346–350. Philadelphia.

Waugh, L. 1982. "Marked and Unmarked: A Choice between Unequals in Semiotic Structure." *Semiotica* 38:299–318.

Wehrli, F. R., ed. 1944-1959. *Die Schule des Aristoteles*. 10 vols. Basel.

Wender, D. 1978. *The Last Scenes of the Odyssey*. Leiden.

West, M. L., ed. 1966. *Hesiod: Theogony*. Oxford.

———. ed. 1978. *Hesiod: Works and Days*. Oxford.

Whitman, C. H. 1958. *Homer and the Heroic Tradition*. Cambridge, Mass.

Wigley, M. 1989. "The Translation of Architecture, the Production of Babel." *Assemblage* 8:7–21.

Wittkower, R. 1988. *Architectural Principles in the Age of Humanism*. New York.

Zanker, P. 1965. *Wandel der Hermesgestalt in der attischen Vasenmalerei*. Bonn.

Zeitlin, F. 1981. "Travesties of Gender and Genre in Aristophanes' *Thesmophoriazusae*." *Critical Inquiry* 8:301–328.

INDEX

Q

R

INDEX LOCORUM

INDEX OF GREEK TERMS

411